D1301266

The media's watching Vault!
Here's a sampling of our coverage.

"For those hoping to climb the ladder of success, [Vault's] insights are priceless."
– *Money* magazine

"The best place on the Web to prepare for a job search."
– *Fortune*

"[Vault guides] make for excellent starting points for job hunters and should be purchased by academic libraries for their career sections [and] university career centers."
– *Library Journal*

"The granddaddy of worker sites."
– *U.S. News & World Report*

"A killer app."
– *The New York Times*

One of *Forbes'* 33 "Favorite Sites."
– *Forbes*

"To get the unvarnished scoop, check out Vault."
– *Smart Money Magazine*

"Vault has a wealth of information about major employers and job-searching strategies as well as comments from workers about their experiences at specific companies."
– *The Washington Post*

"A key reference for those who want to know what it takes to get hired by a law firm and what to expect once they get there."
– *New York Law Journal*

"Vault [provides] the skinny on working conditions at all kinds of companies from current and former employees."
– *USA Today*

EMPLOYER
GUIDE

VAULT GUIDE TO THE TOP

HOSPITALITY
& TOURISM
EMPLOYERS

2009 EDITION

HOSPITALITY &

TOURISM

EDITED BY MICHAELA R. DRAPES AND
NICHOLAS R. LICHTENBERG

Copyright © 2008 by Vault.com Inc. All rights reserved.

All information in this book is subject to change without notice. Vault makes no claims as to the accuracy and reliability of the information contained within and disclaims all warranties. No part of this book may be reproduced or transmitted in any form or by any means, electronic or mechanical, for any purpose, without the express written permission of Vault.com Inc.

Vault, the Vault logo, and "the most trusted name in career information™" are trademarks of Vault.com Inc.

For information about permission to reproduce selections from this book, contact Vault.com Inc., 150 W. 22nd St., 5th Floor, New York, NY 10011, (212) 366-4212.

Library of Congress CIP Data is available.

ISBN 13: 978-1-58131-544-8

ISBN 10: 1-58131-544-9

Printed in the United States of America

ACKNOWLEDGMENTS

We are extremely grateful to Vault's entire staff—especially Laurie Pasiuk, Elena Boldeskou, Mary Sotomayor and Marcy Lerner—for all their help in the editorial, production and marketing processes for this guide. Vault also would like to acknowledge the support of our investors, clients, employees, family and friends. Thank you!

To ensure that our research was thorough and accurate, we relied on a number of people within the companies that we profiled.

To the many employees who took the time to be interviewed or to complete our survey, we could never thank you enough. Your insights about life inside the top hospitality and tourism employers were invaluable, and your willingness to speak candidly will help job seekers for years to come. We also thank the firms who were so helpful in completing this project.

Table of Contents

ABOUT THE EDITOR   380

Visit Vault at **www.vault.com** for insider company profiles, expert advice,
career message boards, expert resume reviews, the Vault Job Board and more.

V∧ULT CAREER LIBRARY

ix

Introduction

HOSPITALITY INDUSTRY

Hospitality everywhere

The hospitality and tourism industry is made up of a variety of interconnected sectors, including lodging (everything from roadside motels to luxury resorts), recreational activities (cruises, theme parks, and the like), rental cars and food services. All of these sectors work in tandem with the transportation industry to bring consumers to the destinations where they'll spend money on the local goods and services. In the industry, this is known as an "upstream" effect: the more likely travelers are to board a plane to get somewhere, for instance, the more in demand the hospitality and tourism industry's services become. According to the American Hotel and Lodging Association (AHLA), spending by overseas and domestic vacationers in the U.S. alone was $654 billion in 2005—about $1.8 billion per day. In the States, after automobiles and food stores, hospitality and tourism is the No. 3 retail industry, and one of the top-three businesses for nearly two-thirds of the 50 states. The World Tourism Organization estimates worldwide growth of travel and tourism in 2007—measured by number of arrivals—at 4 percent.

Lodging, travel agencies and food services are briefly discussed below, followed by an analysis and discussion of opportunities available in the airline industry.

Who wants to go somewhere?

Because of industry's interrelated segments, the aftereffects of the September 11 attacks, along with other turmoil overseas, had a chilling effect from 2001 through 2003. The subsequent dip in the economy also led to slashed budgets for business travel, the bread and butter of the lodging and rental car sectors. But through 2007, a variety of factors—including a perception that the economy is improving, increased confidence about security and lower-cost plane fares—have led to an overall rebound. PKF Hospitality Research predicted hotel revenue (along with costs, unfortunately) would be up for the fourth consecutive year in 2007. Even high gas prices haven't managed to dampen travelers' wanderlust. According to a survey conducted by AAA, 1.7 percent more people will take a trip of 50 miles or more over the last weekend of May, 2007 than did the year before. They also noted travelers would economize on food and hotels in order to reduce the sting of high prices at the pump.

Visit Vault at **www.vault.com** for insider company profiles, expert advice, career message boards, expert resume reviews, the Vault Job Board and more.

VAULT CAREER LIBRARY

1

Checking into hotels

According to the Bureau of Labor Statistics, nearly 62,000 establishments—including upscale hotels, RV parks, motels, resorts, casino hotels, bed-and-breakfasts and boarding houses—provide overnight accommodation in America, with a staggering 4.4 million rooms on offer each night. These employ 1.8 million wage and salary workers in the process; two-thirds of these work in service occupations, such as housekeeping and food prep. All of this helped the lodging industry earn roughly $133 billion in receipts during 2006.

Hotels fall into several categories: commercial, resort, residential, extended-stay and casino. Some commercial hotels are also classified as conference facilities, with spaces designed to accommodate large-scale meetings and events. In recent years, the industry has seen the most growth in extended-stay properties, accommodating guests for visits of five nights or longer. By eliminating traditional services like lobby facilities, 24-hour staff and daily housekeeping, the sector has been able to reap profits. In addition, during the last few years, properties more commonly tack on charges to the room rate (for facilities fees, energy taxes or wireless charges, for example), regardless of whether the guest has actually used the features in question. Partly for these reasons, average revenue per available room (known in the trade as RevPAR) increased 7.7 percent in 2006.

Top hotel corporations include Marriott International, Starwood and the Intercontinental Group. Another hospitality giant is Cendant, considered the world's largest hotel franchiser, with Days Inn, Super 8 and other brands under its roof. In July 2006 Cendant's board voted to divide the company into four parts. Its travel booking services became Travelport, which owns Orbitz; the Cendant name continues to be attached to the company that controls the Avis and Budget car rental firms; and the hotels and timeshares are owned by Wyndham Worldwide. (The Blackstone Group bought Travelport and took it private later that year.) Realogy was created to take over the company's real estate functions. Accor and InterContinental are the segment leaders in Europe.

Inhospitality

If you've had a bad customer service experience in the hospitality and tourism industry, you're not alone—and the industry's trade organizations do care about your plight. The industry has struggled for some time with human resource issues, and "the current bad situation is worsening," says the International Society of Hospitality Consultants (ISHC). The ISHC frets that the "spirit of hospitality is deteriorating," with guest services compromised by staff reductions, high turnover and poorly trained workers.

Other labor issues also dog the industry. As hotels compete with other sectors, like retail and fast food, for unskilled and semi-skilled labor, workers are becoming increasingly demanding of benefits. In addition, for a sector that relied heavily on an immigrant labor population, post-September 11 border tightening has also put strain on the industry. But, according to the ISHC, the challenge that will most affect the lodging industry onward from 2006 is higher operating costs, especially those associated with labor and fuel. Hoteliers must also contend with rising insurance premiums (most notably in areas prone to natural disasters such as hurricanes), escalated competition between accommodations, stiffer "brand standards" and the rising cost of construction and renovation.

Electronic customers

Nearly every portion of the hospitality and tourism industry has adjusted to the increased presence of the Internet in travel planning and spending. Industry analysts predict that, worldwide, 38 percent of travel bookings will be made online by 2011 (amounting to $128 billion in sales); another 33 percent currently use the Internet to research lodging and other travel specifics, but then book by other means. According to a TIA survey in 2007, consumers much prefer the comforting glow of their computer screen to waiting on hold, or, heaven forbid, dealing with someone face-to-face. According to the survey, travel agent bookings were down to a mere 4 percent of all travel booked.

Indeed, across the industry, electronic distribution—a means of allowing travel agencies, consolidators, consumers and other bookers to access available rooms, rental cars, flights and even golf course tee times online—has become the norm. The Internet has had the effect of empowering customers, allowing them to comparison shop for the best deals through so-called "e-mediaries" like Expedia, Orbitz and Travelocity, all of which sell rooms and travel services, such as rental cars, often at discounted rates. Consumers' ability to compare prices before booking has created downward pressure on room rates, which, according to the ISHC, will continue to affect hotels' profitability.

At the same time, hotels have become more reliant on electronic database systems and the Internet to fill rooms, and have upgraded the feel and features of their proprietary web sites. As a result, most people now make their arrangements via specific hotel or brand web sites (as opposed to the e-mediaries), and in 2006, consumers using those online portals were more satisfied with the experience than any other travel site, such as Hotwire, Expedia or Travelocity.

While online hotel and transportation bookings allow customers to minimize large-ticket expenses, travelers who book online do have a tendency to be freer with their

Visit Vault at **www.vault.com** for insider company profiles, expert advice, career message boards, expert resume reviews, the Vault Job Board and more.

VAULT CAREER LIBRARY

3

pinched pennies once they arrive at their destination. The TIA reported in 2005 that online bookers spent more and participated in more activities while on vacation than those who arranged their trips by phone.

Rock me Amadeus (and Galileo, too)

The electronic distribution trend stems from the global distribution system (GDS) and Internet distribution system (IDS) models that form the inner machinery of the travel industry. The GDS sector arose in the 1960s as a means for airlines to keep track of their schedules, seat availability and prices. Formed by airline leaders such as American (which founded Sabre), the GDSs were installed in travel agencies in the 1970s, marking one of the first successful business-to-business e-commerce ventures. A few decades later, e-commerce travel sites like Expedia and Travelocity, using Sabre and other GDS systems as their information engines, made travel booking available to the connected masses. In addition, the more than 500,000 travel agents operating worldwide now have a wealth of electronic methods to plug into and shop from. Entities that want to survive in hospitality and tourism can't afford to be shut out of these systems.

There are four main GDSs, or booking systems, in the world, allowing access to bookings for airlines, car rentals, hotels and cruise reservations. Known by different names in various parts of the world, the GDSs are familiar to American travel bookers as Amadeus, Galileo (a subsidiary of Travelport), Sabre and Worldspan. According to the Hotel Electronic Distribution Network Association (HEDNA), cost per booking for hotels through a GDS or IDS is less expensive than any other distribution method, including bookings made directly through the property.

Decommissioning agencies

Ironically, what started off as a tool to help travel agents access and sell travel to consumers has now led to the steady erosion of the travel agency business itself, since consumers no longer need to rely on a middleman to purchase airline tickets or travel packages. The segment is now dominated by bigger traditional travel retailers like American Express and Carlson Wagonlit; many smaller shops have gone under in the past decade. E-retailer Expedia held the position of the 2006 market leader.

Airlines, once a steady source of income for travel agencies, also contributed to the downturn in the agency system. Beginning in the mid-1990s, major air carriers, after decades of providing at least a 10 percent commission to agents on sales, slashed or eliminated these commissions entirely. The loss of income drove some agencies out of business, while others consolidated. According to the BLS, the number of travel agents in the U.S. was around 88,000 in 2006, while it was 103,000 just two years earlier. Associations such as the American Society of Travel Agents insist that the industry can continue to thrive by providing the extra attention to detail, insider knowledge and customer service that consumers crave and can't get from electronic sources.

Feeding the masses

In the vast lodging and recreation territory, it can be difficult to deliver food and other sundries to guests cheaply and efficiently—and that's where outsourcing companies enter the picture. With revenue of more than €12.8 billion in 2006, French company Sodexho is the biggest firm providing outsourced food and services to hospitality facilities (as well as a host of other institutions from offices to nursing homes and elementary schools). It ranks fourth in market capitalization among all players in the restaurant industry, coming in behind McDonald's, Starbucks and Yum! Brands. And its effectiveness has been recognized by the International Association of Outsourcing Professionals, which voted it No. 1 in its industry group and fourth overall.

Another global contender is Aramark, which returned to private ownership in early 2007. The company collected $10 billion from its worldwide food service business in 2006 (and another $1.6 billion from rental and sales of uniforms and job apparel). It provides services to colleges, universities and corporations, and operates concession services at entertainment venues and sporting events.

WORKING IN THE INDUSTRY

Tours of duty

The good thing about hospitality and tourism is that there's almost always a job to be found. The BLS reports that jobs in accommodation and food services as a whole are expected to increase more than 17 percent through 2014. There is a wide variety of jobs in the industry for people of all skill sets and education levels, and high turnover means wide availability. Except for the mid- to upper-level positions, compensation levels are on the low side.

Most entry-level jobs in hotels require little training. Housekeeper and janitor positions require the least training and education, and have the fewest opportunities for advancement, though they can be attractive to people who might want seasonal or temporary work. Those who work in guest services as a host or hostess or desk clerk

Visit Vault at **www.vault.com** for insider company profiles, expert advice, career message boards, expert resume reviews, the Vault Job Board and more.

VAULT CAREER LIBRARY

5

can advance to supervisory positions with sufficient experience. Completion of a program in hotel management will lead to more rapid advancement. Hotels may also need people in the food service industry, such as chefs and restaurant staff. Hospitality involves 24-hour service, and low seniority usually entails working night and weekend shifts, at least initially. Sales positions are usually fast-paced and often require prior experience.

Travel agents need at least a high school diploma, and good sales, research, and computer skills (a BA in geography or travel services helps as well). Currently, 13 states require travel agents to be certified or registered. The Travel Institute offers a downloadable educational course geared toward certification, and the American Society of Travel Agents (ASTA) provides a wealth of information about the industry and working as an agent.

AIRLINE INDUSTRY

A volatile industry

The airline industry consists of companies that move people and cargo with planes. The International Air Transport Association (IATA) claims that this $470 billion worldwide industry stimulates 8 percent of global GDP through tourism, shipping and business travel. But despite its enormous contribution to world commerce, the industry has historically gone through dizzying booms and alarming busts as it reacts to regulatory changes and economic factors. Airlines are just starting to dig themselves out of the hole caused by September 11th. The IATA says the implementation of security measures has cost the industry $5.6 billion per year. Spats with labor unions, troubles with underfinanced pensions, high jet fuel prices and a string of bankruptcies, from which some carriers are still emerging, have caused further havoc. The July 2007 attack on Glasgow's airport is a reminder that the airline industry is still a target for terrorists. Nevertheless, *The Economist* thinks that once these issues have been resolved (no easy task), the airlines will be in a position to expand.

Cleared for takeoff

The airline industry took to the skies following the Wright brothers' first successful flight in 1905. As with many new technologies, airplanes were first used extensively by the military—namely, during World War I, for reconnaissance, bombing and aerial combat. Following the war, when the U.S. found itself with a surplus of military aircraft and pilots without much to do, the postal service opted in 1918 to start a transcontinental airmail service, which ran from New York to San Francisco. To keep costs down, 12 spur routes were spun off to independent contractors. Thus the familiar scions of the friendly skies—American Airlines, United Airlines, TWA and Northwest—were born.

Passenger flights didn't become a reality until Ford introduced a 12-seat plane in 1925. The Ford Trimotor made carrying people potentially profitable. Pan American Airways, the first airline with international destinations, was founded in 1927. Remarkably, airlines remained generally profitable during the Great Depression. Under the New Deal, the government subsidized airlines to carry mail. In 1934, however, postal reforms reduced the amount of money airlines earned for carrying the mail. By 1938, over a million Americans were flying on airplanes. This industry's rapid growth prompted new government policies. In 1938, Congress enacted the Civil Aeronautics Act. The airlines were happy that an independent agency was in charge of aviation policy. Before 1938 Civil Aeronautics Act passed, numerous government agencies and departments pushed and pulled airlines in many directions.

World War II brought many advances to the civilian air transport sector. Innovations initially intended for bombers made passenger planes larger, faster, and able to carry heavier payloads and to fly at higher altitudes. The 1970s saw the introduction of supersonic air travel with the advent of the Concorde. Due to the Concorde's only crash in 2000, as well as world economic effects after the September 11, 2001 attacks, the supersonic airliner stopped flying in October 2003.

Big trouble for the Big Six

After September 11th, Congress gave well over $20 billion to the airline industry in the form of reimbursements for losses incurred while planes were grounded following the attacks, monetary help for new passenger and plane security requirements, and pension funding relief. But many of the industry's major players were forced to shoulder massive debt loads to continue their operations; this was on top of debt they had been accumulating since even before the terrorist attacks. Of the "Big Six"—United, US Airways, American, Northwest, Continental and Delta—all but two, Continental and American, have been forced to file for Chapter 11. Smaller airlines, including Great Plains, Hawaiian, Midway, National, Sun Country and Vanguard, have also shown up in bankruptcy court.

Though passenger confidence continued to grow in the years following the terrorist attacks, the industry's red ink kept on flowing. The SARS scare in Asia, the Iraq war and a slowdown in the economy also hurt airlines. According to a June 2004 Senate report, the industry carried combined debts of more than $100 billion. Thus, major carriers continued to lobby the feds for financial support in the form of subsidies and loans.

Looking up?

The industry has struggled with profitability due to a combination of factors. Air carriers have been hit hard by rising fuel costs, with jet fuel prices in 2007 averaging about $80 per barrel. The high cost of oil remains a huge challenge to the airline industry. The IATA projects that in 2007, the industry's fuel bill will grow to $119 billion, an increase of $8 billion from 2005, when fuel costs totaled $111 billion. Labor disputes and underfinanced pensions have also been expensive problems for many carriers. Even JetBlue, which had strong profits for several years, suffered loses recently as it continues to grapple with rapid growth and rising expenses.

Overall, however, costs associated with air travel have dropped significantly over the past five years, resulting from price competition and attempts to keep ticket prices low despite high fuel costs. In early 2007, IATA Director General and CEO Giovanni Bisignani said the industry's distribution costs (the cost of selling tickets, such as ticket processing, credit card processing fees, etc.) are down 13 percent. Bisignani added that non-fuel unit costs, the cost per seat mile excluding the price of fuel, have declined 15 percent. Industry belt-tightening seems to be working. The IATA reports that the industry break-even fuel price went from $22 per barrel in 2003 to $65 per barrel in 2006.

Recently, the airline industry has started to show other signs of recovery. According to the IATA, a stronger world economy saw passenger traffic rise by 7 percent between 2005 and 2006, and air freight experienced a 5 percent gain. In order to accommodate this increased demand for air travel and to lower their fuel expenditures, airlines began snapping up new, more fuel-efficient planes. The airline industry's profitability has improved, and the IATA predicts that the industry will see $5 billion in profits in 2007. However, IATA Director General Bisignani pointed out that the airlines still have $200 billion dollars of debt. Moreover, he warned that an event like another terrorist attack or a pandemic scare could put many carriers back in the red.

A global network

Around the world, many airlines still are heavily subsidized—or owned outright—by their home nations. While this has been a successful setup for many, others haven't been so lucky. Swissair and Belgium's airline, Sabena, both crumbled when their respective governments couldn't keep up with demands for subsidies. Subsidized international and U.S. carriers have formed global alliances to avoid some regulatory issues and to maximize profits by sharing resources, including routes and marketing strategies. Well-known alliances include Oneworld—an alliance between American Airlines, British Airways and several other carriers—and SkyTeam, a partnership made up of Delta Air Lines, Air France, AeroMexico and other airlines. Such partnerships aren't always successful. An alliance between Dutch carrier KLM and Alitalia fell apart, for instance, after the Italian airline had trouble securing funding from its government patrons.

Partnerships aside, the airline industry remains remarkably competitive, and in today's tough climate, it's everyone for themselves. Tight regulatory controls in the U.S. make it difficult for major domestic carriers to merge. For example, a plan to join United Airlines and US Airways was shot down due to antitrust regulations. The US Airways name showed up again in merger talks, linked to America West for $1.5 billion, and the two companies made it official in September 2005. Then, in November 2006, US Airways made an offer for Delta. However, in early 2007, Delta's creditors rejected US Airways' $10 billion bid. Even if US Airways had purchased Delta, size (large or small) is no guarantee of profit. Four of the Big Six have gone into bankruptcy since 2001, and smaller budget airlines have also started struggling to make a profit.

Going regional

Regional airlines, which benefit from smaller, newer jets and lower operating costs than the domestic giants, have gained ground in recent years, becoming the fastest growing segment of the airline market. Approximately 25 to 30 regional, or commuter, carriers operate in the industry today, according to the Bureau of Labor Statistics. Recent statistics from the Regional Airline Association reveal that one in five domestic airline passengers travel on a regional airline, and that planes serving regional markets make up one-third of the U.S. commercial airline fleet on the whole. The big carriers have taken notice, and many now have controlling interests in newer regional airlines—Delta controls Comair, for instance, while American has American Eagle. In April 2006, Compass Airlines became a subsidiary of Northwest. The trend is reflected in Europe, too. Both globally and domestically, alliances with major carriers give the upstart regionals access to major airport hubs. In some cases, however, regional and low-budget airlines have skirted the hub question altogether by choosing to operate out of slightly out-of-the-way airports—Southwest's use of Islip airport, in a suburb of New York, and JetBlue's adoption of Long Beach, near Los Angeles, are two examples. And in other instances, regional airlines have decided to spread their wings and join the burgeoning low-cost boom. Some regional airlines now do longer haul flights. For example,

Visit Vault at **www.vault.com** for insider company profiles, expert advice, career message boards, expert resume reviews, the Vault Job Board and more.

VAULT CAREER LIBRARY

9

Midwest Airlines (formerly Midwest Express) connects several cities in the Midwest to destinations like Boston, New York and San Francisco.

The budget boom

The budget airline sector—consisting of top performers like Southwest Airlines and JetBlue, plus a growing number of upstarts—has gotten a good deal of attention lately. But budget flight isn't a new phenomenon in the industry. In fact, Southwest has been around since 1971. The difference is in the branding and public acceptance of these carriers, fueled in part by Southwest's customer-centric approach, and by customers' reduced service expectations post-September 11th. Expanded routes have helped, too. Where once low-budget carriers limited their flights to relatively short hauls in regional markets, today's top discount airlines regularly offer cross-country, and even international, flights.

The budget carrier phenomenon has rocked Europe, too, where about 60 low-cost carriers operated in 2006, compared to just four in 1999. European customers have warmed up to the budget boom as well. British-based easyJet increased its passenger flow more than eightfold between 1999 and 2004, while low-cost carrier Ryanair, operating out of Ireland, ranked as one of the top performers in the industry worldwide. Some of the larger airlines have decided to take advantage of the low-cost boom, such as United's Ted and Delta's Song, but to not much avail; Song, in fact, was reabsorbed into Delta in 2006, three years after its first plane took off.

The boom in low-budget carriers isn't limited to North America and Europe. There are also low-fare carriers in Asia, where there are now about 45 discount airlines. Examples are Singapore-based Tiger Airways, Pakistani carrier Aero Asia and Jakarta-headquartered Adam Air. In June 2007, South Korea's largest airline, Korean Air Lines, announced plans to start a low-fare unit to compete with discount carriers in Asia. Some budget airlines are also branching out into long-haul flights across the Atlantic and Pacific.

Cutting costs

Above all, cost-savings are seen as key to the success of low-budget carriers. One way air carriers measure their fiscal health is through cost per available seat mile (or CASM), a complex formula involving airplane capacity, operating costs, route lengths and other factors. Whereas American Airlines spends about 9.4 cents for each seat on each mile flown, budget competitors like Southwest and JetBlue lighten their loads with CASMs of 7.6 cents and 6.4 cents, respectively, according to an

MSNBC article from December 2003. Those pennies add up over time, and so-called "legacy" carriers are under pressure to pinch them ever harder. But with more liberal work rules and a less-senior workforce overall, low-cost carriers beat their established rivals in terms of labor costs.

Other cost-cutting measures in the airline industry overall include streamlining fleets and retiring older planes, canceling unprofitable routes, greater efficiency in procurement processes involving suppliers and slashing commissions once paid regularly to middlemen such as travel agencies. Airlines have saved money through online booking, and they encourage customers to book directly through airlines web sites by offering incentives such online bonus miles. According to a 2006 *International Herald Tribune* article, online booking saves the airline industry $2 billion a year.

These airlines have also realized that consumers prefer to pick and choose their perks. An in-flight cocktail on JetBlue will still set you back $5, but XM radio and DIRECTV are free. Charging for amenities that previously came gratis allows carriers to keep ticket prices low, yet still turn a profit. Many airlines now charge passengers for meals and snacks. On Air Canada, customers now pay $2 for a pillow and a blanket. Moreover, some airlines now charge people for extra legroom. On Northwest, a bigger exit-row seat costs an additional $15. United's flyers can sign up an Economy Plus subscription, which is $299 a year. Subscribers get seats with five inches of extra legroom.

How low can you go?

Low-fare carriers, such as Southwest and JetBlue, were once the darlings of the airline industry. Recently, however, Southwest and JetBlue have had troubles of their own. When an ice storm hit JetBlue's hub at JFK airport in New York in February 2007, passengers were trapped on the tarmac for eight or more hours. It took JetBlue nearly a week to resume normal operations. JetBlue's founder and CEO David Neeleman apologized publicly for what happened and also introduced a "passenger's bill of rights." In May 2007, Neeleman stepped down as the airline's CEO.

In June 2007, *The Wall Street Journal* reported on a growing profit squeeze at Southwest. Over the past four years, Southwest's unit costs—the expenses to fly each seat one mile—have risen almost 20 percent due to increased labor costs and higher fuel prices. The airline's hedges to lock in low fuel prices have become less successful, and passengers have resisted increases in fares. Low-cost carriers are also facing greater competition from other airlines, which copied budget airlines' low-cost model during the post-September 11 industry downturn. Southwest has said it will respond to these pressures by reining in its rapid growth.

The lap of luxury

Some of the newest carriers attempt to attract the super-wealthy and business travelers instead of the budget-minded traveler. Upscale airlines MaxJet, SilverJet and Eos fly between New York and London. On Eos, which was launched in 2005, the airline's "guests" travel in style—they sleep on 6'6" beds and dine on gourmet meals. L'Avion, a business-class airline that offers service between Paris and New York, boasts that passengers can enjoy comfy seats and French food. In the Middle East, luxury airline Al Khayala aims to attract well-heeled customers by providing service that's somewhere between first class and a private jet. The airline uses specially modified Airbus A319s, which the company has configured to seat just 44 people instead of the usual 170 passengers. The wealthy also have the option of the Eclipse 500. Eclipse Aviation makes this "very light jet," which sells for about $1.5 million. Florida-based company DayJet owns several of the small jets and runs an air taxi service for business travelers.

Established airlines are also trying to cater to the luxury market. For example, Lufthansa is expanding the airline's first-class lounge in the Munich airport. New additions to the lounge will include day beds, showers, a gourmet restaurant and a bigger bar. Lufthansa is also spending millions of dollars to upgrade luxe lounges in Paris, New York's JFK, Berlin and Düsseldorf. In addition, Singapore Airlines is upgrading its business and first-class cabins on certain flights. The airline announced that, on some flights, it was rolling out 35-inch wide seats in first class. According to Singapore Air, the seats, which fold into beds, are "the largest seat in the sky" and are "exquisitely upholstered in fine-grained leather with mahogany wood trimming."

Investing in a dream(liner)

Major carriers hope to save money in the future by investing in new planes that offer a lower cost of ownership and operation. In late 2003, Boeing's board of directors gave the company the go-ahead to offer the 787 Dreamliner for sale. The following April, Japan's All Nippon was the first airline to order Boeing's new passenger jet, which promises fuel savings of up to 20 percent. By December 2006, Boeing had nearly 450 orders for the new Dreamliner, and the number had soared to more than 580 by June 2007.

Meanwhile, Airbus, the French firm and Boeing's rival for No. 1 aircraft maker in the world, unveiled a brand new high-scale jumbo-jet, the A380, at the start of 2005 at a gala event during the Le Bourget air show in Toulouse, France. Designed to comfortably seat 555, the A380 rocked the airline industry and represented a joint effort with France, Britain, Germany and Spain, all of whom contributed to the 10-year, $13 billion program that designed the plane. The double-decker leviathan, the largest plane ever built, boasts a 262-foot wingspan and extra space companies can use to install bedrooms, gyms, bars and lounges.

The conservation end, though, is where the A380 packs its biggest punch: its carbon fiber components and fuel-efficient technology are estimated to match or exceed Boeing's 20 percent fuel savings, and slash cost per passenger. However, in October 2006, Airbus announced that the delivery of the new jet would be delayed until the second half of 2007, with the industrial ramp-up finished in 2010. As of June 2007, Airbus had 13 signed contracts from two airlines for the A350, and another five customers had agreed to purchase 148 A350s.

It's not easy being green

Global warming is a hot topic, and airplanes are one of the biggest contributors to carbon emissions. Environmentalists have also criticized the airline industry for planes' air pollution in general. In 2006, Al Gore's documentary *An Inconvenient Truth* was a surprise hit, and a number of businesses have started going "carbon-neutral." Members of the airline and aviation industries are finally starting to address concerns about airplanes' emissions. In June 2007, the IATA has asked the aerospace industry to build zero-emissions airplanes within the next 50 years. Later that month, Louis Gallois, the CEO of Airbus, called on aircraft makers to work together to invent more environmentally-friendly technology. In addition, the European Commission proposed a $2.13 billion public-private plan, dubbed the Clean Sky program. The program, which would start in 2008, would help Europe's air-transportation sector develop technologies to reduce planes' pollution.

Labor pains

According to the Bureau of Labor Statistics, labor costs make up roughly 38 percent of many airlines' operating costs—that's around 40 cents for every dollar spent by an air carrier. Passenger safety regulations and a workforce made up of highly specialized and rarely cross-trained professionals, half of whom are unionized, make it tough for airlines to trim costs from their labor budgets. One way they've done this is by cutting staffs to the bare bones. Following September 11th, Continental Airlines and US Airways were the first to make dramatic cuts, laying off about 20 percent of their respective workforces and paring flight schedules. Most other carriers followed suit.

Cuts in salaries and benefits

At many airlines, employees have agreed to salary and benefit cuts to help keep airlines from going bankrupt. For example, in June 2006, Delta's pilots union agreed to a 14 percent pay cut. Other employees at Delta also agreed to pay cuts, including CEO Gerald Grinstein, whose pay was chopped by 25 percent. In May 2007, Northwest Airlines departed bankruptcy protection following a 20-month reorganization. The restructuring attempted to make the airline competitive for future years. Among other things, Northwest's new labor contracts pay employees less. Flight attendants for the airline used to make as much as $44,190, but now their pay tops out at $35,400.

Although American Airlines posted an annual profit for the first time in six years, many workers were angry during the airline's annual stockholder meeting in May 2007. These employees, who agreed to salary cuts in recent years to keep the airline flying, were unhappy because top executives got bonuses worth millions of dollars. At Northwest, the airline cut pilots' wages by 40 percent and increased their hours. In protest, pilots regularly call in sick to take days off, which results in more cancelled flights.

In order to save money, airlines have also started outsourcing many jobs that used to be filled with airline employees. For example, in 2005, Alaska Airlines replaced its baggage handlers with lower-paid outside contractors. In 2006, Northwest hired non-union employees to clean airplanes. In some cases, airlines have also replaced people with machines—just think of the self-service check-in kiosks that have sprung up at airports in recent years.

WORKING IN THE INDUSTRY

Not just plane jobs

One manager for a major airline says, "This is not a place for the faint of heart. The airline industry is chaotic, and [it has been] particularly brutal for the traditional or legacy carriers since 2001." This source feels career development opportunities are extremely limited. The contact adds, "There is a glut of MBAs that have never moved up due to the incredibly heavy toll exacted by several world events (the dot-com bust, September 11th, SARS, the Iraq war). However, work hours are pretty light, and the travel benefits can be fantastic." An insider at American Airlines agrees that working for the airline industry is tough, explaining, "If making lots of money, getting big bonuses and securing promotion opportunities are important to you, AA may not be the best place to work. However, if you value work/life balance, enjoy solving challenging business problems and love flying first class to any destination across the globe, American really isn't that bad."

The airline industry hires a wide variety of employees ranging from pilots and flight attendants to ticket agents, sales people and managers. Although flight crews are the most visible in the industry, most airline employees don't fly the friendly skies. Rather, they work in airport terminals or in offices. Due to the fact the flights leave at all hours, many who work in the industry have schedules that are variable or irregular. Most jobs with the airline industry are in or near the cities that serve as major airlines hubs. For example, many of Northwest Airlines' jobs are in Minneapolis-St. Paul.

In the airline industry, most recieve standard benefits, such as health insurance and paid vacation—and many also have benefits like retirement plans and profit sharing. One perk that attracts many people to the industry is free or reduced-fare flights for airline employees and sometimes even their family members.

Many airline jobs are also unionized. Unions include the Air Line Pilots Association, International (ALPA), the International Association of Machinists and Aerospace Workers (IAM), and the Association of Flight Attendants-CWA (AFA-CWA). The AFA, which represents 55,000 flight attendants at 20 airlines, claims it is the largest flight attendant union.

FLYING HIGH: FLIGHT ATTENDANTS AND PILOTS

Flight attendants

They are not all pneumatic babes, they're not called stewardesses anymore and, no, they don't want to hear about your cockpit. Flight attendants are both male and female, they vary in appearance, age (age restrictions were recently abolished), and ethnicity, and they can make the difference between a comfortable flight and a nightmarish one. And while you may think that getting your bag of pretzels is of paramount importance, the primary responsibility of a flight attendant is the safety of the passengers. Competition for the few attendant jobs at the "Big Six" carriers is stiff, but smaller regional carriers and airlines are a good place to start a career in teh skies. According the U.S. Bureau of Labor Statistics, the median salary for flight attendants was $43,470 in 2004, the most recent year for which data is available. Bucking industry trends, Southwest pays its flight attendants per trip.

Tested and trained

Flight attendants are trained and tested professionals: they undergo weeks of (often unpaid) training; most large airline companies require them to pass a grueling exam that tests them on every nut and bolt of the aircraft on which they serve. In the wake of the September 11 hijackings, many flight attendants have also undergone training in self-defense.

Flight attendant training lasts about four to six weeks, during which trainees learn emergency procedures, such as how to operate an oxygen system and give first aid. Trainees for international routes get additional instruction in passport and customs regulations and terrorism coping techniques. The training is rigorous and not all trainees pass the examinations. The lure of free travel to exotic locales attracts applicants, but the often unglamorous process of being cloistered with 100 trainees at a budget hotel in Houston or Cleveland weeds many would-be flight attendants out of the group.

At home and away

The hours for flight attendants vary widely, and many flight attendants work at night, on weekends and on holidays. They spend about 75 to 80 hours a month on the ground preparing planes for flights, writing reports following completed flights and waiting (just like passengers) for planes that arrive late. In-flight work can be strenuous because of demanding passengers and crowded flights. Attendants are on their feet during much of the flight and must remain helpful and friendly regardless of how they feel or how obnoxious their passengers are. As a result of scheduling variations and limitations on flying time, many flight attendants have 11 or more days off a month. Attendants can be away from their home base—often the hub city of the airline they work for—a great deal of the time, and are compensated by the airlines with hotel accommodations, meal allowances and, of course, discounted or free tickets for both themselves and their immediate families.

Save yourself

It takes a patient, extroverted personality to become a flight attendant. It also takes steady nerves and a sense of duty. In the event of an emergency, atttendants must take the passengers' safety into account before their own. This can entail anything from simple reassurance to directing passengers during evacuation following an emergency landing. Though the chances of a plane crash are small, flight attendants must be undaunted by the prospect of disaster. Airlines that serve international destinations also look for individuals who are fluent in foreign languages, such as Spanish, French, German, Chinese, Japanese, Greek, Italian and Russian.

Pilots

Senior pilots are among the best-paid employees in the United States. According to the Bureau of Labor Statistics, the median salary for pilots, co-pilots and flight engineers was $137,160 in 2004, the most recent year for which data was available. Because pilots have such good incomes, competition for these jobs is understandably intense. Pilots need a commercial pilot's license with an instrument rating. They also must have a medical certificate. Pilots need to have 20/20 vision, with or without corrective lenses; good hearing; and be in excellent health overall. In addition, they have to be certified to fly the types of aircraft the airline operates. In early 2007, the FAA said the agency would allow pilots, who previously had been allowed to fly until they were 60 years old, to keep working in the cockpit until age 65.

Most planes have a pilot and co-pilot. Generally, the captain, who is the most experienced pilot, supervises all other crew members. The pilot and co-pilot share the job of flying. They also split other duties, such as monitoring instruments and communicating with air traffic controllers. In a handful of airplanes, there's a third pilot—called a second officer or flight engineer—who helps the other pilots.

Calling Ted Striker

The more FAA licenses a pilot has—that is, the more flying time he has on complex, modern equipment—the more in demand his services will be. For this reason, military-trained pilots are particularly desirable. However, recent military actions mean they are in short supply.

If you don't want to become an Air Force fighter pilot, there are other ways to get experience flying planes. Civilians can learn to fly at a private flight school and gain practice flying on progressively larger aircraft; they may work their way up from private jets to regional carriers and from there to the larger airlines. One pilot, who is now the captain of an Airbus A320 passenger airline, says he "first spent several years flying for charter and mail contract carriers." Before a major U.S. airline hired the pilot, he flew for a smaller regional airline.

Initially, a newly hired pilot will be a flight engineer or co-pilot, assisting the captain with communications with control towers, instrument readings and flight duties. Work assignments for flight attendants and pilots are frequently given on a seniority basis, with the most senior employees having the pick of the litter. New hires, therefore, must be prepared to receive less desirable assignments initially.

Jobs on the ground

If you're afraid of flying, there still might be a job for you in the airline industry. Positions on the ground vary greatly. They include a wide range of jobs, such as mechanics, baggage handlers, ticket agents, customer service representatives and reservations agents. Airlines also hire people to work in information technology, marketing and sales, finance and administration and more.

The skills and education you need depend on the on-the-ground position for which you are applying. For most administrative positions, employees need strong computer skills. A recent posting for a finance associate with United required an MBA and two years of related work experience in an area such as banking, consulting or accounting. Mechanics need to have licenses. Often, airlines are seeking reservations representatives who speak languages other than English, including Spanish, Japanese, Mandarin Chinese, Creole, French and German.

Salaries for these jobs vary as well. According to the BLS, the 2004 median salary for aircraft mechanics and service technicians was $54,890. Reservation ticket agents and travel clerks' median salary was $31,450, and customer service representatives typically earned $28,420.

Some airlines also need temporary and seasonal workers, usually in jobs such as customer service and ramp service. Working in a temporary job can sometimes give you a foot in the door for a more permanent position. In addition, airlines including United and Northwest have paid and unpaid internships.

Navigating airline interviews

Most sources at airlines, regardless of their position, say the interview process can be long and usually involves multiple meetings. A reservations agent for Continental says, "The hiring process was very long. It took about six months from resume submitted to being hired." The contact says there were two rounds of interviews. One HR person with American Airlines says, "The interview process can be lengthy and meeting with a number of people the norm." A mechanic with Continental says getting the job entailed three interviews. Flight attendants for various airlines say a group interview is part of the hiring process.

An airline agent says interview questions included "Where do you see yourself 10 years from now?", "How do you deal with difficult people?", "Do you work better by yourself or in a group?", "Do you loose you temper easily?" and "How important it is to spend the holidays with your loved ones?" Another ticket agent says one question was, "Describe the most difficult problem you dealt with at a previous job and how you handled it." A manager says questions included "What is your greatest accomplishment?" Some say they also needed to pass a medical examination or psychological tests.

The future of airline careers

Industry employment is largely at the mercy of the economy, though the BLS expects jobs to increase somewhat independently due to a growing population and greater demand for air travel. The BLS predicts employment growth initially in low-cost and local carriers. After larger airlines recover from bankruptcy, the BLS says, larger airlines will start hiring again. However, the airline industry is often as turbulent as the skies it flies, and salaries and perks aren't what they used to be.

RECOMMENDED READING:

Periodicals and web sites

World Tourism Association—www.world-tourism.org
American Hotel and Lodging Association (AHLA)—www.ahla.com
The Travel Institute—www.thetravelinstitute.com
American Society of Travel Agents—www.astanet.com

International Air Transport Association—www.iata.org
Air Transport World—www.atwonline.com
Airwise—news.airwise.com
Pilot Jobs—www.pilotjobs.com
AV Jobs—www.avjobs.com

Aircraft Maintenance Technology—www.amtonline.com
Airways—www.airways.com

Books

Bock, B. *Welcome Aboard!: Your Career as a Flight Attendant.* Aviation Supplies & Academics, Inc., 2005.

Brown, G. *Job Hunting for Pilots: Networking Your Way to a Flying Job.* Aviation Supplies & Academics, Inc., 2001.

Havers, R. and Chris Tiffney. *Airline Confidential: Lifting the Lid on the Airline Industry.* Sutton Publishing, 2007.

Mark, R. *Professional Pilot Career Guide.* McGraw-Hill Professional, 1999.

Marks, M. *Flying by the Seat of My Pants: Flight Attendant Adventures on a Wing and a Prayer.* WaterBrook Press, 2005.

McCoy, M. *Airline Wings as a Career.* Trafford Publishing, 2006.

Ward, K. *The Essential Guide To Becoming A Flight Attendant.* Kiwi Productions, 2001.

EMPLOYER GUIDE

PROFILES

Top Hospitality & Tourism Employers

Accor

2, rue de la Mare-Neuve
91021 Evry Cedex
France
Phone: +33-1-69-36-80-80
Fax: +33-1-69-36-79-00
www.accor.com

LOCATIONS

Cedex, France (HQ)
Bangkok
São Paulo
Segrate, Italy
Sydney
Carrollton, TX

Additional locations throughout the US and international operations in 98 countries.

THE STATS

Employer Type: Public Company
Stock Symbol: AC
Stock Exchange: Euronext Paris
Chairman: Serge Weinberg
CEO: Gilles Pélisson
2007 Employees: 150,000
2007 Revenue (€ mil.): €8,121

DEPARTMENTS

Communications/Public Relations
Conference & Banqueting
Customer Services
Development/Franchise
Entertainment/Sport/Leisure
Finance/Accounting
Food & Beverage
Front Office
Hotel Management
Housekeeping
HR/Training
IT Systems
Kitchen
Legal
Maintenance/Technical/Security
Marketing/Quality
Purchasing
Region/Multi Unit Management
Reservation
Sales/Distribution
Secretariat/Administration
Sustainable Development
Thalassotherapy/SPA

KEY COMPETITORS

Hilton Hotels
InterContinental Hotels
Marriott international

EMPLOYMENT CONTACT

www.accor.com/gb/rh/accueil.asp

THE SCOOP

Chain, chain, chain

One of the world's largest hotel groups, Accor is the leading European exemplar of the budget hotel, putting people to sleep for cheap in a sector once known for its bed-and-breakfasts and small, independent hotels. Now, Accor's hotel chains span the world. Its Ibis, Formule 1 and Motel 6 brands, among others, proudly house cost-conscious lodgers in over 100 countries. The company is sticking with what it knows best: of its more than 4,000 hotels, only about 320 (8 percent) are upscale establishments. Of the rest, 56 percent are economy and 36 percent are mid-scale.

While this approach to the hotel business may not be glamorous, it has largely shielded Accor from cyclical downturns in the hospitality industry. Simply put, the average thrifty traveler is likelier to choose a Motel 6 than a more expensive alternative; the same holds true for businesses sending employees on work-related trips. While Accor's hotels might not attract the most tourists, at least they don't suffer when tourist travel dries up. This occurred recently in the aftermath of the attacks of September 11th and the war in Iraq, and Accor emerged much better off financially than its well-heeled competition.

Also in Accor's favor, budget travel received a boost in the 1990s with the rise of discount airlines such as EasyJet and Ryan Air, making the erstwhile-unaffordable weekend trip easier to manage for Europe's penny-pinchers. As the leading European budget hotel group, Accor gained from these trends.

Rest easy

Accor got its footing in France in 1967, with the opening of the first Novotel, which filled the void between big city luxury lodging and small town inns with is highway-side hotel chains. The company built and acquired other hotel chains throughout France and then expanded internationally during the 1970s. The company held 195 hotels in 22 countries by 1978, including properties in South and North America, Africa and Asia.

A 1980 investment in Jacques Borel International, which operated restaurants and the high-end Sofitel hotel chain, led Accor to purchase that company's operations outright in 1982. The sale made Accor one of the top-10 hoteliers in the world, with a hotel count of 452, more than 1,500 restaurants and a staff of 39,000.

Free lunch

Accor began to enter the business of providing employee vouchers in the 1980s, first with the 1982 purchase of Jacques Borel International and then with the 1985 acquisition of British firm Luncheon Voucher. Employee vouchers, usually of the "luncheon" variety, are tickets (i.e., "vouchers") given to employees as a benefit or bonus. Accor took on the task of coordinating these vouchers, both with the companies dispensing them and the various restaurants sponsoring them.

Accor soon expanded beyond vouchers for food, introducing employee benefit programs to cover health care, transportation, parking costs, uniform cleaning and even housework. By 1987, Accor led the world in providing vouchers. The business has now evolved beyond paper ticket stubs and into electronic gift cards and consumer loyalty programs. Through its Accor Services arm, the firm sells voucher services to corporations, governments and nonprofit organizations.

Formule 1 goes off to the races

With the debut of its Formule 1 hotel in 1985, Accor introduced the idea of saving money by reducing staff. Inexpensive both for Accor and its customers, Formule 1 hotels came without restaurants, private bathrooms or reception staff, and pre-fabricated construction kept setup costs low. Each 60-room facility required just two workers to maintain its operations; visitors merely swiped a credit card and then carried their own bags to their room. After the successful launch of its first two Formule 1 hotels in France, Accor began building more throughout Europe. On top of expanding its Formule 1 chain, Accor was opening hotels and restaurants at breakneck speed, averaging one new operation a day through 1989.

Although Accor opened Sofitel, Novotel and Ibis hotels in the U.S. in the 1980s, the company didn't make much headway in the market until 1990, when it purchased the Motel 6 chain and its 650 hotels for $1.3 billion. Motel 6 was established during the same period as Accor—the 1960s, that golden age of motels—with a facility in Santa Barbara, California. In 1991, Accor purchased fellow hospitality firm Compagnie Internationale des Wagons-Lits et du Tourisme, which had operations in hotels, car rental, trains, travel agencies and food service.

Accor reversed course in the mid-1990s and sold off some non-core businesses, including its catering and rental car interests. In 1997, Accor was back to splashing around the cash, entering into a 50/50 joint venture with Carlson Companies, merging its Wagonlit travel agencies with Carlson's operations to create—you guessed it—Carlson Wagonlit Travel, a travel booking company. Also in 1997,

Visit Vault at **www.vault.com** for insider company profiles, expert advice, career message boards, expert resume reviews, the Vault Job Board and more.

VAULT CAREER LIBRARY

25

Accor purchased a majority interest in a casino chain and promptly renamed the enterprise Accor Casinos. A spate of acquisitions in 1999 brought the U.S.-based Red Roof Inn chain (founded in Columbus, Ohio, 1972) and Vivendi hotels into Accor's holdings.

Eastward, ho!

In the new millennium, threats of terrorism, SARS, avian bird flu and high gas prices combined to put a strain on the travel industry. Accor's income fell accordingly; while the company netted €430 million in profit for 2002, that figure fell 37 percent the next year to €270 million. The company responded by diversifying into international locales, adding hotels in China, Panama and Peru, on top of new locations for its luxury Sofitel hotel chain.

Over the course of 2004, Accor added 188 new properties and became the largest shareholder in Club Med, purchasing a 30 percent share. In February 2005, Accor won an international bid for a luxury hotel in Mecca, Saudi Arabia. A month later, it garnered a €1 billion investment from, actually, the investment firm Colony Capital. With the extra cash flow, Accor announced it would increase its capacity by 20 percent within three years, upping its companywide hotel room count to 550,000.

Log on, sleep in

After coming a little late to the Internet game—the company web site didn't launch until 2000—Accor has recently stepped up efforts to integrate the World Wide Web into its booking and the services it offers guests. In August 2004, the company announced a partnership with T-mobile to enable wireless Internet access in its Red Roof Inns.

In February 2005, the hotel group reported a 44 percent increase in online bookings from 2003 to 2004, primarily due to added language functionality. Accorhotels.com is now available in French, English, German and Spanish, with regional sites in Brazilian, Chinese, Japanese and Thai, which reflects the company's mission to provide hotel rooms in every corner of the globe.

Do the corporate shuffle

After leading the hotel giant for nine years, CEO Jean-Marc Espalioux announced he would step down from his post in October 2005. His successor was named in January 2006, after months of bickering among the company's leaders. Behind the bickering?

Company Chairman (and co-founder) Gérard Pélisson was accused of nepotism for backing the bid of his nephew, Gilles Pélisson.

Additionally, loose lips in the headhunting process caused one executive at tech firm Capgemini to lose his job when his employers discovered he was considering a move to Accor. Looking for an expedient end to the drama, Gilles Pelisson was given the CEO position in January, on the condition that Gerard Pelisson resign from his chairman seat, which went to former retail executive Serge Weinberg.

Sell, sell, sell!

The junior Pélisson immediately set to work reshaping the gargantuan company, with the intention of refocusing on hotels and voucher services. Since his promotion to the executive boardroom, Pélisson has shed non-core operations, selling off Accor's half of Carlson Wagonlit Travel to its in the venture for $465 million in April 2006.

The company's stake in Club Med went on the auction block a few months later—Accor sold most of its 30 percent share in the luxury resort chain. In February 2007, Accor's Go Voyages tour operation went to luxury brand mogul Bernard Arnault, for $364 million, followed by the sale of the Red Roof Inn chain in April 2007, for $1.3 billion. Accor rounded out its sell-off spree by dumping its Italian restaurant business to a private equity firm for €135 million in August 2007.

Moving and shaking

Meanwhile, the company has gone about its hotel and services business with gusto. In March 2006, Accor announced an ambitious plan to open more than 200,000 new rooms and a little over 4,000 total hotels by 2010, mostly in the economy and budget hotel market, with two-thirds of the openings in emerging markets. The company grew even more ambitious by November 2007, increasing its projections for 2010 to a room count of 600,000 and new hotels to 5,000.

On the services front, Accor bought out other companies' shares in the Brazil voucher company Ticket Servicos in December 2006 to bring that firm's €500 million annual revenue completely into Accor's coffers. The purchase of French gift card and voucher seller Kadeos in March 2007 made Accor the national leader in the gift card market—Accor now sells its voucher services and loyalty programs in 35 countries. Accor amped up its Asian services presence with the June 2007 purchase of Surf Gold, which provides loyalty programs to businesses in China, South Korea, Hong Kong, India and Taiwan.

Visit Vault at **www.vault.com** for insider company profiles, expert advice, career message boards, expert resume reviews, the Vault Job Board and more.

VAULT CAREER LIBRARY   27

In November 2007, CEO Pélisson unveiled a brand new business model, the cause of which was advice (or pressure) from billion-euro investor Colony Capital, according to analysts. It's a multipronged strategy, reflective of Accor's truly international reach; the firm will open up a slew of new budget- and mid-range hotels in "emerging countries," such as India and China, while also revitalizing Motel 6 in the States and debuting new hotel brands across Europe. Two of those brands are All Seasons, a European budget chain, and Sofitel, which is being repackaged as a "luxury" hotel.

At the same time, the firm is looking to reduce the number of hotels it owns. Accor currently owns outright about 50 percent of its properties; it's aiming to own only about 23 percent by 2010. It will probably sell its hotels to professional property managers, keeping a partial stake in real estate while avoiding unforeseen developments in the local economy (can you say "housing bubble?"). Although it is still too early to tell if Pélisson's efforts will pay off, Accor finished strong in 2006, with revenue in the services business growing 20 percent for the year, and overall revenue increasing 6 percent to €7.6 billion.

GETTING HIRED

Come one, come all

With 170,000 employees all over the planet, Accor has a job for pretty much everybody. You can look up these jobs at its web site: www.accor.com/gb/rh/accueil.asp

They have everything from the maids who clean bedrooms to the managers who keep the hotels running smoothly to the executives who oversee the company's regional operations. If that seems like too many possibilities to wrap your mind around, Accor helpfully publishes a guide to the professions under its purview on this web site, which is also home to a database of openings searchable by location, department and hotel chain. Applicants may submit their cover letter and resume online upon finding a position that seems a good fit.

Accor emphasizes promoting from within the organization—the company estimates that 90 percent of its managers have worked their way up to that position. Accor also hires interns and apprentices; people starting in these positions are often end up with permanent positions at the company.

To facilitate the upward mobility of its workers, Accor started the Academie Accor, a company-run university to train hotel professionals, in 1985. The university's services have since been taken worldwide, so that all of Accor's employees can benefit from the training. In addition to education and training, Accor's workers enjoy perks that come with the business, like voucher cards good for deals at company hotels and restaurants, on top of special travel promotions. Accor also shares its spoils with annual profit-sharing payouts.

OUR SURVEY SAYS

Small for something so big

Although Accor has an army of hotel staffers across the globe, opportunities for advancement at the company seem to be readily available, probably because of the budget nature of most of its chains. "I have been promoted every 18 months since commencement," remarks an Australian sales director, "and [I] have tripled my salary in seven years." A general manager type agrees: "Anyone that is capable, dedicated, and is open to continuing education, is assured a successful career [at Accor]."

This could also mean that there aren't enough able bodies around, as one source writes that "The biggest need for personnel at present is in operations." This category includes managerial types and even VPs of operations. "Although Accor has a strong 'promote from within' culture," the source adds, "it will, in my opinion, not be possible to meet these needs solely by this method."

Also, as the company continues its massive international expansion, that can only mean more job for these managerial types, especially as the firm looks to sell off its real estate holdings and just administer its hotels. "An aggressive expansion of [Accor's] brands is planned for the next five years," claims one source, adding that "Accor will continue to recruit operations people, as well as more employees for home office support positions." Another seems positively enamored, writing, "corporate culture is second to none" and "people love working for Accor, it is like family (with the family politics and passion)."

Visit Vault at **www.vault.com** for insider company profiles, expert advice, career message boards, expert resume reviews, the Vault Job Board and more.

VAULT CAREER LIBRARY   29

Air Canada

Air Canada Centre, 7373 Côte-
Vertu Boulevard West
Dorval, Quebec H4Y 1H4
Canada
Phone: (514) 205-7856
Fax: (514) 205-7859
www.aircanada.com

LOCATION

Dorval, Quebec (HQ)

THE STATS

Employer Type: Public Company
Stock Symbol: AC.A, AC.B
Stock Exchange: Toronto
Chairman: Robert A. Milton
President & CEO: Montie Brewer
2007 Employees: 31,800
2007 Revenue ($mil.): C$10,599

DEPARTMENTS

Administrative & Professional
Aircraft Maintenance
Airport Ground Services
Facilities/Building Maintenance
Flight Attendants
Passengers Services
Pilots

KEY COMPETITORS

American Airlines
Northwest Airlines
WestJet

EMPLOYMENT CONTACT

www.aircanada.com/en/about/career

THE SCOOP

Like so many Canada geese

Canada's largest airline, Air Canada keeps over 32 million passengers airborne every year, eh? The airline offers direct flights to 170 locales on five continents. And its reach extends even farther, to 855 destinations, through its affiliation with the Star Alliance—a codesharing brotherhood of airlines that also includes United Airlines, Lufthansa and Air New Zealand.

The airline also gets pro sports teams and corporate groups to their very important appointments on chartered flights through Air Canada Jetz, sets up Canada-bound travelers with plane and cruise vacation packages through Air Canada Vacations, and ships cargo to 150 destinations worldwide through Air Canada Cargo. For about five million loyal customers, Air Canada hosts a frequent flyer program, Aeroplan. Finally, the airline's aircraft maintenance arm, ACTS, provides repairs for several other companies, including JetBlue, United Airlines and Canada's Department of National Defence. These various subsidiaries are all housed under the auspices of Air Canada's parent company, ACE (Air Canada Enterprises) Aviation Holdings. The firm has maintained this structure since emerging from bankruptcy in late 2004.

Headquartered in Dorval, Quebec—a city just outside of Montreal—Air Canada was voted Best Airline in North America in 2007 by readers of *Global Traveler*, a U.S. magazine. Air Canada employs 31,800 pilots, flight attendants, travel agents, ground workers, mechanics and the like.

TCA stand for Totally Controlling the Air

In the late 1930s, Canada was just starting to rebound from the Great Depression, partly through the recovery of the worldwide economy and also due to the Canadian government's increasing propensity towards social welfare programs. One of these programs was a government-owned airline. Now known as Air Canada, the airline began corporate life in 1937 as Trans-Canada Airlines (TCA).

The government gave TCA, and its founding fleet of three planes, a near complete monopoly over the nation's airspace. Its only competitor was the Vancouver-based Canadian Pacific Airlines, which was founded in the 1940s by Canadian Pacific Railway to fly mail routes on the West Coast.

NEW YORK INSTITUTE OF
TECHNOLOGY

Visit Vault at **www.vault.com** for insider company profiles, expert advice, career message boards, expert resume reviews, the Vault Job Board and more.

VAULT CAREER LIBRARY   31

By 1942, Canada's prime minister had designated TCA as Canada's only international and transcontinential airline. The government expanded TCA's fleet and reach significantly during the post-World War II economic boom of the 1950s, as demand for passenger air travel increased. Rival CPA refused to perish, however, and in 1959 the government allowed it one transcontinental flight in each direction per day.

Air Canada gets company

Unperturbed by its new neighbor in the sky, TCA added routes to Europe and Asia in the 1960s. The company changed its name in 1965 to Air Canada, and the next year the government enacted further legislation, directing small, regional airlines not to compete with Air Canada and CPA. Also, it ordered all airlines to work together, in terms of sharing equipment and establishing airfares. In 1969, the government refined the system by limiting regional airlines' operations to specific boundaries.

However, this heavy regulation of the airline industry didn't result in lower fares and more competition. Although Air Canada's revenue reached all-time highs in the 1970s, the U.S. began to deregulate its airlines during the decade, and Canada wasn't far behind. The Air Canada Act of 1978 ended the government's regulatory control over airlines' prices, routes and operations. In the process, Canadian Pacific's transcontinental service was freed from its restraints, giving it the chance to nab more of Air Canada's market share.

Canadian Pacific debuted its international service in 1980 and Air Canada was slow to adapt to this unaccustomed feeling of competition. The company took on heavy debt to overhaul its aging, nigh-obsolete fleet, as well as purchase some of its regional competitors. This left it especially weakened when a recession hit in 1982— Air Canada ended that year with a loss of $15 million.

In 1985, Canada's transport minister, Donald Mazankowski, announced plans to take Air Canada private, to better compete in the deregulation era. Two years later, the industry was completely deregulated with the 1987 passing of the National Transportation Act. Air Canada launched new trans-Atlantic routes that year, including flights to Glasgow, Paris, Munich, Bombay and Singapore. Air Canada pulled in C$3 billion and enjoyed a 54 percent share of the domestic air travel market in 1987, and then it went up for sale in 1988. Air Canada was fully privatized by 1989.

Aerial gymnastics

Air Canada and many of its peers in the industry faced trouble in the early 1990s as the war in the Persian Gulf hurt international travel. In an effort to cushion itself against the blow—and to trim about C$570 million from its annual costs—Air Canada announced in October 1990 that it would cut nearly 3,000 jobs. After the cuts, the airline reported a loss of C$74 million in 1990, followed by a deeper loss of C$128 in 1991.

CEO Pierre J. Jeanniot bowed out from his executive role in the middle of the trouble, and was replaced in 1992 by former Delta Airlines executive Hollis L. Harris. The new boss instituted a cost-cutting plan, aimed at saving C$300 million by 1993—he immediately saved C$20 million by eliminating 100 clerical positions and 250 management positions, including four SVPs and the COO. The airline also sold a number of non-core businesses, and relocated its headquarters from downtown Montreal to Dorval Airport. By 1994, Air Canada was profitable again.

Air Canada focused on enjoying a pleasant ride into the end of the century, signing an "open skies" agreement with the U.S. in 1995 that introduced 30 new U.S. routes (soon to be very popular). As the company celebrated its 60th birthday in 1997, its annual revenue was in excess of C$5 billion, a company record. Also that year, Air Canada started the Star Alliance, its networking and codesharing coalition with Lufthansa, Scandinavian Airlines, Thai Airways International and United Airlines.

In 1996, Harris passed the CEO role on to his protégé, Lamar Durrett, who quickly earned the ire of investors through mismanagement. After a less than impressive turn at the helm, including a 13-day pilot strike in September 1998 that cost the airline C$250 million, Durrett stepped down in August 1999. He was replaced by Robert Milton, a seven-year veteran of the company.

We'll call it "Air Canadian Airlines"

Meanwhile, Air Canada's longtime adversary Canadian Airlines (formerly Canadian Pacific) had gone through its own crisis in the 1990s. Air Canada had made an offer to take over the airline in 1992, only to back out, wary of the C$7 billion debt it would have to shoulder if the airlines combined. However, Canadian possessed some enviable international routes and remained an attractive prospect.

As Air Canada readied another bid in 1999, Toronto-based buyout firm Onex entered the fray, and soon formulated a plan to buy both Canadian and Air Canada and merge them together. Onex also had a secret partner in the plan—AMR Corporation, parent

Visit Vault at **www.vault.com** for insider company profiles, expert advice, career message boards, expert resume reviews, the Vault Job Board and more.

VAULT CAREER LIBRARY

33

company of American Airlines. Air Canada responded by taking Onex to court and launching its own bid for Canadian. The court ruled in favor of an obscure law, which stipulated that no shareholder could own over 10 percent of Air Canada, thus scuttling Onex's plans. Then, in July 2000, Air Canada bought its longtime rival for only C$61 million.

Chapter 11: the Bankruptcy

After the merger, Air Canada realized it had bought a company that was losing roughly C$2 million per day, with C$12 billion in debt (hence the low selling price). Although Air Canada now controlled 80 percent of the Canadian airline market, it struggled to integrate Canadian Airlines' network. Soon, low-cost and no-frills airlines like WestJet exposed Air Canada for the relative dinosaur it was. Matters got so bad that CEO Milton was featured in a series of ads in August 2000, promising that Air Canada would work out its operational problems soon.

Air Canada started up two low-cost airlines of its own; Tango hit the skies in November 2001, followed by Zip in September 2002. But they were too late to avoid the unavoidable—the terrorist attacks of September 11, 2001, which caused security costs to rise dramatically and passengers to temporarily retreat from air travel. Then, when the U.S. went to war in Iraq in 2003, fuel costs rose dramatically. And finally, the SARS outbreak in Asia in 2003 crippled Air Canada's routes in the region. It was a recipe for disaster, and Air Canada's losses exceeded C$1.6 billion between 2001 and 2003. The airline filed for bankruptcy in April 2003.

After entering bankruptcy proceedings, the airline announced it would cut 3,600 jobs from its 40,000-strong workforce to realize savings of C$770 million. The company also cut 20 percent of its management team, with remaining executives taking a 15 percent pay cut. In July 2003, pilots agreed to a 15 percent pay cut and a reduction in their ranks by 317.

Invest in the Air

Despite this restructuring, Air Canada struggled to line up an investor to propel the airline out of bankruptcy. A C$650 million equity deal that Air Canada struck with Trinity Time Investments in December 2003 fell through the following April after Air Canada couldn't get its unions to accept Trinity's proposed changes to their pension plans. A judge then extended Air Canada's bankruptcy protection for four months as the company scrambled to find investors.

Deutsche Bank stepped up its investment offer from C$450 million to C$850 million and New York firm Cerberus—which had lost out to Trinity just months earlier—came through with another C$250 million. Along with C$1.1 billion in concessions from its unions, the airline was able to emerge from bankruptcy in September 2004. At this time, ACE (Air Canada Enterprises) Aviation Holdings was organized to house Air Canada and its related subsidiaries, and Air Canada was taken private. CEO Milton now leads the larger ACE Aviation organization, with Montie Brewer stepping in as Air Canada's CEO in December 2004.

The password is ...

To keep its tenuous grip on financial viability, Air Canada announced it would pare down its fleet of planes and dissolve Zip, the low-cost carrier it debuted in 2002. Low-cost airlines continued to drive down Air Canada's market share; as its domestic capacity shrank from 87 percent in 2000 to 51 percent in 2004, low-cost WestJet's capacity grew from 5 percent to 23 percent in the same period.

Soon, Air Canada and WestJet clashed directly, with Air Canada taking its rival to court in July 2004. Air Canada accused WestJet of stealing information from its computer system and using a pilfered password to log onto Air Canada's reservations database over 240,000 times. WestJet countered that Air Canada hired private investigators to sift through its executive's garbage. The conflict went on for two years, until WestJet admitted to the information mining in May 2006 and paid Air Canada's court expenses ($5 million), on top of donating C$10 million to children's charities.

Taking off, eventually

Air Canada now tries to use its size to its advantage, adding more services to its flights instead of paring them down for low-budget rides. Passenger loads improved from 2004 to 2005, and the company just rolled out more in-flight goodies. In August 2005, for instance, the airline added web check-in for flights from the U.S. to Canada—a service it already supplied for domestic flights. The following November, the company updated its fleet's business class cabins with fully reclining seats. Satellite radio became available on flights in March 2007, provided by XM Canada, the Canadian licensee of XM Satellite Radio.

Even as the airline improved the comfort of its aircrafts, however, it tussled with its unions over a $6 billion order for 32 jets from Boeing. After agreeing to purchase 18 Boeing 777s and 14 of the newfangled 787 Dreamliners in April 2005, Air Canada

Visit Vault at **www.vault.com** for insider company profiles, expert advice, career message boards, expert resume reviews, the Vault Job Board and more.

VAULT CAREER LIBRARY

35

was forced to retract its bid when pilots didn't agree to the costs of training for the new planes. However, talks between Boeing and Air Canada resumed and the deal was back on again in November 2005. Boeing 787s will begin entering the fleet in 2010; Air Canada ultimately expects to add 60 of them to its fleet. In the midst of the scuffle, Air Canada's revenue grew to C$9.5 billion in fiscal 2005, with year-end losses relatively minor, at C$33 million.

Spin-offs

To raise money, Air Canada's parent company, ACE Aviation, began spinning off portions of the Air Canada family in 2005, starting with a 50 percent share of Air Canada's frequent flyer program, Aeroplan. A quarter of the regional airline Jazz went on the auction block in February 2006. The following November, it was Air Canada's turn, and ACE raised C$525 million by selling a quarter of Air Canada's shares on the public market—the largest North American IPO in three years.

In February 2007, ACE announced it would completely sell off ACTS, the airline's repair unit, by the end of the year; it raised $723 million by selling 70 percent of it in October. Also in October 2007, the firm raised some funding through offerings of its Aeroplan Income Fund and Jazz Air Income Fund.

Fiscal 2006 results show Air Canada's revenue steadily growing, reaching C$10.1 billion for the year. Profit remains elusive, but analysts point to rising passenger capacity and the airline's devotion to international expansion as signs that Air Canada will continue its recovery.

GETTING HIRED

Oh, Canada

Air Canada lists its current openings at its career web site, www.aircanada.com/en/about/career. Applications can be filed online. With its international reach, Air Canada employs folks beyond its home country's borders, and many positions are found within the contiguous 48 U.S. states. However, the company's headquarters are just outside of Montreal, so many administrative and professional positions are located there.

The web site also provides information on the benefits enjoyed by Air Canadians, which include health insurance, pension plan and minimum vacation time of two weeks per year. Air Canada also gives its employees training, of both the classroom and online varieties—because the airline flies to many nations, Air Canada also provides language instruction in French, English, Spanish and German. Best of all is the industry-standard perk of travel privileges. Workers and their immediate families enjoy airfare discounts and deals on hotel, car rental and tour reservations through Air Canada's travel industry affiliations.

Air Canada is also looking to swoop in and carry away the fresh-from-college set. Recent MBAs and undergraduates in the finance, marketing/sales, HR/industrial relations, IT or engineering are welcome to apply for Air Canada's Graduate and Undergraduate Hire Program. These 18-month assignments place graduates one of the airline's operational divisions—at the airport, in the call center or on board an aircraft—for three months before pairing them with an executive or senior director mentor to learn more about the finer details of the company. These positions are available in Montreal, Toronto and Vancouver, and questions about the program may be referred to grad@aircanada.ca.

Air France-KLM

45, Rue de Paris
75747 Roissy
Cedex-CDG
France
Phone: +33-1-41-56-78-00
Fax: +33-1-41-56-56-00
www.airfranceklm-finance.com

www.klm.com

LOCATIONS

Roissy, France (HQ)
New York, NY (US HQ)
Atlanta, GA • Boston, MA •
Chicago, IL • Cincinnati, OH •
Detroit, MI • Houston, TX • Los
Angeles, CA • Miami, FL • Newark,
NJ • Philadelphia, PA • San
Francisco, CA • Sunrise, FL •
Washington, DC

International locations in 114
countries.

THE STATS

Employer Type: Public Company
Stock Symbol: AKH
Stock Exchange: Euronext Paris
Chairman & CEO: Jean-Cyril Spinetta
2007 Employees: 104,991
2007 Revenue ($mil.): $30,768

KEY COMPETITORS

American Airlines
British Airways
Lufthansa

EMPLOYMENT CONTACT

Air France:
emploi.airfrance.com/FR/fr/home/
home_accueil.jsp

KLM:
www.klm.com/corporate/jobs/en

THE SCOOP

Titan of European industry

The European airline giant Air France-KLM is Europe's No. 1 carrier and the worldwide leader in terms of revenue. It employs more than 103,000 people, and ranks No. 1 in terms of international passenger traffic and No. 2 in cargo services. The company is a member of the SkyTeam alliance, an international codesharing alliance of airlines that includes Alitalia, Delta Air Lines and Korean Air.

The firm operates as a holding company for its two namesake airlines, Air France and KLM Royal Dutch Airlines, which merged together in 2004. And it runs a number of smaller airlines: the regional carriers Brit Air (in the U.K.), CityJet (U.K. and Western Europe), Regional (France) and KLM Cityhopper (Holland), the low-cost European carrier Transavia and the freight carrier Sodexi. Other subsidiaries include Air France Consulting (airline consulting services), CRMA (maintenance) and Servair (airline catering).

Air France and KLM operate separately from one another, maintaining independent fleets and routes. Both Air France and KLM were national airlines before the merger, and the French and Dutch governments still own significant stakes in Air France-KLM. The firm earned €23 billion (about $30 billion) in revenue in 2007.

The states' rights

When Air France and KLM merged together in 2004, it was the first instance of one national airline's acquisition by another (in this case, Air France acquiring KLM), and the first formation of a holding company for two national airlines. The merger created a new No. 1 European airline, vaulting Air France-KLM ahead of rival European carriers British Airways and Lufthansa, which had dominated the top-two spots in the marketplace. The French government relinquished its majority stake in Air France but the Dutch government kept a measure of control, retaining 51 percent voting rights on the new company's board.

The Low Countries take to the air

KLM Royal Dutch Airlines—the initials stand for Koniklijke Luchtvaart Maatsch, or "Royal Dutch Airlines"—is the oldest continuously operating airline in the world. It was founded in 1919 as Dutch Airlines (Luchtvaart Maatsch). The company's first plane took off from Amsterdam, headed for London, in 1920. By 1929, the company

Visit Vault at www.vault.com for insider company profiles, expert advice, career message boards, expert resume reviews, the Vault Job Board and more.

VAULT CAREER LIBRARY   39

was making regular flights from Amsterdam to the Dutch colonies in the East Indies, an 11-day undertaking. Service to Sydney, Australia, followed in the 1930s.

Nazi forces invaded the Netherlands in 1940 and KLM's planes remained grounded until the end of World War II in 1945. In 1958 the firm began flying a great circle route, over Northern Russia, between Amsterdam and Japan. KLM purchased its first jetliners in 1960, just as airlines around the world experienced a drastic and unexplained drop in business. The company struggled to turn a profit for much of the 1960s and 1970s and became a fierce advocate of European deregulation, which occurred in the early 1990s. The company's low-cost regional European airline, KLM Cityhopper, made its debut in 1991, and immediately reported consistent profits.

Vive l'Air France!

Air France has its own story, beginning in 1932, when the French government, tired of subsidizing five competing airlines, merged them all into a single company. The company's operations changed dramatically under the Vichy government during World War II, effectively becoming an arm of the Nazi army. In 1946 the airline re-emerged into the Western world, flying decommissioned war planes between Paris and New York—a 20-hour trip.

Following the war, the French government controlled most of the company's shares, and expanded the number of miles the airline covered by a third between 1953 and 1960. The company made history with its Concorde supersonic jet, which it flew with glamorous regularity daily between Paris and New York from 1976 to 2003, when mounting losses during the post-September 11 downturn led Air France to shelve its operations.

A public company, privately owned

In 2002, the French government started looking for ways to privatize Air France and began courting KLM, which had also posted losses in the aftermath of September 11th. The airlines agreed to merge in September 2003, and finalized the transaction in May 2004, when Air France-KLM's stock began trading on the New York and Paris Stock Exchanges. The merger effectively privatized Air France, as the government reduced its stake from 55 percent to 44 percent (it now owns less than 20 percent of the airline's shares).

The new company has a distinctly French flavor: former Air France shareholders control over 80 percent of the new company's shares; it operates under French corporate laws and its chairman and CEO, Jean-Cyril Spinetta, was the Air France CEO who initiated the merger. The firm's headquarters are even located at Charles de Gaulle International Airport in Roissy, France. Such a Francophone identity could spell the end of the KLM Royal Dutch Airlines brand—KLM is contracted to fly under that name until 2008, but analysts expect that it will most likely merge its operations into Air France after that, ending more than 80 years of aviation history.

Since the merger, Air France-KLM hasn't posted a single loss, racking up $445 million in profits in 2004 and $1.3 billion in 2005. The new firm combined its airlines' frequent flyer programs into a new system called Flying Blue in June 2005. In 2006, despite a sharp rise in oil prices, and still recording hefty merger-related charges of about €500 million, the company's revenue improved by about 10 percent to €21.4 billion and profits by 29 percent to €913 million.

The modern way

In June 2007, both Air France and KLM invested in a fleet modernization program, placing orders on new Boeing 777 and 737 jets. Air France will replace 18 of its old 747 jets with flashy new 777s and KLM will take delivery of seven new Boeing 737s; the planes should all arrive in summer 2008. In November 2007, KLM increased its order to include five more Boeing craft for 2010 and 2011—two 777s and three 737s—as well as two Airbus A380s.

Most of the new aircraft are more fuel-efficient and will cut down on long-haul flights' fuel emissions. KLM has been particularly outspoken on the problem of climate change, with executives calling for drastic action at the Dutch Aviation Agenda Conference in November 2006. Air France and KLM are currently the only airlines listed on the Dow Jones and FTSE4Good sustainability indices.

The cabin crew strike

In October 2007, Air France's cabin crews went on strike, crippling long-haul departures out of Paris for five days. Unlike in the U.S., flight attendants and crew members have many unions to choose from in France, and all these unions participated in the October strike. Union representatives claimed that cabin employees hadn't received salary raises in 10 years, despite the firm's consistent financial success. Air France managed to run about 70 percent of its flights during the strike.

Visit Vault at www.vault.com for insider company profiles, expert advice, career message boards, expert resume reviews, the Vault Job Board and more.

VAULT CAREER LIBRARY

41

After the strike ended and contract negotiations resumed, the National Federation of Travel Agents (SNAV) sued Air France-KLM for lost proceeds. In turn, Air France-KLM requested compensation from three labor unions for lack of notification that a strike was pending, as required by a March 2007 labor agreement. In late October, Air France teamed with SNAV to speed up the process of refunding customers and placed an initial estimate on the costs of the strike: €60 million.

KLM meets VLM

In December 2007, Air France-KLM agreed to terms with Dutch firm Panta Holdings to acquire the regional Flemish carrier Vlaamse Luchttransportmaatschappij (VLM). Primarily a business class airline, VLM is based out of London City Airport. Under Air France-KLM ownership, it will cooperate with Air France-KLM's subsidiary CityJet, another regional carrier based out of London City.

Al-aboard!

Just as Air France-KLM was formed out of the French and Dutch governments wishing to privatize their national airlines, the Italian government has wanted to privatize national carrier Alitalia, entertaining bids from June 2006 onwards. During that period, four of Alitalia's six board members resigned, all of them airline executives whose companies worked closely with the Italian airline. Only two directors were left on Alitalia's board: the chairman and a government representative. The last to resign, in January 2007, was Air France-KLM CEO Jean-Cyril Spinetta. (Immediately afterwards, Alitalia CEO Giancarlo Cimoli resigned from Air France-KLM's board). Analysts stated that Spinetta's resignation was probably an indication that Air France-KLM would place a bid.

Spinetta confirmed Air France-KLM's interest in November 2007, and stated that if the company's bid for Alitalia was successful, it would shift the hub from Milan to Rome and eliminate approximately 1,700 jobs—touching off a furor in Northern Italy. However, Alitalia's board recommended Air France-KLM's bid to the Italian government in December 2007, which then approved exclusive talks between the airlines.

In January 2008, Spinetta flew to Rome to reassure Alitalia executives about his restructuring plans. Spinetta said the new company would be a "European champion," and apparently Alitalia shared his views, as he told reporters that the Rome talks were "very positive." The deal was thrown into question again in late January, when the Italian government—a major stakeholder in Alitalia—effectively came to a halt with the resignation of Prime Minister Romano Prodi due to a vote of no confidence. Although the Italian government must sign off on any Alitalia merger, executives of both airlines said they would continue their discussions with the precarious government.

Watching its buddy's back

Across the pond, news emerged in January 2008 that Delta Air Lines was in merger talks with other major U.S. carriers, including Northwest Airlines and United Airlines. Air France-KLM has a major stake in the outcome of these talks, as it has partnered with Delta in the lucrative SkyTeam codesharing alliance since 2000, connecting its customers to Delta's flights.

According to published reports, Air France-KLM is lobbying Delta on behalf of Northwest, or as *The Wall Street Journal* put it, it's "playing cupid" in the two firms' merger discussions. Air France-KLM doesn't want Delta to choose United as that airline is a close ally of its archrival, German carrier Lufthansa, and is a member of rival codesharing group the Star Alliance. A merger with Northwest makes sense from Air France-KLM's point of view, as Northwest is already a Sky Team member. But more importantly, Air France-KLM and Delta have agreements in place for the future "open skies" agreement between the U.S. and the EU, which will free up trans-Atlantic routes when it takes effect in April 2008. Air France-KLM and Delta agreed to a joint venture to share trans-Atlantic costs in October 2007, and in November the two agreed to include Northwest in the venture. If Delta and Northwest agree to merge (which would take all of 2008 to complete), Air France-KLM could partner with that airline for years to come.

Bye bye, Broadway

One place Air France-KLM will not go in 2008 is Wall Street. In November 2007, the airline announced plans to delist from the New York Stock Exchange, as more than 95 percent of the previous year's share trades occurred in Paris on the Euronext exchange. Air France-KLM's board of directors approved the delisting in January 2008, and the firm currently has delisting applications in front of the NYSE and the Securities and Exchange Commission.

GETTING HIRED

Enter the royal service

As Air France and KLM operate separately, they maintain separate careers sites. Air France's careers site, located at www.airfrance.us/US/en/local/toutsurairfrance/emploi/ af_career_opportunities.htm, offers information on working for Air France in the U.S., the application process, current employment opportunities and benefits. To apply, one should e-mail a resume and cover letter to mail.resume@airfrance.fr, indicating the desired position, job title, location and job code, if applicable. Resumes remain on file for six months. Air France stresses that it offers no application form, and only takes applications, even for jobs posted on the web site, as original resumes and cover letters. At press time, Air France had postings for passenger service agents in New York and Washington, D.C., and a cargo service agent in Chicago. Benefits for U.S. employees include medical, dental and vision coverage, 401(k) and a pension plan, worldwide flight discounts, paid time off and certain incentive programs, depending on the position.

KLM's careers site, at www.klm.com/corporate/jobs/en, provides information about internships and careers with the company. Applicants must fill out an online form with past work experience, which they can then submit to the jobs that interest them. Those interested in flight attendant jobs must speak English, though a command of other European languages is helpful, and should have previous customer service experience. Applicants for these positions must also meet minimum height requirements, must have a weight proportional to their height, and must know how to swim.

Some 80 percent of KLM's employees are based in the Netherlands. Benefits include an 8 percent holiday bonus (as well as an annual variable bonus), 24 days of vacation (plus seven other days off during the year), health insurance, pension, continuing education—and, of course, discounted or free travel options.

KLM offers 400 internships per year to students who work at the company in a capacity connected to their studies. Students can apply to listed openings on KLM's web site. KLM also offers a two-year management training course for new graduates.

OUR SURVEY SAYS

Meeting of the minds

Sources say that KLM's Dutch origins give it "openness" and lead to the "direct addressing of issues … in an open environment, discussing and correcting where it is needed." On the other hand, "Air France['s] culture is more hierarchical but also [has] openness and a change in culture." Overall, the merger has resulted in "teaming up and internal communication," leading to "success." "The company is special," says a long-time staffer, "you find not the big earning[s] but you find friends … and a place you like to work for a long time." It's still work, though, says a sales contact who works 70 hours per week. And "in our business," says another, "there is no stock option or [hope of a] bonus."

Visit Vault at **www.vault.com** for insider company profiles, expert advice, career message boards, expert resume reviews, the Vault Job Board and more.

V/\ULT CAREER LIBRARY

45

Air New Zealand Limited

Quay Tower, Level 19
29 Customs Street West
Auckland, 1020
New Zealand
Phone: +64-9-336-2400
Fax: +64-9-336-2401
www.airnz.co.nz

LOCATIONS

Auckland (HQ)
Christchurch
Wellington

THE STATS

Employer Type: Public Company
Stock Symbol: NZE
Stock Exchange: New Zealand
Chairman: John Palmer
CEO: Rob Fyfe
2007 Employees: 10,713
2007 Revenue ($NZ mil.): $NZ 4,297

DEPARTMENTS

Administration, Secretarial & Clerical
Airline Services
   Commercial • Customer Service •
   Loaders
Business Analysis
Cabin Crew
Contact Centre
Customer Service
Engineering
   Aeronautical • Applications •
   Maintenance
Finance
Human Resources
Information Technology
Legal
Management
Marketing
Operations
   Airline & Planning • Standards &
   Safety
Pilots
Procurement
Public Affairs
Sales
   Business Direct • Holiday Store •
   Travel Centers • Web

KEY COMPETITORS

AMR Corporation
Qantas
Virgin Blue

EMPLOYMENT CONTACT

www.airnz.co.nz/aboutus/careers

THE SCOOP

Up in the air from Down Under

They were probably flying Air New Zealand. This high-flying firm operates a fleet of 95 jets (60 owned, 35 leased). It flies about 4,000 flights per week to 46 destinations, both short-haul (i.e., domestic) throughout Australia and New Zealand, and long-haul to Asia, North America, the Southwest Pacific and the U.K. These long-haul flights are generally over five hours in length.

A TEAL background

The airline began as Tasman Empire Airways Ltd. (TEAL) in 1940, primarily connecting New Zealanders and Aussies with flights over the Tasman Sea. The Australian and New Zealand governments each bought 50 percent stakes in TEAL in 1953, and New Zealand took full ownership of the airline in 1961. The government changed its name to Air New Zealand (ANZ) in 1965, and the airline became the country's major carrier for domestic and international flights. In 1978, it merged with New Zealand's leading regional airline, National Airways Corporation.

Public, private, wait, no, public

In 1988, the Australian and New Zealand governments struck a deal to merge together their state-owned airlines: the Aussie-owned Australian Airlines and Qantas and Air New Zealand. News of the plan aroused political opposition in New Zealand, however, and the government decided to privatize ANZ instead. It entertained a number of offers from consortiums including British Airways and Qantas, and the Qantas faction won the bidding in 1989. A few months later, with Qantas holding a 19.9 percent stake in ANZ, the airline went public on the New Zealand Stock Exchange.

Qantas maintained its stake in Air New Zealand until 1997, when ANZ completed purchase of a 50 percent stake in rival Aussie airline Ansett Airlines. Qantas duly sold off its stake, and Ansett went bankrupt in the aftermath of September 11th, nearly taking Air New Zealand with it. Later in 2001, the government provided ANZ with a capital injection of nearly $370 million, which led to state ownership of the airline once more (the government now owns 76 percent of the company).

Air New Zealand cares

Air New Zealand revamped nearly all of its services, from ticket options to customer loyalty programs. In November 2002, it introduced Express class for domestic service, including no-frills class-less seating, no meals or alcoholic beverages, self-check in and lower fares. Also in November, the airline added Pacific Premium Economy class for high-end travelers. On average, Pacific Premium fares are about 25 percent more expensive than standard economy fares, but passengers enjoy lie-flat beds with aisle access and on-demand entertainment on a personal 8.4-inch high resolution screen.

As another recovery effort, in 2004 the airline introduced Airpoints Dollars, awarded based on dollars spent rather than miles traveled, which can be used toward purchasing any seat on any Air New Zealand flight. The program, which assigns NZ$1 for every Airpoints Dollar, won the Best Award Redemption category at the Freddie Awards ("the frequent traveler's answer to the Oscar[s]") in May 2005.

In July 2002, the company began a revamp of its short-haul fleet with the purchase of 15 new Airbus jets. In June 2004, Air New Zealand turned its attention to its long-haul planes, contracting with Boeing for 10 new planes and the future acquisition of an additional 46 long-haul aircraft.

Deal? No deal

For fiscal 2004, Air New Zealand reported revenue of NZ$3.5 billion (about $2.2 billion), down from NZ$3.6 billion the year before. These results were stronger than they appeared—Air New Zealand said that the decrease primarily resulted from the stronger New Zealand dollar.

Competition is also hitting the company's profitability—Air New Zealand is coping with too many planes flying the Tasman Sea route, driving down prices from an expected NZ$189 one-way ticket to NZ$149 or even NZ$99. In 2004, ANZ and Qantas worked out a partnership to reduce costs, which involved Qantas buying a minority ANZ stake (about 22.5 percent), so that the two firms could cooperate on routes across the Tasman Sea. Australian authorities approved the coalition, but the New Zealand High Court rejected it in September 2004.

Labor troubles

Air New Zealand faced an unexpected challenge when CEO Ralph Norris resigned in August 2005, to become chief of the Commonwealth Bank of Australia. Norris came on after the near-bankruptcy of 2001, and many saw him as integral to the airline's subsequent turnaround. Furthermore, Norris was in the middle of negotiating new labor deals when he departed.

The company promoted its general manager, Rob Fyfe, to the CEO spot, and in October 2005 it announced the elimination of its engineering unit (about 600 jobs), in favor of outsourced labor. The cuts were designed to save $100 million. Engineering unions hastily resumed negotiations and in February 2006 they struck a deal with ANZ to save 300 of the threatened jobs, in exchange for pay cuts across the board.

Later in 2006, Air New Zealand announced another, altogether different labor-related issue. In June 2006, the airline launched an internal inquiry over an alleged sex-for-travel scam. Apparently, Air New Zealand employees in Auckland worked out a system to receive sexual favors from local prostitutes, and to return the favor by providing the hookers with their employee-discounted plane tickets. The investigation has not yet resulted in any action on Air New Zealand's part.

That Tasmanian devil

Air New Zealand took another stab at solving its Tasman Sea route dilemma in 2006. With eight airlines offering so-called trans-Tasman flights, the route is one of the most competitive in the world. In April 2006 the company again tried to strike a deal with Qantas, this one a codesharing agreement, under which Air New Zealand customers would ride Qantas flights across the Tasman, saving ANZ two trans-Tasman flights and $40 million per year.

But, like the previous deal, this one was nixed in November 2006, this time by the Australian Competition and Consumer Commission. At the time, the Commission stated that the deal would have reduced customer's options. Upon getting the bad news, Air New Zealand upped its end of the competition by adding back-of-seat entertainment systems to its Tasman Sea and Pacific flights in June 2007.

Fast plane to China

Air New Zealand wagered on the surging interest in China when it introduced flights to Shanghai in November 2006. Also, the company has been recruiting Mandarin-speaking staff, in hopes that Chinese tourists will increasingly visit New Zealand's shores. The service runs three flights per week and it should get a boost with a $4

Visit Vault at **www.vault.com** for insider company profiles, expert advice, career message boards, expert resume reviews, the Vault Job Board and more.

VAULT CAREER LIBRARY   49

million ad campaign, launched in conjunction with ad firm Tourism NZ. The airline expects to expand to daily flights once the new service gains notoriety.

Air New Zealand showed further dedication to expanding its direct flight menu when it purchased eight of Boeing's new 787 Dreamliner planes in July 2007 for $1.2 billion. Smaller and more fuel-efficient than 747s, the planes will allow Air New Zealand to offer direct flights farther afield than is now possible. After the first of the new planes go into service in 2010, Air New Zealand plans to add between 20 to 25 new routes to its current list of 10 long-haul destinations.

This airline rocks

In June 2007, Air New Zealand's booking web site, www.grabaseat.com, turned one year old, and the company celebrated with a massively popular gimmick—domestic fares as low as NZ$1. Also, in March 2007, the airline teamed up with über-cool cable network MTV to introduce a Mile High Gig promotion, offering live in-flight music en route to the MTV Australia Video Music Awards. The flight sold out.

These measures, on top of lowered domestic fares and the aforementioned increased destinations abroad, largely allowed the airline to rise above the challenges of recent years in 2007. Flights were robustly full through the year, with the company flying at 78 percent capacity on average, up more than 7 percent from 2006.

GETTING HIRED

The way in

Air New Zealand's career web site, at www.airnz.co.nz/aboutus/careers, makes it easy and efficient to land a job with this skybound firm. Interested candidates can use the job search tool on the company's web site to find current openings, sign up for job alerts to be notified of open positions, save applications on the company web site and fill out an employment profile to be matched with jobs for which the company is recruiting. A careers newsletter, the *HiFlyer*, comes out monthly with job listings, company news and day-in-the-life profiles of Air New Zealand employees. The helpful "I Want to Work in …" link provides overviews of the different arms of this many-tentacled airline to help candidates determine where their best fit is within the company.

Alaska Air Group, Inc.

19300 International Boulevard
Seattle, WA 98188
Phone: (206) 392-5040
Fax: (206) 392-2804
www.alaskaair.com

LOCATIONS

Seattle, WA (HQ)
Anchorage, AK • Bethel, AK • Boise,
ID • Chicago, IL • Juneau, AK •
Kent, WA • Ketchikan, AK • Los
Angeles, CA • Nome, AK • Orange
County, CA • Reno, NV • Sitka, AK
• Tempe, AZ • Washington, DC

THE STATS

Employer Type: Public Company
Stock Symbol: ALK
Stock Exchange: NYSE
Chairman, President & CEO: William
  S. Ayer
2007 Employees: 14,710
2007 Revenue ($mil.): $3,506

DEPARTMENTS

Administrative
Accounting
Applications Analysis
Cargo Control Center
Customer Service
Government Affairs
Engineering
Flight—Pilots/Flight
Attendants/Instructors
Human Resources
Quality Assurance
Ramp Service
Management
Marketing
Systems Analysis
Work Control

KEY COMPETITORS

American Airlines
Southwest Airlines
United Airlines

EMPLOYMENT CONTACT

www.alaskaair.com/as/www2/
Company/Careers.html

THE SCOOP

Juneau there's an airline serving Alaska?

The Alaska Air Group is a holding company with two principal subsidiaries, Alaska Airlines and Horizon Air Industries. Alaska Airline is the ninth-largest airline in the U.S., operating a fleet of 108 Boeing jets, and Horizon is a regional Alaskan carrier, with a fleet of small jets and turboprop (propeller) aircraft. These airlines primarily serve Canada, Mexico and the Western U.S., but also fly to major Eastern and Midwestern hubs like Boston, Chicago, Denver, Miami and Newark. In 2006, Alaska and Horizon flew nearly 24 million passengers to 90 destinations throughout North America. And don't let the name fool you—the company is based in the contiguous 48, with headquarters in Seattle, Washington.

From fur to flying

Linious "Mac" McGee, an Indiana transplant, moved to Alaska during the Great Depression and founded Alaska Air Group in 1932. Mac was a jack-of-all-trades, and only turned to aviation after working as a dishwasher, fur buyer, miner and truck driver. In fact, he bought his first plane (a three-seat Stinson, for $5,000) for his fur-buying business, and only offered passenger service as an afterthought. But the flight he offered between the Alaskan cities Anchorage and Bristol Bay proved popular, and he founded a small passenger line named McGee Airways. After a few more incarnations, merging with local rival Star Air System later in the 1930s and renaming itself Alaska Star Airlines in 1942, the company changed its name for the final time in 1944, to Alaska Airlines.

Horizon Air first took flight nearly four decades later, after the U.S. government deregulated the airline industry in 1978 and large carriers abandoned routes in the Pacific Northwest en masse. In 1981, a 20-year Boeing veteran named Milt Kuolt teamed with a group of venture capitalists to found Horizon in Washington, with two planes and one service between Seattle and Yakima. By the time Alaska Air acquired Horizon in 1987, it was the fifth-largest regional airline in the U.S., flying 32 aircraft to 30 cities. Horizon wields a large influence on its parent company, especially in the executive suite—before becoming Alaska Air's chairman and CEO, William Ayer worked for Horizon Air from its 1981 founding to 1995.

Competition for Alaskan airspace heated up in the 1990s, as smaller, low-cost outfits like Southwest Airlines horned in on the company's airspace. Alaska Air held its own by sticking to its award-winning customer service and investing in technology. For example, Alaska Air became the first U.S. air carrier to sell tickets online in 1995, and it was the first commercial air carrier to use the global positioning system (GPS) in 1996.

Safety concerns

In January 2000, one of Alaska Airlines's McDonnell-Douglas M80 jets crashed into the Pacific Ocean and killed all 88 people onboard; it was one of the deadliest airplane accidents of the last decade. A government investigation concluded in December 2002 that both Alaska Airlines and the FAA had contributed to the crash through lax maintenance policies. The findings were so worrisome that the government then audited every major carrier's maintenance, although it decided not to press criminal charges against Alaska Airlines in 2003. By that point, the airline had settled nearly every lawsuit related to the crash. Neither side disclosed financial terms, but attorneys told the AP that each of the 88 lawsuits settled for millions of dollars apiece.

The entire affair affected Alaska Airlines' employees as well. In 2002, a terminated maintenance supervisor named Mansour Fadaie sued the company, alleging that Alaska Airlines refused to promote him because he is Muslim, and that he was fired for refusing to certify incomplete safety inspections. Alaska Airlines settled with Fadaie in October 2005 for undisclosed terms.

The red and the black

Alaska Air posted year-end losses in 2000, and the economic climate worsened for the airline industry the next year, after the terrorist attacks of September 11th. While Alaska Air wasn't hit as hard as competitors, many of which soon filed for bankruptcy protection, it has only recorded one profitable year (2003) since the attacks. The company's position in the West Coast remains strong—in 2003, Alaska Airlines accounted for 89 percent of flights between Alaska and the West Coast—but employment at the company is tenuous, due to seemingly never-ending restructuring efforts.

The company's retooling began in 2003, when it started negotiating a new deal with its 1,465 pilots and their union, the Air Line Pilots Association (ALPA). In 2004, the company laid off 900 employees, retired old aircraft from its fleet and took about $53 million in restructuring charges. The airline finally reached an agreement with its pilots in May 2005. The pilots all kept their jobs, but took a 20 percent (!) pay cut for the privilege. The same month, Alaska Air signed agreements with its 2,400-odd flight attendants and laid off 474 baggage handlers at its hub Seattle-Tacoma airport. Customers disliked this last move, which caused delays and lost baggage for months afterward.

Alaska Air invested some of the savings from restructuring in cost-efficient fleet updates. In March 2005, the company spent extra money to equip its new shipment of Boeing 737 aircraft with leather seats and winglets. Leather seats are easier to clean and last more than three times as long as the cloth seat alternative, and winglets improve takeoff and cruise performance, resulting in fuel savings of approximately 5 percent. In another cost-saving measure, the airline discontinued paper tickets in September 2005. The airline reported year-end losses by the slimmest of margins in 2005—they came in at $5.9 million.

The company's transitional efforts continued in 2006, when it announced in March that it planned to convert its fleet from a mongrel mix of aircraft to an all-Boeing 737 flock by 2008. Alaska Air expects to save $115 million a year from the switch, as the planes are more fuel efficient and the lack of aircraft diversity will cut down on training and maintenance costs. However, the plan required an up-front investment of $750 million. As of October 2007, it only had to retire 16 Boeing MD80s to complete the switch. Despite the cost-cutting efforts, Alaska Air actually hired about 700 new employees in 2006, increasing its ranks to 14,485 (just below its number of employees in 2004, 14,584).

Habla español?

Alaska Air added more flights to its schedule in spring 2006, including new nonstop flights from the Pacific Northwest to Mexican resorts just in time for the summer exodus to Southern climes. As unlikely as it may seem, Alaska Air now leads all U.S. airlines in flights between the West Coast and Mexico, shuttling 1.3 million passengers annually between the locales.

The airline is making itself more accessible to potential Hispanic customers, as well. In October 2006 the company launched a Spanish-language web site for booking and check-ins and, around the same time, began staffing its West Coast-Mexico flights with bilingual flight attendants. Early in 2007, Spanish-language check-in kiosks opened in 82 of the 90 airports through which Alaska Air flies.

Eye on the bottom line

In 2007, the company continued negotiations with its pilots, after Alaska Airlines' pilot contracts became amendable in May 2007 and Horizon's in September 2006. To smooth the flow of negotiations, Alaska Air appointed a new managing director of labor relations in January 2008—Elizabeth Ryan, who previously negotiated for Alaska Air with the mechanics' union in 2005 and the Transport Workers Union in 2002.

In October 2007, Alaska Air's hub Seattle Tacoma International Airport premiered the first phase of its "Airport of the Future," an extended version of the check-in kiosks it started introducing in 1999. Seattle's "Future" should be complete in mid-2008, and is aimed at reducing customer wait times; it will also probably mean fewer Alaska Air employees at each check-in counter.

GETTING HIRED

Opportunities galore

Alaska Air offers a wide range of job opportunities in areas including administration, customer service, human resources, finance and accounting, maintenance and engineering, and information technology—to name a few. Through the company's career web site (www.alaskaair.com/as/www2/Company/Careers.html), job seekers can find opportunities at Alaska Airlines and Horizon Air, listed by type and location. Employee benefits include health insurance, 401(k) and profit sharing. But the real perks are the travel deals—discounts on company fares in addition to discounts on cruises, hotels, car rentals and theme parks for employees and their families.

The company participates in campus recruiting and also offers internships for current students in its customer service, maintenance, accounting, marketing, sales and information technology departments. Internship openings are listed with the other job openings on the company's main career search page. Finally, Alaska has a management development program that provides participants with hands-on and classroom training, and exposure to a variety of divisions.

Visit Vault at **www.vault.com** for insider company profiles, expert advice, career message boards, expert resume reviews, the Vault Job Board and more.

VAULT CAREER LIBRARY

55

OUR SURVEY SAYS

Still a great atmosphere

Sources at Alaska Air echo what the newspapers report, saying that "Labor challenges have a significant effect on the morale and performance of the company." However, most report a "great corporate culture" and one Seattle insider says that "working at Alaska is a very social experience. There is great [camaraderie] and many friendships develop among co-workers." Still, the work "tends to involve long hours" and one contact who made "many lateral moves" says that "advancement has been limited." Finally, a director at Seattle headquarters says the "potential at Alaska Airlines is great, and highly undertapped. I sense that the leaders in our company do not fully believe in and support the employees, but I do not fully understand the basis of this perception."

All Nippon Airways Co., Ltd.

Shiodome City Center
1-5-2 Higashi-Shimbashi
Minato-ku, Tokyo 105-7133
Japan
Phone: +81-3-6735-1000
Fax: +81-3-6735-1005
www.ana.co.jp

LOCATIONS

Tokyo (HQ)
Burlingame, CA • Chicago, IL •
Honolulu, HI • Los Angeles, CA •
New York, NY • San Francisco, CA
• Washington, DC • Bangkok •
Beijing • Brussels • Dalian, China •
Düsseldorf • Frankfurt • Fukuoka,
Japan • Geneva • Guangzhou,
China • Hamburg • Hangzhou,
China • Ho Chi Minh City • Hong
Kong • Kuala Lumpur • London •
Nagoya • Okinawa • Osaka •
Madrid • Moscow • Paris •
Qingdao, China • Rome • Sapporo,
Japan • Seoul • Shanghai •
Shenyang, China • Singapore •
Tamuning, Guam • Tianjin, China •
Xiamen, China • Yangon, Myanmar
• Zurich

THE STATS

Employer Type: Public Company
Stock Symbol: 9202
Stock Exchange: Tokyo
Chairman: Yoji Ohashi
President & CEO: Mineo Yamamoto
2007 Employees: 32,460
2007 Revenue (¥mil.): ¥1,489,658

DEPARTMENTS

Administration
Customer Service
Sales

KEY COMPETITORS

American Airlines
Japan Airlines
Singapore Airlines

EMPLOYMENT CONTACT

www.ana.co.jp/wws/us/e/about_ana/
employ

THE SCOOP

Flying into the sunrise

From the land of the Rising Sun comes All Nippon Airways (ANA), ranked No. 7 in the world by number of passengers carried—nearly 50 million in 2006. The company mostly serves cities in its own region, with planes flying to 60 cities in Japan, 18 cities in Asia and a handful of major European and American cities. In addition to its passenger service, ANA offers cargo service and owns a chain of Japanese hotels in a joint venture with InterContinental Hotels Group.

All about All Nippon

In 1952, the U.S. and Japanese governments signed the San Francisco Peace Treaty, effectively ending America's postwar occupation of Japan. Almost immediately afterwards, the Japanese government passed a law allowing private airlines to begin operations, and a number of small outfits took flight, including Nippon Helicopter and Far East Airlines. Demand for domestic air travel grew alongside Japan's burgeoning postwar economy, and the companies agreed to merge in 1956, instantly becoming the largest private airline in Japan's fledgling and rapidly growing flight industry. ANA went public on the Tokyo stock exchange in 1964, and the following year entered the jet age with the purchase of Boeing 727s. ANA used this model of aircraft for the next 30 years.

Japan's economy liberalized in the 1970s, keying both the demand for air travel and All Nippon's growth. In 1971, ANA sent its first flight outside of Japan, to Hong Kong. And in 1973 the company began a major diversification effort, establishing ANA Enterprises Ltd., a hotel management business with lodgings near its main airports. The next year, the company established another subsidiary, All Nippon Co., to provide regional flights within Japan. Both strategies paid off: by the turn of the 1980s, ANA's hotel business accounted for a large part of company revenue and the company possessed Japan's most extensive domestic route system.

All Nippon's business expanded again in the mid-1980s, after the Japanese government deregulated the country's airline industry, breaking up Japan Airlines' (JAL) effective monopoly over international flights. In 1986, ANA started offering more international flights, making its first trips to Guam, Los Angeles and Washington, D.C. ANA still maintained a secondary status to JAL in terms of international flights, but the company's international presence continued to expand.

The firm floated its stock on European exchanges in 1991 and invested the proceeds in Airbus A320 jets.

ANA's weight loss plan

In the early 1990s, however, a generally sluggish world economy and a disastrous economic downturn in Japan severely affected both All Nippon and Japan Airlines. ANA only maintained profitability in 1993 by selling off a number of its aircraft. And in 1994, the company posted its first year-end loss in 27 years. Later in 1994, ANA cut 1,500 jobs from its 14,800-strong workforce, one of the first times a major Japanese firm deviated from that country's employee-for-life tradition.

The beleaguered giant shortly faced further problems due to the entry of two low-fare competitors in 1996—Skymark and Hokkaido International Airlines. To keep itself in the black, ANA reduced the salaries of its highest-paid employees (by as much as 25 percent!), sold more of its planes and instituted a restructuring plan to return to profitability. In 2000, still losing out to the discount carriers, ANA decided to fight fire with fire and created its own entrant into the category, Air Nippon. Also that year, the company joined the Star Alliance, an international codesharing partnership of airlines that includes United Airlines.

Nippon it in the bud

In 2001, ANA suffered along with every other airline after the events of September 11th. Also that year, JAL acquired ANA's main domestic rival, Japan Air System. This strengthening of JAL's services threatened the weakened ANA, which had posted losses in five of the last seven years. Having already cut many jobs and sold off many planes, ANA enacted another restructuring plan, and continued to post losses in 2002 and 2003. Against many analysts' expectations, though, the firm posted a profit in 2004. It stayed in the black in 2005 and 2006 as well, in spite of spiraling fuel prices. In 2006, ANA took in $11.6 billion in revenue, a 6 percent increase over 2005. Profits remained essentially the same as the year before, increasing by just under 1 percent, which the firm attributed to high fuel prices.

How do they do it?

In 2007, *Air Transport World* magazine named ANA its Airline of the Year, and pulled back the curtain on the company's unlikely turnaround. For one, the company's participation in the Star Alliance started paying dividends. It accounts for

Visit Vault at **www.vault.com** for insider company profiles, expert advice, career message boards, expert resume reviews, the Vault Job Board and more.

VAULT CAREER LIBRARY

59

roughly $130 million annually and also compensates for ANA's secondary status to JAL in terms of international flights.

But the true champion of ANA's resurgence is an innovative approach that blends technology and customer service. ANA invests about $300 million annually in IT, which its passengers appreciate in the form of a comprehensive, ticket-selling web site, self-check units at airports (available to all Star partners), and, starting July 2007, a "Skip" system that permits domestic travelers to bypass the check-in area with tips from their mobile phones. These passengers also use mobile phones to confirm their tickets at the security line. The airline also offers passengers all kinds of nifty, non-tech options. In 2002, the company introduced its New Style service, with "lie-flat seatbeds" in business class and other convertible seat options to transform underbooked flights into more spacious, fully booked affairs.

ANA's IT emphasis has occasionally backfired, as in May 2007, when a system failure caused the cancellation of a whopping 103 ANA flights and delayed an additional 306, affecting about 69,300 travelers. This was surely exceptional, as in 2006 the company reported departure rates of 92 percent for domestic flights and 80 percent for international ones.

Finally, ANA's hotels are not to be forgotten in its improved economic fortunes. The hotel group was thrust front and center in October 2006, when ANA announced a joint venture with InterContinental Hotels Group, creating Japan's leading hotel operating firm. The joint venture, called IHG ANA Hotels Group Japan, will rebrand both companies' Japanese hotels, a process that started in April 2007, when the ANA Hotel Tokyo became the ANA-InterContinental Tokyo.

Dreaming of the Dreamliner

In July 2007, when ANA debuted its Skip system for mobile-wielding flyers, the airline announced an even cooler feature for the future. Starting in May 2008, the company will buy six Boeing 787 Dreamliner jumbo jets every year until 2015. And ANA's Dreamliners will come equipped with bidets, a sort of toilet for cleaning purposes that is common in Europe and Japan. At the time, CEO Mineo Yamamoto proudly announced this feature would "refresh the parts other airlines cannot reach." The airline has high hopes for its new Dreamliner fleet, the first installment of which it plans to use in August 2008 for flights to the Beijing Summer Olympics. By late 2009 or 2010, the airline also expects the Dreamliner to be flying its New York-Tokyo route.

GETTING HIRED

Say ohayou gozaimasu to ANA

ANA's careers site, at www.ana.co.jp/wws/us/e/about_ana/employ/index.html, provides information about job opportunities and benefits at the company. Jobs are located in Los Angeles and San Francisco, whether at the company's offices in those cities or at the Los Angeles and San Francisco International Airports. It lists open positions on the front page, and resumes can be sent to laxhr@fly-ana.com (for positions at LAX) or sfohr@fly-ana.com (for positions at SFO). Applicants must have a command of English and Japanese, and Chinese language skills are helpful, too. The company offers benefits, including health and dental, 401(k) and travel discounts.

Visit Vault at **www.vault.com** for insider company profiles, expert advice, career message boards, expert resume reviews, the Vault Job Board and more.

VAULT CAREER LIBRARY

61

Amadeus IT Group SA

Calle Salvador de Madariaga 1
E- 28027 Madrid
Spain
Phone: +34 91 582 0100
Fax: +34-91-582-0188
www.amadeus.com

LOCATIONS

Madrid, Spain (HQ)
Miami, FL (US HQ)
Antwerp
Benelux
Crawley, UK
Douala, Cameroon
Erding, Germany
London
Madrid
Mississauga, Canada
Munich
Nice
Paris
Sydney

THE STATS

Employer Type: Private Company
President & CEO: José A. Tazón
2007 Employees: 7,660
2006 Revenue ($mil.): $3,423

DEPARTMENTS

Accounting—E-Commerce Solutions
• Accounting—Multinational
Accounts • Airline Business Group •
Application Development •
Application Support • Commercial •
Corporate Finance & Administration •
Corporate Human Resources •
Development • Engineering • E-Travel
Business Unit • Group Internal Audit
• Hospitality Business Group •
Human Resources • Information
Technology • Internship • Marketing
• Marketing Communications •
Markets EMEA & LA • Multinational
Customer Group • Product
Development • Quality Assurance •
Sales & Marketing—Direct Sales •
Sales & Marketing—Project
Management • Software & Support
Services • Software Development •
Technical Planning & Central
Services

KEY COMPETITORS

Pegasus Solutions
Sabre
Travelport

EMPLOYMENT CONTACT

www.amadeus.com/careers

THE SCOOP

Wunderkind of the skies

Amadeus is Europe's leading computerized reservation system (CRS) for air travel, handling 95 percent of the world's airline seats. And, as the world's leading global distribution system (GDS), Amadeus books computerized reservations for virtually every other travel industry—over 70,000 hotels, 27 car rental companies and 18 cruise lines. All told, it handled nearly 500 million reservations in 2006. The company increasingly fashions itself as an all-purpose IT group, and provides IT services and consulting to airlines and travel businesses.

Making music from a welter of schedules

American Airlines developed Sabre, the original computerized reservation system, during the 1950s. Sabre was first introduced in Europe in 1986, and four European airlines (Air France, Iberia, Lufthansa and SAS) immediately teamed together to create a competitor, fearful that American Airlines would take advantage of its monopoly on the GDS market. Their $300 million system, called Amadeus after the great composer Mozart, started operating in 1987.

By 1990, Amadeus had over 550 employees (from 38 nationalities), and offices in Asia, Europe and South America. It started developing its GDS the next year, which debuted in 1992, and signed up 60 percent of Europe's travel agencies by 1993. With an important acquisition in 1995, Amadeus vaulted itself into the front ranks of worldwide GDS systems. That year, it teamed with Continental Airlines and outsourcing firm Electronic Data Systems in purchasing System One Direct Access, a travel agency-focused reservations system that was founded in 1984. By 1998, Amadeus took full ownership of System One and completed the integration of its 8,000 customers into its database, entrenching its status as the world's No. 1 GDS system, both in terms of customers and technical sophistication. Amadeus launched its web site, www.Amadeus.net, in 1996 and acquired www.Vacation.com, North America's largest vacation-selling network, in 1999.

Can you dig IT?

Amadeus expanded into bookings for corporate travel in 2000 and became the first GDS to provide rail schedules in 2001. The next year, it acquired Smart AB, a Scandinavian GDS, and added the important airline accounts of British Airways and

Visit Vault at **www.vault.com** for insider company profiles, expert advice, career message boards, expert resume reviews, the Vault Job Board and more.

VAULT CAREER LIBRARY   63

Qantas. Around this time, the company started its transformation into an all-purpose IT business. In 2003, the company built a new IT platform for Finnair, invested in Europe's leading hotel IT provider Optims and established a partnership with IBM to provide "airline IT solutions."

In July 2005, the private equity firms BC Partners and Cinven and a group of company managers and took Amadeus private for €4.3 billion. But that didn't change the company's long-term goals. In a January 2006 Latin American Leaders Forum, CEO José Tazón stated that by 2010, Amadeus wanted "to be the world's top IT service provider for the travel industry." To reflect these ambitions, in February 2006 Amadeus changed its name from Amadeus Global Travel Distribution SA to Amadeus IT Group SA. "While travel distribution remains a significant part of our global business," said CEO Tazón, "it is now one element of a broader IT portfolio."

In terms of GDS business, Amadeus stored the flight schedules of 766 different airlines in 2006, and booked reservations for 490 of them. The company's IT credentials emerge upon further inspection, however: over 70 of the world's leading airlines power some 250 web sites using Amadeus' IT expertise. And according to market analysts, Amadeus controls 65 percent of the European market for online travel reservations and 20 percent in Asia. In 2006, Amadeus took in €2.68 billion in revenue, an 11 percent increase over 2005.

Show them the money

To drive more bookings, Amadeus teamed up with rival GDS system Sabre in August 2007 to announce the joint venture MoneyDirect, a unified payment system for travel arrangements. Both companies hope MoneyDirect will become the industry standard for payments in the travel industry. Already, the system funnels $2 billion per annum to the right people at the right time. It's not as easy as it sounds—the system has to deal with different countries, currencies and payment methods (like credit or debit). In September 2007 the EU approved MoneyDirect for the common market.

A cheaper alternative

Amadeus is also trying to establish itself as the GDS of choice among low-cost carriers in Asia. With the area's rapidly growing economies and emerging middle class, demand for air travel is expected to outpace that of the world's largest current market by 2027. Low-cost carriers are the fastest-growing sector of the air-travel arena, as consumers eschew the extra trappings of air travel that accumulated during the Pan Am age—and the high fares that went with them. Amadeus is already realizing this goal, signing Australia's leading low-cost carrier Virgin Blue to a deal in December 2007. Amadeus will provide Virgin, and its startup long-haul carrier V Australia, with new distribution and e-ticketing systems and with its patented IT support.

GETTING HIRED

Eine kleine travelmusik

There's info aplenty on Amadeus' careers site, at www.amadeus.com/careers?src=corporatehomepage for students seeking internships and old hands alike. The company offers internships in the areas of applied mathematics, business and marketing, software engineering, support and administration, and work process administration. Technical internships are also available in the areas of programming, database management and operating systems. Experienced hires can search for jobs by location. In order to apply, they can submit resumes and cover letters through the site. Positions may involve some travel.

Visit Vault at **www.vault.com** for insider company profiles, expert advice, career message boards, expert resume reviews, the Vault Job Board and more.

V/\ULT CAREER LIBRARY

65

American Automobile Association

1000 AAA Drive
Heathrow, FL 32746
Phone: (407) 444-7000
Fax: (407) 444-7380
www.aaa.com

LOCATIONS

Heathrow, FL (HQ)
Orlando, FL
Seattle, WA
Calgary

THE STATS

Employer Type: Not-for-Profit
Chairman: Jeanette Gamba
President & CEO: Robert L. Darbelnet

DEPARTMENTS

Administrative and Support Services
Advertising/Marketing/Public
 Relations
Automotive/Motor Vehicle/Parts
Executive Management
Hospitality/Tourism

KEY COMPETITORS

Allstate
American Express
State Farm

EMPLOYMENT CONTACT

www.aaa.com/jobs

THE SCOOP

Little help?

Car in a ditch? Got a flat tire? Being tailed by a mad trucker across the desert? Just call AAA, and leave the rest to them. The not-for-profit American Automobile Association (AAA) is a nationwide federation of more than 80 regional motor clubs, providing road-related benefits to 50 million members in the U.S. and Canada. AAA members partake in health, life, vehicle and homeowners' insurance policies, in addition to the association's signature maps and travel guides—the organization annually publishes more than 160 million copies of its travel books and brochures.

AAA's best-loved service is probably its 24-hour roadside assistance, which has helped many a driver get out of a jam quickly and efficiently. Through its 1,000 travel agency locations, the association also hooks its members up with reservations and discounts on air, cruise ship, railway, hotel and rental car transactions.

AAA maintains a sizable legal presence, lobbying the federal government on behalf of motorists everywhere, notably for vehicle safety amongst children, teenagers and senior citizens, those most at risk in traffic accidents. Headquartered in Heathrow, Florida (just a hop and skip down the road from Orlando), AAA operates more than 1,100 offices throughout the U.S. and Canada.

Putting the car before the horse

AAA traces its history back to the early 20th century, when an equine-centric America referred to newfangled cars as "horseless carriages" and America's highways were little more than muddy paths rutted by wagon wheels. In those early years of the automobile, drivers had to fight for their right to cruise—horses outnumbered cars in 1902 by 17 million to a paltry 23,000. At the time, roads were unsurprisingly much better suited to hooves than tires, and there was no infrastructure to handle the faster, further-reaching travel enabled by automobiles. AAA started as a loose affiliation of car enthusiast clubs scattered throughout Midwestern and Northeastern states, which were desperate for appropriate roads to make automobile driving safer; they banded together in Chicago in 1902 to form a national club—the American Automobile Association.

AAA and its growing membership set to work convincing Uncle Sam to improve the national highway system and won its first major victory in 1915, when President Woodrow Wilson signed the Federal Aid Highway Act. This bill appropriated federal

Visit Vault at www.vault.com for insider company profiles, expert advice, career message boards, expert resume reviews, the Vault Job Board and more.

VAULT CAREER LIBRARY

67

funds to build and maintain roadways. Also in 1915, AAA offered the earliest incarnation of its now-famous roadside assistance service, when a St. Louis chapter engaged five of its members to cruise the streets of the city atop motorcycles, looking for motorists in need of engine and tire repairs. This vigilante mechanic squad caught on quickly, and grew to become a standard AAA service nationwide.

Indeed, the abundance of highway mishaps convinced AAA that the American population needed a little help learning the rules of the road. To this end, AAA established a traffic safety department in the 1920s, charged with getting automobile safety lessons into schools. In the 1930s, the organization also began publishing driving manuals, including *Responsible Driving* and *Sportsmanlike Driving*.

Making maps, making roads

As the use of automobiles became more widespread in the U.S., AAA got into the business of mapmaking. In 1932, the organization trademarked its TripTik maps, which provided all the necessary details on a trip, including driving time, mileage, roadside diversions and construction detours. Then, in the 1940s, AAA lent its mapmaking services to the war effort, working hand in hand with America's armed forces during World War II. The practice was repeated during the Korean War in the 1950s.

Also in the 1950s, a little thing called the highway played a major part in creating suburban culture, in which cars became indispensable, even revered objects. And, just as AAA's lobbying was instrumental in President Wilson's 1915 Federal Highway Act, so it proved in 1956, when President Eisenhower passed the $25 billion Federal-Aid Highway Act. It was the largest public works program in American history, and created much of America's current Interstate system (signs on which still read "Eisenhower Interstate System").

Crisis, of the energy and roadside varieties

As the family road trip became an American institution in the 1950s and 1960s, AAA began offering more information on hotel and restaurant ratings to its eight million-odd members, introduced in 1963. AAA also forged agreements with foreign auto clubs in the 1960s, so its members could enjoy roadside assistance benefits while traveling abroad.

But U.S. motorists hit a red light in the 1970s, when an oil embargo caused an increase in gas prices. In response, AAA began monitoring gas prices in 200 cities throughout the U.S. and issued a weekly *Fuel Gauge Report* to let members know where prices were low and gas plentiful. Along with the reports came a *Gas Watcher's Guide*, which supplied drivers with tips on how to save fuel. Both of these publications continue to inform members today, with the *Fuel Gauge Report* becoming a daily feature at AAA's web site in 2000.

As AAA became a go-to source for all its members' auto-related questions, the organization began giving its seal of approval to trusted auto repair shops. The Approved Auto Repair program, launched in 1975, gave members a trusted place to go with their dents, dings and pings. This rating system came in handy in 1981, when AAA launched its nationwide toll-free number, 1-800-AAA-HELP. In 1984, AAA gave back to the mechanic community, co-sponsoring a competition for students interested in automotive repair, which continues to this day, in partnership with Ford Motors.

Beware of teenagers and seniors

In 1993, the club launched its "Show Your Card and Save" program, through which a flash of AAA plastic brings members discounts at more than 46,000 businesses. In 1995 Robert Darbelnet, a one-time emergency road service driver for the Quebec Automobile Club, became president and CEO of AAA, which he remains today. The same year, AAA created a financial services arm, offering members mortgages, home and auto loans, and credit cards.

AAA began advocating for highway safety with the 1996 launch of a campaign to invest in the maintenance of America's aging transportation infrastructure. AAA also set its sight on the notoriously dangerous ranks of teenage drivers, and began pushing for Graduated Driver Licensing (GDL) laws—which put teenagers on a probationary schedule before granting them their full rights to the road—in 1997. By 2005, GDL laws were adopted in all 50 states. In 2005, AAA also debuted its national web site, a one-stop shop for members in the U.S. and Canada.

In addition to its initiatives on teenage driving safety, AAA has stepped up efforts to address child safety in automobiles. Through its Seated, Safe & Secure campaign, which started in 2002, AAA calls for stricter enforcement of child restraint laws in the U.S., along with releasing reports on the safest vehicles for children. Concerned with the safety of senior citizens behind the wheel, AAA launched its Life-Long Safe Mobility program in 2004 to advocate for driving alternatives to serve an aging population. The club also created a CD-ROM designed to help seniors assess their ability to drive safely in 2005. A collaboration with AARP and the American

Visit Vault at **www.vault.com** for insider company profiles, expert advice, career message boards, expert resume reviews, the Vault Job Board and more.

VAULT CAREER LIBRARY

69

Occupational Therapy Association spawned CarFit in 2007, a program that helps seniors determine ways to make their car safer for driving.

Who's got gas?

When the war in Iraq caused gas prices to rise in 2003, AAA started offering members a 5 percent gas rebate and reporting on price fluctuations diligently. As of May 2007, the rebate card has saved members $142 million at gas pumps all over the country. Also in 2003, AAA launched its National Travel Barometer program, to provide weekly reports on America's travel trends. After initially reporting drops in cruise bookings, tour packages, car rentals and hotel reservations in March 2003, AAA happily noted that travel bookings returned to 2002 levels by June of that year, with travel on July Fourth the heaviest in nine years.

Life in the fast lane

Besides AAA's diligent and earnest support of automobile safety and efficiency, the organization admits that cars can be fun, too. AAA sanctioned auto racing in its early years, and even officiated at such races as the Indianapolis 500, until driver deaths prompted its withdrawal from the racing scene in 1955. The siren song of screeching tires eventually called the organization back to the track, however, and in 2005 AAA became the "official auto club" of NASCAR racing. The next year, AAA began sponsoring Rousch Racing's No. 6 Ford in the Nextel Cup tour.

After AAA's 50-year absence from American racing, the organization's return was seen by many as an affirmation of auto racing's improved safety record and overwhelming popularity. Indeed, AAA took advantage of NASCAR's popularity to spread its message of safe driving to teenagers, enlisting its drivers—NASCAR veteran Mark Martin and rookie David Ragan—to make pit stops at high schools across the country and teach teenagers safe driving techniques.

AAA goes digital?

AAA has recently upgraded its longstanding traveler services, offering all of its trademark roadside assistance, maps and other goodies on the Internet. AAA noticed that 35 percent of its calls for aid came from people at home or in the office, and began offering roadside assistance over the Web in February 2003. The following June, AAA debuted an online auto shopping service to help its members choose their next sedan, pickup truck, minivan or Hummer.

The May 2004 launch of the AAAmaps.com web site made AAA routing and mapping technology available for free to members and nonmembers alike, although its members-only Internet TripTik provides more extensive mapping and trip-planning services. In March 2007, AAA teamed up with navigation firm Magellan to bring GPS services to portable navigation devices, from which members can access AAA-approved maps, repair shops, restaurants, hotels and attractions. The service became available on GPS-enabled cell phones in August 2007.

AAA celebrated a milestone in May 2007, as it elected the first female chair to its board of directors. The honor went to Jeanette Gamba, chairwoman of Jordan Associates, an Oklahoma City-based communications and marketing agency. So far in her tenure, AAA is spreading its trademark automobile awareness, as evidenced by a recent "reminder from AAA," which simply advised motorists that "red means stop." Also, in a more specific AAA news release, the association revealed on November 19, 2007 that Tucson, Ariz., was selling the cheapest gas in the United States.

GETTING HIRED

For driven professionals

If you passionately believe in America's right to drive, coupled with a yen for travel, AAA may be the place for you. Interested parties are directed to the organization's career web site, www.aaa.com/jobs. Job seekers can browse the site for opportunities at AAA's main U.S. and Canadian offices in Calgary and Heathrow, Fla. Upon applying online, promising candidates will be contacted by AAA for an interview by phone or a one-on-one meeting with a hiring manager, depending on the position. Opportunities at local offices can be found by contacting individual branches, which are accessible through the zip code search at AAA's main web site or through the "AAA/CAA clubs" link on AAA's employment page.

Benefits for full-time AAAers include 21 to 37 vacation days a year, based on how long workers have been with the club, on top of eight paid holidays. AAA also offers extensive health insurance benefits after 30 days of employment, along with 401(k) and retirement plans. Extra perks include an employee credit union, tuition reimbursement, health club reimbursement and a 50 percent discount on AAA membership.

Visit Vault at **www.vault.com** for insider company profiles, expert advice, career message boards, expert resume reviews, the Vault Job Board and more.

VAULT CAREER LIBRARY

71

Making inroads

AAA also offers internships to full-time undergrads. These are posted with the rest of the employment opportunities in AAA's main job search. The club also collaborates with the INROADS organization to employ minority college students in internships. Students with a strong academic record are directed to www.inroads.org to learn more about AAA's INROADS internship program.

American Express Travel Related Services Company, Inc.

200 Vesey Street
3 World Financial Center
New York, NY 10285
Phone: (212) 640-5130
Fax: (212) 640-9365
www.americanexpres.com/travel

LOCATIONS

New York, NY (HQ)
Los Angeles, CA
London
Melbourne
Mexico City
Paris
Sydney
Tokyo
Toronto

2,200 locations worldwide.

THE STATS

Employer Type: Subsidiary of
American Express Company
Chairman & CEO: Kenneth I.
Chenault
2007 Revenue ($mil.): $24.3

DEPARTMENTS

Administrative Support/Clerical
Human Resources
Information Sales
Management
Marketing
Sales

KEY COMPETITORS

Expedia
priceline.com
Travelport

EMPLOYMENT CONTACT

www10.americanexpress.com/sif/
cda/page/0,1641,19188,00.asp

THE SCOOP

Put it on the card

American Express, best known for its credit cards, also takes good care of its customers' traveling needs. The company offers travel services for business and pleasure, like currency exchanges, traveler's checks and reservations for planes, hotels and cruises.

At a loss as to where to go? The company also publishes *Travel and Leisure* magazine and its offshoots, *Travel and Leisure Family* and *Travel and Leisure Golf*. It purchases wholesale travel reservations through its Travel Impressions business, and offers its credit card holders deals on hotel rooms, plane tickets and toys, such as private jets and yachts. If the worst happens on its customers' vacations, American Express offers travel insurance, travel medical insurance, insurance for lost luggage and help for travelers who have lost passports or credit cards while away from home. American Express is a member of the S&P 500 stock index.

Checks and balances

Back in 1841, Buffalo, N.Y., was a wild and thriving frontier town. The Western terminus of the Erie Canal, it was a bridge for people and goods between the developed Eastern states and the wide-open Northwest Territory. A man named Henry Wells recognized the need for a service that would provide safe transport of goods, valuables and bank remittances in and out of Buffalo.

Wells started an express service, initially carrying precious metals and securities between Albany and Buffalo (the trip took four days). In 1850, Wells merged his service with two competitors to form American Express. Wells soon wanted to expand into the gold rush state of the moment (California), and started another venture there in 1952 with Amex's then-secretary William G. Fargo. While establishing the venture, which they called Wells & Fargo, the two men continued working at American Express.

American Express merged with a competing company in 1868, the same year that William Fargo took over the presidency from Henry Wells. During Fargo's 33-year tenure the company developed the American Express Money Order, in 1882 and the famed American Express Travelers Cheque arrived in 1891. The Traveler's Cheque allowed travelers to carry liquid funds with them that could be replaced in the event that they were lost or stolen. It replaced an inefficient system of prearranged letters of credit exchanged between banks, which often left travelers stranded and without access to their money. Traveler's Cheques became immensely popular with Americans touring Europe—by 1901, the company sold checks worth more than $6 million. The company followed its customers across the pond, establishing a Paris office in 1895 and a London outpost in 1896. By 1910, there were a dozen American Express offices from Copenhagen to Naples.

For all your traveling needs!

Shortly before World War I, American Express began providing visitors with advice on hotels, restaurants and sightseeing. And its offices provided outlets for tourists to send and receive mail and packages, store their luggage, buy boat tickets and, of course, exchange money. The company formalized these services in 1915 under the umbrella of its travel department, just before the U.S. government nationalized its express services as a wartime measure. This enabled the company to deliver packages and handle the finances of Allied countries in Europe.

Following the Paris peace conference, American Express began setting up luxury tours for travelers to Asia, Europe, the Far East and other far-flung locales. In 1922, the company chartered the RMS Laconia, a Cunard Line steamship, for a 'round-the-world cruise. This move to travel products benefited the company during the Great Depression. In 1933, when President Franklin Roosevelt closed all U.S. banks for four days to stop a run on bank funds, American Express remained open for business, cashing a great amount of Travelers' Cheques and money orders. American Express struggled to keep its offices open during World War II, but boomed after the war, as soldiers often kept their pay in Traveler's Cheques. The company's number of offices quadrupled between 1944 and 1951.

By the 1950s, an American Express charge card seemed a logical extension of the company's services. Introduced in 1958, the card enjoyed immediate popularity—within three months, half a million people wouldn't leave home without them. The postwar boom continued in the 1960s, as sales of Traveler's Cheques increased exponentially and the firm expanded into more overseas markets. In 1968, the company purchased an insurance company called the Fireman's Fund, a publishing concern that went on to produce the popular *Travel and Leisure* magazine, and investment banking firm Equitable Securities.

Express for the modern era

In the 1980s, in a bid to transform itself into a one-stop financial supermarket, American Express acquired three brokerage firms (E.F. Hutton, Investors Diversified Services and Shearson Loeb Rhoades), two banks (the Boston Company and Lehman Brothers) and one real estate company (Balcor). In 1986, annual revenue surpassed $1 billion for the first time.

This financial supermarket strategy ultimately failed, as the U.S. entered a recession in the late 1980s, rocking the stability of Amex's recently assembled network of financial units. Shearson lost $1 billion during the market's 1989 downturn and American Express pumped an additional $1 billion into the unit in 1990 to keep it viable. However, the company started divesting its banking and brokerage assets after the appointment of CEO Harvey Golub in 1993, selling most of Shearson to Primerica Corp. for $1 billion that year and spinning the rest of its operations off to shareholders as Lehman Brothers in 1994.

The Boston fee party

The company's biggest headaches came from its credit card division, as rivals Mastercard and Visa charged small businesses with lower rates than American Express, and rapidly chipped into its market share. News reports credited a Bostonian restaurant with refusing to accept American Express' credit cards in 1991, inspiring other local businesses to do so. Analysts excitedly labeled the incident the "Boston fee party." Visa capitalized on the climate by launching an ad campaign, stressing to Amex cardholders that many businesses simply "won't take American Express." Amex worked hard to repair its damaged relationships with businesses, especially restaurants, and the company's stock was on the rise again by the mid-1990s.

Moving on

The tech bust of the late 1990s, followed shortly by the attacks of September 11th, put a major crimp in travel spending and greatly depressed American Express' core businesses. The attacks also damaged American Express' headquarters building, located across the street from Ground Zero—11 employees died and several others were injured. Thousands of American Express employees worked in interim locations for at least the next eight months as the company repaired its Downtown Manhattan facilities.

Kenneth Chenault, who rose through company ranks to become Amex's CEO in January 2001, pushed the company's recovery effort by emphasizing the need for change. Amex cut staff by about 16 percent (14,000 people) in the months after the attacks, and the leaner, more efficient company was profitable again by 2002. He brought American Express into places unthinkable during the "Boston fee party" era, selling gift cards through drugstores as of 2004 and overhauling Traveler's Cheques in 2005 for the first time in their 114-year history, debuting the Traveler's Cheque debit card for ATM withdrawals.

Chenault also took on rivals Visa and Mastercard in 2004, suing them for stipulating that their bank partners not issue American Express credit cards. In 2005, the Department of Justice agreed with American Express that this was an anti-competitive business practice, and ordered both Visa and Mastercard to terminate these policies. American Express then sued for damages; a trial was scheduled for September 2008. Rather than go to court and expose these business practices, Visa settled with American Express for $2.25 billion in November 2007. The settlement also covers Visa's bank affiliates Capital One Financial, J.P. Morgan Chase, U.S. Bancorp, Washington Mutual and (ironically) Wells Fargo. In a customer-friendly flourish, American Express vowed to use the settlement funds for customer reward programs. The case against Mastercard is still pending.

All about the customer

In June 2007, CEO Chenault reorganized American Express' corporate structure into "two distinct customer-focused groups." The two divisions will be the Global Consumer Group and the Global Business-to-Business Group, streamlined to better serve laypersons and lay-corporations, respectively. This means the company will continue to expand its business-to-business assets, like its January 2007 purchase of leading corporate e-invoice and e-payment firm Harbor Payments. Yet it also means more of the customer-friendly American Express, familiar from its recent ad campaigns with celebrities like Robert DeNiro and Tina Fey waxing rhapsodic about what their Amex card means to them. It all means a further move away from the financial supermarket approach of the 1980s, and in September 2007 Amex agreed to sell its banking subsidiary American Express Bank Ltd. to Standard Chartered plc for $1.1 billion. The transaction is expected to close in first quarter 2007.

Visit Vault at **www.vault.com** for insider company profiles, expert advice, career message boards, expert resume reviews, the Vault Job Board and more.

VAULT CAREER LIBRARY

77

Evident expenses

In 2006, American Express took in $27 billion in revenue, a 13 percent increase over 2005. Profits came in at $3.7 billion, essentially unchanged from 2005. Also in 2006, American Express introduced Axiom, an online device designed for employees making travel arrangements for business trips. Axiom lets employees book everything from airport parking to hotels to rental cars to restaurant reservations. And the service saves companies' money, since employees are prone to choose less pricey accommodations than would, say, a travel agent.

GETTING HIRED

Get away from it all

American Express' careers site, at www10.americanexpress.com/sif/cda/page/ 0,1641,19188,00.asp, provides gobs of information for aspiring Amex employees. The site clearly lays out career path options—everything from upper management to field sales to financial positions.

The company recruits at a number of career fairs for diversity candidates, including the United Negro College Fund's National Alumni Conference, the National Association of Asian American Professionals National Conference, National Society of Hispanic MBA's Annual Conference & Career Fair and the ReachingOut Lesbian, Gay, Bisexual, Transgender MBA Conference. There's also a helpful FAQ section, as well as information on benefits, which include work/life programs and help funding retirement. Job seekers can search open positions in numerous ways, and must create an online profile in order to apply.

Charge ahead

Ready for your interview? American Express is fond of introducing interviewees to several layers of management. "I interviewed with six different people of various positions (manager to VP)," recalls one hire. "I interviewed with four people," said another. "Generally, you will interview with two to five people, depending on the job, if you are coming from the outside." "Most interviews are capabilities-focused," adds another source.

OUR SURVEY SAYS

Distinctive culture, yet customer-focused

Company culture is distinctive. Insiders say to be prepared for a workplace "hyper-focused on gaining consensus" and that "Teamwork is encouraged and vital since the organization has a matrix structure. Another source adds that "Projects might take time to be implemented since buy in from higher ups is necessary." Other workers aren't so happy with the constant need for agreement, which they call "touchy-feely" and "stifling." Diversity gets high marks. "Diversity is strong as there are many women and minorities in leadership positions," explains a source.

One insider notes that "The closer you are to the customer, the more pressure, as there is a lot of customer focus within the company." One hire recalls, "During the tsunami, Amex customer service reps called every single cardholder in the region, employees and those who had purchased tickets/travel services to the region to ensure that they were [all right] and see what type of assistance they needed."

A relaxed Express

American Express is also distinguished by a fairly relaxed working day. The company "tends to the needs of employees very well, such as accommodating telecommuting requests, enhancing skills with coaching or classes," says one insider. "You need to make sure you are always 'on' and know the buzzwords that management loves to throw around constantly. Hours depend on the job, level and how much you want to put in, but are generally not bad until you get to the director level or above," agrees a co-worker. "The company is addicted to PowerPoint and upper management is generally incapable of reading anything not in bullet-point form, so know your PowerPoint!" Another source praises the "reasonable working hours," but adds that "salaries are slightly lower than average." But it can't be that bad, since "many employees stay with the company for years."

And you won't be doing the same thing day after day for your entire career. "There are decent opportunities for advancement, as the company encourages movement and promotion from within. However, you are 'tracked' and if you are not one of the chosen ones, it can be difficult to advance," advises one insider. "Card business is core," adds another, "and if you do want to advance, you need to work in this group at some point in your Amex tenure."

Visit Vault at **www.vault.com** for insider company profiles, expert advice, career message boards, expert resume reviews, the Vault Job Board and more.

VAULT CAREER LIBRARY

79

AMR Corporation

4333 Amon Carter Boulevard
Fort Worth, TX 76155
Phone: (817) 963-1234
Fax: (817) 967-9641
www.aa.com

LOCATIONS

Fort Worth, TX (HQ)
Albuquerque, NM
Boston, MA
Cary, NC
Chicago, IL
Fort Lauderdale, FL
Jamaica, NY
Miami, FL
New York, NY
Newark, NJ
Philadelphia, PA
San Francisco, CA
San Antonio, TX
San Jose, CA
Tucson, AZ
Tulsa, OK

Additional locations throughout the
US and in Canada.

THE STATS

Employer Type: Public Company
Stock Symbol: AMR
Stock Exchange: NYSE
Chairman, President & CEO: Gerard
  J. Arpey
2007 Employees: 85,500
2007 Revenue ($mil.): $22,935

DEPARTMENTS

Communications/Public Relations
Engineering
Executive Management
Finance/Accounting/Audit
Human Resources
Information Technology
Legal
Marketing/Sales
Medical
Operations
Procurement/Logistics
Project Management
Safety/Security/Environmental

KEY COMPETITORS

Delta Air Lines
Northwest Airlines
United Airlines

EMPLOYMENT CONTACT

www.aacareers.com

THE SCOOP

Not easy being No. 1

American Airlines, the main subsidiary of AMR Corporation, edges out United Airlines as the top airline in the U.S. and the world, thanks largely to its 2001 acquisition of TWA Airlines. From its five air travel hubs in Chicago, Dallas/Fort Worth, Miami, St. Louis and San Juan, American and its affiliate regional carrier American Eagle offer trips to over 250 destinations worldwide on more than 600 aircraft.

Recently, the company has experienced its share of financial woes and internal scandals. These culminated in April 2003, with the forced resignation of then-CEO Donald Carty. The company largely recovered under Carty's replacement as chairman and CEO, Gerald Arpey, in 2006 proudly posting its first year-end profit in five years, totaling $231 million. Revenue has grown each year since 2002, and came in at $22.5 billion for 2006.

Getting off the ground

American Airlines traces its roots back to 1929, when the Aviation Corporation formed to assemble a group of small aviation companies, then mostly regional airmail carriers. One of the companies it acquired, Missouri's Robertson Aircraft Corporation, employed a chief pilot by the name of Charles Lindbergh. The company incorporated the name American Airlines in 1934, and rapidly switched its business model from airmail to passenger flight. By the end of the 1930s, American led the U.S. flight industry in terms of revenue from passenger miles. The airline began European service in 1945 and was the first carrier to offer coast-to-coast flights in the U.S. in 1959.

In the early 1960s, the company introduced the first automated reservation system in the industry, Sabre. Among other things, Sabre enabled American to track mileage records, and the company used this technology to introduce AAdvantage in 1981, the industry's first frequent flyer program. (American spun off Sabre completely in 2000; for more information on that company, please see Sabre Holdings, later in this guide).

After the U.S. government deregulated the airline industry in 1978, American greatly expanded its service in the U.S. and the Caribbean, and moved its headquarters from New York City to Dallas/Fort Worth. The company reorganized in 1982 to form a

Visit Vault at **www.vault.com** for insider company profiles, expert advice, career message boards, expert resume reviews, the Vault Job Board and more.

VAULT CAREER LIBRARY

81

new parent entity, the holding company AMR Corporation In 1984, American continued with its reorganization, integrating a new regional carrier, American Eagle, into its domestic route system.

American further enhanced its carrier capacity in 1999, launching the oneworld global alliance with a number of other international airlines: Ireland's Aer Lingus, the U.K.'s British Airways, Finland's Finnair, Spain's Iberia, Chile's LanChile and Australia's Qantas. Oneworld allows customers to transfer frequent flyer miles among these member airlines, resulting in service to over 550 destinations in approximately 135 countries worldwide.

The TWA acquisition

A few years later, in 2001, American catapulted ahead of United as the biggest domestic and international airline with its acquisition of TWA (Trans World Airlines) for $724 million. TWA was founded in 1930, when Transcontinental Air Transport and Western Air Express merged to form a major airmail carrier. The company dominated American flights across the Atlantic Ocean for most of its history, but after deregulation in 1978, it suffered tremendously from other firms' encroachment on its market. Although it was the eighth-largest U.S. carrier in 2001, it hadn't turned a profit since 1988 and had twice filed for bankruptcy protection. By the end of 2001, the TWA flights, web site and ticket counters were all integrated into American's system.

The ramifications of September 11th

On September 11, 2001, two of American Airlines' jets were hijacked and crashed in terrorist attacks. In the following months, the airline industry went into a terrible slump, and American laid off 20,000 employees and cut flight capacity, even in spite of a $414 million bailout from the U.S. government. Then, disaster struck again in November 2001, when an American Airlines jet crashed near John F. Kennedy airport in New York City, killing 265 people. At first, many feared it was another terrorist attack, but American's internal investigation revealed that the plane's tail snapped off just before the incident. In January 2002, when AMR released results for fiscal 2001, it reported a quarterly loss of $798 million—its biggest quarterly loss ever—and year-end losses of $1.7 billion.

Pride goeth before a fall

In the wake of September 11th, travel conditions worsened with a sluggish wartime economy, competition from discount airlines and SARS-related travel scares. The company's economic profile continued to decline, hitting a low point in March 2003, when American's stock fell so low that Standard & Poor's removed it from its 500-stock index. The company was close to declaring bankruptcy for protection.

Immediately, then-CEO Donald Carty responded with drastic measures, asking American's labor leaders for about $1.8 billion in wage and benefit cuts for employees. Despite initial resistance, union representatives accepted these conditions on March 31, 2003. That same day, in a show of good faith, Carty announced that he would take substantial cuts in his base salary, voluntarily forgo his bonus for the third year in a row, and ask AMR's board to scale back other senior officers' salaries. Carty secured further concessions from the flight attendants' union on April 16, 2003.

On April 17th, less than 24 hours after flight attendants voted to accept Carty's restructuring efforts, workers at American discovered that Carty had secretly convinced AMR's board to approve huge retention bonuses for six top executives, worth twice their annual salary (the board allocated $1.6 million for Carty alone). The board also earmarked $41 billion in extra pension benefits for 45 top executives—to be paid even if the company filed for bankruptcy. These revelations were a staggering blow to Carty's promises of "shared sacrifice," and Carty resigned in the midst of the ensuing scandal, on April 24th.

New leadership—again

Effective immediately, AMR's board named one of its directors, Edward Brennan, as the new company chairman, and promoted Gerard Arpey, company president, to chief executive (Arpey became chairman of the board in May 2004). The board dropped its executives' exorbitant bonuses, although it kept the $41 billion pension package. And, after some negotiation between Arpey and AMR's constituent unions, the concessions agreed to under Carty stayed in place. The planned layoffs of 7,000 employees began to take effect in May 2003. Workers who kept their jobs took pay cuts of 15 to 23 percent, with longer hours and fewer benefits as their reward.

A ray of hope amid mounting losses

In lieu of downsizing the airline's already-shrinking number of routes, Arpey introduced a turnaround plan with such features as significantly lower air fares, the reintroduction of standard seating in 23 percent of the fleet, a higher minimum number of frequent-flyer miles customers could redeem for travel awards, and a substantial reduction of business conducted in hub city St. Louis. American's financial results improved in 2003, with year-end losses 53 percent smaller than in 2002, an indication that Arpey's plan was working.

Fueling a comeback

Arpey's virtuosic cost-cutting brought the company $500 million closer to profit in 2004, and the company celebrated by opening a new terminal at its Dallas/Fort Worth hub in July 2005 and a new terminal at New York's JFK in August. One cost the company couldn't cut, though, was the price of gas. In September 2005, when jet fuel prices spiked by 39 percent, American canceled 15 roundtrip flights out of its Chicago and Dallas/Fort Worth hubs.

More cutbacks in service came in April 2006, when American cut 27 planes from its fleet and began flying planes at higher capacities to defray fuel costs. From 2001, when the company had 880 planes in service, it now had only 673. Investors liked the strategy, though; public offerings of stock raised nearly $1 billion in fiscal 2006, and AMR turned its first year-end profit in five years.

They'll get theirs

American reported this good financial news in January 2007, and months later, in April 2007, the company's executive staff received $21 million in bonuses. This infuriated AMR's union employees, whose pay cuts were then worth $1.62 billion a year. At the next stockholders' meeting, two unions sponsored resolutions to curb executive compensation, but stockholders rejected the proposals in May 2007, apparently satisfied with a profitable year. And in all fairness, American's employees benefited from the company's peachy financial returns—in spring 2007, the company began handing jobs back to furloughed flight attendants and mechanics.

Immune to competition

The U.S. government, doing its part to encourage air travel, struck a deal with the European Union in summer 2007. Called the "open skies" treaty, it allowed for a greater amount of trans-Atlantic flights. In July 2007, American and its European cohorts in the oneworld alliance duly filed with the U.S. Department of Justice for antitrust immunity. The airlines want to offer essentially monopolistic practices—more codesharing and frequent flyer programs—to capitalize on the opportunities offered by "open skies." American's rivals United Airlines and Delta also applied for immunity, on behalf of Star Alliance and SkyTeam, their respective international consortiums.

Upgrades for a better tomorrow

American is trying hard to maintain its recent profitability, recently upgrading its fleet to attract as many customers as possible. In May 2007, the company equipped transcontinental flights with free audio and video on-demand services and, later that spring, announced new LC monitors and digital media file servers onboard all flights. In August 2007, American contracted with aviation communication firm AirCell to add Internet access to its list of in-flight niceties.

Not all upgrades are for the benefit of flyers. In 2007, American instituted a range of fuel-conserving modifications to its fleet. The largest upgrade occurred in June 2007, when American announced the purchase of new, more fuel-efficient Boeing 737-800s. These planes were originally slated for purchase in 2016, but will now enter the fleet in 2009. Other American innovations occur on a much smaller scale, and actually seem more like downgrades—smoothing out the tail cones on MD-80 aircraft to make them more aerodynamic, using lighter catering carts, even applying less paint to a plane's exterior, as chipped paint can cause an airplane to drag and use unnecessary fuel.

Easy does it

These might seem like desperate measures for a firm that reported its sixth straight profitable quarter in October 2007, and expects to report its second straight profitable year in January 2008. But they don't seem so outlandish considering the company's stock price, which fell by nearly 60 percent over the course of 2007. The company's prospects for 2008 only darkened in December 2007, when the Air Transport Association and International Air Transport Association tempered their forecasts for the year, stating that airlines would make less money in 2008 due to high fuel costs.

Perhaps in a move related to the industry's current woes, AMR Corporation announced in November 2007 that, after an "ongoing strategic value review process," it would seek to divest its American Eagle regional carrier subsidiary. For now, AMR hasn't stated whether it will spin American Eagle off to its shareholders, sell it to a third party or choose a third option. After the divestiture, though, American Eagle will continue to operate as a regional airline complementary to American, under their "mutually beneficial air services agreement."

Visit Vault at **www.vault.com** for insider company profiles, expert advice, career message boards, expert resume reviews, the Vault Job Board and more.

VAULT CAREER LIBRARY

85

GETTING HIRED

Get on board

Prospective job seekers can browse a descriptive listing of the latest openings by consulting American Airlines' employment web site at www.aacareers.com. Here, the company allows interested applicants to create and submit an online resume. There are separate listings for job opportunities in Mexico and with the American Eagle subsidiary (for now). On top of travel privileges and discounts available for employees and their families, American offers a 401(k) plan with company match, health insurance, profit sharing and training opportunities to help its workers climb the company ladder.

Throughout the year, American appears at several colleges and job fairs in its search for the best talent, and publishes a calendar of its recruitment schedule on its career page. The company seeks out a diverse workforce through partnerships with professional organizations like the American Indian Science and Engineering Society, the Association of Latinos in Finance and Accounting, the National Black MBA Association and the National Association of Women MBAs. American has long taken pride in its diversity efforts; it was the first major airline to hire a female pilot, after all. In 2007, *Black Enterprise* named AMR Corporation one of the 15 Best Companies in Marketing Diversity, and in 2006 *Profiles in Diversity Journal* ranked it in the top-10 Companies for Innovation in Diversity.

OUR SURVEY SAYS

Unlimited opportunity for more hours, unlimited flights

One respondent, a revenue analyst at AMR's Fort Worth headquarters, came to the company via a campus visit. AMR "came on campus" for an interview, says the source, "Although I know for a fact that [AMR does] look seriously at candidates from schools they don't [visit]." A fleet services clerk reports "really good diversity down on the ramp," although "There are not really … many opportunities for advancement." On the other hand, the source observes "unlimited opportunity for more hours. You could [work] 80 hours a week if you want."

"The real reason anyone works for the airline industry," says one contact, "is the travel benefits. Unlimited standby travel (sometimes in first class) for you and a companion … Many people fly out after work on Friday night and return Monday. If you love to

ARAMARK Corporation

1101 Market Street
Philadelphia, PA 19107
Phone: (215) 238-3000
Fax: (215) 238-3333
www.aramark.com

LOCATIONS

Philadelphia, PA (HQ)
Boston, MA
Charlotte, NC
Chicago, IL
Dallas, TX
Little Rock, AR
Minneapolis, MN
New York, NY
Orlando, FL
San Francisco, CA
Washington, DC

Additional locations nationwide and in Canada.

THE STATS

Employer Type: Private Company
Chairman & CEO: Joseph Neubauer
2007 Employees: 167,000
2007 Revenue ($mil.): $11,863

DEPARTMENTS

Administrative/Clerical • Architecture & Design • Art/Creative • Aviation • Biomedical/Imaging Technology • Communications • Construction Management • Culinary • Customer Services • Engineering • Finance/Accounting • Food Service Management • General Management • Grounds Management • Healthcare —Non-clinical • Hotel/Conference Centers • Housekeeping/Custodial/Laundry • Human Resources • Information Technology • Legal • Marketing • Nutrition/Dietetics • Operations/Manufacturing/Production • Purchasing/Supply Chain • Retail/Merchandising • Risk Management • Sales

KEY COMPETITORS

Cintas
Compass Group
Sodexho Alliance

EMPLOYMENT CONTACT

www.aramark.com/Careers

Visit Vault at **www.vault.com** for insider company profiles, expert advice, career message boards, expert resume reviews, the Vault Job Board and more.

VAULT CAREER LIBRARY   87

THE SCOOP

Large and in charge

Aramark is the U.S.'s top provider of managed services, providing other corporations and institutions with outsourced services such as catering, uniforms, facilities management, lodging and cleaning. That grease-stained uniform you wore during your stint as an auto mechanic: probably from Aramark. That hot dog you ate at the baseball game you skipped work to see: probably from Aramark. The industrial strength detergent you used to get the grease stains out before returning the uniform: again, probably from Aramark.

To convey a sense of the variety of the company's client base, Aramark provides concessions at 90 arenas, ballparks and stadiums, feeds children at more than 600 K-12 schools around the world and feeds prisoners at 700 correctional facilities. The company fed the 2004 Olympic Games in Greece, the 2005 FIFA Confederation Cup in Germany and the revelers at former-President George H.W. Bush's 80th birthday bash. The company also serves colleges, hospitals and plain old businesses.

One of Aramark's biggest customers is the U.S. government, which contracts with Aramark for cleaning services at major museums, such as New York's Museum of Natural History, and for lodging and visitor tours at Ellis Island and national parks. Based in Philadelphia, Pa., Aramark operates in 18 countries worldwide and employs more than 240,000 people.

A tale of two vendors

Aramark started out in 1959, when vendors Dave Davidson and William Fishman formed Automatic Retailers of America (ARA). By combining Davidson's West Coast-based vending machine business with Fishman's Midwestern one, ARA aimed to put a vending machine (or two or three) in every factory and office across America. The foundling firm surrendered itself up to investors with a public offering in 1960 and gained a nationwide presence in 1961 with the acquisition of Philadelphia-based Slater Systems. The Slater purchase also brought ARA into manual (that is, not coin-operated) food services.

Name game

In the mid-1960s, the firm began providing food for air travel and sporting events. The company's first international assignment came in 1968, when it fed fans in the stands for Mexico City's Summer Olympic Games. That year, the company re-dubbed itself ARA Services, a reflection of its expansion into large-scale catering and other "service"-based pursuits. In accordance with its new title, ARA Services expanded into all kinds of services in the 1970s: housekeeping, student bussing, trucking, even nursing home management. Later in the decade, it ventured into work uniform rental and developed an international presence, operating cafeterias in Canada, Mexico, Japan and the U.K.

CEO Joseph Neubauer led ARA Services' privatization in 1984. At this point, the company began collaborating more actively with its clients, working to meet their food, uniform and what-have-you needs as they developed, instead of simply complying with orders. The company also hired some advertising firms to build its brand into a household name. They suggested changing the company's name, and ARA renamed itself Aramark in 1994. Whether attributable to the rebranding or not, in the mid- to late-1990s Aramark landed food service and uniforms contracts with big corporate clients like McDonald's and Sprint. By 1999, Aramark's annual sales exceeded $6 billion.

Hitting the Ara-mark

Aramark purchased concessionaire Ogden Corp. in 2000, making it the largest entertainment and sports arena concessions provider in the country. The company then beefed up its facilities division with the 2001 purchase of ServiceMaster Management Services for $800 million. The company went public on the New York Stock Exchange the same year and used its IPO funds to purchase more service companies, including Clinical Technology Services in September 2002 and Fine Host Corporation in December 2002.

Out with the new, in with the old

After serving as chairman and CEO since 1984, Joseph Neubauer scaled back his duties at Aramark in 2003. A 20-year company veteran, William Leonard, took his place as CEO, only to quit a year later in September 2004. The company was mum as to why Leonard left so suddenly, but analysts suspected that the company's sagging quarterly earnings had something to do with it.

When fiscal 2004 financials came in the following December, they showed revenue growth of more than $500 million, to $10 billion. But rising labor costs and expenditures associated with new accounts took a bite out of profit, which fell by $40 million from 2003. Neubauer was back in the saddle again in no time, agreeing to lead the company for at least three more years.

Aramark's world domination continued in 2004 with the purchase of a 90 percent stake in Bright China Service Industries, a Beijing-based food service provider for hospitals and businesses in mainland China. Also in 2004, Aramark acquired food service companies in the U.K. and Spain. Sales outside of the U.S. accounted for 15 percent of Aramark's revenue in 2004.

A Giant-sized legal headache

Back on the home front, in January 2005, Aramark found itself on the wrong end of a lawsuit concerning a drunk driver striking and paralyzing a small girl after a football game at Giants Stadium in New Jersey. Where does Aramark fit in? The driver reached his state of dangerous intoxication after downing at least six beers at the stadium, where Aramark sells concessions.

A New Jersey jury determined that Aramark was partly responsible for the accident because it had served the man more than two beers after he was visibly intoxicated. The New Jersey Supreme Court dismissed the ruling in August 2006, but the entire affair brought bad publicity on the company and on stadium alcohol sales in general. Aramark settled with the family in November 2007 for an undisclosed amount.

Eat your heart out

In January 2006, Aramark opened a new "innovation center" in Philadelphia to house its consumer research and product development operations. The 53,000-square-foot space includes a test kitchen where 24 chefs slave away to produce the very best food for America's bellies. Innovation is a primary concern for Aramark, which must keep abreast of eating trends around the globe to best serve each of its markets.

One of Aramark's recent innovations is the addition of more nutritious food to its menus, in line with the health-consciousness now sweeping popular culture. Its Just4U line of low fat, vegetarian and low carb foods debuted in October 2005. Another element of mainstream health-consciousness is legislation against trans-fats, as enacted by local governments such as New York City. Aramark's 24 chefs got to work, and the company overhauled its product line to be trans-fat free in March 2007. And, to ring in the new year and for all those with resolutions about going on diets, in January 2008 Aramark unveiled its "5 under 500" menu of five meals, each under 500 calories.

Private business

In May 2006, CEO Neubauer was back to his old tricks again, teaming with Goldman Sachs, J.P. Morgan Chase and other private equity firms to take Aramark private once again, in a $5.8 billion buyout. Shareholders approved the deal after the company finished strong in fiscal 2006, with revenue growing to $11.6 billion and profit holding steady at $261 million. The takeover went down in January 2007, with the investment group paying about $8 billion for Aramark, including the assumption of $2 billion of debt. As a whole, Aramark's debt now stands in excess of $6 billion.

One special interest wasn't pleased at Aramark's buyout and its massive amount of debt: its employees. A number of Aramark's union contracts are set to expire in early 2008, and in late 2007 select groups of chefs, cashiers and other service workers went on strike in New York City. They might have a legitimate gripe, since Aramark has a history of under-compensating its employees. In April 2007, for instance, the U.S. Department of Labor concluded a two-year investigation (from July 2004 to July 2006), finding that Aramark failed to pay proper wages to 72 employees in Los Alamos, N.M. The company responded by shelling out $153,440 in back wages and fringe benefits to the affected employees. Perhaps Aramark can come to terms with its New York employees' demands—they are asking for a raise of approximately $0.70 per hour.

GETTING HIRED

Ara-mark it down

Aramark's career web site (www.aramark.com/Careers) offers a database of open positions searchable by type and location for those looking to join the ranks of its 240,000-strong army of workers. All candidates are required to apply online, and to that end the company asks applicants to create an online profile and upload their resumes. The web site also provides helpful interview tips and day-in-the-life rundowns of several jobs at Aramark. The company offers a "full array" of benefits, including medical, dental and vision insurance, 401(k) and paid vacation.

Winning the hearts and minds of college students through the seduction of school cafeterias, Aramark also visits university job fairs in search of those looking to make their (Ara)mark. The company hires interns, usually at or near its Philadelphia headquarters, in addition to welcoming recent grads to entry-level positions. The company offers its accredited dietetic internship program in New York City, Kansas

Visit Vault at **www.vault.com** for insider company profiles, expert advice, career message boards, expert resume reviews, the Vault Job Board and more.

VAULT CAREER LIBRARY   91

City and Philadelphia. In the program, interns train in the rigors of health and food science to prepare for entry-level dietician work—Aramark is, incidentally, one of the nation's largest employers of dieticians. Details on the application process and program dates are available through Aramark's main employment page.

Aramark has won a slew of awards for its employment policies. In 2005, *Fortune* listed the company as one of its Top 50 Employers for Minorities in 2005, and *Black Enterprise Magazine* agreed in 2007. In 2006, the Diversity Network named it one of the Top 30 Companies for Minorities.

The Aramark interview

Sources report varied interview techniques, depending on which of the 240,000 jobs one applies for at Aramark. For instance, a director at the company's corporate offices in Philadelphia met with "several people in the company at various levels, including the executive VP of corporate affairs." The source went through three rounds of interviews, and found the lengthy process "quite acceptable," since Aramark's philosophy "was to interview people, find the best talent and create a position that best fits their skills and interests, that also brought benefit to the company."

On the other hand, an HR insider reports just two interviews and a hasty job offer, since the company "needed someone desperately." The contact met with an operations manager and general manager, and concluded that "The process was a breeze." And down at the ground level, a seasonal part-timer at one of the company's national park locations says "There aren't several rounds of interviews. Usually just one. Interviews are conducted in person and over the phone (for out-of-state potential employees) … Interview questions are generally focused on basic customer service and hospitality.

OUR SURVEY SAYS

Good ole' Aramark

An operations manager in New York reports that Aramark's "corporate culture is typical, but more of a 'good ole' boys' club. Women are still underpaid and overlooked." And a food service director in Tennessee states that she sees "a lot of 'good ole' boy' politics" and that Aramark's "women [employees] are still paid less than men in the same positions," although "salaries for women with this company have finally become more competitive."

The food service business is tough

Another source observes that "the bottom line, with no concern for employees or clients, seems to be the [company's] primary objective." This emphasis on cost-consciousness is evident at some of Aramark's far-flung job sites, such as at Virginia's Shenandoah National Park, where a contact revealed that, as of 2006, Aramark was "still using a program that seems DOS-based (instead of Windows-based) for reservations. No mouse. Just arrow keys."

Sources also report confusion about the company's direction. "Our corporate culture," says one, "seems to have no clear direction at this time. Over the last six months we have been given totally contradictory directives, [which] makes it very difficult to perform one's job well." An HR assistant at the company's New York staffing center reports a similar experience, although that could be particular to the job: "the environment was always changing and unpredictable ... [and] as time went by, the atmosphere became pretty intense because everyone was [given] new responsibilities and new projects." The same source concedes that the industry itself could cause these operational difficulties. "Aramark is a food service provider, so working in the kitchens and facilities [is] very stressful and there is a very high turnover, even in the staffing center itself. To work here, you have to have a very tough skin, great customer service skills, [and] always [be] attentive to what employees and managers want ... The weakness for this company is that the turnover rate [will] always be [high], you can't stop it."

Visit Vault at **www.vault.com** for insider company profiles, expert advice, career message boards, expert resume reviews, the Vault Job Board and more.

VAULT CAREER LIBRARY   93

Avis Budget Group, Inc.

6 Sylvan Way
Parsippany, NJ 07054
Phone: (973) 496-3500
Fax: (888) 304-2315
www.avisbudgetgroup.com

LOCATIONS

Parsippany, NJ (HQ)

590 operations throughout the US, with additional locations in Canada and Mexico.

THE STATS

Employer Type: Public Company
Stock Symbol: CAR
Stock Exchange: NYSE
Chairman & CEO: Ronald L. Nelson
President & COO: F. Robert Salerno
2007 Employees: 30,000
2007 Revenue ($mil.): $5,986

DEPARTMENTS

Administrative
Automotive
Business Operations
Call Center
Client Services
Communications
Customer Service
Finance/Accounting
Ground Product
Human Resources
Information Technology
Interline and Incentives
Legal
Marketing/Advertising
Operations
Real Estate
Reception
Resort Operations
Revenue Management
Risk Management/Insurance
Sales
Supplier Strategy
Travel Industry

KEY COMPETITORS

Enterprise Rent-A-Car
Hertz
Vanguard Car Rental

EMPLOYMENT CONTACT

www.avisbudgetgroup.com/careers

THE SCOOP

An as-Cendant company

The Avis Budget Group is the parent company of Avis Rent-a-Car and Budget Rentals, two of the world's largest rental firms, operating some 6,700 car and truck rental outlets worldwide. Avis is all that remains of the larger entity called Cendant, which split into four separate companies in late 2006. The other companies comprised of former Cendant properties are Realogy, Travelport and Wyndham Worldwide Corp.

A bright idea

In the mid-1940s, no American car rental agency had airport operations. The first entrepreneur to address this reality was Warren Avis, a former Army pilot running a car dealership in Detroit. In 1946 he opened rental outlets at airports in Detroit and Miami, using some cars from his dealership. The strategy was an immediate success, and the Avis brand expanded across the U.S. in the late 1940s. The company picked up its first international franchises in 1953, in Canada, Mexico and Europe.

Who owns Avis?

Investors took notice of Avis' nearly overnight success and clamored to purchase the company, resulting in a series of ownership changes in the 1950s and 1960s. Boston financier Richard Robie purchased the company for $8 million in 1954, selling it only two years later to an investment group led by Amoskeag Company. Investment bank Lazard Freres & Co. acquired Avis in 1962, for $51 million, and then the giant industrial conglomerate ITT Corporation purchased it in 1965. Avis made great strides under these corporate owners, growing into the U.S.'s second-largest rental firm, behind Hertz, and expanding into Africa and the Middle East. In fact, the company introduced its "we try harder" motto in 1963, as an effort to chip away at Hertz's market share.

Avis went public in 1972, the same year it introduced Wizard, the car rental industry's first real-time electronic reservation system. (The first electronic reservation system in the travel industry as a whole was American Airlines' Sabre, which debuted in 1960.) By 1973, Avis led its competitors in Africa, Europe and the Middle East. The company changed ownership six more times between 1977 and 1987, becoming part of four successive entities that were purchased by other companies. Norton Simon

Visit Vault at **www.vault.com** for insider company profiles, expert advice, career message boards, expert resume reviews, the Vault Job Board and more.

V\ULT CAREER LIBRARY

95

Inc. purchased Avis in 1977. Norton Simon was purchased by Esmark Inc. in 1983, which was purchased by Beatrice Foods in 1984; Beatrice was then acquired by investment firm Kohlberg Kravis Roberts & Co. (KKR) in 1986. Avis escaped this cycle later in 1986, when KKR sold it to Wesray Capital Corp. for $263 million.

Evidence of Avis trying harder

On the ground level, Avis constantly improved its services from the 1970s onward, remaining near the top of its industry. In 1979, the company struck an advertising and marketing deal with General Motors, updating its fleet with a full array of GM vehicles. In 1985, the company took its Wizard system into Europe (it operated in more than 34 countries by 1994). The company flexed its tech muscles in 1987 and launched its Roving Rapid Return handheld computer screen, which helps customers pick up cars without waiting at a check-in counter.

More ownership changes!

Avis gained an unlikely new owner in 1987, after many years of operating under corporate interests. That year, through an employee stock ownership plan, Avis staffers spent $750 million for a 71 percent stake in the company, turning Avis into one of the largest employee-owned companies in the U.S.

The company became a minority shareholder in its African, European and Middle East operations in 1989, when it sold Avis Europe to Cilva Holdings, a consortium of investment firms. To this day, Avis Budget Group and Avis Europe operate under different ownership.

Employee ownership of Avis lasted until 1996, when real estate and hotel concern Hospitality Franchise Systems (HFS) acquired the company for $800 million. HFS spun off Avis the next year, although HFS' CEO Henry Silverman retained ownership of the Avis name and the Wizard system, along with an 18 percent Avis stake.

Cendant's penance

In 1997, HFS merged with CUC International, a direct marketer and one of the first e-commerce companies, in a deal valued at over $14 billion. The resulting firm, called Cendant, provided travel and real estate services to customers worldwide. Cendant's recognizable brand names included Century 21, Coldwell Banker, Days Inn, Howard Johnson, Ramada and Super 8. Avis joined the fold in 2001, when

Cendant purchased all of its public shares and Henry Silverman's 18 percent stake in the company.

However, the previous few years of Cendant's corporate history were marked by scandal and a great amount of internal upheaval. The corporate unrest concerned accounting fraud committed by CUC International in the mid-1990s, directly before its merger with HFS. When this fraud came to light in the late 1990s, many Cendant directors and executives resigned, and many shareholders and investors sued the company. Cendant shelled out lots of money in settlements, including a record $2.83 billion agreement in December 1999.

Adding to its Budget

The dust had largely settled from this turmoil in 2002, when Cendant acquired the bankrupt Budget Group for $108 million. Cendant then combined Budget's operations—including Budget Car Rental and Truck Rental—with Avis to form the world's No. 2 rental firm. Over the next few years, Cendant overhauled Budget's fleet, replacing its once ubiquitous yellow Ryder trucks with white Budget-branded ones. By 2005, the firm also added roughly 12,000 new trucks to Budget's 2,500 locations across the U.S.

Cendant descending

In October 2005, Cendant announced plans to split itself into four companies. In June 2006 the company sold its electronic reservation system, Travelport Inc., to The Blacksone Group for $4.3 billion. The following July, it spun off two other units to its shareholders—the Wyndham hotel business, including Days Inn, Howard Johnson and Ramada, and the Realogy real estate services business, with Century 21, Coldwell Banker, ERA, Sotheby's International Realty Affiliates and other assets. All of these deals closed by August 23, 2006, and the company renamed itself Avis Budget Group Inc. on August 29th.

Today, Avis maintains cooperative agreements with complementary former Cendant properties, such as online travel sites Orbitz and ebooker, and Wright Express, a payment processing and information management service for the vehicle fleet industry.

So, back to Avis and Budget, then

Avis Rent A Car and Budget Rent A Car currently share a fleet of approximately 400,000 vehicles. The two firms also use much of the same corporate infrastructure, but they maintain largely separate operations. Avis Rent A Car targets the upscale traveler, operating some 1,700 rental counters in Australia, Canada, the Caribbean, Latin America, New Zealand and the U.S. On the other hand, Budget Rent A Car does exactly what its name implies—offers rentals for the budget-minded consumer at 1,900 locations in all corners of the globe. Budget's Truck Rental unit dwarfs its car rental brother with 2,800 locations (in the U.S. only), and provides cargo vans and utility trucks for moves and commercial transport.

Cool stuff

Avis wants to make renting a car fun again (or fun for the first time). In May 2006 the company debuted a "cool car collection" that it markets as "fun-to-drive." The line includes the Chrysler Crossfire, the Lincoln MKX and the irresistibly over-the-top Hummer H3, and aims to tap into drivers looking for thrill rides. In July 2007 the firm responded to charges that renting out Hummers was bad for the environment by adding hybrid vehicles to the collection—500 Nissan Altimas and 1,000 Toyota Priuses.

In August 2006, for those who consider it cool not to be lost, Avis and Budget added Where2 global positioning system (GPS) navigation instruments to their cars. In January 2007, Avis introduced optional mobile Wi-Fi to its rental cars. For an additional $10.95 per day, customers can equip their vehicles with these Autonet Mobile Service units and enjoy the pleasures of the Internet from inside their cars (hopefully not while driving), provided they have a laptop or personal digital assistant. The notebook-sized Autonet gadget is portable, so Avis customers can take it with them from their rental cars into their hotel rooms, conference rooms or wherever the family vacation might lead. The device uses 3G cellular networks, so it should work wherever a cell phone gets a signal.

In response to high demand for these gadgets, Avis premiered the "next generation" of its Where2 GPS systems in January 2008. The new batch features bigger screens in brighter colors, with more languages; it's also easier to detach and fit in one's pocket. Avis also tailored its GPS machines to appeal to business travelers, adding new services to the Where2 in December 2007 that offers customers tips on concerts, sporting events, museums and other local events, wherever they may be traveling. These are available on the company web site at www.avis.com/mywhere2.

Business travelers should be pleased with another recent Avis initiative: the October 2007 purchase of a majority stake in Carey International, the worldwide leader in "chauffeured ground transportation services." For $60 million, Avis bought 45 percent of Carey's stock and a one-year option to increase its ownership to 80 percent. Carey operates its fancy cars in 550 cities in 60 different countries. For now, Carey's investor group Chartwell Investments continues to own a majority stake.

Tougher times

The increasingly unstable state of the American auto industry has resulted in at least one major change for car rental firms. In previous years, rental firms sold cars back to their manufacturers after using them for about six months or a year. Nowadays, manufacturers usually don't buy back any vehicles from rental firms, leaving the agencies to sell the cars themselves.

As rental firms adapt to this reality, Avis is leading the way. In May 2007, Avis announced a program by which dealers could purchase its cars while they were still in the rental fleet. The program makes Avis cars available to dealerships across the country through an alliance with online auction service ATC Open. Soon after the program started, in June 2007, ATC's SVP Clive Kinross told *AutoRemarketing* magazine that "the rental segment of our industry is going through significant change at the moment ... [and ATC] and the Avis Budget Group have been exceptionally delighted with the initial adoption and results [of this program.]"

Indebted to Cendant

In its first year out from under the Cendant umbrella, Avis Budget Group's revenue broke a company record in fiscal 2006, increasing by 5 percent to $5.7 billion. However, costs incurred in Cendant's breakup led the company to year-end losses of $677 million. As of September 2007, Avis was operating under $8.7 billion of debt, of which $6.9 billion came from vehicle programs, such as financing and leasing the company's fleet.

Revenue from non-airport locations grew by an impressive 18 percent over the year, thanks to the opening of 197 such locations in 2006. Coincidentally, off-airport revenue accounts for 18 percent of the company's overall sales.

Visit Vault at **www.vault.com** for insider company profiles, expert advice, career message boards, expert resume reviews, the Vault Job Board and more.

VAULT CAREER LIBRARY   99

GETTING HIRED

Hiring overview

Avis Budget Group's careers site, at www.avisbudgetgroup.com/careers, contains information about corporate positions as well as at individual Avis Rent-A-Car, Budget Rent-A-Car and Budget Truck Rental locations. The North American search only queries locations in the U.S., Canada and Mexico, but the Campus search queries open positions in locations worldwide. Applications may be filed online after job seekers set up a profile, saving their details for future applications to Avis.

Avis Budget Group's slogan is "we try harder"; harder than what, we can't say, but the company does put some effort into keeping its employees content through a generous benefits package. In addition to health insurance and a 401(k) plan with company match, those working for the Avis Budget Group enjoy tuition reimbursement, an employee stock purchase program and discounts on company car rentals. The Management Fast Track program assists those looking to climb the corporate ladder. Avis Budget Group also hires college students for internships, which are posted at Monstertrak.com.

Avis interviews

A pricing analyst in New Jersey reported one day of three interviews, lasting about three hours. The contact met with "HR and two sets of two managers … and they asked the usual interview questions, and also showed a report used by analysts. They asked various questions about these reports, but helped with the answers." A finance operations manager also had three interviews, one with "myself [and an] HR representative, my manger and her manager," and then "an informal chat structure with us chatting about my experience and items on my CV." The questions included "my ability to adapt in [a] fast-changing environment and how I cope under pressure."

A beneficial company

Avis contacts reported some very good benefits packages, with one manager receiving a "company performance bonus paid out biannually," a pension scheme, a car allowance and 26 days of vacation per year. Another talks of "special perks," with discounts at "Verizon, Sprint, Cingular, Ford, GM," and others. "There is tuition reimbursement," he continues, "however, one must stay at the company a year after the course is over in order to receive it, and the maximum amount is $6,000 a year (I think), if one receives all A's."

OUR SURVEY SAYS

Having fun at Avis

Insiders say Avis was a "fun, casual work environment" and that "the atmosphere seems to be on the way up," as "everyone in the business is targeted with finding better ways of working." Although the business climate for Avis is somewhat shaky after Cendant's recent breakup, sources are optimistic. "I think [Avis and Budget] are in good positions compared to [their] competitors," says one, and another agrees: "The outlook for [Avis] is promising, with current investment levels … and the focus shift to a worldwide [Avis] brand, which is aligning management objectives and defining employees' role[s] more." Another takes the long view, stating that "One contributing factor is the deteriorating domestic auto industry, since all rental cars are leased from Ford or GM, and increased auto prices, as well as gas prices, are increasing costs for the company."

If you work at Avis, expect to wear a tie. "The dress code is business casual," says a contact at Parsippany headquarters. A U.K.-based insider says the dress code is "smart" from Monday to Thursday, and "generally involves a shirt [and] tie for men." Opinion is similar on advancement, as one notes that opportunities "are available, especially if you enjoy finding answers and are willing to work hard to get new processes implemented." Another reveals that "due to the high retention rate within the department, promotions typically occur within a year." The same source reported starting out "at $35,000" and leaving "after a year at a base salary of $42,000."

Boyd Gaming Corporation

3883 Howard Hughes Parkway
Ninth Floor
Las Vegas, NV 89169
Phone: (702) 792-7200
Fax: (702) 792-7313
www.boydgaming.com

LOCATIONS

Las Vegas, NV (HQ)
Dania Beach, FL
East Peoria, IL
Henderson, NV
Kenner, LA
Michigan City, IN
Robinsonville, MS
Shreveport, LA
Vinton, LA

THE STATS

Employer Type: Public Company
Stock Symbol: BYD
Stock Exchange: NYSE
Chairman: William S. Boyd
President & CEO: Keith Smith
2007 Employees: 16,900
2007 Revenue ($mil.): $1,997

DEPARTMENTS

Administration
Arena
Casino
Card Room
Facility Maintenance
Finance
Food & Beverage
Hotel Operations
Linen & Uniform Services
Sales & Marketing
Warehouse

KEY COMPETITORS

Harrah's Entertainment
Las Vegas Sands
MGM MIRAGE

EMPLOYMENT CONTACT

www.jobflash.com/websub/user/
reg.jsp?company_id=324

THE SCOOP

Life's a gamble

The Boyd Gaming Corporation is pretty well addicted to gambling, having operated slot machines, roulette wheels, blackjack tables and poker games for over 30 years. It is one of the largest gaming corporations in the United States, boasting 17 casinos in Nevada, Illinois, Indiana, Louisiana, Mississippi, Florida and New Jersey. These facilities house 23,500 slot machines, 500 table games and 7,500 hotel rooms. (Casino giants Harrah's and MGM Mirage are still bigger, though.) Boyd Gaming employs a staff of nearly 20,000 and brings in over $2 billion in sales.

$80 and a dream

Boyd Gaming got is start in 1941, when Sam Boyd arrived in Las Vegas with just $80 in his pocket. The industrious Boyd took a job in the gaming industry and worked his way up from dealer to pit boss to shift supervisor to, eventually, general manager and partner at The Mint hotel. He and his son William first ventured into the casino and hotel management business in 1962, purchasing the Eldorado Club in Henderson, Nevada.

In 1975, Boyd Gaming became a corporation with the opening of the California Hotel and Casino in Las Vegas. Just a few years later, in 1979, the Boyds hit the big time, opening Sam's Town Hotel and Gambling Hall in southeastern Las Vegas. Sam's was one of the first resorts to cater to the local population, and local yokels remain a principal source of revenue and profits at Boyd's Vegas-based casinos.

The Boyds continued to expand their holdings through acquisitions in the following decades. In 1985, the company gained a larger share of Vegas' tourist business, acquiring two downtown properties, the Stardust and the Fremont. After going public on the NYSE in 1993, Boyd Gaming took its gambling know-how to the road in 1994, opening Sam's Town Hotel and Gambling Hall in Mississippi, its first property outside of Nevada. In April 1996, the company acquired an Illinois riverboat gambling casino, the Par-A-Dice Gaming Corporation, for $163 million. The Blue Chip riverboat casino, outside of Chicago, came into Boyd Gaming's grasp in 1999, for $273 million.

Nice niche

For nearly all of its corporate history, Boyd Gaming has cultivated a far-flung (and lucrative) niche market: Hawaiians. In the 1970s, Boyd first tapped Hawaiian travel agents to send their customers to its California Hotel and Casino. Boyd Gaming now runs its own travel agency, Vacations Hawaii, which shuttles Hawaiians to Nevada with six charter flights from Honolulu to Las Vegas per week.

Boyd Gaming also contracts with other Hawaiian travel agencies to offer all-inclusive vacation packages at its resorts. The scheme has worked wonders for three of the company's downtown Vegas hotels—the California, the Fremont and Main Street Station—each of which reported that Hawaiians occupied more than half of their hotel rooms in 2006.

Nationwide dreams and schemes

After spreading the Boyd brand all across Las Vegas, the company expanded farther across the United States in the new millennium. Since 2001, Boyd has established operations in Indiana, Louisiana, Florida and New Jersey, often buying old casinos, expanding upon them, and reopening them with spiffy new names.

The firm entered Louisiana in 2001 with the acquisition of Delta Downs in Vinton, Louisiana. Upon acquisition, Boyd invested $65 million on a two-phase expansion project, including a new entrance, reconfiguring the casino and adding a 206-room hotel, which opened in March 2005. The new features transformed Delta Downs from a racetrack with slots to a vacation destination, one of many in a rapidly growing population of racinos. And, while renovating Delta Downs, Boyd purchased another Louisiana property for $197 million in 2003: the Shreveport Hotel and Casino. After a typical Boyd-style renovation, the establishment reopened as Sam's Town Hotel and Casino in May 2004.

Meet me tonight in Atlantic City

Perhaps Boyd's grandest non-Las Vegas expansion scheme is located in America's other gambling paradise, Atlantic City, New Jersey. Around the turn of the century, Boyd began looking for investment opportunities in the area with MGM Mirage, owner of some of Las Vegas' most fabulous hotels. The result was the MGM- and Boyd-co-owned Borgata, a luxury resort featuring hip restaurants, 300-thread count sheets, glass chandeliers and a 50,000-square-foot spa. The property opened in July 2003 and caters to a younger audience in search of a little Las Vegas glitz east of the Rockies, keeping its restaurants open past midnight and specifically targeting the just-over-21 crowd in marketing efforts for its Mixx nightclub. Despite soft margins in its early days, the Borgata quickly began pulling its own weight, accounting for 13 percent of Boyd's profits in 2004.

Staying in Vegas

Despite its investment in gaming beyond Nevada's borders, Boyd Gaming's heart is still in Las Vegas. In July 2004, the company cemented its leadership of the local market when it merged with Coast Casinos in a $1.3 billion deal. Under the terms of the agreement, Coast became a wholly owned subsidiary of Boyd, and Coast's properties—Barbary Coast, Gold Coast, The Orleans, Suncoast and South Coast— retained their brand and management (although South Coast was sold off in 2006, for $513 million).

This investment in Las Vegas' high-rolling gambling industry couldn't have come at a better time, as "Sin City" had recently returned to its wild-and-sexy image after selling itself in the 1990s as a sufficiently mild destination for families and retirees. Around the turn of the century, the city adopted a nationwide marketing campaign, telling potential visitors that "What happens in Vegas, stays in Vegas." But the city has not completely returned to the rough and tumble days of the 1960s; it houses the largest number of huge corporations in its history (Harrah's, MGM Mirage), as well as non-gambling, entertainment acts (Cirque du Soleil). As a result, the city has enjoyed a resurgence in popularity and profitability, with its vibrant economy attracting young people in unprecedented numbers.

Stardust memories

The best example of Boyd's commitment to Las Vegas is Echelon Place, an ambitious new downtown Vegas development project, scheduled to complete in 2010. At press time, the Echelon was budgeted at about $4.5 billion, the second-largest ever development in Vegas history, behind only MGM Mirage's $7 billion Project CityCenter.

The Echelon is scheduled to open its lavish doors in early 2010, revealing a complex with four hotels, containing 5,300 guest rooms and luxury suites. The development's centerpiece, the wholly owned Echelon Resort, will include a tower with 2,600 rooms, another with 700 suites, a 140,000-square-foot casino, and 25 restaurants and bars. The Hong Kong-based Shangri-La Hotels and Resorts will operate a signature hotel within the complex, and Morgans Hotel Group has reached a deal with Boyd to add two namesake hotels, each costing $700 million.

Visit Vault at **www.vault.com** for insider company profiles, expert advice,
career message boards, expert resume reviews, the Vault Job Board and more.

VAULT CAREER LIBRARY   **105**

This enormous development comes at the expense of an iconic piece of the city's history, the Stardust casino, a Boyd asset for over two decades. Boyd has accumulated real estate around the Stardust since 2004, which will be the site for the new Echelon. In November 2004, Boyd acquired a 13-acre site, increasing the size of the Stardust's lot to approximately 63 acres. In November 2006, Boyd ceased operations at the Stardust, and in February 2007, the company traded its Barbary Coast Hotel and Casino to Harrah's in exchange for 24 more acres bordering on the Stardust property. Finally, in March 2007, the 32-story Stardust became the tallest building to be demolished on the Las Vegas Strip, as 428 pounds of explosives brought almost half a century of gambling history down in under 10 seconds. Ironically, Boyd's commitment to gambling in Las Vegas has cost the city one of its signature casinos.

To ensure Echelon's success, Boyd is bringing in the all-star team behind the success of Atlantic City's Borgata. Bob Boughner, the Borgata's founding CEO, will travel West to become Echelon's president and CEO (he should not be confused with the former hockey player, of the same name). Kevin Sullivan, also on the Borgata team, will be Echelon's senior vice president. Even the lead construction firm, Tishman Construction Corp., will be retained.

Boyd is bad, it's nationwide

Boyd isn't neglecting its nationwide properties, especially its crown jewel in Atlantic City. The company broke ground on a second hotel at the Borgata in January 2006. The project, budgeted at $400 million, started in the midst of another addition to the Borgata compound; in June 2006, Boyd Gaming opened a $200 million expansion of the resort's public space, including more restaurants, gaming, meeting and convention space and an even bigger spa.

Also in 2006, Boyd invested in its Blue Chip floating casino, which straddles both Illinois and Indiana. In January, the company added a new floating casino boat and the following October, Boyd announced a $170 million expansion of the Blue Chip hotel. The expansion, to be completed in 2008, will add 300 guest rooms, more than doubling the Blue Chip's capacity.

Boyd Gaming is still breaking into new markets, too. In March 2007, just as the Stardust imploded in Las Vegas, Boyd spent $152 million on the Dania Jai Alai facility near Fort Lauderdale, Fla., along with 50 acres of adjacent land. Immediately after the acquisitions, Boyd announced plans to build a casino on the site that will feature off-track betting and live jai alai (the super-fast Spanish ballgame) matches, to open by the end of 2008. However, the firm put its expansion plans on hold in August 2007; slot machines were drawing only an average of $85 per machine per day, far short of the company's hoped-for draw of $212 per machine per day.

Bye bye, Bill Boyd

In July 2007, Bill Boyd announced he would step down as CEO of the company he co-founded with his father, ceding the position to Keith Smith. Smith is a 17-year veteran of Boyd Gaming, having served as COO since 2001, and president since 2005. Boyd will stay on as executive chairman and continue to work on his company's customer and employee relations.

When Smith took over the top spot in January 2008, he inherited a company that has not been able to significantly increase its market share in recent years, as gaming has become an increasingly national industry. Boyd Gaming drew $2.19 billion in sales for 2006, up only $29 million from the year previous. Profits for the same period were $117 million, a total very close to profits of $111 million in 2004 and far below 2005's earnings of $164 million.

While Echelon Place is expected to give the company a shot in the arm and a spike in sales, the completion of that project is still a few years off, and until then Boyd Gaming will have to stay on its toes against the constant competition in Las Vegas to maintain its profitability. Boyd might not be able to maintain its pace, as evidenced by its July 2006 sale of South Coast Casino. With the Stardust now only a memory, the pressure will be on Boyd's other casinos to perform.

GETTING HIRED

Hiring overview

Boyd Gaming offers employment opportunities at corporate headquarters as well as at each of its 17 properties located in Nevada, Illinois, Indiana, Florida, Louisiana, Mississippi and New Jersey. Interested applicants can search the company's web site for job openings by location or use the listing of phone numbers to contact the properties directly. Candidates wishing to apply online must sign up for JobFlash.

Visit Vault at **www.vault.com** for insider company profiles, expert advice, career message boards, expert resume reviews, the Vault Job Board and more.

VAULT CAREER LIBRARY   107

British Airways Plc

Waterside, Harmondsworth
London, UB7 0GB
United Kingdom
Phone: +44-870-850-8503
Fax: +44-20-8759-4314
www.britishairways.com

LOCATIONS

London (HQ)
Atlanta, GA • Chicago, IL • New
York, NY • Amsterdam • Bangkok •
Barcelona • Beijing • Berlin •
Brussels • Delhi • Frankfurt •
Glasgow • Hong Kong • Inverness

Additional locations in Algeria,
Angola, Antigua, Australia, Bahrain,
Bangladesh, Brazil, Bulgaria,
Denmark, Dubai, Finland, France,
Germany, Iceland, India, Iran, Italy,
Japan, Norway, Portugal, Romania,
Singapore, South Africa, Spain,
Sweden, Trinidad and Tobago and
Turkey.

THE STATS

Employer Type: Public Company
Stock Symbol: BAY
Stock Exchange: London
Chairman: Martin F. Broughton
CEO: Willie Walsh
2007 Employees: 48,070
2007 Revenue (£mil.): £8,492

DEPARTMENTS

Commercial
Corporate Services
Customer Contact
eBusiness & IT
Technical & Operations

KEY COMPETITORS

Air France-KLM
Lufthansa
United Airlines

EMPLOYMENT CONTACT

www.britishairwaysjobs.com

THE SCOOP

Flying British

British Airways, the U.K.'s No. 1 and Europe's No. 3 carrier, flies about 35.5 million passengers annually on 284 aircraft to more than 148 destinations in some 75 countries. Subsidiary companies include British Airways Holidays Limited and British Airways Travel Shops Limited. British Airways also holds interests in the Australian carrier Qantas and the Spanish airline Iberia. The airline considers London's Gatwick and Heathrow airports as its main hubs, although it has been reducing its operations at Gatwick since 2000. A new terminal that will exclusively serve British Airways flights at Heathrow airport is slated to open in March 2008.

Imperial beginnings

The company's origins lie in a handful of groups that began international flights just after World War I: Aircraft Transport and Travel, Daimler Airways, Handley Page Transport and Instone Airlines. These were all private enterprises, largely formed in the direct aftermath of John Alcock and A. Whitten Brown's famous flight from Newfoundland to Ireland in June 1919, the first direct flight of the North Atlantic. In August 1919, Aircraft Transport and Travel began the world's first scheduled international service, flying a consignment of leather, several brace of grouse and some jars of Devonshire cream from London to Paris. The same year, Handley Page Transport Ltd. first took the air, using converted World War I bombers to traverse from London to Paris. Instone Airlines also formed in 1919.

By the early 1920s, these private enterprises faced stiff competition from state-subsidized foreign airlines. The British government duly intervened, and in 1924 merged the fleets of British Marine Air Navigation Co. (which operated a flying boat service), Daimler Airway (a successor to AT&T), Handley Page Transport and Instone. The government called the new operation Imperial Air Transport. Imperial was an apt title for the airline, as it focused on quick, reliable courses to every part of the British Empire, especially India, and by 1932, it offered flights to India, Singapore and Australia (beginning the firm's association with Australia's Qantas airline, then known as Queensland and Northern Territories Air Service). Imperial also began flying to Africa in the same period, establishing a hub in Cairo in 1931. Five years later, the airline offered routes to Cape Town, Khartoum and Nigeria.

Visit Vault at **www.vault.com** for insider company profiles, expert advice, career message boards, expert resume reviews, the Vault Job Board and more.

V/\ULT CAREER LIBRARY   109

British Airways is born

Meanwhile, private airlines had regained some liveliness, three of which—Hillman's Airways, Spartan Airlines and United Airways (not that United)—merged in October 1935, forming British Airways Limited. At the dawn of 1936, the upstart BA purchased a fleet of Lockheed 10 Electras, then the fastest airplanes in the world. In November 1937, British Parliament proposed the nationalization of British Airways, and its merger with Imperial Airways. This was completed by November 1939, and saddled with a lengthy new title: the British Overseas Airways Corporation (BOAC).

However, the U.K. declared war on Germany in October 1939, eliminating nearly all of BOAC's continental European routes. BOAC went the other route, and offered about 54,000 miles of international routes by war's end, in 1945. The postwar Labour government divided BOAC's operations into three new entities; BOAC for routes to the Empire, Far East and North America, British European Airways (BEA) for services to Europe and domestically within the U.K., and British South American Airways (BSAA) for new services to South American and Caribbean destinations. However, equipment failures in BSAA led the government to remerge it with BOAC in 1949.

British Airways is born (again)

BOAC suffered from "excess capacity," or too many empty seats, in 1961. The company ended the year with losses of £64 million, and the government saved the firm from certain bankruptcy. The airline spent the rest of the 1960s paying the government back and regaining solvency, a process that included the resignations of its chairman and managing director, Sir Matthew Slattery and Sir Basil Smallpiece, respectively.

When the books were balanced in March 1972, BOAC and BEA started exploring merger options. In July of the same year, the two airlines retained their routes and separate names but condensed management into a new parent company, called the British Airways Group. The BOAC and BEA names fell by the wayside in April 1974, replaced by the catch-all moniker British Airways.

In 1979, newly elected Conservative Prime Minister Margaret Thatcher almost privatized the airline, but recession delayed this measure. Two years later, Thatcher appointed John King as chairman of British Airways, hoping he could whip the airline into shape for eventual privatization. King instituted drastic changes, firing 22,000 employees (nearly 50 percent of headcount), replacing old aircraft with more modern carriers and canceling unprofitable routes.

Within two years, King also axed over half of the company's board—on one infamous day in 1983 he fired 50 senior executives—and replaced them with younger appointees. When British Airways was finally privatized in 1987, the market proved King's brutal efficiency effective—BA's initial share offering was 11 times oversubscribed.

Virgin territory

In addition to tightening its operations under King, British Airways grew by virtue of acquisitions through the 1980s and 1990s—most notably the 1987 purchase of its former domestic rival, British Caledonian, and its 1993 purchase of a stake in Qantas. Still, even as the company secured its position as the U.K.'s leading airline, its primacy was challenged by the emergence of a completely unexpected but dangerous rival, Sir Richard Branson's Virgin Atlantic.

Virgin, which began with one route and one Boeing 747 in 1984, soon began seriously threatening some of BA's most lucrative routes. Virgin enjoyed tremendous publicity in 1991, when it flew British citizens held hostage in Iraq by Saddam Hussein back to the U.K. This event allegedly prompted John King to tell Colin Marshall and David Burnside, BA's CEO and public affairs director, to "do something about Branson."

Over the next few years, British Airways launched what BBC reporter Martyn Gregory called a "secret war" against Virgin, involving "dirty tricks," such as hacking into Virgin's computer system and organizing a smear campaign against Branson and the safety of his aircraft. Gregory reported that BA paid private investigators as much as £15,000 a month to make Branson's life difficult. Branson sued King and British Airways for libel in 1992. Branson won a settlement of £500,000 for himself and £110,000 for his airline, and John King resigned shortly afterwards. Litigation dragged on for several more years, and CEO Marshall stepped down in 1996, replaced by four-year BA veteran Robert Ayling. Marshall stayed on as part-time BA chairman.

Changing its spots

After the "dirty tricks" scandal, new CEO Ayling had more to repair than the company's reputation. Increased competition, high oil prices, a strong pound and repeated disagreements between the company and its trade unions all hurt profits in the mid- to late-1990s. Ayling repeatedly pursued a merger with American Airlines, but was ultimately unsuccessful due to the conditions placed on the deal by regulatory authorities. Ayling also changed the company's longtime tradition of featuring the Union Jack on the tail fins of its aircraft. Partly due to political sensitivities, the planes were repainted in 1997 with abstract ethnic images representing the countries they were flying to, such as Egyptian scrolls, Celtic designs or Gothic calligraphy. Other major airlines followed suit, such as Dutch carrier KLM.

But British Airways' new look made the planes harder for air traffic controllers to identify, and some public figures disliked them for more aesthetic reasons. At the 1997 Conservative party conference, Margaret Thatcher is said to have placed her handkerchief over the tail fin of a model aircraft featuring the new design, opining that it made British Airways look like a third-world airline. "We fly the British flag, not these awful things," she said.

Ayling ailing

The firm reported a 50 percent slump in profits in 1999, its worst since privatization. The board removed Ayling in 2000, replacing him with Rod Eddington, a veteran of the airline industry who clocked in 18 years at Cathay Pacific Airways, a partner in British Airways' oneworld codesharing alliance. Also in 2000, the world-famous supersonic Concorde jet, which had carried passengers across the Atlantic in record time for decades, was pulled from the skies after an Air France Concorde crashed in July 2000. After British Airways spent millions of pounds, euros and dollars on safety checks and maintenance to its Concorde fleet, it permanently retired the model in October 2003.

Eddington to the rescue

To pull British Airways out of its tailspin, CEO Eddington enacted workforce reductions across the board and attempted to whittle the giant airline down to its core customer base of business travelers. He also reversed his predecessor's rebranding attempt, declaring that the tail fins of all British Airways planes would be repainted with the Chatham Dockyard Union Flag, a design first used on the Concorde. In June 2001, Eddington initiated a campaign to divest non-core assets, selling off the discount airline Go (an independent subsidiary founded in 1997 that competed with cheap Euro-travel players Ryanair and easyJet) to its management team for £110 million.

In 2001, the entire airline industry reeled from the terrorist attacks of September 11th. British Airways expected the worst and quickly moved to shore up against an industrywide slump, cutting 7,000 workers and reducing flights by 10 percent. In February 2002, the company announced its Future Size and Shape initiative, a package of measures (some of them desperate) aimed at seeing British Airways through the turbulence. The plan cut another 5,800 jobs from the company payroll. It seemed to work, as British Airways saved £869 million in 2003 and reported profits of £396 million in 2004, while many competitors reported losses or even entered bankruptcy proceedings.

A striking proposition

Eddington's maneuvers were naturally unpopular with British Airways' staff, and union disputes abounded as his job reductions were implemented. In July 2003, BA counter agents mounted a "wildcat" strike (an unofficial strike that unions neither condoned nor condemned), causing the cancellation of 500 flights and disrupting 80,000 customers' travel plans. Two years later, in British Airways' second straight year of profitability, another strike—this one by ground workers at Heathrow Airport—left 70,000 passengers stranded and punctured the airline's swelling optimism.

Aussie love

Amid these labor woes, CEO Eddington retired in October 2005, transferring his position to Willie Walsh, former CEO of Aer Lingus (another oneworld alliance member). Also signing onto the British Airways payroll in 2005 was Australian singer Kylie Minogue, as a British Airways' spokesperson. Minogue's sponsorship deal followed the renewal of a deal between BA and Australian carrier Qantas to cooperate on the so-called "kangaroo route" between Australia and Britain.

Thrifty Brits

Amid the recent waves of fuel cost increases and terrorist threats, British Airways continues to lower its costs and survive on smaller staff. Technology assisted with the latter, as e-tickets have cut down on paper tickets and online check-in has eliminated many check-in counters.

Technology also enabled British Airways to reach out to its flyers. In August 2006, when a suicide-bomb alert at Heathrow Airport grounded flights and stranded passengers, British Airways responded by sending text-message warnings of delays and cancellations. Although messages only went out to members of the service, the airline estimated that it notified, on average, 23 people from each affected flight.

Making nice at being naughty

After a long and highly publicized rivalry, British Airways and Virgin Atlantic have worked together in recent years. Unfortunately, their collaboration concerned the illegal fixing of prices, specifically concerning fuel surcharges added onto plane ticket prices. In June 2006, after investigators raided British Airways' offices and the price-fixing scandal unfolded, two BA executives—Martin George and Iain Burns— hastily resigned. Virgin Atlantic escaped prosecution by admitting its involvement early in the proceedings, but the British Office of Fair Trading and the U.S. Department of Justice fined British Airways £270 million in an August 2007 dual action. BA and Virgin settled a class-action lawsuit on the matter for $204 million in February 2008, with $59 million going to passengers affected in the U.S. and £73.5 million to those in the U.K.

Aside from illegal collusion, British Airways also joined forces with Virgin in March 2007 to lobby against an "open skies" agreement between the European Union and the United States. They argued that the agreement was imbalanced in favor of U.S. carriers, but the open skies agreement was approved in April 2007. The initiative will allow more airlines to operate flights between the U.S. and Heathrow airport, a landing pad dominated for decades by American, British, United and Virgin Airlines. Heathrow's opening will threaten British Airways' clout in trans-Atlantic travel, which currently makes up 60 percent of the company's revenue. Analysts say that British Airways doesn't have all that much to worry about in terms of the new Heathrow—it will still control 40 percent of the airport's actual terminal slots.

Still airborne

Under CEO Walsh's tenure, British Airways' revenue has consistently grown. For fiscal 2007 (which ran from April 2006 through March 2007), British Airways reported revenue growth of 3.4 percent to £8.5 billion. Profit was down slightly from 2006, falling from £616 million to £611 million. The airline expects that its new, exclusive terminal at Heathrow will increase revenue and profits in 2008. Also from fiscal 2006 to 2007, the company's employee headcount fell by more than 6,000.

GETTING HIRED

Positions

Those interested in flying with the Brits are welcome to peruse British Airways' career web site (www.britishairwaysjobs.com). British Airways breaks its careers down into five job groups: customer contact, commercial, e-business and IT, technical and operations, and corporate services. Descriptions of the careers that fall into each category are provided on the web site. Here, open positions may be searched by location and type, and applications may be filed online. Should British Airways like what it sees, the company will invite applicants for a round of interviews or assessment days, conducted by human resources and specialized staff. These days may be comprised of a mixture of classroom-based tests, psychometric tests, role play, group exercises, presentations, fact-finding exercises, or interviews at one or more stages.

Once on the company payroll, employees at British Airways enjoy vacation time, contributory pension and private health care plans, employee profit sharing, and sports and social facilities, including employee clubs. Best of all, the staff at British Airways benefits from the fruits of its labor with reduced airfare deals and travel discounts.

British Airways also offers a program to get undergraduates in the pilot's seat, so to speak. Through its Industrial Placements plan, undergrads work for six months to a year in HR, engineering, finance, airline operations, customer services, marketing, sales or IT. Eligibility requirements and application instructions for these positions are provided on the British Airways career site.

Visit Vault at **www.vault.com** for insider company profiles, expert advice,
career message boards, expert resume reviews, the Vault Job Board and more.

VAULT CAREER LIBRARY   **115**

Carlson Companies

701 Carlson Parkway
Minnetonka, MN 55305
Phone: (763) 212-1000
Fax: (763) 212-2219
www.carlson.com

LOCATIONS

Minnetonka, MN (HQ)
Birmingham, AL
Boston, MA
New York, NY
Philadelphia, PA
Phoenix, AZ

Additional locations nationwide.

THE STATS

Employer Type: Private Company
Chairwoman & CEO: Marilyn
  Carlson Nelson
2006 Employees: 176,000
2006 Revenue ($mil): $37,100

DEPARTMENTS

Administrative Services
Communications
Consulting
Customer Service
Family Services
Finance
Human Resources
Information Technology
Legal
Marketing
Operations
Operations Management
Operations Support
Procurement
Property Management/Development
Quality/Measurement
Restaurant & Food Service
Sales/Account Management
Travel

KEY COMPETITORS

American Express Travel Related
  Services
Darden
Marriott international

EMPLOYMENT CONTACT

www.carlson.com/careers

THE SCOOP

For all of your leisure needs

Carlson Companies have the hospitality and leisure travel industries covered. Need a place to stay? Carlson can put you up in its Regent International Hotels, Radisson Hotels, Park Plaza Hotels, Country Inns & Suites or Park Inn Hotels. Need to get out on the open seas? Check out Carlson's Radisson Seven Seas Cruises, Cruise Holidays and SeaMaster Cruises, not to mention its SinglesCruise.com web site. Got a rumbly in your tummy? Chow down at Carlson's T.G.I. Friday's and Pick Up Stix restaurant chains.

And that's not all, folks. Carlson's travel agencies can book you trips through Carlson Wagonlit Travel, Cruise Holidays, Results Travel, Carlson Destination Marketing Services, Carlson Leisure Travel Services and CW Government Travel. The firm also markets myriad wares through its Peppers & Rogers Group and the aptly named Carlson Marketing Group. The Carlson Real Estate Company can even find you a home. And don't forget the Gold Points Reward Network, which offers coupon discounts at supermarket-type places.

Headquartered in Minneapolis, Minnesota, Carlson is one of the largest privately held corporations in the U.S. It employs about 170,000 people in 150 countries and territories.

Putting his stamp on the industry

Company founder Curtis L. Carlson created the Gold Bond Stamp Company in Minneapolis in 1938 with a $55 loan. In the cash-strapped era of the Great Depression and World War II, his idea was that, over time, faithful consumers of certain stores would rack up stamps through the purchase of certain items. Once the consumer filled a Gold Bond stamp book, he or she redeemed it at the local grocery store for $3 and merchandise from a Gold Bond catalog.

The company's big break came in 1953, when it succeeded in winning the Super Valu supermarket chain as a sponsor. Throughout the 1950s and 1960s, a stamp-trading craze swept the nation and Gold Bond grew by leaps and bounds along with its sister company, Top Value Stamps. In the 1960s, as stamp collecting reached its peak, Gold Bond competed with over 400 rival stamp firms. But there's more to life (and business) than stamps, and the company was soon looking to diversify. In 1960, it purchased 50 percent of the Minneapolis Radisson Hotel, which had just refurbished

Visit Vault at www.vault.com for insider company profiles, expert advice, career message boards, expert resume reviews, the Vault Job Board and more.

VAULT CAREER LIBRARY 117

its interior and needed an investor to cover the costs. Within two years, Carlson held a majority stake in the hotel.

Under Carlson, new Radissons opened up in the Minnesotan towns of Bloomington and Duluth, and then in suburbs across the state. The success of the hotels spurred the company to annual growth of around 33 percent during the period, and Gold Bond changed its name to Carlson Companies in 1973, reorganizing into four major business divisions. These were: Carlson Hospitality Group, Carlson Travel Group, Carlson Marketing Group and Carlson Promotion Group (which included Gold Bond).

Following the name change, Carlson purchased the T.G.I. Friday's restaurant chain, Ask Mr. Foster travel agencies (later renamed Carlson Travel Network) and Country Kitchen International. The company reached $1 billion in annual revenue by 1977, and grew even larger in the 1980s, acquiring Provisions, a global purchasing and project management company, while founding the Country Inns & Suites hotel brand.

Travel opportunities

The 1990s kicked off with the purchase of the A.T. Mays Group, a British-oriented travel agency, which signaled Carlson's increasing interest in the leisure and travel industries. Throughout the decade, the Radisson Hotel brand spread rapidly; at one point, a new Radisson opened worldwide every 10 days. And in 1992, the Radisson Diamond, the largest twin-hull ship ever built, launched Carlson into the international cruise market.

Carlson was busy in 1994, acquiring Cruise Holidays and Seven Seas Cruise Line, and forming a partnership with SAS hotels. In 1997, Carlson Travel Network and Paris-based Wagonlit Travel signed an alliance to form (naturally) Carlson Wagonlit Travel, currently one of the world's largest business travel management companies. Also in 1997, the company founded Carlson Destination Marketing Services and debuted its Gold Points program, which Curtis Carlson referred to as "trading stamps gone electric." By this point, Carlson was a hospitality industry behemoth, with $20 billion in annual revenue.

All in the family

Curtis Carlton retired at a gala 60th Anniversary celebration in 1998, where he named his daughter, Marilyn Carlson Nelson, as the company's next president and CEO. Following her father's death the next year, Marilyn Carlson Nelson also became chairwoman of the board. In 2000, the company founded the Results Travel agency franchise and added more hotels, acquiring the Park Plaza and Park Inn brands. T.G.I. Friday's celebrated its 500th restaurant opening in 2001, the same year that Carlson picked up the Pick Up Stix restaurant brand. Having saturated the Western Hemisphere with its restaurants and hotels, Carlson announced an expansion into Asia Pacific with the 2002 creation of Carlson Hotels Asia Pacific.

Marilyn's son, Curtis Nelson, became president and COO in 2003, as Carlson's hotel and cruise line businesses expanded with the purchase of Radisson Aruba Resort & Casino and the launch of Seven Seas Voyager, a luxurious all-suite, all-balcony cruise ship. The same year, Carlson also acquired the Peppers & Rogers Group, a business-consulting firm. The cruise line division grew yet again in 2004, as Carlson purchased SinglesCruise.com and All Aboard Travel of Fort Myers, Fla. That year, the systemwide sales for Carlson (the revenue of both company-owned and franchised businesses) reached a record $26.1 billion, representing a 25 percent increase over 2003; company-owned enterprises alone brought in $8.4 billion for the year.

Fun with franchisees

Much of the revenue Carlson so cheerily reports doesn't actually enter company coffers—it's the money that Carlson-branded properties earn for franchisees. In 2005, of the 900 Carlson-branded hotels, only about 300 were fully owned by the company. The company made money off the other 600 through franchising fees, but that income source is far from guaranteed, as franchised properties can switch affiliations to another hotel brand. In fact, the nationwide number of Radisson rooms shrank by 34 percent between 2002 and 2007.

Since 2005, Carlson has attempted to secure more of its franchises; that year, it purchased a 25 percent stake in Belgium-based Rezidor SAS Hospitality, which operates 250 Carlson hotels throughout Europe and the Middle East. The deal gave Carlson two seats on Rezidor's board of directors, along with some decision-making clout. Rezidor quickly set about launching mutually beneficial projects with its new stockholder, opening several locations of a "new breed" of Carlson's Radisson brand in Europe in 2006. In May 2007, in a bid to retain a high number of franchisees, Carlson announced plans to remodel all existing Radisson properties and open 100 new hotels by the end of 2009.

Travel boom

Carlson gained majority ownership of Carlson Wagonlit travel in April 2006, when it teamed up with One Equity Partners in April 2006 to buy out the French hotelier Accor, its partner in the travel firm. The $465 million transaction upped Carlson's stake to 55 percent. Also in 2006, Carlson Wagonlit purchased the corporate travel company Navigant International for $530 million, thereby doubling its size in North America and becoming the world's second-largest travel management company, in terms of revenue, after American Express. By the end of 2006, Carlson Wagonlit's revenue was $17.6 billion, more than double that of 2003.

It's a family affair

Being a family-owned and -operated corporation gives Carlson a certain cuddly, Waltons-esque public persona, but mixing business with bloodlines comes with its own hazards. When CEO Marilyn Carlson Nelson reorganized the company's management structure in August 2006, she tellingly eliminated the president of operations position held by her son, Curtis Nelson. The vice chairman position was offered to Nelson as a consolation prize, but Nelson refused the job—effectively quitting the company.

The shake-up raised serious questions about the future leadership of the company, as Curtis Nelson was widely assumed to carry on the family business after his mother's retirement. That retirement, however, has been repeatedly postponed, prompting many to suppose that the CEO doubted her son's ability to run the company. Gumming up the already-sticky situation is the fact that six Carlson family members sit on the company board, which approved Nelson's appointment to the vice chairmanship. Nelson was banned from Carlson's corporate campus in January 2007, at which point his employment with the company was officially terminated.

In May 2007, Curtis Nelson sued his mother and the Carlson Companies, contending that his grandfather, the company's founder, handpicked him for the CEO position. The company quickly filed a countersuit, charging that Nelson failed to meet agreed-upon conditions for promotion, including sobriety. As the family drama rages on, it remains unclear who the company will choose as its next CEO.

Giving back

Much of Carlson's philanthropic activity is centered in its home state of Minnesota. The company is a charter member of a group of Minnesota-based organizations that donate 5 percent of annual pre-tax earnings to public service causes in the Land of

10,000 Lakes. Carlson has also sunk over $46 million over the years into various programs at the University of Minnesota, Curtis Carlson's alma mater, including the Carlson School of Management, the Distinguished Carlson Lecture Series at the Hubert H. Humphrey Institute of Public Affairs and the University of Minnesota Tourism Center.

Carlson encourages employee volunteerism through the company intranet site, The Volunteer Connection, which matches employees to volunteer opportunities by shared interest and need. On a national scale, the company is involved with the United Way and the National Minority Supplier Development Council, and is also an active participant in the global fight to prevent exploitation of children through affiliations with the World Childhood Foundation and The Code, an international guideline by which travel and tourism companies have pledged to protect children and end the commercial sex trade.

GETTING HIRED

Joining the Carlson family

The Carlson career web site (www.carlson.com/careers) offers job searches by location, functional area and position. Applications and resumes can be submitted online here, and resumes will be kept in the Carlson database for one year. In recent years, Carlson has been ranked among the 100 Best Companies to Work For by *Fortune* magazine, and the 100 Best Companies for Working Mothers by *Working Mother* magazine.

Part of the reason the company receives such accolades is its extensive benefits package, which offers a full slate of health insurance, a 401(k) retirement program, leave of absence, and purchased time off on top of standard vacation and holidays. On top of offering tuition reimbursement for workers pursuing advanced degrees, Carlson's runs an in-house learning program that offers management training and skills development classes.

For Carlson-workers-to-be, the company sponsors an annual summer internship for undergraduates, which runs full time for 10 to 12 weeks at the Minneapolis corporate campus. Internships cover the fields of accounting and finance, auditing, marketing, HR, IT, and communications and public relations. Carlson also sponsors a 12-week summer program for MBA students, and a yearlong, full-time rotational program for graduates with an MBA.

Visit Vault at **www.vault.com** for insider company profiles, expert advice, career message boards, expert resume reviews, the Vault Job Board and more.

VAULT CAREER LIBRARY 121

For an upper-level or management position, expect a few rounds of interviews. One product manager reported that she spoke with "an HR generalist" for an hour over the phone, then with the "hiring supervisor" for 90 minutes face-to-face, and then finally with the "team on site," followed by a meeting with another HR contact.

OUR SURVEY SAYS

Achieving a balance

Apparently, Carlson lives up to its "family-friendly, work/life balance-friendly" reputation, with a "relaxed but professional" atmosphere, "approachable" executives and even "flexible" hours. One working parent describes how one can "work four 10-hour days rather than five eight-hour days" and how "a summer hours policy allows employees to work 30 minutes extra [for] four days a week, in exchange for leaving early on Friday afternoons."

In terms of diversity, a high-ranking female reports that the "majority of [Carlson's] employees are women, and many of them hold VP or EVP positions," although the firm hires "mostly white males" at the "highest executive level ... famous CEO notwithstanding. And a source indicates that the CEO has "star quality" and "there tends to be trust in [her]." Realistically, however, a source admits that the company is based in Minnesota, "so there isn't much diversity to work with in the population."

Carnival Corporation

3655 NW 87th Avenue
Miami, FL 33178
Phone: (305) 599-2600
Fax: (305) 406-4700
www.carnivalcorp.com

LOCATIONS

Miami, FL (HQ)
Colorado Springs, CO • Fort Pierce,
FL • Long Beach, CA • Miramar, FL
• New Mexico, NM • New York, NY
• Santa Clarita, CA • Seattle, WA •
Genoa • London • Rostock,
Germany • Sydney • Toronto

THE STATS

Employer Type: Public Company
Stock Symbol: CCL
Stock Exchange: NYSE
Chairman & CEO: Micky Arison
2007 Employees: 76,500
2007 Revenue ($mil.): $13,033

KEY COMPETITORS

Disney Cruise Line
Royal Caribbean Cruises
Star Cruises

EMPLOYMENT CONTACT

www.carnival.com/CMS/Fun_Jobs/
ccl_fun_jobs_landing.aspx

DEPARTMENTS

Air/Sea
Bon Voyage
Colorado Reservations
Corporate Audit Services
Corporate Casino
Corporate Tax
Domestic Sales
Embarkation—Los Angeles
Embarkation—Miami
Guest Programming & Entertainment
Hotel Operations
  Commercial
  Transportation
Information Systems
  Application Development
  Business Systems
  PMO
  Quality Assurance/Quality Control
  Systems & Technology
International Sales—International
Marketing Services
Miramar—Consumer Research
Port Operations—Los Angeles
Port St. Lucie—Consumer Research
Reservations
Revenue Accounting
Revenue Management
  Analysis
Revenue Management
  Decision Support
Seabourn
Technical Operations
  Manning & Training
  Safety & Quality Assurance

THE SCOOP

A boatload of fun

Carnival Corporation is the world's largest cruise operator, serving 7.6 million passengers in 2007 (nearly half of the estimated cruise ship passengers worldwide) on its 11 cruise lines and 85 ships. At any given time, roughly 175,000 people are at sea on Carnival ships, en route to sunny locations like the Bahamas, the Canary Islands the Caribbean, Hawaii, the Mediterranean, the Mexican Riviera, the Panama Canal, the South Pacific and less sunny, more scenic locations like Alaska and Europe. And Carnival is still growing; it will take delivery of 20 more cruise ships by 2011.

In North America, the company operates its flagship Carnival Cruise Lines as well as the luxury cruise brands Holland America, Princess Cruise Line and Seabourn. In Europe, the company serves patrons through the AIDA, P&O Cruise and Costa Cruise brands. The Cunard Line operates the ocean liners Queen Mary 2 and Queen Elizabeth 2. Also, Holland America Tours and Princess Tours operate 16 hotels and 560 motorcoaches for sightseers in Alaska and the Canadian Yukon.

Carnival is a dual-listed company, with British operations under the Carnival Plc name. Roughly one-third of Carnival's stock is controlled by CEO Micky Arison and his family, which founded the company. Headquartered in Miami, Fla., Carnival employs 72,000 workers worldwide.

Creating Carnival

After helping launch Norwegian Cruise Lines in the late 1960s, Israeli entrepreneur Ted Arison launched Carnival Cruise Lines in 1972. Besides hitting a few snags—the company's inaugural cruise ran aground on a sandbar—the company's cruising-and-boozing formula quickly gained popularity. By the end of the 1970s, it was one of the world's most popular cruise lines, and an IPO of common stock in 1987 generated cash flow for the company to expand through acquisitions.

Carnival's acquisition expedition kicked off with the purchase of Holland America Line in 1989 and Seabourn Cruise, Windstar Cruises and Alaskan/Canadian tour operator Holland America Tours in 1992. In February 1996, the company bought a 29.6 percent stake in the British tour operator Airtours Plc, and in 1997 it acquired Europe's leading cruise company, Costa Cruises. The crown jewel of the decade was the 1998, $500 million purchase of the Cunard Line—owner of the world's largest ocean liner, the 150,000-ton Queen Mary 2. This spending spree was followed by the collapse of two deals: a $1.7 billion hostile bid for Norwegian Cruises (founder Arison's old company) in December 1999, and an abortive merger with Fairfield Communities, an Orlando, Fla.-based vacation firm, in February 2000.

The Love Boat, soon to be making another run ...

The attacks of September 11th greatly hurt the tourism industry, and bookings for the days immediately following the attacks fell 50 to 60 percent below their usual levels. Many cruise companies scrambled to cut costs, often merging together. The third-largest cruise firm in the world, P&O Princess Cruises (featured on the 1970s TV show *The Love Boat*), was no exception.

In December 2001, Princess announced a deal to join forces with No. 2 cruise operator Royal Caribbean for $2.9 billion. Carnival then tendered its own Princess bid, only to be rebuffed. Carnival responded with a hostile $4.6 billion takeover attempt and, when that didn't work, upped its offer to $5.3 billion in January 2002. Princess rejected this bid the following month, recommending to its shareholders instead that they approve the Royal Caribbean deal. However, the shareholders were sympathetic to Carnival and the extra $2 billion-plus it was offering.

Princess' board recommended that it look into each deal equally. The European Commission approved the Princess-Royal Caribbean plan in June 2002 and the Princess-Carnival in July 2002. The Federal Trade Commission approved both bids in October 2002. Finally, in January 2003, Princess' board formally recommended the merger with Carnival. Princess shareholders voted in favor of the Carnival deal by 99.7 percent, and the acquisition wrapped up in April 2003. After the Princess purchase, Carnival's 12 brands and 66 ships constituted one of the largest leisure travel companies in the world.

Cutting costs and gaining profit

Carnival absorbed its Princess prize by eliminating 300 positions in summer 2004. Roughly half of the workers affected were offered other jobs in the company, while the rest were given severance packages. Higher ticket prices and onboard sales boosted sales to $3.25 billion, from $2.52 billion the year prior. In September 2004, Hurricane Jeanne cut into profits by forcing the company to close several of its Florida ports and end a number of trips ahead of schedule.

Visit Vault at www.vault.com for insider company profiles, expert advice, career message boards, expert resume reviews, the Vault Job Board and more.

VAULT CAREER LIBRARY   125

Katrina wreaks havoc

The next year, in September 2005, Hurricane Katrina devastated the Gulf of Mexico and displaced thousands of people. It disrupted Carnival's business as well, but the U.S. government floated it $192 million so it could break even for the rest of the year. The government also requested Carnival's services for displaced Louisianans, chartering three of its ships to house those rendered homeless by the storms.

The trouble was, evacuees weren't onboard with this plan. After being turned down by people taking shelter at Houston's Astrodome, two Carnival ships sat empty for days off the coast of Galveston, Texas, before cruising over to New Orleans, where relief workers preferred to make a temporary home on the water. Although some, including Senator Barack Obama, voiced concern that the cruise line was handed a "sweetheart deal" by Uncle Sam, Carnival offered further help to relief efforts, donating $7 million in December 2005.

Cruising into Shanghai

Like every other company on the planet, Carnival is making efforts to tap the opening markets in China. Unlike many others, Carnival has already met with success in the region. In March 2006, Carnival announced that China had awarded it access to its ports. Carnival was the first big cruise company to win these rights. In July 2006, Carnival began offering five-day cruises out of Shanghai. And in winter 2006, Carnival's Costa subsidiary started a new Costa Asia division, which began operating cruises to the Persian Gulf.

Seasickness is nothing

Carnival took a blow to its credibility in November 2006, when a highly contagious stomach virus broke out on one of its cruises, infecting over 700 people. The perpetrator was norovirus, a form of stomach flu most commonly found in catering operations. This norovirus outbreak was one of the largest in industry history, but by no means was it the first. The virus infected 1,400 cruise passengers overall in 2004, and a 2006 Royal Caribbean cruise reported 300 passengers with the illness. Industry lobbyists argue that only one in every 3,600 passengers get sick and that the average Joe or Josephine is likelier to catch the stomach flu on land than on a cruise.

Despite such bad publicity, Carnival revenue rose to $11.8 billion in 2006 and $13 billion in 2007. Profits increased to the company record $2.4 billion, despite rising fuel costs. Carnival's sales have recently decreased in the Caribbean and haven't sold as well as expected in China, but CEO Micky Arison stated that "demand for

Caribbean cruises strengthened considerably as [2007] progressed and we expect this trend to continue into 2008." And the company's European operations "enjoyed another record year," due to continually growing capacity. In October 2006, Carnival ordered two new ultra-luxe Seabourn ships for $500 million and placed an order for its largest Carnival Cruise "Fun Ship" yet, a 130,000-ton liner that will cost $740 million and hit the ocean in 2010.

GETTING HIRED

Cruising toward a career

Want to sail the seven seas without taking on the bad reputation that plagues the pirate set? Visit Carnival's career web site (phx.corporate-ir.net/phoenix.zhtml?c=200767 &p=irol-careers), which can be reached through the "About Us" link at the main Carnival Corporation page. The site links to each of the Carnival brands' job listings. Corporate listings are found through Carnival's flagship brand career page, at www.carnival.com/funjobs. These positions are listed by job title, department and location. Applicants are invited to build an online profile and submit their resume via the web site. Carnival's 60,000-odd ship workers make up the bulk of its 72,000 employees, managing everything from the control room to the casino hall.

Visit Vault at **www.vault.com** for insider company profiles, expert advice,
career message boards, expert resume reviews, the Vault Job Board and more.

VAULT CAREER LIBRARY   127

Choice Hotels International, Inc.

10750 Columbia Pike
Silver Spring, MD 20901
Phone: (301) 592-5000
Fax: (301) 592-6157
www.choicehotels.com

LOCATIONS

Silver Spring, MD (HQ)
Grand Junction, CO
Minot, ND
Phoenix, AZ

THE STATS

Employer Type: Public Company
Stock Symbol: CHH
Stock Exchange: NYSE
Chairman: Stewart Bainum Jr.
CEO: Charles A. Ledsinger Jr.
2007 Employees: 1,816
2007 Revenue ($mil.): $615.5

DEPARTMENTS

Administration
Advertising
Architecture, Construction & Design
Brand Management
Brand Performance
Business Strategy
Communications
Customer Service/Reservations
Facilities
Finance/Accounting
Franchise Growth (Sales)
Franchise Services Operations
Human Resources
Information Systems
International
Legal
Marketing, Sales & Business
  Development
Organizational Development/Diversity
  & Learning
Performance Training
Property Systems
Strategic Partner/Vendor

KEY COMPETITORS

Carlson
Marriott International
Wyndham Worldwide

EMPLOYMENT CONTACT

careers.choicehotels.com/careers

THE SCOOP

The hotelier of Choice

One of the largest lodging franchisors in the world, Choice Hotels franchises over 5,300 hotels and motels, dotting highway roadsides and downtown centers in over 40 countries. The company is all about giving its consumer a full smorgasbord of options, offering rooms under 10 brand names in four price ranges (economy, mid-scale, luxury and extended-stay). Choice's brands are familiar to any road tripper: Cambria Suites, Clarion, Comfort Inn, Comfort Suites, EconoLodge, MainStay Suites, Quality Inn, Rodeway Inn, Sleep Inn and Suburban.

Through its business structure, Choice owns its hotels' brand names, logos and reservation systems, and licenses them to franchisees, which own and operate the physical property. The company makes money by charging fees to its franchisees, including an initial startup fee, a percentage of sales and reimbursement for use of Choice's brands and marketing campaigns. This system displaces onto the franchisee much of the overhead costs (and risk) of running a hotel, while bestowing smaller hoteliers with the well-established reputation of Choice's brands.

Choice's revenue has steadily grown since the company's founding over 60 years ago, reaching $545 million in 2006. The company hopes to boost its sales further, with more hotels on the way—Choice was developed 950 hotels in late 2006.

Motel roots

In 1941, a group of seven motel operators banded together in Daytona Beach, Fla., forming a nonprofit membership organization called Quality Courts United. The organization set quality standards for its seven members' hotels, thus combating motels' negative image as seedy roadside dens of the criminal class. It also provided mutually beneficial services, such as referring guests to other motels under the Quality Courts seal.

With its commitment to improving motels' services and standards, Quality Courts was well positioned to take advantage of the explosion of a national car culture in 1950s America. And by 1952, 100 motel firms joined the organization, each of them bearing a sunburst logo to let potential lodgers know it was a Quality motel. Also by 1952, all Quality motels featured wall-to-wall carpeting and 24-hour desk service. By 1954 they all featured swimming pools and in-room telephones.

When hotelier and nursing home operator Stewart Bainum joined the association's board of directors in 1961, he argued for it to exit the nonprofit sector. The association followed Bainum's advice, incorporating in 1963 as Quality Courts Motels Inc. Soon after, the company started a training school and centralized reservation system to shape its hotels into a more uniform fleet. In 1968 Bainum became Quality Courts' president and CEO, and merged it with his hotel company, Park Consolidated. The same year, Quality moved its headquarters to Silver Spring, Maryland.

Growth Hazards

In 1970 Quality rolled out its toll-free, 24-hour reservation hotline, an industry first. The company now boasted 375 hotels in more than 33 states, and began expanding its brand internationally. A blip in the company's 1970s success was the oil embargo of 1973, which drove down automobile vacations, and hence motel revenue, across the world. Nevertheless, Quality-brand hotels soon opened for business in Belgium, Canada, Germany, Mexico and New Zealand.

In 1980, CEO Bainum's nursing home chain, Manor Care, bought Quality for $37 million. Soon afterwards, Bainum hired two new executives away from rival Best Western to lead Quality: CEO Robert Hazard and COO Gerald Pettit. Under their direction, Quality raised uniformity standards throughout its motels and debuted a number of new brands to attract customers beyond the motel-set. Some industry analysts credit the two men with pioneering the hotel industry's now standard practice of "segmenting the market," or creating chains for specific types of travelers. Quality debuted the Comfort brand in 1981 and Sleep Inn and Comfort Suites in 1986. Also in 1986, Quality purchased the luxe Clarion brand. The lower-end EconoLodge and Rodeway Inn brands entered the company ranks in 1990, and Quality changed its name to Choice Hotels International later in the year, to reflect its new array of brand options. By 1992, Choice Hotels had 2,800 franchised locations in the U.S., owning 12 hotels itself.

A public affair

A recession in the early 1990s cut down on leisure travel, hitting the hotel industry hard, and Choice switched its focus to international expansion. The chain purchased France-based Inovest in 1993, adding 160 European hotels. Joint ventures and partnerships also beefed up the company's presence in Canada, Italy, Mexico, Singapore and the U.K.

Hazard and Pettit retired into Manor Care's board of directors in 1995, promoting Choice COO Don Landry to the chief executive's seat. But he was merely keeping the seat warm, as it happened, for former Taco Bell COO William Floyd, who became Choice CEO in October 1996 (Landry remained Choice's president and COO). The same month as this executive reshuffling, Choice went public on the New York Stock Exchange. However, CEO Floyd resigned in June 1998, merely 18 months after being named to the job. Charles Ledsinger Jr. stepped into the role the following August, bringing with him 20 years of experience in the hospitality industry.

Internet firsts

Choice made like Al Gore in the 1990s: embracing the Internet as its own. Choice debuted its web site, with a real-time reservation service, in 1995. Two years later, it launched a web site just for travel agents, and in 1999, added an online ordering system for its franchisees. The sites allowed travel agents everywhere to book clients into Choice's myriad rooms, and owner and operators of Choice-branded hotels to order supplies directly from company-endorsed vendors. In 2002, the company joined with Chicago-based Viator Networks to begin providing high-speed Internet access in its hotels.

Rooms empty out, then fill up again

The terrorist attacks of September 11, 2001, brought setbacks to the travel industry, as Americans tightened their purse strings. Choice quickly launched its "Thanks for Traveling" campaign in an effort to reawaken the nation's dormant travel bug and get people back into the company's 3,500 franchised U.S. locations. Still, year-end revenue took a hit, falling from the company's 2000 total of $353 million to $341 million. Revenue quickly recovered its upward momentum, though, and has grown steadily ever since.

Choice soon set about adding more brands to its roster. In February 2003 it purchased the remaining shares of Flag Hotels, an Australian brand in which it first bought a controlling interest in 2002. Choice debuted Cambria Suites in January 2005, a "lower-upscale" brand featuring large units decked out with plasma TVs, refrigerators, microwaves and wireless Internet access. Later in 2005, Choice spent $10 million to acquire the Suburban Franchise Holding Company, franchisor of 67 Suburban Extended Stay hotels. This purchase made Choice the largest franchisor of extended-stay lodging, offering 9,000 rooms under its MainStay and Suburban

Visit Vault at **www.vault.com** for insider company profiles, expert advice, career message boards, expert resume reviews, the Vault Job Board and more.

VAULT CAREER LIBRARY

131

brands. In 2005, Choice boasted year-end revenue of $477 million and profits of $87 million.

Choice rests easy

In summer 2006, after Choice's quarterly profits failed to meet Wall Street's expectations, the company's shares dropped by 25 percent in one day. The company attributed the slowdown to rising gas prices, which have plagued every corner of the travel industry, from air carriers to cruise ships to, apparently, motor lodges. Luckily, Choice's fortunes turned around quickly thanks to increases in room rates and new hotel openings.

The company is actively diversifying into Europe, purchasing the operating rights of its franchises there to guard against a weak domestic market. In October 2006, the company bought out one of its European franchisees, CHE Hotel Group, gaining control of CHE's properties in Austria, Belgium, the Czech Republic, France, Italy, Portugal, Spain and Switzerland. The company executed a similar deal in December 2007, buying operating rights for 78 U.K. franchises from Real Hotel Group. Elsewhere in international efforts, Choice's subsidiary Choice Hotels India is growing rapidly. The unit currently franchises 32 properties in 22 destinations, and was negotiating with various investors in December 2007 to open 20 new establishments by 2009.

In 2006, Choice amassed $545 million in revenue, up by nearly $70 million from 2005. Profit increased by a whopping 29 percent to $113 million. Analysts warn that the company may not be able to keep up such impressive growth because of the budget-minded clientele served by Choice's brands—the company can't raise rates very much without losing customers.

GETTING HIRED

It's your Choice

For those looking to get in with this major player in the hospitality world, Choice Hotels hosts a web site with open positions at careers.choicehotels.com/careers. A quick search allows potential job candidates to search for openings by department or location and applications may be submitted online. Corporate careers are found at company headquarters in Silver Spring, Md., and at the company's Western outpost in Phoenix, Ariz. Jobs with Choice's contact center are centered in Grand Junction, Colo., and Minot, N.D. Choice also appears at several recruiting events throughout the year—schedules for these can be found through the main career page.

Benefits for those who choose Choice include 401(k), an employee stock purchase plan, health coverage, and paid vacation and sick days. Tuition reimbursement is also available, along with industry-specific perks like hotel discounts and deals with Choice-affiliated companies, such as Cingular Wireless, Dell (computers) and Serta (mattresses).

Looking for new faces

Hoping to bring new entrepreneurs into its franchising fold, Choice recently launched a number of initiatives to attract minority groups to hotel management. The company created an Emerging Markets division in 2003, charged with the task of diversifying Choice's franchisee base. And in May 2005, the company created the Choice Hotels African American Owners Alliance and the Choice Hotels Hispanic Owners and Managers Alliance, to connect existing franchisees and attract new ones. Choice followed that up with a web site designed to help minority and nontraditional hoteliers start up their own locations. Launched in March 2006, the site provides resources for newcomers, including step-by-step guides to setting up a franchised hotel and an online crash course in hotel operations.

Visit Vault at **www.vault.com** for insider company profiles, expert advice, career message boards, expert resume reviews, the Vault Job Board and more.

VAULT CAREER LIBRARY 133

Club Méditerranée

11 rue Cambrai
75019 Paris
France
Phone: +33-1-53-35-35-53
Fax: +33-1-53-35-32-01
www.clubmed.com

LOCATIONS

Paris (HQ)

Additional locations in the US;
International locations in Austria,
Belgium, Canada, Germany, Greece,
Ireland, Israel, Italy, Mexico,
Morocco, Netherlands, Portugal,
Spain, Switzerland, Tunisia, Turkey,
the UK and West Africa.

THE STATS

Employer Type: Public Company
Stock Symbol: CU
Stock Exchange: Euronext Paris
Chairman & CEO: Henri Giscard
 d'Estaing
2007 Employees: 15,465
2007 Revenue (€mil.): €1,727

DEPARTMENTS

Catering
Child Supervision
Corporate Office
Entertainment
Excursions
Health/Well-being
Hotel Services
Housekeeping/Maintenance
Sales
Water & Land Sports

KEY COMPETITORS

Carnival
Hilton Hotels
Sol Meliá

EMPLOYMENT CONTACT

www.clubmedjobs.com

THE SCOOP

A good time was had by all

Ladies and gentlemen, prepare for a brightly-colored cocktail of a vacation, complete with more fruit on the rim than in the glass, and a full complement of plastic swords and little folding umbrellas. And you can thank Club Méditerranée ("Club Med," to the English speaking world) for developing the concept of the all-inclusive vacation—coladas and snacks at the bar, currency bead necklaces, communal campfires, trapeze lessons, the whole shebang.

Club Med's resorts offer a variety of activities and services to visitors under one single package. These include facilities, food, games, lodging, shows and sports activities. Staff members intermingle freely with guests and lead the activities. Everyone dines, plays sports, participates in nightly shows and generally socializes with each other. The resorts also have a tradition of spontaneous dancing—called crazy signs—that erupts throughout the day. Club Med staff, called GOs (or gracious organisers, from the French *gentils organisateurs*) move among resorts, working the summer and winter seasons. Support staff, such as housekeepers and cooks, is generally local.

The French resort chain holds 90 properties in exotic locations throughout Africa, Australia, the Caribbean, Europe, French Polynesia, South America, Southern Asia and the U.S. Though best known for its vacation "villages," the company also owns and operates a chain of French gyms, bar/restaurant complexes and a cruise line.

No man is an island ...

Well, perhaps not, but Gerard Blitz certainly helped make them popular vacation destinations. In 1950, the Belgian diamond cutter and water polo champion (now *that's* a varied resume) established a small vacation village on the Spanish island of Mallorca. Blitz's vision was to provide affordable respite from the devastation of a war-torn Europe, via a low frills holiday resort where guests could enjoy the natural environment. The original village was rather bare bones, a far cry from the luxury that Club Med exemplifies today. Guests stayed in tents and helped out with the cooking and cleaning.

The first village was a success, though, and led to the opening of a second location in Italy. The addition of Italian managing director Gilbert Trigano in 1954 brought out the club's true potential. Trigano pushed the Club's concept, opening its doors in locales around the world and extending its offerings year-round. The company also opened to outside investment under Trigano's guidance, and the Rothschild Group came on as the company's largest investor in 1961, which it remained until 1988. The company's flush finances led to the 1963 promotion of Trigano as chairman and CEO, and expansion into the U.S. market in 1968, with clubs in the Caribbean and Florida.

Succession drama

Club Med almost became too successful, spreading all over the world in the 1970s and 1980s and then watching competitors copy its business model, to equally impressive success. Also, the company's guiding light Gilbert Trigano was growing old. In 1993, he stepped down, handing the chief executive's job to his son Serge. The new chief switched the company from a nonprofit association to a for-profit public limited company in 1995, and then came under fire in 1996 for predicting a large profit and instead revealing $130 million in year-end losses.

The company's board reacted quickly, placing Serge in the largely ceremonial chairman's position and hiring former EuroDisney Chief Philippe Bourguignon as the new CEO in 1997. Bourguignon turned the club's finances around by modernizing it, bringing it into the fitness industry, opening bar/restaurant complexes in Paris and Montreal, and unveiling budget resorts aimed at a younger clientele.

Following the September 11th attacks in the new millennium, Club Med and the recreation industry as a whole took a severe hit. After two straight years of losses, CEO Bourguignon resigned in December 2002. The company replaced him with Henri Giscard d'Estaing, son of the former French president. The new chief closed more than 50 villages, opened more than 20 new ones and overhauled corporate culture, all while courting high-end travelers ("pashas"). Guests no longer washed dishes alongside employees; now they resided behind the walls of quiet, exclusive luxury quarters. The club returned to profitability by 2005.

A change in tactic

The organization hopes to complete its transition to the upscale family market by December 2008. The club committed $530 million to renew and revamp its properties in 2006 and 2007, and even closed five of its more basic resorts in order to upgrade seven others. Benefiting from refurbishment will be clubs in Brazil, Mauritius, Mexico, Guadeloupe, the French Alps and Provence. On the horizon are more clubs in Belize, Costa Rica, the Dominican Republic and Mexico. Other countries trying to foster tourism, like Guatemala, Honduras and Nicaragua, are also of locations of interest.

Babies, grown-ups and everything in 'tween

Among the organization's tactical shifts is a new focus on families. Long gone are the resorts catering solely to (usually single) adults. These days, Club Med can't afford to ignore the family vacation market. In November 2006, Club Med's Yucatan resort dropped its adults-only policy and reopened as a family resort, leaving the company with only one adults-only club in 2007.

The company aims for families to make up nearly 70 percent of future visitors, married couples another 20 percent, and those singles as the final 10 percent. In 2007, Club Med continued to roll out the family-friendly amenities, like bottle warmers for babies and babysitting services. For older children, Mini-Club Med offers child-centered outdoor activities like flying trapezes and in-line skating. Teens and 'tweens can find age-appropriate activities—like music mixing facilities—in the Junior Club Med.

Liberté, Fraternité, Responsibility

In November 2006, no doubt with some help from its CEO's famous diplomat father, Club Med announced a partnership with the World Heritage Alliance, an undertaking of the United Nations Foundation. The World Heritage Alliance works to foster conservation, sustainable tourism and the local economy of World Heritage sites. The alliance underscores Club Med's commitment to supporting the local culture of its Club's many locations. Rather than just highlighting leisure activities, resorts will place equal emphasis on the local culture, with excursions and explorations of historical sites. The club terms these locations "Discovery Resorts," and encourages guests to experience local archaeology, cuisine and scenery. In the Cancun Yucatan resort, for instance, guests can tour archaeological sites in Coba and Tulum and visit Sian Ka'an, Mexico's largest protected marine area.

GETTING HIRED

GO get a job at Club Med

Club Med's careers site, at www.clubmedjobs.com, provides job seekers with information about openings at the company's various villages. Positions include everything from housekeeping to child-minding to costume and set design, as well as instructors in windsurfing, sailing, trapeze and SCUBA. The kitchens are run by the French system, and there are openings for pastry chefs, butchers, bakers and chefs de partie (line cooks) who might like to spend some time in paradise.

In any case, the company hires its employees for six-month tours of duty. Insurance, meals and lodging are provided, as is one day off per week. Unlike other resort places, employees are expected to interact with guests, and even eat with them. Since Club Med draws a lot of its customers from Europe, knowledge of several languages is an asset.

Compass Group PLC

Compass House
Guildford Street
Chertsey, Surrey KT16 9BQ
United Kingdom
Phone: +44-1932-573-000
Fax: +44-1932-569-956
www.compass-group.com

LOCATIONS

Chertsey, UK (HQ)

International operations in
Argentina, Australia, Austria,
Belgium, Chile, Czech Republic,
Denmark, France, Germany, Ireland,
Japan, Luxembourg, The
Netherlands, Portugal, Romania,
Russia, South Africa, Spain,
Sweden, Switzerland, the UK, and
throughout Africa, Central Asia and
the Middle East.

THE STATS

Employer Type: Public Company
Stock Symbol: CPG
Stock Exchange: London Stock
  Exchange
Chairman: Sir Roy A. Gardner
CEO: Richard Cousins
2007 Employees: 360,000
2007 Revenue (£mil.): £10,268

DEPARTMENTS

Accounting/Auditing
Administrative & Support Services
Environmental Services
Facilities Management
Finance
Foodservice
 Airports
 Business/Corporate Dining
 Corrections
 Cultural Center
 Education
 Healthcare
 Hotels/Conference Center
 Restaurants
 Retail
 Sports/Entertainment
 Vending
Hotel/Conference Center
Management
Housekeeping
Human Resources
Information Technology
Legal
Marketing
Nutrition/Dietetics
Patient Transport
Purchasing/Procurement
Sales

KEY COMPETITORS

Aramark
Elior
Sodexho Alliance

EMPLOYMENT CONTACT

www.compass-group.com/Careers

Visit Vault at **www.vault.com** for insider company profiles, expert advice,
career message boards, expert resume reviews, the Vault Job Board and more.

VAULT CAREER LIBRARY   **139**

THE SCOOP

World-class service

The Compass Group is one of the world's largest food service companies, employing over 400,000 people in over 70 countries. Compass provides food, catering, vending and related services at concession stands, airports, colleges, hospitals and rest stops around the world, to the tune of $20 billion in annual revenue.

Some of the company's major clients include Time Warner, Condé Nast, Avon Products, Bank of America, Nissan, Sony, IBM, ChevronTexaco and Symantec. The firm also covers major events, such as when it catered the 2002 Winter Olympic Games in Salt Lake City, Utah. The company operates a variety of restaurant chains as well, including Upper Crust and Caffé Ritazza, and franchises a number of Burger King outlets.

Creating and catering

Compass was born in 1987 when managers of Grand Metropolitan Plc—a British business group devoted mostly to hotels, casinos, entertainment, and food and drink manufacture and distribution—bought the firm's catering arm for about $266 million. At the time, this was the U.K.'s largest management buyout ever, and the company was listed on the London Stock Exchange the following year under its new title, the Compass Group.

Francis Mackay, who was Compass' finance director during the 1987 buyout, was appointed CEO of the company in 1991. The next year, the Mackay-led Compass undertook the first of many acquisitions, buying food service firm Letheby & Chrisopher and caterer Traveller's Fare from British Rail. The company got into airline catering in 1993 with the purchase of Select Service Partner from Scandinavian Airlines Systems. Eurest Dining Services International, a division of French hotelier Accor, joined the team in 1995.

The spending spree continued in the late 1990s, as Compass bought a laundry list of catering concerns to keep ahead of its similarly expanding competitors, Sodexho and Aramark. By the end of the decade, Compass snapped up Roberts Catering, Payne & Gunter (a sports catering business), National Leisure Catering, SHRM (a French food service company) and Restaurant Associates. Compass also signed some major food service contracts with companies like Philips Electronics, IBM, EuroDisney and even the Australian armed forces.

Compass in North America

Compass entered the U.S. market for the first time in 1994 with its $450 million acquisition of Flagstar Companies' Canteen Vending Corp. It was quite an entrance, given Canteen's 12,000-odd business, education, health care, retirement and correctional accounts, primarily in Southeastern states.

Compass went upscale, New York-style, with the May 1995 purchase of Flik International, and it even got into higher learning in 1996, buying the Florida-based university caterer Professional Food-Service Management. Another American food peddler, Daka International, came aboard in 1997. Unsurprisingly, American operations accounted for nearly 35 percent of Compass' total revenue by 1998.

Food service regurgitated

CEO Mackay retired to the chairman's seat in 1999, and was replaced by Michael Bailey, erstwhile head of North American operations. One of Bailey's first big deals—a $26.3 billion merger with media and hospitality firm Granada Group PLC—resulted in an entirely new company known as Granada Compass PLC.

Compass retained control of one-third of Granada Compass and shareholders were initially unhappy with the deal. In spring 2001, Compass "de-merged" from Granada as part of the deal, taking with it Granada's hospitality businesses. When Compass Hospitality was relisted on the London Stock Exchange as Compass Group Plc in April 2001, it was the world's largest food service conglomerate.

Booming business

The "new" Compass continued to grow with a series of multimillion-dollar deals and acquisitions in 2001 and 2002. Again, Compass added a bevy of business from both sides of the Atlantic, including catering contractors Selecta Group, Morrison Management Specialists, Restorama, Rail Gourmet and Woodin & Johns. Compass also bought Vendepac, a supplier of vending machines, the Castle Independent school meals business and Bon Appetit Management, a U.S. food service company. During this period, the firm gained food services contracts from a wide range of partners, including the Royal Bank of Scotland, the BBC, Crown Cork & Seal packaging group in Europe, the Reno-Tahoe International Airport in Nevada and Abu Dhabi National Hotels in the Middle East.

Buying and selling

Compass also shed many of its non-food service operations, accumulated from its numerous acquisitions. Within the first few years of the millennium, the company raised $2.7 billion through the sales of its two London hotels, 48 Heritage country hotels, 79 Posthouse hotels and its Le Meridien chain of hotels. In December 2002, the firm shed 368 Little Chef restaurants and 220 Travelodge budget hotels, raising another $1.1 billion.

But mostly buying

What was a food company to do with so many billions of dollars? Discover a taste for sushi, of course. In March 2001, Compass formed a joint venture with Itochu Corporation to move into the Japanese food service game. One of their first deals together was the December 2001 acquisition of Seiyo Food Systems for $274 million.

Clouds gather

Despite Compass' brisk business, investors grew worried in September 2004, when the company warned that U.K. sales had slackened and its profits might not meet forecasts. Months later, celebrity chef Jamie Oliver began a publicity campaign in the beginning of 2005—he claimed that school food in the U.K., much of it supplied by Compass, was unhealthy. Compass shares fell by a third and the firm lost some business as schools attempted to prepare their own food.

When another profit warning hit in March 2005 (this one due to shrinking revenue in Iraq, where Compass was contracted to feed soldiers), shareholders began clamoring for a management change. Months later, in May 2005, Sir Francis Mackay announced he would step down from his chairmanship in 2006, after 20 years with the company. The company issued two more major announcements in September 2005: that Sir Roy Gardner, CEO of Centrica Plc, would take Mackay's place and that CEO Mike Bailey would also leave the company in 2006.

Thunder rolls

Compass' announcements of executive reshuffling occurred directly before the storm broke. In October 2005, the United Nations began investigating whether Compass had employed bribery to gain a $62 million food service contract for UN peacekeepers in Liberia. The UN suspended the company as a vendor and its shares fell to a five-year low. The following November, Compass fired three executives involved with the scandal.

As UN investigations, now paired with probes by the U.S. Department of Justice, wore on, two competitors sued the company in March 2006. Es-Ko and Supreme Foodservice both claimed that Compass' dishonest dealings had deprived them of $800 million worth of revenue. Compass settled with both firms for about $75 million in October 2006, although UN and U.S. investigations of the possible bribery continue.

Buying back shares and cutting costs

In March 2006, Compass named Richard Cousins, former chief of BPB Plc, as its new CEO. Under his direction, Compass is reigning in its sprawling operation. The company sold its travel unit to a consortium of investors for $3.2 billion in April 2006. Approximately $870 million of the travel unit sale was funneled to a share buyback program. Also in April 2006, Compass spent $250 million to purchase the remaining 51 percent of Chicago-based sports arena caterer Levy Restaurants (Compass had owned a 49 percent stake in Levy since 2000). In September 2006, Compass issued its annual report, and stated that the year had been a "transitional" one, and that it would "learn from mistakes" and "take responsibility for our actions."

In May 2007, Compass sold its vending machine business, Selecta, to private equity group Allianz, providing shareholders another $900 million in the ongoing buyback scheme. In September 2007, Compass reported fiscal results for the year, with startlingly good results: profit had grown from the previous year by 81 percent, from $646 million to $1 billion. With its financial house seemingly in order, Compass is still working to improve its ethical business model. In December 2007, for example, the company inked a five-year strategic partnership with Pura Vida Coffee, a fair trade coffee firm. For every pound of Pura Vida beans purchased through Compass, the company will donate 25 cents to Pura Vida's Create Good fund-raising program for at-risk children in "coffee-growing communities."

Visit Vault at www.vault.com for insider company profiles, expert advice, career message boards, expert resume reviews, the Vault Job Board and more.

VAULT CAREER LIBRARY   143

GETTING HIRED

Point your compass here

At the company's career web site (www.compass-group.com/Careers), applicants can search for employment opportunities, apply for specific jobs, upload a resume and fill out an online application form. Through its various subsidiaries scattered across the globe, Compass Group serves up about 25 million meals a day: that's one heck of a cafeteria, and it requires loads of manpower. Compass lists its job offerings by specific country location. Compass will contact applicants for interview, a step that generally involves a skills test and occasionally requires an assessment day of interviews, problem-solving activities and job location tours.

Continental Airlines, Inc.

1600 Smith Street
Department HQSEO
Houston, TX 77002
Phone: (713) 324-2950
Fax: (713) 324-2687
www.continental.com

LOCATIONS

Houston, TX (HQ)
Fort Lauderdale, FL
Los Angeles, CA
Newark, NJ
Seattle, WA
Washington, DC

Additional US locations in California, Colorado, Florida, Hawaii, Illinois, Indiana, Louisiana, New Jersey, New Mexico, New York, Ohio, Oklahoma, Pennsylvania, Utah, Texas & Washington; International operations in France, Guatemala, Ireland, Mexico, Spain, St. Maarten and the UK.

THE STATS

Employer Type: Public Company
Stock Symbol: CAL
Stock Exchange: NYSE
Chairman & CEO: Lawrence W. Kellner
2007 Employees: 42,370
2007 Revenue ($mil.): $14,232

DEPARTMENTS

Agent
Airport/Flight Operations
Chelsea Catering
Continental Micronesia
Corporate
Engineering
Flight Attendants
Internships
Pilot
Reservations
Technical Operations
Technology

KEY COMPETITORS

American Airlines
Southwest Airlines
United Airlines

EMPLOYMENT CONTACT

www.continental.com/web/en-US/
content/company/career

Visit Vault at **www.vault.com** for insider company profiles, expert advice, career message boards, expert resume reviews, the Vault Job Board and more.

VAULT CAREER LIBRARY   145

THE SCOOP

Troubled airline turns around

Continental Airlines is the world's fifth-largest airline. From its hubs in Cleveland, Houston and Newark, it operates about 3,100 flights per day to 140 U.S. cities and 130 international locations. Its Continental Micronesia subsidiary flies out of a hub in Guam to Western Pacific locales—including more flights to Japanese cities than any other U.S. carrier. The company runs a small jet service, Continental Express, and a turboprop (propeller-driven plane) service, Continental Connection, through two contractors: ExpressJet and Chautaqua Airlines, respectively. Both ExpressJet and Chautaqua license the Continental name for their flights to about 120 regional airports in the U.S., Canada and Mexico.

Flying high

After selling Varney Airlines to United Airlines in 1930, aviation pioneer Walter T. Varney co-founded Varney Speed Lines with Louis Mueller in 1934. Primarily an airmail outfit, Varney Speed's first flight covered 530 miles from Pueblo, Colo., to El Paso, Texas, with stops in Las Vegas, Santa Fe and Albuquerque, N.M. By the end of the year, Varney sold his interest in the company to Mueller, who, in turn, sold a majority (40 percent) stake to Robert F. Six in 1936. Under Six, the company changed its name to Continental Airlines and moved its headquarters from El Paso to Denver.

Continental aided the war effort during World War II, building its Denver Modification Center to engineer B-17 Flying Fortresses and B-29 Super Fortresses for the Army. After the war, the company returned to its Western routes from Denver to Texas and New Mexico. It added 16 new stops in the region in 1953, through an agreement with Pioneer Airlines. By the end of the 1950s it completed its first jet flight, on a Boeing 707-120. The company moved its headquarters in 1963, leaving Denver behind in favor of Los Angeles.

Covering new territory ... or not?

Continental formed its Air Micronesia subsidiary in 1968 to transport U.S. troops to the Asia Pacific region in the Vietnam War. Air Micronesia's first flight, from Honolulu to the Northern Mariana Islands, covered more than 4,000 miles. Before leaving office, President Johnson awarded Continental the rights to fly to Hawaii,

Australia and New Zealand. The airline excitedly placed orders on four new Boeing 747 jets.

Immediately after taking office in 1968, President Nixon revoked Continental's flights to the same three Pacific destinations Johnson had granted. Continental thus had no use for its new shipment of jets, and stored them in a New Mexico hangar, which cost $13 million per year. Continental posted the second annual losses in its history in 1968, and suffered through financial insecurity for the better part of the next decade. The Airline Deregulation Act of 1978 injected more competition into Continental's stalwart routes, further worsening the airline's plight.

A bankrupt pioneer

In 1980, the company's longtime chief, Robert Six, retired from active duty at the age of 72, and his successors began looking for merger candidates to revive Continental's fortunes. The company found a potential merger-mate in Western Airlines, another Los Angeles-based firm struggling after deregulation. However, in late 1981, Texas Air Corporation increased its stake in Continental from around 4 to over 50 percent. This met with opposition from Continental employees, who launched their own takeover attempt of Continental with the aid of nine different banks. The employees' deal fell through, though, and Texas Air took over Continental in October 1982. Robert Six, now a nonexecutive chairman and 74 years old, publicly vouched for Texas Air's ability to bring Continental back to profitability.

The post-merger Continental now offered service to four continents (Asia, Australia, and North and South America), but it was also insolvent. Less than a year after the merger, in September 1983, Continental filed for Chapter 11 bankruptcy protection. Determined to recover, the company started offering flights mere days later, becoming the first airline to operate while in bankruptcy negotiations. Infuriated Continental workers went on strike but the company reported profits in 1984 of $50 million. Striking employees changed course and returned to the airline; pilots even denounced their union for questionable strike tactics. Continental offered its first European flights (to London) in April 1985, while still bankrupt. It later added routes to Frankfurt, Madrid, Munich and Paris. Continental successfully emerged from Chapter 11 in June 1986 as a nonunion airline with the industry's lowest labor costs and some of its lowest fares.

The newly solvent Continental immediately started buying up other bankrupt airlines, within six months adding Eastern Airlines, Frontier Airlines and People Express Airlines. By January 1987, Continental was the third-largest U.S. airline,

Visit Vault at **www.vault.com** for insider company profiles, expert advice, career message boards, expert resume reviews, the Vault Job Board and more.

VAULT CAREER LIBRARY   **147**

operating under $4.6 billion of debt. The airline was profitable and on pace to pay off its debts, but rising fuel costs and the onset of Operation Desert Storm in the Persian Gulf led Continental to declare bankruptcy again in December 1990.

Bethune's big turn around

Air Partners and Air Canada invested $450 million in Continental in November 1992, helping the company to emerge from bankruptcy by April 1993. By the time CEO Gordon Bethune joined Continental in 1994, the airline was dead last in federal rankings for on-time performance, baggage handling and the involuntary bumping of passengers off flights.

Bethune made it his mission to turn the company's performance around. Among other strategies, he created employee incentives (e.g., a $65 bonus for every month Continental finished in the top half of the performance rankings) to improve the company's service. By 1995, the airline was ranked No. 1 for on-time domestic performance and domestic baggage handling. And in July 1995, Continental announced the largest quarterly profit in its history. The following December, *BusinessWeek* named Continental the Best NYSE Stock of 1995. Officially rebounded, Continental moved its headquarters to Houston in September 1997.

Continental plays nice with its airline buddies

In 1998, Northwest Airlines paid $370 million for a 13 percent stake in Continental, now a hot property. The two airlines began participating in codesharing arrangements, linking up their flights for the benefits of passengers. These agreements continue today, as Northwest and Continental link flight schedules on 850 flights to 95 destinations. Continental struck another codesharing deal in April 1999 with Alaska Airlines, and in the summer struck a codesharing agreement with Panama's Copa Airlines.

To close out the 20th century, in December 1999 Continental bought a minority stake in the Florida-based Gulfstream International Airlines. In October 2000, CEO Bethune and Houston Mayor Lee Brown broke ground on a $350 million expansion project at Bush Intercontinental Airport, the airport's largest facility expansion in over two decades.

September 11th stuns airlines

The terrorist attacks of September 11, 2001, sent the entire tourism industry into a tailspin, and especially affected U.S. air travel firms. Four days after the attack, Continental said it would reduce its long-term flight schedule by 20 percent and lay off 12,000 employees. Despite the government legislating nearly $4.5 billion in relief funding for the industry, Continental lost $95 million on nearly $9 billion in revenue in 2001. It was a far cry from just a year before, when the airline was flying high with profits of $342 million and just under $10 billion in sales.

Carrier carries on

Continental pushed ahead despite the tough operating environment, launching daily nonstop service between Houston and Amsterdam in 2002, and picking up codesharing agreements with Amtrak and KLM Royal Dutch Airlines. The company continued its cooperative work with other travel firms in 2003, co-launching interline e-ticketing with Delta Airlines and US Airways, signing codesharing agreements with Denmark's Maersk Air and TAP Air Portugal, and entering into an alliance agreement with AeroMexico.

The company wasn't able to turn a profit in 2002, but reported the (humble) result of $28 million in 2003. Another positive sign: sales via www.continental.com reached $1.16 billion overall in 2003, an impressive jump of nearly 82 percent over the previous year. Any profits were impressive that year, since the beginning of military action in Iraq in March 2003 forced temporary reductions in international capacity. Shortly after combat began, Continental laid off a large segment of its workforce, cutting its senior management by 25 percent and eliminating 1,200 jobs for savings of $500 million.

At the start of 2004, CEO Bethune announced he would retire by the end of the year, to be replaced by Larry Kellner, the company's president and COO. Before he departed, Bethune enacted a number of other cost-cutting measures, including the elimination of paper tickets and a further reduction in staff, saving $200 million by cutting 425 more jobs. It wasn't enough to maintain profitability, as soaring fuel prices drove the company back into the red for fiscal 2004.

As soon as new CEO Kellner took over, in January 2005, Continental and its employees agreed to a $99 million cut in wages and benefits for cargo, gate, operations, ramp and ticket workers at domestic airports. This was just part of a larger $500 million savings plan to prevent a liquidity crisis due to the soaring cost of jet fuel. The next month, the board agreed to reduce fees for most directors by 30 percent and to forgo stock-option grants. On a more positive note, Continental Express' regional operations enjoyed record results in the first half of 2005, and the company's international operations continued to expand at a double-digit rate of growth. Nevertheless, Continental posted a loss of $68 million in 2005, despite revenue increasing by more than $1 billion to $11.2 billion.

Still the tops

Fuel costs actually increased in 2006 (by about 24 percent from 2005), but Continental increased its passenger revenue by about 17 percent and sold 40 percent more tickets on its web site. The airline also raised more funds, selling off about 30 percent of its interest in Copa Airlines in December 2006. Full year results for 2006 were a dramatic improvement—the company squeezed profits of $343 million out of $13 billion in revenue.

A fleet to beat

Continental seized the initiative in March 2007, increasing its order of new Boeing 787 Dreamliner jets from 12 to 25. The Dreamliner is a fuel-efficient jet for making long-haul (usually international) flights, and Continental hopes to lower its expenses by taking advantage of better fuel economies. In July 2007, on the heels of an "open skies" agreement opening up air travel between the U.S. and China, Continental applied to the U.S. Department of Transportation for rights to the first nonstop route from New York to Shanghai. The company won approval in September 2007, and flights from Newark/New York to Shanghai will begin in 2009.

Continental is hot for international travel largely because of trouble at home. Competition from low-cost carriers (including Virgin America, the upcoming U.S. arm of Sir Richard Branson's British airline) within the U.S. threatens Continental's profitability in the domestic market. And in July 2007, Continental announced it would cut capacity on domestic flights, creating a scarcity that would allow it to raise fares. Shortly afterwards, Continental sold 10 of its Boeing 737 airplanes to Russian air carrier Transaero. The company added another international route in October 2007, beginning nonstop service from New York to Mumbai.

Paying attention to pensions

While Continental was enjoying consistent profits in 2007, the company set aside large chunks of money for its employee pension plan. At the beginning of the year, the airline aimed to set aside $328 million, and set a minimum of $187 million.

Continental ended up contributing $336 million after putting money aside in January, April, July, September and October (it surpassed the minimum of $187 million in July). Also, in February, the airline distributed $111 million in profit sharing to its employees, the largest such distribution in company history. As soon as the new year began, Continental was at it again, contributing $60 million to its employees' pension plan in January 2008.

Corporate love matches

Continental might grow larger in 2008, as a result of heated merger talks with a number of other American carriers: Delta, Northwest and United Airlines. Delta started the whole affair in January 2008, approaching both Northwest and United with merger proposals and keeping Continental on the back burner. The talks with Northwest apparently escalated in February, and in response Continental took up serious talks with United. Continental CEO Larry Kellner actually said he would prefer not to merge, but a marriage of Delta and Northwest would create such a giant new airline that he wouldn't want Continental to be dwarfed.

GETTING HIRED

You career could take off

Go to www.continental.com/web/en%2DUS/content/company/career to explore positions sorted into several job categories, including flight attendants, pilots, corporate jobs, engineering, internships and reservations. Job seekers can also search the entire database of job listings by location and division. Upon finding an opening to their liking, wannabe Continentals can submit their resume and cover letter online.

Benefits for the initiated include a 401(k) savings plan, vacation and sick pay, profit sharing and stock purchase plans, and the full gamut of health insurance coverage. Employees still enjoy monthly bonuses when the airline meets its on-time goals—a holdover from the days of CEO Gordon Bethune. Continental workers and their families also enjoy a popular, industry-standard perk—travel discounts.

For seven consecutive years from 1998 to 2004, *Fortune* magazine ranked Continental one of its Top 100 Companies to work for. Recently, Continental won the No. 1 spot on *Fortune*'s 2006 list of Most Admired Global Companies.

OUR SURVEY SAYS

There's more to life than flying privileges

Some of our sources are frustrated with Continental's benefits package. One says that "flight benefits are touted as an integral part of compensation, indeed why compensation is below market. But the benefits don't pan out." Another says the company "assigns a bogus [salary] value for … flying privileges." A more level-headed contact reports that the "industry is fragile, with mergers and possible mergers being explored," and hence "Overtime is available on a limited basis, awarded by seniority … profit sharing up until [September 11th] was good." And "401(k) was suspended as part of cutbacks." Some of these should come back in 2007, he says, "after a good year in aviation."

Across the board, contacts say that employee cutbacks have inevitably created more work for everyone. "Headcount reductions have left office workers understaffed and overworked," says one manager. "Work hours are the normal in the business," says a maintenance worker, "with graveyard hours being the norm for most new hires." Another engineering veteran says that he tells "every intern not to go into the airline side of this business and stick with Boeing, Lockheed Martin, Honeywell, etc. Continental cannot attract industry veterans (because of the salary disparity) and has to hire graduates with limited experience. These newbies hang around for [three to five] years and then move on, once they realize what other companies will pay."

Delta Air Lines, Inc.

1030 Delta Boulevard
Atlanta, GA 30320
Phone: (404) 715-2600
Fax: (404) 715-5042
www.delta.com

LOCATIONS

Atlanta, GA (HQ)
Albany, NY • Austin, TX • Boston,
MA • Cincinnati, OH • Columbia, SC
• Dulles, VA • Flushing, NY •
Honolulu, HI • Houston, TX •
Jacksonville, FL • Kahlului, HI • Las
Vegas, NV • Los Angeles, CA
• Minneapolis, MN • New Orleans, LA
• New York, NY • Newark, NJ •
Philadelphia, PA • Phoenix, AZ •
Pittsburgh, PA • Raleigh, NC •
Richmond, VA • Sacramento, CA •
Salt Lake City, UT • San Francisco,
CA • San Jose, CA • Santa Ana, CA
• Syracuse, NY • Warwick, RI •
Washington, DC • West Palm Beach,
FL

International locations in Canada,
Costa Rica, France, Guatemala,
Honduras, Italy, Nigeria, Puerto
Rico, Russia and the UK.

THE STATS

Employer Type: Public Company
Stock Symbol: DAL
Stock Exchange: NYSE
Chairman: Daniel A. Carp
CEO: Richard Anderson
President: Edward Bastian
2007 Employees: 55,044
2007 Revenue ($mil.): $19,154

DEPARTMENTS

Accounting/Auditing/Finance
Administrative & Support Services
Airport Operations/Management
Engineering
Flight Operations/Management
Legal
Maintenance/Technical Operations
Marketing/Sales/Account
Management
Reservations/Call Center &
Management

KEY COMPETITORS

American Airlines
Southwest Airlines
United Airlines

EMPLOYMENT CONTACT

www.delta.com/about_delta/
career_opportunities

Visit Vault at **www.vault.com** for insider company profiles, expert advice,
career message boards, expert resume reviews, the Vault Job Board and more.

VAULT CAREER LIBRARY 153

THE SCOOP

No. 3 in the skies

In terms of revenue, Atlanta-based Delta Air Lines is the third-largest U.S. carrier, behind American and United. Together with its network of regional carriers—including its Comair and Atlantic Southeast subsidiaries—Delta takes off 2,533 times every day. Delta filed for Chapter 11 protection in September 2005, and successfully emerged from bankruptcy at the end of April 2007.

At home and abroad

Delta's North American operations account for roughly 77 percent of the airline's passenger revenue, with hubs in Atlanta, Cincinnati, Salt Lake City and New York City. Many of its regional flights operate under the Delta Connection network, which includes ASA, Comair and SkyWest. The airline also runs the Delta Shuttle, which provides weekday service from New York's La Guardia airport to both Boston and Washington, D.C.

Delta's international service leads all domestic competition in trans-Atlantic service, with 29 daily departures, generating about 23 percent of the company's passenger revenue. On its own, Delta flies to 307 destinations in 52 countries around the world. But through its international SkyTeam partners (Aeromexico, Air France, Alitalia, CSA Czech Airlines, KLM and Korean Air), Delta serves 460 locales in 96 countries.

Delta through the decades

Delta began as a crop dusting division of Huff Daland Manufacturing in Macon, Ga., in 1924. Upon hearing Huff Daland was planning on selling the company, a longtime crop-dusting entrepreneur named C.E. Wollman organized a group of investors and bought the division in 1928. The new owners renamed it Delta Air Service, after the Mississippi Delta region it called home. A year later, Delta launched its first passenger flight from Dallas to Jackson, Mississippi.

The company cut back on costly passenger flights during the early years of the Great Depression, focusing on crop dusting operations and other aircraft-related businesses. In 1934, the company was granted an airmail contract, and then resumed its passenger service. Corporate headquarters moved to Atlanta in 1941, and the company officially changed its name to Delta Air Lines Inc. four years later.

Growth slowed during World War II, as Delta focused much of its operations on aiding the war effort. But flight routes grew side-by-side with the baby boom throughout the 1950s, adding service to Chicago, Washington, D.C., New York and the Caribbean. The company was soon listed on the New York Stock Exchange, and adopted its now-ubiquitous red, white and blue triangle logo (which has the swept-wing appearance of a jet) in 1959.

Delta flights expanded from coast to coast in the 1960s, with the first nonstop flight between Atlanta and Los Angeles in 1961. Delta merged with Northeast Airlines in 1972, giving it a large presence in Boston and New York. In 1987, it merged with Western Airlines to become the fourth-largest airline in the U.S. Delta made its largest acquisition to date in 1991, buying almost all of Pan Am's trans-Atlantic routes and the Pan Am Shuttle.

The calm before the storm

To compete with low-cost startups like ValueJet (now Airtrain), which were beginning to take a bite out of Delta's business, the air carrier launched its own low-fare airline in 1996, Delta Express. The next year, Leo Mullin was appointed Delta's president and CEO, replacing Ronald Allen, chairman and CEO since 1987.

In 2000, Delta acquired Atlantic Southeast Airlines (ASA) and Comair as wholly owned subsidiaries. Also that year, Delta collaborated in the launch of SkyTeam, a codesharing alliance that gave Delta a further global reach. (Codesharing is an agreement that allows passengers to buy connecting flights through different airlines.) SkyTeam's founding members included AeroMexico, Air France and Korean Air, but the coalition has since expanded to include 10 airlines, including U.S. carriers Northwest Airlines and Continental Airlines.

The effects of September 11th

Delta was having a bad year in 2001 even before the terrorist attacks of September 11th. Like the rest of the airline industry, Delta was experiencing a slump in business due to the weak, post-tech bubble economy. But it had also been hurt financially by labor disputes, including a three-month strike by Comair pilots.

After September 11th, the entire industry experienced a sharp and sudden decline in travel. Delta responded by cutting almost 11,000 jobs (!) and lowering capacity by 16 percent. The airline lost $1.2 billion for the fiscal year—the biggest annual loss

Visit Vault at **www.vault.com** for insider company profiles, expert advice, career message boards, expert resume reviews, the Vault Job Board and more.

VAULT CAREER LIBRARY   155

in its history. And the company still reported this result with a $556 million shot in the arm from the government, as part of its $15 billion bailout of the airline industry.

Although traffic began to pick up by 2002, Delta—and the rest of the industry—faced skyrocketing costs for tighter airline security and insurance. Part of CEO Mullin's proposal to get the industry back on its feet included making security screening as hassle-free as possible, and lowering passenger taxes and fees. Additionally, to cut back costs, Delta announced in June 2002 it would no longer provide traditional paper tickets for most itineraries, moving to e-ticketing instead.

Airfare for a Song

Delta debuted a new low-fare carrier in November 2002. Called Song, it was basically a relaunch of the Delta Express subsidiary, which premiered to some success in 1996, but fell victim to rising costs with its unionized pilots and high-maintenance fleet of planes. As Song boss John Selvaggio put it in 2003, "we were dabbling [with Delta Express]. There wasn't a real commitment to win in the market."

But any excitement over Song's formation was trumped by disheartening news from its parent company in March 2003, when CEO Mullin announced that Delta might be forced to cut over 1,000 jobs to fend off filing for Chapter 11 bankruptcy. Delta also announced that it would cut back service as the travel industry entered an Iraq war-related slump, and nearly 1,000 employees accepted voluntary leave offers from the company, effectively retiring. After major fighting in the Middle East ended shortly afterwards, 250 pilots that had gone on leave filed a grievance, insisting they should be put back to work.

Song emerged in April 2003, with fancy perks for passengers like video-screens, MP3 music, live satellite television, pay-per-view movies and interactive video games. The airline's first flight was between West Palm Beach, Fla., and New York City. By September, the airline announced additional flights between Los Angeles and other Florida cities.

Big job for the new boss

Leo Mullin stepped down as CEO in January 2004, succeeded by Gerald Grinstein, a former Western Airlines CEO and 16-year veteran on Delta's board. John "Jack" Smith Jr. took over chairmanship duties the following April. That month, Delta battled with its pilots union, again trying to stave off bankruptcy. Pilots twice rejected a plan to reduce pay by 30 percent, although they offered to accept a 9 percent reduction, an amount Grinstein said "[didn't] come near enough to close the gap." The next month, Delta announced it had hired The Blackstone Group, an investment bank, for advice on "business reassessment and planning efforts" for a possible Chapter 11 filing.

Piloting a resolution

Delta's debt swelled to $20.6 billion by summer 2004, and executives acknowledged that bankruptcy seemed imminent. Grinstein cut $700 million from Delta's overhead through a series of cost-cutting efforts, but to no avail. Stock hit a 52-week low in September, as Delta announced it would sell eight D11 aircraft and four spare engines to FedEx Express. Grinstein then unveiled a plan to get his company back on track, including restructuring more than half of Delta's network, de-hubbing the Dallas/Fort Worth airport, expanding Song's flight routes and eliminating over 7,000 more jobs. The company estimated that, just to stay afloat, it would need to cut $2.7 billion by 2006.

Finally, in October 2004, Delta and its pilots union reached an agreement through a combination of wage and benefit cuts and work rules to increase productivity. Pilots were given the option to purchase nearly 30 million shares of Delta common stock in return for a 33 percent wage reduction and no contractual raises for a five-year period. The deal was closed in the nick of time, just hours before the Delta board was scheduled to meet to discuss a possible bankruptcy filing. In December 2004, Grinstein announced that he and other executives and salaried workers at Delta would receive no bonuses for 2004 and take a 10 percent pay cut in 2005. The money saved was badly needed—Delta suffered a net loss of $5.2 billion for 2004.

Fueling debt

In spring 2005, the rapidly rising cost of jet fuel put a serious cramp in Delta's restructuring and the company announced more job cuts and more sell-offs of aircraft in September of the same year. Fuel costs never decreased and the travel industry took another blow with the catastrophic devastation of the Gulf Coast from Hurricane Katrina. By mid-September 2005, Delta gave up the ghost and filed for Chapter 11 bankruptcy protection.

Desperate to get back on its feet, Delta announced another mind-boggling elimination of jobs (between 7,000 and 9,000) and a drop in domestic capacity by 15 to 20 percent. These cuts were designed to save $930 million annually, of which

Visit Vault at **www.vault.com** for insider company profiles, expert advice, career message boards, expert resume reviews, the Vault Job Board and more.

VAULT CAREER LIBRARY

157

$325 million was from pilot salaries and $605 million from the balance of staff. In addition, Grinstein took a 25 percent pay cut, while other executives took a 15 percent pay cut. These layoffs came on top of the roughly 24,000 Delta layoffs since the September 11 attacks.

Chief ends bankruptcy, takes off

In October 2006, Delta CEO Gerald Grinstein announced his plans to retire once the company emerged from bankruptcy in the first half of 2007. A month after this announcement, in November, US Airways made an unexpected $8 billion offer to purchase Delta. Grinstein rebuffed the offer, stating that, "Delta's plan has always been to emerge from bankruptcy in the first half of 2007 as a strong, stand-alone carrier. Our plan is working and we are proud of the progress." US Airways insisted that it would leave the Delta name and much of its business untouched, but Delta rejected the bid in December 2006 and has resisted all subsequent acquisition attempts.

The airline reported losses of $6.21 billion for fiscal 2006, a number that was close to double Delta's $3.84 billion loss in fiscal 2005. Although Delta's revenue increased by 6.1 percent in 2006, to $17 billion, the results brought the carrier's five-year losses to a grand total of $18.5 billion. Also in 2006, Delta discontinued its low-cost carrier Song, after less than four years in operation.

Clearer skies

Delta emerged from Chapter 11 bankruptcy protection in April 2007; it slashed $3 billion in annual costs, dropped 6,000 jobs and restructured its fleet. As part of the reorganization plan, Delta's creditors can receive between 60 and 80 percent of the value of their claims in new Delta stock, which started trading under the symbol DAL on the New York Stock Exchange in May 2007. The company's existing stock, trading for pennies the previous week, became worthless.

Delta's staff will get something, too: a 3.5 percent stake in the company (worth $480 million) for employees and a 2.5 percent share (worth $240 million) for managers. In August 2007, Delta announced the retirement of CEO Gerald Grinstein. His replacement was former Northwest CEO Richard Anderson, who had beaten out two candidates from within Delta's ranks, Edward Bastian and James Whitehurst. What happened to the runners-up? In August 2007, simultaneous with Anderson becoming the new CEO, Delta promoted Bastian to president and CFO and Whitehurst resigned his post as COO.

Also in August, new CEO Anderson dispelled rumors that a merger between Delta and fellow-ex-bankruptee Northwest was in the offing, stating that an alliance relationship between the two would be equally beneficial. Months later, Anderson denied another merger rumor, involving United Airlines.

Good cop, bad cop

Although new CEO Anderson repeatedly dispelled the Northwest merger rumors, Delta's employees were nervous about losing former CEO Grinstein, who was beloved because he shouldered the burdens of Chapter 11 restructuring alongside his workers. He gave up stock options and bonuses while the company was under restructuring, ate lunch with his employees and even volunteered to clean out planes. On the other hand, Richard Anderson might not have it so easy. Northwest is infamous for having less than chummy relationships with its employees and many staffers were afraid Anderson might carry over that tradition. Delta flight attendants are agitating to unionize, and the company's slim profits might be further reduced if workers drive a tough bargain for higher pay and better benefits.

Merger complications

As 2007 turned into 2008, the rumors about a Northwest merger gained legitimacy. The two airlines' executive staffs met by February 2008, and soon worked out a deal that would create the world's largest airline. As a sign of good faith, Anderson told Delta's board that should the deal go through, he would waive millions of dollars in compensation. At the same time, he assured Delta employees that all of their benefits would stay intact after the merger. But it wasn't meant to be, as the two airlines' pilot unions simply couldn't agree on the issue of seniority. For pilots, the issue of seniority is hugely important, as it determines things like raises and vacation time. Apparently, Northwest's union wanted to shake up the two fleets' levels of seniority, and Delta refused to budge on the issue.

On March 18, 2008, the leader of Delta's pilots union told the company that the negotiations with Northwest's union had failed. Although neither airline said the deal was definitely dead, the very same day Delta announced a massive wave of employee cutbacks. In a letter to employees, Richard Anderson said the firm would offer buyouts to 30,000 of its 55,000 employees, with the hope of reducing overall headcount by about 2,000. He didn't mention the merger, instead noting that the cost of fuel had jumped by 20 percent in the previous quarter alone, and that the annual budget would probably be $900 million more than expected.

Visit Vault at **www.vault.com** for insider company profiles, expert advice, career message boards, expert resume reviews, the Vault Job Board and more.

VAULT CAREER LIBRARY   **159**

GETTING HIRED

Work your way up, up, up ...

For those who want to team up with Delta, the company's career web site (www.delta.com/about_delta/career_opportunities) has the lowdown on open positions in the air and on the ground. These are searchable by job title, division and location. If your browsing of the listings turns up a good fit, you'll need to create a job profile with the web site before uploading cover letters and resumes online.

Benefits for those flying with Delta include 401(k) with company match, vacation and sick pay, and extensive health benefits. Employees also enjoy worldwide travel discounts and a company credit union.

Internships and co-ops are also available at Delta, which is always swooping in to pluck up fresh young talent. Internships last one semester for undergraduates and graduates alike, and co-ops span an entire year, but are for undergrads alone. Both programs pay their young worker bees, and Delta graciously extends its attractive travel benefits to its college-aged employees.

Deutsche Lufthansa AG

Von-Gablenz-Straße 2-6
D-50679 Cologne, 21
Germany
Phone: +49-0221-826-3992
Fax: +49-221-826-3646
www.lufthansa.com

LOCATIONS

Cologne, Germany (HQ)
Chicago, IL
Los Angeles, CA
New York, NY
Bangalore
Bangkok
Delhi
Dubai
Johannesburg
London
Madrid
Milan
Moscow
Paris
Sao Paulo
Shanghai
Shannon, Ireland
Singapore
Stockholm

THE STATS

Employer Type: Public Company
Stock Symbol: LHA
Stock Exchange: Frankfurt
Chairman: Juergen Weber
CEO: Wolfgang Mayrhuber
2007 Employees: 105,261
2007 Revenue (€mil.): €22,420

DEPARTMENTS

Accounting
Auditing/Revision
Banking
Consultancy
Controlling
Design
Finances
Human Resources
Investments/M&A
Law/Patent Laws
Logistics/Material Management
Marketing/Product Management
Marketing/Sales
Medicine/Social Affairs
Planning/Organization
PR/Communication/Advertising
Production
Purchasing/Procurement
R&D/Procurement
Service/Customer Assistance
Strategy/Corporate Development
Taxes/Insurances
Technology
Training

KEY COMPETITORS

Air France-KLM
American Airlines
British Airways

EMPLOYMENT CONTACT

www.be-lufthansa.com

Visit Vault at **www.vault.com** for insider company profiles, expert advice,
career message boards, expert resume reviews, the Vault Job Board and more.

VAULT CAREER LIBRARY   161

THE SCOOP

Lufthansa gives flyers a lift

With its fleet of more than 300 Boeings and Airbuses, the Germany-based Lufthansa hauled over 50 million passengers to and "frau" in 2006. The airline is Europe's second-largest, after Air France-KLM, and includes subsidiary carriers Air Dolomiti, Lufthansa CityLine and Eurowings. In all, Lufthansa Group houses about 400 subsidiaries in five segments: passenger business (the airline proper), logistics (Lufthansa Cargo), mantenance/repair/overhaul (Lufthansa Technik), catering (LSG Sky Chefs), IT services (Lufthansa Systems) and a miscellaneous catch-all division, which includes Lufthansa's flight training and aviation insurance operations.

Sputtering into action

Lufthansa formed in a 1926 merger of two German airlines, Deutsche Aero Lloyd and Junkers Luftverkehr. Originally named Deutsche Luft Hansa Aktiengesellschaft, the moniker was, thankfully, shortened to Deutsche Lufthansa in 1933. The firm started out with an impressive fleet of 162 planes and stunned the world with an expedition to China at the end of its inaugural year. The company started the first trans-oceanic airmail service in 1934, flying to Buenos Aires via the South Atlantic.

The airline further expanded its routes in the 1930s, but was taken over by the German air force, the Luftwaffe, in World War II. The Luftwaffe converted many of Lufthansa's planes for military use (and drafted many of its employees) during the war. Lufthansa was earthbound from 1945 to 1951, as the West German republic began its postwar economic recovery.

Hans Bongers, Lufthansa's former traffic chief, was tapped to lead the company, which was briefly known as Luftag before readopting the Lufthansa name. Scheduled flights resumed in 1955 and the company incorporated jets in 1961, with the purchase of several new-fangled Boeing 707s. These planes introduced economy-class seating, opening up air travel to a broader swathe of society than ever before.

As its propeller-driven planes were taken out of rotation, Lufthansa expanded its international routes, introducing service to Nigeria and South Africa in 1962. The airline became profitable for the first time in 1964, earning an income of DM35 million (approximately €18 million). As the airline proved independently successful, the government offered some of its stock to the public in 1966, retaining 75 percent ownership of the company.

Gaining some privacy

In 1970, Lufthansa began employing Boeing's wide-body 747 jumbo jets, allowing for long-distance hauls with high passenger capacity. The last of the old-fashioned propeller-driven planes were put out to pasture the next year. Lufthansa purchased its first Airbus A300 jet in 1976, also the first commercial aircraft to be built primarily in Germany in over 30 years. Airbus craft became fixtures in Lufthansa's fleet, with A310s, A319s, A320s, A231s and A340s to follow in the 1980s.

Lufthansa also expanded into travel-industry services, such as hotels and car rentals, in the 1980s. The added revenue from these divisions nearly tripled the airline's profits in one year, going from $22 million in 1983 to $57 million in 1984. West Germany's government then issued more of the company's stock on the public market, which raised political controversy about foreign investors potentially snapping up too many shares. By 1989, the government owned only 51 percent of the firm.

With the reunification of Germany in 1990, Lufthansa triumphantly flew into Berlin for the first time in 45 years. The glee was short-lived, however, as a number of factors soon took a toll on Lufthansa's profitability. Competition for domestic and continental routes both became heavier in the 1990s, as a reunited Germany and a more deregulated European airline industry allowed more carriers to cut into Lufthansa's market share. Also, the Gulf War negatively affected all kinds of travel. Lufthansa posted losses in 1991 and 1992.

Jurgen Weber, who came aboard as Lufthansa chairman and CEO in 1991, immediately instituted a $1 billion savings plan. By 1994, the company was back in the black, having cut 8,400 jobs, frozen wage increases for a year and cut routes and services. The firm also restructured its cargo, aircraft maintenance, catering and training divisions into wholly owned subsidiaries of the Lufthansa Group. In May 1997, Lufthansa partnered with Air Canada, SAS, Thai Airways and United Airlines to create the Star Alliance, a codesharing and cross-promotion affiliation. The government sold its remaining shares of Lufthansa in October 1997, making the airline a fully privatized entity.

Visit Vault at **www.vault.com** for insider company profiles, expert advice, career message boards, expert resume reviews, the Vault Job Board and more.

VAULT CAREER LIBRARY   **163**

Survival through diversification

Lufthansa grew through acquisition in the early years of the new century, with major share purchases in 2000 of OSFI/Sky Chefs, an airline catering group, and Thomas Cook, a travel agency. The same year, the airline's technical arm began outfitting Airbus A340 planes with satellite TV and Internet access. In April 2001, Lufthansa launched its "D-Check" program—so named for the top-down inspection a plane gets before its determined airworthy—to examine and improve the minute processes of the sprawling airline.

When the terrorist attacks of September 11, 2001 crippled the travel industry, Lufthansa was able to remain profitable. Thanks to a low debt load, the company didn't have to resort to layoffs; instead, it kept employees but reduced salaries. It also grounded 43 planes, returning them to service gradually as customers trickled back in. And it didn't hurt that most of its businesses were No. 1 or No. 2 in their respective fields. In 2002, Lufthansa posted profits of $751 million as its U.S. contemporaries lost a collective $9 billion.

One bad year won't spoil the whole batch

Lufthansa didn't wear its told-you-so smile for long, as SARS and the war in Iraq eroded revenue in 2003. In June of that year, Jurgen Weber stepped down as chairman and CEO, passing the duties on to Wolfgang Mayrhuber. The company eventually posted losses of €980 million for the year, with the catering division writing off an accounting charge of €800 million. More belt-tightening followed in 2004, with pilots accepting a wage freeze in December, as Lufthansa aimed at saving €1.2 billion by 2006. As the industry recovered from the challenges of 2003, Lufthansa happily broke a company record in 2004, carrying more than 50 million passengers that year.

Taking on the competition

In March 2005 the company celebrated its 50th birthday. Its biggest present that year was the €310 million acquisition of Swiss International Airlines. The purchase brought Lufthansa into closer competition with the world's largest airline, Air France-KLM (itself the product of a recent merger). Because of complications over foreign landing rights, Lufthansa staggered the purchase over several years, assuming full control in August 2007.

However, since the appearance of low-cost carriers like Ryanair and easyJet in Europe (and JetBlue in the U.S.), Lufthansa has lost many of its customers to no-frills, ultra-cheap flights. Lufthansa gained some leverage in the field in January 2006, when it secured majority voting rights in low-cost airline Eurowings. And Lufthansa began offering its own low fare flights around Europe in March 2006, offering flights to 181 locations for prices as low as $138 (€99).

Heavy dealings

In February 2006 the European Commission and the U.S. Justice Department began investing possible price-fixing in the air cargo divisions of eight major airlines, including Lufthansa. Specifically, the probe concerned possible collusion to cover rising fuel costs since the start of the war in Iraq. The chairman of Lufthansa's cargo division, Jean-Peter Jansen, stepped down in March 2006, citing health concerns. Lufthansa settled the issue in September 2006, paying $85 million and receiving immunity from further penalties related to the price-fixing.

Big money

The financial reports for fiscal 2006 showed Lufthansa to be in fine form, with revenue growing by nearly 10 percent to €19.8 billion and profit nearly doubling to €803 billion. The airline wagered on continued growth in December 2006, ordering 20 Boeing 747s and 30 Airbus A320s. After nursing the travel agency Thomas Cook—in which it owned a 50 percent stake—back to financial health, Lufthansa sold off its share early in 2007, boosting the company's revenue forecast.

Later, in December 2007, Lufthansa and JetBlue agreed on a $300 million deal, in which Lufthansa will acquire a 19 percent stake in the budget airline. The announcement came amid reports linking both Lufthansa and Air France-KLM to troubled Italian carrier Alitalia, and Lufthansa CEO Mayhuber remarked at the time that he assumed Air France-KLM would consummate that purchase. He also stated that Lufthansa was still interested in taking over Spanish carrier Iberia; this purchase would create a carrier of about 70 million passengers per year, rivaling Air France-KLM for the largest airline in the world.

Visit Vault at **www.vault.com** for insider company profiles, expert advice, career message boards, expert resume reviews, the Vault Job Board and more.

VAULT CAREER LIBRARY　165

GETTING HIRED

Fly like the Germans

Job seekers should visit Lufthansa's careers web site, www.be-lufthansa.com. Available in English (but go ahead and read it in German for practice), the web site provides listings of company openings searchable by division, department and location. Applications may be filed online, and job seekers can create and save a job skills profile on the site.

Competition for positions at this airline is tight—in 2006, Lufthansa reported 97,000 applicants for a scant 2,500 open jobs. Still, the company is planning on expanding, announcing plans in August 2007 to hire 3,000 new employees, and then in December 2007 to hire 4,300 more by the end of 2008. Most of the hires will be assigned to Lufthansa's operations in Frankfurt and Munich, according to news reports.

Lufthansa takes applications for internships as well for currently enrolled students. Knowledge of both German and English is required for successful interns, who work three to six months with the firm and are paid €550 a month. Lufthansa Technik, the airline's maintenance, repair and overhaul division, accepts students-to-be for its 10-week basic internship program, in addition to hosting an expert internship with those who have already begun their studies. The company also has a pilot training program on top of training in business informatics, applied informatics, aircraft engineering, mechanical engineering, electrical engineering and business administration.

Nearly all those surveyed reported two rounds of face-to-face interviews. A human resources contact even met with "a psychologist and various VPs." In terms of hiring, a sales manager states that "it usually takes me at least two to three rounds before we shortlist [our candidate] … The focus is mainly on qualifications, age, attitude, expertise, experience [and] communication skills."

OUR SURVEY SAYS

How good is it at Lufthansa?

Our sources note that Lufthansa is "a great company to work for" and "a great company." In less glowing terms, another observed that, "Financially, it is a very stable company to be working for." Other contacts are mixed on Lufthansa's outlook, however. "It's a great time to work for a strong European airline like Lufthansa," states an American manager, only to be contradicted by a counterpart in Russia: "Competitors are coming to the market, so difficult years are ahead." A human resources associate in New York sums it up: "Being in the airline industry is exciting, but frustrating at the same time, as business goes up and down [along with] the economy."

German discipline

Our sources agree on a few central facts of life at Lufthansa: "Our company is very cost-conscious," says one respondent in New York, and another in Oman agrees that Lufthansa "is very strongly financially controlled, with very strict audit checks and [a] strong emphasis on cost management." This emphasis on cost extends to salaries, as contacts remark that "pay is mediocre," and a "back-of-the-mind feeling [persists] that Lufthansa is still not the best paying company." Also, as a result of finance-first thinking, Lufthansa "often [places] limits on employee numbers, creating stress and long work hours." Another respondent simply states that "due to bad personnel policy, the office is currently understaffed."

Another common theme is the German culture of the firm. "Although the company does not want to admit it," says one, "it still is a predominantly German culture" at Lufthansa. Others remark that the "head office is mainly populated by Germans and EU-citizens," although "corporate culture is very dependent on the department where you are working" and "there is a lot of diversity in terms of multicultural [and multi]national employees based worldwide." Although one respondent goes so far as to say "if you are not a German, [then] I would say one's [advancement] chances could be rated very low," another simply states that "if you don't know the German language, you are at a distinct disadvantage."

Dollar Thrifty Automotive Group, Inc.

5330 East 31st Street
Tulsa, OK 74135
Phone: (918) 660-7700
Fax: (918) 669-2934
www.dtag.com

LOCATIONS

Tulsa, OK (HQ)
Albuquerque, NM • Allentown, PA •
Aspen, CO • Camp Springs, MD •
College Park, GA • Naples, FL •
Washington, DC

Additional locations throughout the
United States; International
locations in Anguilla, Antigua,
Argentina, Aruba, Australia, Austria,
Bahamas, Belize, Bosnia
Herzegovina, Brazil, Canada,
Cayman Islands, Costa Rica,
Croatia, Cyprus, Czech Republic,
Dominican Republic, El Salvador,
Estonia, Fiji, France, Germany,
Greece, Guadeloupe, Guam,
Guatemala, Hungary, India, Ireland,
Israel, Italy, Jamaica, Jordan,
Kuwait, Latvia, Lebanon, Malta,
Mariana Island, Mexico, Netherlands
Antilles, New Caledonia, New
Zealand, Nicaragua, Oman, Panama,
Papua New Guinea, Portugal, Qatar,
Romania, Russia, Serbia, Seychelles
Islands, Slovakia, Slovenia, South
Africa, Spain, St. Kitts & Nevis, St.
Martin, Trinidad & Tobago, Turkey,
the United Arab Emirates, Uruguay,
the UK, Venezuela and the Virgin
Islands.

THE STATS

Employer Type: Public Company
Stock Symbol: DTG
Stock Exchange: NYSE
Chairman: Thomas P. Capo
President & CEO: Gary L. Paxton
2007 Employees: 8,500
2007 Revenue ($mil.): $1,761

DEPARTMENTS

Administrative Support •
Audit/Compliance • Communications
• Customer Service •
Driver/Mechanic/Service • Executive
• Finance/Accounting • Fleet
Operations/Sales • Fleet/Maintenance
Management • Field Operations
Management • Field Operations Non-
Management • Franchise
Sales/Support • Human Resources •
Information Technology • Legal •
Marketing • Properties/Concessions •
Purchasing/Distribution • Risk
Management/Collections • Rental
Sales Agent • Reservations • Sales •
Security • Training/Development

KEY COMPETITORS

Avis Budget
Enterprise Rent-A-Car
Hertz Global

EMPLOYMENT CONTACT

www.dtag.com/phoenix.zhtml?c=71
946&p=irol-aboutcareers

THE SCOOP

Here's a Dollar for the Thrifty driver

For the vehicularly and fiscally challenged among us, Dollar Thrifty Automotive Group is here to help. Through its Dollar Rent-A-Car and Thrifty Car Rental chains, the company offers Americans their pick of about 140,000 vehicles at both company-owned and franchised locations. The brands' revenue comes mainly from tourists and business travelers, and they are usually located close to airports.

Dollar's 647 locations span 53 countries worldwide; about half of them are in the U.S. and Canada. Thrifty is a larger operation, with over 1,000 locations in 68 countries. Despite its large international presence, Dollar Thrifty reaps only a fraction of its revenue from outside North America; the company generally franchises its overseas locations, collecting only franchise, reservation and advertising fees from these locations, rather than sales.

A bargain at twice the price

Thrifty got its start in 1958 as a car-rental outfit with a double-barreled approach, courting the local and travel markets with locations near both mechanics' shops and airports. Once its brand was established, the company swiftly moved to a franchise-intensive business model. William Lobeck acquired Thrifty in 1981, becoming its president and CEO. The firm went public in 1987.

Dollar began in 1966, when the operatically-named Henry Caruso, the son of Italian immigrants, started a car-rental business near Los Angeles. Initially named Dollar A Day Rent-a-Car, Caruso's operation started out with six Volkswagen Beetles, which it rented out for (duh) $1 per day. The company was popular with tourists visiting the area, and soon expanded its operations to other touristy places like Hawaii, Orlando and Nevada. A decade later, during the fuel shortages of the 1970s, the company grabbed customers from gas lines with the promise of a rental car with a full tank. The fuel crisis passed, but Dollar Rent a Car continued to grow. By 1990, the firm boasted 1,400 locations worldwide.

Gathering the troops

These two car-rental companies minded their own respective businesses until the late 1980s, when the major American car manufacturers—General Motors, Ford and Chrysler—began purchasing rental firms. Rental car demand conveniently kept their production lines busy, and provided a place to park poorly-selling models while they were rented out to recoup their production costs.

By 1989, Chrysler had already purchased General Rent-a-Car and Snappy Rent-a-Car, and later that year it created a subsidiary rental unit, the Pentastar Transportation Group. It purchased Thrifty late in the year, and Dollar in 1990. General Rent-a-Car's sales began to flag and it was closed in 1993; Chrysler sold off Snappy in 1994. Although Thrifty and Dollar weren't in such bad shape, Chrysler sold them off in a 1997 IPO, renaming them the Dollar Thrifty Automotive Group.

A public divorce

After gaining independence, Dollar and Thrifty continued to function as they had under Chrysler. Effectively separate companies with overlapping managment, each brand had its own sales, marketing, administrative and technical staff. The group restructured in 2002, merging together their technical, administrative and fleet management arms. The streamlining made the company more efficient, and in 2003 Dollar Thrifty premiered on the Fortune 1000 at No. 999.

Eyes on franchises

In 2004, the company began a revenue-boosting program, with the goal of acquiring its franchisees in the top 75 U.S. airport markets and key tourist areas. That year, it purchased several franchisees in popular tourist destinations, including Colorado, Florida, North Carolina, Texas and Illinois. In 2005, the firm acquired more franchises in Louisiana, Oklahoma and New Mexico, among others. Company revenue and profits increased each year, to $1.4 billion and $66 million, respectively, in 2004, and to $1.5 billion and $76 million in 2005. However, profits dipped by 40 percent in 2006 to $51 million, even though revenue increased to $1.6 billion. The company attributed the results to the acquisition program and increased costs in fleet management. On a positive note, Dollar Thrifty announced the purchase of franchisees in 18 more key markets, "complet[ing] the majority of" its acquisition program.

Vanguard of the movement

Dollar Thrifty isn't just after its franchisees. In February 2007, word got out about a possible merger with Vanguard Car Rental, owner of rival rental firms Alamo and National. A deal between the two would result in one of the top four car rental companies, in terms of revenue. The next month, however, Vanguard agreed to a merger with Enterprise Rent-A-Car, the largest American carrier, creating a formidable new force in the market.

Dollar Thrifty lives up to its name

Dollar Thrifty soon felt the repercussions of missing out on this deal. In August 2007, the company announced a "reorganization, implementing "aggressive initiatives to streamline" its organization. The changes resulted in a 25 percent reduction in management positions at the company's Tulsa, Okla., headquarters, outsourcing "certain call center operations" and IT services to Electronic Data Systems and introducing "lean management techniques" in all field locations, to improve productivity. CEO Gary Paxton stated that certain conditions within the auto industry necessitated these changes: vehicle manufacturers are selling fewer cars, at higher costs, to rental firms, and the act of financing vehicles recently became more expensive due to lower credit ratings.

Investing in IT

In its bid to reduce operating costs and become more efficient, Dollar Thrifty is embracing information technology. In October 2007, the company hired Rick Morris as its new chief information officer, a position he previously occupied at Capital One Financial Corporation. The link between his appointment and Dollar Thrifty's, well, thriftiness, is obvious. In a press release, the company specifically stated that Morris will aim to develop and implement "technology initiatives that improve cost-effectiveness, service quality and business development" and "achieve more cost-beneficial enterprisewide IT operations."

In December 2007, Dollar Thrifty introduced new software for its Thrifty Car Sales division, located in Tulsa at its centralized business development center (BDC). Developed in conjunction with customer relationship management firm MyGoalTracking, the new system will funnel all data management to the BDC, freeing up salespeople nationwide to spend more time with customers. It will automatically schedule follow-up calls, letters and e-mails to rental customers. Dollar Thrifty estimates that it will double the company's "lead-management capabilities," improve customer satisfaction and help with the company's marketing efforts.

Visit Vault at **www.vault.com** for insider company profiles, expert advice, career message boards, expert resume reviews, the Vault Job Board and more.

VAULT CAREER LIBRARY   171

GETTING HIRED

Baby, you can drive my car

Because of its corporate setup, Dollar Thrifty runs three different career web sites: one for Thrifty Car Rental, one for Dollar Rent A Car and one for the Dollar Thrifty corporate hub that oversees both businesses. Accordingly, job openings for Dollar Rent A Car and Thrifty are located with each brand's field locations scattered throughout the country, whereas most Dollar Thrifty openings are located at the company's headquarters in Tulsa, Oklahoma. Regardless of which part of the corporate trinity you want to work for, job listings can be found online, searchable by department and location. Applications may be submitted online as well, and candidates can create a profile to make the process of applying for multiple positions just that much easier.

Enterprise Rent-A-Car Company

600 Corporate Park Drive
St. Louis, MO 63105
Phone: (314) 512-5000
Fax: (314) 512-4706
www.enterprise.com

LOCATIONS

St. Louis, MO (HQ)

Additional locations throughout the US; International locations in Canada, Germany, Ireland and the UK.

THE STATS

Employer Type: Private Company
Chairman & CEO: Andrew C. Taylor
2006 Employees: 75,700
2006 Revenue ($mil.): $9,000

DEPARTMENTS

Accounting/Finance
Information Systems
Internships

KEY COMPETITORS

Avis Budget
Dollar Thrifty Automotive
Hertz Global Holdings

EMPLOYMENT CONTACT

www.erac.com

Visit Vault at **www.vault.com** for insider company profiles, expert advice, career message boards, expert resume reviews, the Vault Job Board and more.

VAULT CAREER LIBRARY   173

THE SCOOP

Taylor made

North America's largest car rental company, Enterprise Rent-a-Car operates a fleet of more than one million automobiles, with branches located within 15 miles of 90 percent of the U.S. population. Perhaps most remarkable, though, is how steadily Enterprise has grown throughout its 50-year history; still a privately held company, ranked No. 21 on *Forbes'* Largest Private Companies in America list, Enterprise has never experienced a single downsizing or unprofitable year.

The company is truly "Taylor Made"—longtime CEO Andy Taylor is the son of Enterprise founder, Jack Taylor—and the family's involvement doesn't look to be diminishing anytime soon. Enterprise still runs the Enterprise Rent-A-Car Foundation, established by Jack Taylor upon the company's 25th anniversary in 1982, awarding funds to charitable organizations nationwide.

Segmented business

Besides its rental car division, which manages over 6,500 rental offices in five countries, Enterprise has a fleet management services, car sales and truck rental divisions. The fleet management services division helps businesses manage their own fleets (generally ranging from 15 to 125 vehicles) and deals with financing, licensing, taxes and fuel in addition to providing vehicles. Enterprise's Car Sales division established a "haggle-free buying" policy 40 years ago that remains in place, with prices clearly posted on every vehicle and no negotiations involved. For businesses needing to rent a truck, there's the Rent-a-Truck division.

Boldly going where there are no airports

In 1957, Cadillac salesman Jack Taylor had a hunch that a market existed for leasing automobiles, and he founded Executive Leasing Company. At first, the company operated out of the basement of Taylor's employer, a St. Louis Cadillac dealership, leasing a grand total of seven cars. It wasn't until 1962 that Taylor added a rental car division, as customers had been telling him that they wanted to rent cars, not lease them. The rental division had a tiny original fleet of 17 vehicles.

The company expanded beyond St. Louis in 1969, and Taylor changed its name to Enterprise, in honor of the U.S.S. Enterprise, an aircraft carrier he served on as during World War II. The company grew in the 1970s by taking a different approach to rental cars. While other agencies competed for business at airports—trying to snag vacationing families and traveling businessfolk—Enterprise focused on making cars available for rent in small towns and neighborhoods. Today, Enterprise still has a very small share of the airport rental market; around 90 percent of the company's total transactions occur in its neighborhood braches.

In 1974, Enterprise began offering customers free rides to the rental office to get their cars, further enticing the local car-less masses. This practice continues today, advertised by Enterprise in its "We'll Pick You Up" campaign. As Enterprise thrived in local markets, it saw the need for a centralized reservation system to coordinate its far-reaching branches into one network. In 1980, the company opened a national reservation center that allowed people to call just one phone number from anywhere in the country to rent a car from Enterprise's now 6,000-strong fleet from any location.

The fleet rapidly expanded, reaching 50,000 cars by 1989. The firm reached a milestone in 1992, surpassing $1 billion in annual revenue. That year, the company returned to Jack Taylor's leasing idea, debuting its Fleet Services division to lease small fleets of cars to businesses.

Many different Enterprises

The company finally tried its hand at the already-crowded airport car rental business in 1995, opening its first on-airport location in Denver, Colorado. It wasn't an admission of defeat, however. The firm had grown so large and so successful by this point, that it was expanding all of its other operations, too. Enterprise added truck rentals to its product line in 1999, by which point it leased over 500,000 vehicles out of 4,000 locations per year. From 2000 onward, Enterprise opened an average of 415 new branches every year. By 2005, the company boasted 200 airport locations nationwide.

Going global

Besides growing into every sector of the U.S. rental car industry, Enterprise began expanding internationally in the 1990s. Enterprise opened its first international office in Windsor, Canada, in 1993, and entered the U.K. in 1994. The company has since moved into Germany, in 1997, and Ireland, in 1998, and opened a Belfast office in Northern Ireland in 2003.

In fiscal 2004, Enterprise generated over $500 million in revenue outside of the U.S., an increase of more than 20 percent year-over-year. By 2005, Enterprise had nearly 800 locations throughout the U.K., Canada, Germany and Ireland. The company's international wing rents cars to individuals, corporate rentals for companies, fleet rentals, and courtesy car rentals to auto dealers and body shops.

Dunn in

Enterprise became involved in a particularly nasty lawsuit in 2003, when Thomas P. Dunn, the company's former controller and vice president, filed a lawsuit alleging he was fired in July 2001 from his $650,000-a-year position for raising concerns about questionable Enterprise business practices. Dunn claimed that the company overbilled customers for repairs, levied deceptive surcharges on customers and registered vehicles so as to avoid paying sales tax, thus boosting the bottom dollar in preparation for a proposed IPO.

In March 2003, the jury voted 9-3 in Dunn's favor, awarding him $4 million for wrongful termination. Enterprise moved for the judge to disregard the verdict, pointing out that because the company never went public with its stock, its accounting could not have violated applicable laws. Enterprise also claimed Dunn was fired due to poor performance, citing more than 30 employee complaints regarding Dunn's behavior. Senior Judge Jack Koehr complied, overturning the verdict. An appeals court agreed with both jury and judge, finding that Dunn was wrongfully terminated but that Enterprise violated no laws in regards to its accounting practices.

Cruising into success

Courtroom snafus aside, Enterprise's corporate story may bore those looking for white collar noir and scandalous thrills—few shake-ups, no takeovers and little employee turmoil. This lack of drama is a testament to the company's strength, as Enterprise has continued to bring in the big bucks. By 2005, annual sales hit a company record $8.23 billion, with revenue growth of 11 percent over 2004.

Enterprise also reached record fleet size in fiscal 2005, with a combined total exceeding 818,000 vehicles. It also opened 494 new locations, for a worldwide total of over 6,500. And despite its relative eschewing of the airport business, in 2005 J.D. Power and Associates ranked highest in customer satisfaction among airport car rentals for the fifth time in six years.

At the Vanguard of airport rentals

Although Enterprise built its empire on the main streets of small towns and urban centers across the country, its competitors are closing the gap. Since opening its first airport location in 1995, Enterprise is now the fifth-highest selling airport car rental firm, but its rivals are now eating into Enterprise's urban and suburban customer bases.

But Enterprise is still the biggest game in town, and in March 2007 acquired Vanguard Car Rental, owner of the National and Alamo rental brands. Vanguard raked in over 30 percent of the market share in airport rentals in 2006, which should combine with Enterprise's 7 percent share to create a major player in the sector. The purchase also enlarged Enterprise's fleet by 300,000 vehicles—it now numbers over one million cars! In 2006, Vanguard earned about $2 billion in revenue.

Drive green

But airports aren't everything. The latest trend in the car rental industry is so-called "green fleets," fuel-efficient hybrid cars that appeal to environment-conscious customers. In June 2007 Enterprise launched a new marketing strategy, boasting that it offered more fuel-efficient cars than any other rental agency, pointing to its 3,000 gas-electric hybrids available for rent in the U.S.

Enterprise has also donated money to the environmental cause, including a $25 million gift to the Danforth Plant Science Center in March 2007 for research on ethanol and other alternative fuels. The focus on planet-conscious cars is especially useful in offsetting the declines suffered by the rental car industry as gas prices climb, especially in rentals of gas-guzzling SUVs. Now consumers can rest easy driving one of Enterprise's 41,000 ethanol-guzzlers, instead.

GETTING HIRED

A growing fleet

Job seekers should visit Enterprise's extensive career web site: www.erac.com. Here, they may search for open positions by location and job type. The company says most employees begin their Enterprise careers in the management training program, gradually rising through the ranks, although there are also opportunities for some administrative positions, IS professionals, accounting/finance, and part-time drivers and lot attendants.

To keep up with its continued growth, Enterprise estimates that it hires more than 6,000 college graduates a year. According to a variety of publications, the company's not a bad place to be: in September 2004 the venerable Princeton Review cited Enterprise as one of 66 employers with the best entry-level jobs. In 2006, *The Globe and Mail* recognized it as one of the 50 Best Employers in Canada and *BusinessWeek* ranked it at No. 5 on its Best Places to Launch a Career list. Enterprise earned the No. 1 slot on the Top 500 Entry Level Employers for 2006 list for the fourth consecutive year at CollegeGrad.com, an entry level job site.

From the ground up

Nearly all of Enterprise's executives get their start in the Management Training Program, and Enterprise prides itself in recruiting motivated college educated individuals who learn the business from the ground up, sometimes even washing cars when they first begin. The company says that normally employees who successfully complete the program can expect to become assistant managers after one year and a branch manager after two-and-a-half years with the company. Enterprise says that with this accelerated career growth process, employees could earn an income in two to three years that would take 10 years at other companies.

No one can argue that the program is the surest way to climb the ranks: nearly all of the company's senior managers, including Chairman and CEO Andy Taylor, got their start there. Interested candidates can fill out an online application that will be channeled to a recruiter who will get back to them in seven to 10 days. Enterprise also consistently hires interns, mostly for full-time, temporary paid summer positions after sophomore or junior year. However, the company does have some part-time interns during the school year, and college credit is a possibility. The company says that an impressive internship performance definitely helps in acquiring a full-time position after graduation. All full-time employees receive a comprehensive package of benefits and the company also offers a paid time-off program to help "balance the needs of work and family life."

OUR SURVEY SAYS

Opportunities for Enterprise-ing young graduates

One graduate of Enterprise's management trainee told our survey that "as an entry-level job, [Enterprise] is a great resume builder." Other grads agreed, saying that "I can't imagine anybody getting better experience of how to run a business" and "it gave me exactly what I needed, experience!" "There is always an opportunity to advance in this company," says a corporate account manager, but entry-level employees have to meet high standards, including a 90 percent customer satisfaction rate and a 30 percent sales record (selling car insurance to renters who often already have it).

As for the nuts and bolts of the management program, "it's a ton of work," and trainees "do everything, [including] customer service, telephones, accounts receivables, trash, car wash with a brush and your arm strength, and [picking] customers up like a taxi, and 30 more [responsibilities] at least." "It is hard [work] with long hours," says another, and while "there is opportunity to advance at Enterprise … it depends on how long you can take the low quality of life, stress and long hours." "Be prepared to come home exhausted," says one contact.

And even for the lucky trainees who get promoted to management, the work remains the same. "You will do [the same work] as a management trainee, management assistant, assistant manager and branch manager. And the only things that change in those positions are responsibility and income." In terms of promotion, a former trainee and assistant manager states that "once you have been consistent with your sales you qualify to take 'The Grill.' This is an oral test that takes about six to eight hours. You have to know everything about the business … basically how to run your own branch." The same source remarked that "former [Enterprise] employees seem to have no problem getting other jobs elsewhere. In fact, many times you will be recruited for another job. Unless you have love for the business I recommend staying there until you pass your 'Grill,' then mov[ing] on."

Visit Vault at **www.vault.com** for insider company profiles, expert advice, career message boards, expert resume reviews, the Vault Job Board and more.

VAULT CAREER LIBRARY

179

Expedia, Inc.

3150 139th Avenue SE
Bellevue, WA 98005
Phone: (425) 679-7200
Fax: (425) 679-7240
www.expediainc.com

LOCATIONS

Bellevue, WA (HQ)
Boston, MA • Cleveland, OH •
Dallas, TX • Lahaina, HI • Las
Vegas, NV • Montreal, Canada •
New York, NY • San Francisco, CA
• San Jose, CA • Seattle, WA

International locations in Argentina,
Australia, Belgium, Brazil, China,
Colombia, Denmark, Egypt, Finland,
France, Germany, Greece, Hong
Kong, Italy, Ireland, Japan, Mexico,
the Netherlands, Norway, the
Philippines, Portugal, Singapore,
Spain, Sweden, Venezuela and the
UK.

THE STATS

Employer Type: Public Company
Stock Symbol: EXPE
Stock Exchange: Nasdaq
Chairman: Barry Diller
President & CEO: Dara
Khosrowshahi
2007 Employees: 7,150
2007 Revenue ($mil.): $2,665

DEPARTMENTS

Accounting/Auditing
Administrative & Support Services
Advertising/Marketing/Public
  Relations
Computers/Software
Consulting Services
Customer Service & Call Center
Executive Management
Finance/Economics
Financial Services
Hospitality/Tourism
Human Resources/Recruiting
Information Technology
Internet/E-Commerce
Operations Management
Production Management/Marketing
Project/Program Management
Purchasing
Sales
Sales-Account Management
Sales-Telemarketing
Supply Chain/Logistics
Transportation & Warehousing

KEY COMPETITORS

Orbitz Worldwide
priceline.com
Travelocity

EMPLOYMENT CONTACT

www.expediajobs.com

THE SCOOP

Planes, trains and automobiles

Going someplace? Expedia, the online provider of low-cost plane tickets, rental cars, and hotel rooms, will be happy to get you there. The company allows people to book everything from a flight or rental car to a full-blown, all-the-trimmings vacation through its sites: Expedia, Hotwire, Hotels.com, Classic Vacations, eLong (which caters to the growing demand for travel products in China) and TripAdvisor. These web sites supported the bulk of Expedia's $2.2 billion in 2006 sales. The company claims that nearly half of all Americans now book flights, hotel rooms and other travel products over the Internet, a proportion that should only rise in the future.

here do you want to go today?

Expedia got its start in 1996, as a travel service offshoot of Microsoft's MSN portal. The site proved popular, and the folks behind Windows expanded its services to the U.K. in 1998. The next year, Microsoft set Expedia (mostly) free on the open markets, raising $80 million with an IPO while keeping a large portion of its shares—not bad for a company that had yet to turn a profit.

In 2001, InterActive Corp (then USA Networks) acquired a controlling stake in the company. IAC completed the acquisition in 2002—just in time to see the market for travel products plunge after September 11th. Still, Expedia recorded a profit in 2002 and expanded into corporate travel arrangements in 2003.

The firm sprouted new wings in July 2005, when IAC decided to spin off Expedia.com and its related travel services (Hotels.com, Hotwire, TripAdvisor, Expedia Corporate Travel and Classic Vacations). This deal made Expedia, Inc. the largest online travel agency in the world.

Steady does it

In 2006, Expedia took in $2.2 billion in sales, of which $250 million was profit. Revenue increased modestly, along with the recovering travel industry. Airlines cut back on their number of flights, reducing the number of seats Expedia could sell. Nonetheless, the firm's 2006 results represented moderate increases over the previous year, with revenue growing by 5 percent and profits by 7 percent.

Visit Vault at **www.vault.com** for insider company profiles, expert advice, career message boards, expert resume reviews, the Vault Job Board and more.

VAULT CAREER LIBRARY

181

Room for growth

In January 2007 Expedia inked a deal with China's largest hotel management company, Jin Jiang International Hotel Management. Jin Jiang has 250 hotels in various cities, and the agreement gives Expedia license to fill all of them with online-happy travelers. Expedia is surely hoping to get business from China's emerging middle class, the ever-growing flow of international business travelers into China and, in the short term, visitors for the 2008 Olympics, to be held in Beijing.

In November 2007, the firm announced a partnership with eLong Inc. to launch its online travel service in China, its first foray into the Asia-Pacific region. And the next month, CEO Dara Khosrowshahi announced plans to expand its operations larger within Europe and into India in 2008. Within five to six years, he said, more than half of Expedia's revenue should come from outside the United States.

GETTING HIRED

Have a well-traveled career

Expedia maintains a careers page at www.expediajobs.com, which provides information on benefits, recruiting events and job openings. While it does attend recruiting events at colleges, it had none listed on its online calendar at press time. Jobs are searchable by keyword and location. Those interested in keeping abreast of the latest developments at the company can sign up for their talent network, which will allow company recruiters to contact individuals with positions that match skills on their resumes.

The company offers its employees medical, dental, disability and life insurance, as well as a 401(k) with company match, fitness stipend and discounts on travel (of course). The company also claims that it has "no stuffy dress code."

What an interview!

The interview process at Expedia is intense. Company insiders warn interviewees that "candidates can expect to sit through at least three interviews before receiving a job offer." A hire adds, "There are no set questions, no expected interview style and little coordination through the process." Other hires note that it can take several weeks for Expedia to get back to new hires. "Questions asked included, 'Tell me about yourself,' 'What is the best lesson you have learned in the workplace,' and 'what do you like the least about your current job?'"

OUR SURVEY SAYS

Expedia is speeding up

Insiders warn that the company is undergoing some tumultuous changes. "The company is going through the throes of moving from being an entrepreneurial, fast-growth, just-do-it company to being a big business with serious competition and a need for solid processes," explains a manager.

"Expedia is currently undergoing numerous organizational and cultural challenges. Over the past two years or so, there has been a constant trickle of turnover in leadership positions from the director level on up," explains his colleague from IT. An insider concurs: "There is much upheaval and frequent turnover. Numerous recent and long-time employees have moved on." The source concludes that "Candidates most comfortable in small, nurturing environments will not like working for Expedia, since it tends to be an aggressive, performance-based evaluator, and executives feel the need to restructure on an annual basis," sums up his associate.

Going boldly into the unknown

With all this turmoil, there's room to move up in the ranks. "Opportunities for advancement are vast but require patience, flexibility and a certain affinity for the unknown, since the company rarely sticks with a structured corporate ladder," observes a source. "Expedia Inc. is constantly opening up new offices and closing old ones, satisfying the sense of adventure in younger, unattached employees and dread and insecurity in employees striving to stay geographically put," notes a colleague.

Expedia seems to have inherited some of Microsoft's hardworking ethic. "Most employees—including management are working extremely long hours ... 60 hours per week is standard," explains a member of the IT department. "Eighty hours per week is not unusual." But fear not, potential Expedia worker bees! Though hours may be long, other departments report that their "Hours are open—no one even has core hours." The dress code is similarly relaxed. "Dress is wide open [and] Seattle weird—and people take advantage of it."

Fairmont Raffles Hotels International Inc.

Canadian Pacific Tower
100 Wellington Street West
Suite 1600, TD Center
Toronto, Ontario M5K 1B7
Canada
Phone: (416) 874-2600
Fax: (416) 874-2601
www.fairmont.com
www.raffles.com

LOCATIONS

Toronto (HQ)
Algonquin, IL • Boston, MA •
Chicago, IL • Dallas, TX • Kohala
Coast, HI • Maui, HI • Miami, FL •
New Orleans, LA • Newport Beach,
CA • San Francisco, CA • San Jose,
CA • Santa Monica, CA • Scottsdale,
AZ • Seattle, WA • Sonoma, CA •
Telluride, CO • Washington, DC •
Acapulco • Banff, Canada • Calgary •
Dubai • Edmonton • Hamburg •
Hamilton, Bermuda • Jasper, Canada
• Kenya • London • Mont Tremblant,
Canada • Monte Carlo • Montebello,
Canada • Montreal • Montreux,
Switzerland • Nairobi • Newfoundland
• Nile City, Cairo • Ottawa • Riviera
Maya, Mexico • Southampton,
Bermuda • St. Andrews, UK • St.
James, Barbados • Whistler, Canada •
Victoria, Canada • Vancouver •
Winnipeg

THE STATS

Employer Type: Private Company
CEO: William R. Fatt
President & COO: Chris J. Cahill

DEPARTMENTS

Accounting
Administration
Food & Beverage
Golf
Housekeeping
Human Resources
Kitchen
Maintenance
Public Relations
Retail
Revenue Management
Rooms
Sales
Spa
Technology

KEY COMPETITORS

Four Seasons Hotels
Starwood Hotels & Resorts
Wynn Resorts

EMPLOYMENT CONTACT

www.fairmontcareers.com
www.raffles.com/about_raffles/
careers.html
E-mail: careers@raffles.com

Fairest of them all

Fairmont Raffles Hotels represents the results of the 2006 merger of Fairmont Hotels and Raffles Hotels, two major luxury lodgings groups. The resulting company has 120 hotels in two dozen countries the world over. The company operates hotels under the Fairmont, Swissotel and Raffles names, and also manages spas and timeshare programs.

"The symbol of all the fables of the exotic East"

The Raffles Hotel is a Singaporean landmark. Four Armenian brothers founded it as a 10-room outfit in 1887, and the building expanded to its present form in 1899. Named for Thomas Stamford Raffles, the founder of Singapore, the hotel is best known as the place where the first Singapore Sling was made in the 1910s. It played host to many notables during the 1920s and 1930s, including Charlie Chaplin, Rudyard Kipling and W. Somerset Maugham, who wrote that the hotel represented "all the fables of the exotic East."

The Raffles' heyday was not to last, as its fortunes dwindled along with its supply of visitors during the Great Depression. The Raffles declared bankruptcy in 1933 and fell even farther from its former grace in World War II, when occupying Japanese forces used it as a prison camp! However, British forces restored it to a luxury hotel upon recapturing the city in 1945. Through it all, the hotel maintained its striking looks, and was used as a location for the 1955 film *The Barefoot Contessa*.

A fair hotel for a fair city

San Francisco's Fairmont hotel has a similar back-story to the Raffles. Founded by the Fair sisters in 1907, the hotel flourished in the 1910s and 1920s and hit a low period during the Great Depression. It stayed in business, and notably hosted the signing of the United Nations' charter in 1945. A few months after the UN Conference left town, Benjamin Swig purchased the hotel and hired Dorothy Draper, inventor of the American Baroque style, to renovate the place. The hotel's famed Venetian Room opened in 1947, going on to host performances by Ella Fitzgerald and Nat King Cole. In 1958, Alfred Hitchcock shot Vertigo in the Fairmont.

Modern days

The Fairmont got a second lease on life sooner than the Raffles, which wasn't renovated until 1989. The success of San Francisco's Fairmont enabled Benjamin Swig to acquire and refurbish similar grande dame hotels in other American cities.

By the 1990s, Swig's company Fairmont LP operated luxury hotels in Boston, Chicago, Dallas, New Orleans, New York and San Jose. Some of these hotels had historical pedigrees as impressive as the Fairmont itself, such as New Orleans' Grunewald and New York's Plaza Hotel.

Meanwhile, the Raffles fell into disrepair and reported low occupancy rates in the 1970s and 1980s. The government helped restore the hotel to its former glory, declaring it a national monument in 1987 and approving a massive $160 million restoration plan in 1989. Raffles Hotels and Resorts, a Singaporean firm, formed with the sole intention of renovating the hotel; it reopened the Raffles in 1991, with a number of new facilities such as restaurants, a theater and a shopping arcade. All the work, however, was completed with an eye to maintaining the hotel's original style. By 1997, the company completed the renovations of other colonial-era hotels in Phnom Penh and Siem Reap. Also that year, the company expanded into Europe, purchasing Brown's Hotel in London and the Hotel Vier Jahreszeitin in Germany.

Millennial occurences

Around the same time, in 1999, Fairmont merged with Canadian Pacific Hotels, a massive Canadian conglomerate that opened its first hotel, Mount Stephen House, in 1886. By that point, Saudi Prince Al-Waleed Bin Talal and American high-end hotelier Lewis Wolff controlled Canadian Pacific (Prince Al-Waleed is a notable investor in Four Seasons Hotels, that other Canadian hotel group). Canadian Pacific restructured in 2001, spinning off all of its assets, including Fairmont. Shortly afterward, the terrorist attacks of September 11th rocked the travel industry, and Fairmont stopped construction on new hotels and began seeking out less risky management contracts.

Fairmont scored a number of management contracts at super-luxe hotels around the world. In 2002, Fairmont won management rights to California's 75-year-old Sonoma Mission Inn & Spa, Washington, D.C.'s Monarch Hotel and Hawaii's Orchid. In 2003 and 2004, it won rights to Floridian, Mexican and Puerto Rican hotels. It even sold off some of its own properties and signed on to manage them afterwards. The company still opened some properties in super-luxurious locations, like the Fairmont Dubai, in 2002.

In the new millennium, Raffles Hotels and Resorts expanded into North America, purchasing the Californian Hotel L'Ermitage in 2000. The company rebranded all of its hotels under the Raffles name in 2002 and continued on with its pursuit of luxury. In 2004 it acquired an actual palace, Switzerland's Le Montreaux, and added luxury hotels in Beijing and Dubai in 2005.

Deal-making aplenty

In October 2005, Raffles' parent company Raffles Holdings Ltd. agreed to sell all 41 of its hotels (14 owned and 27 managed) to the Los Angeles-based real estate firm Colony Capital LLC for $1.72 billion. The two sides struck the deal in Hong Kong, at the 16th annual Hotel Investment Conference Asia Pacific (HICAP), and it was of such magnitude it won HICAP's Deal of the Year award.

Mere months later, in January 2006, Colony Capital struck a deal with former Fairmont investor Prince Al-Waleed and his company Kingdom Hotel Investments. In the deal, Kingdom purchased Fairmont Hotels & Resorts for $3.2 billion and combined its 87 hotels (28 owned and 57 managed) with Colony Capital's Raffles chain, in return for a significant stake in the new company. Instrumental in the deal was corporate raider Carl Icahn, who purchased 6.7 million Fairmont shares for $185 million in November 2005 and immediately began agitating for a deal.

With their powers combined ...

The new company kept both the Fairmont and Raffles brands, and announced plans for nine new hotels in 2007. It opened one new hotel in 2007, the Fairmont Zanzibar, in November. North American luxury seekers will be disappointed with the company's news, as most new locations will be located overseas. The company currently has plans to open 30 more hotels (either owned or managed) over the next five years, and one-third of them will be in Asia. Two of the most high-profile new establishments opening in 2008 will both be located in China, operating under management contracts: Raffles Tianjin and Fairmont Beijing.

Travel further than your food

While demand for both business and leisure travel is booming in Asia and the Middle East, North American consumers are increasingly aware of the environmental effects of everyday activities. Fairmont Raffles' green campaign involves efforts to reduce trash and water use. And as of 2007, the company's hotels will showcase seasonal, local and organic foods purchased from the regions in which they are located. The new menus have items such as organic and biodynamic wines, meats, fruits and vegetables raised using sustainable and organic farming practices and hotels will serve fair-trade tea. Some hotels even grow their own seasonings in on-site herb gardens. Visitors to Fairmont hotels can opt to take classes in wines, cooking or go shopping for local goodies with the kitchen staff.

GETTING HIRED

Have a Raffling career

Raffles' careers site, at www.raffles.com/about_raffles/careers.html, provides information for job seekers who wish to work at one of the company's hotels. Candidates are invited to submit their resumes via an online form. The HR department can be contacted via e-mail at careers@raffles.com, or by snail mail at:

Raffles Hotels & Resorts
250 North Bridge Road
#10-00 Raffles City Tower
Singapore 179101
Phone: +65 6339 8377
Fax: +65 6333 3215

Fairmont's careers site is a bit more extensive, with information on the company's programs for students and recent graduates. Jobs are searchable by location, title, keyword and position. In order to apply, job seekers must first create a profile.

Four Seasons Hotels Limited

1165 Leslie Street
Toronto, Ontario M3C 2K8
Canada
Phone: (416) 449-1750
Fax: (416) 441-4374
www.fourseasons.com

LOCATIONS

Toronto, Canada (HQ)
Atlanta, GA • Austin, TX • Boston,
MA • Chicago, IL • Dallas, TX •
Houston, TX • Hualalai, HI • Jackson
Hole, WY • Lana'i, HI • Las Vegas,
NV • Los Angeles, CA • Miami, FL •
Maui, HI • New York, NY • Palm
Beach, FL • Palo Alto, CA •
Philadelphia, PA • San Diego, CA •
San Francisco, CA • Santa Barbara,
CA • Scottsdale, AZ • Washington,
DC

International locations in Argentina,
Australia, Bahamas, Bali, Canada,
China, Costa Rica, Czech Republic,
Egypt, England, France, Hungary,
Indonesia, Ireland, Italy, Japan,
Jordan, Malaysia, Mexico, Nevis,
Portugal, Qatar, Saudi Arabia,
Singapore, Switzerland, Syria,
Taiwan, Thailand, Turkey and
Uruguay.

THE STATS

Employer Type: Private Company
Chairman & CEO: Isadore ("Issy")
 Sharp
President & COO: Kathleen P. Taylor
2007 Employees: 33,185
2006 Revenue ($mil.): $2,981

DEPARTMENTS

Accounting/Finance
Banquets
Catering
Concierge
Convention/Conference Services
Employee Restaurant
Engineering
Executive Offices
Fitness
Front Office/Reservations
Golf Services and Operations
Housekeeping
Human Resources
In-Room Dining
Kitchen
Laundry/Valet
Purchasing
Residence Clubs
Restaurants
Sales and Marketing
Security
Spa
Stewarding
Systems/MIS
Telecommunications
Uniform Room

KEY COMPETITORS

Fairmont Raffles Hotels
Hilton Hotels
Starwood Hotels & Resorts

EMPLOYMENT CONTACT

www.fourseasons.com/employment

THE SCOOP

Stay Gold

Known the world over for their impeccable service, Four Seasons hotels provide posh accommodations for well-heeled business and pleasure travelers at 70 locations in 31 countries. Not related to the restaurant of the same name in New York, or the singing group, the hotels are well known for their impeccable customer service—based on the golden rule, "do unto others as you would have them do unto you."

Four Seasons hotels were the first to have a number of perks for their guests, including hair dryers, robes, in-hotel spas and those little bottles of shampoo that have since popped up in hotel rooms the world over. Most of its properties operate under the Four Seasons name, but the company also operates a number of Regent hotels, mostly in Asia.

A hotel for all seasons

In 1961, a certain New Jersey-based doo-wop group changed its name from the Four Lovers to the Four Seasons. The same year, a young Jewish Canadian real estate investor named Isadore Sharp opened the Four Seasons Motor Hotel in an area of Toronto that was known for its prostitutes and homeless population. But the motel had one notable neighbor—the Canadian Broadcast System, or CBS, now known as CBC—and it soon became a popular watering hole for its employees.

Sharp launched a second hotel in 1963, the Inn on the Park. Located in a desolate Northern suburb of Toronto, close to a large garbage dump, it was another risk for the fledgling company. However, the hotel's commitment to detail and fine service turned the luxury hotel into a hit and eventually transformed the surrounding neighborhood. Corporate headquarters are still located nearby, although Four Seasons sold the hotel in the late 1980s.

The company went public in 1969 and soon had its eyes on one of the most competitive hotel markets in the world: London. In 1970, the firm opened an Inn on the Park in the U.K. capital, directly off of Hyde Park. Now known as the Four Seasons London, the hotel soon became one of the most profitable hotels in the world, as its small size (just 227 rooms) allowed it to spare few expenses in pursuit of luxury. In the next few years, the company was unable to expand to other European capitals, as it found no willing partners in Paris or Athens, and its construction on a Roman hotel kept being halted, as it unearthed a number of ancient ruins.

Sheraton interlude

In a change of strategy, CEO Sharp struck a deal with Sheraton in 1972 to open the Toronto Four Seasons Sheraton, a much larger endeavor than anything previous, with 1,450 rooms. After four years, Sharp sold his shares in the venture, and again set his sights on smaller upscale establishments.

The Season-ing of America

In 1976, immediately after departing his deal with Sheraton, Sharp made his first American purchase, buying the beautiful, antique Clift hotel in San Francisco. The company went on a spending spree over the next decade, buying similarly beautiful and aged properties all across America and Canada. By 1981, Four Seasons had opened venues in Vancouver, Texas, Washington, D.C., downtown Toronto and New York City, in the form of the notably beautiful Pierre, which developed into a showcase Four Seasons' property after a multimillion dollar renovation.

Debts and booms

So many purchases and renovations came at a hefty price, and Four Seasons was staggering under a large load of debt by the mid-1980s. The company tried to balance its books by selling off its real estate holdings, while continuing to manage the hotels on which they were located. The company sold $30 million worth of assets and went public again by 1985. The IPO raised enough funds to pay off the remainder of its debt, and the company boomed towards the end of the decade, as it opened a Tokyo hotel in 1988 and began eyeing other financial centers, notably Paris and Frankfurt.

During an economic downturn in the early 1990s, Four Seasons briefly became the world's largest chain of luxury hotels, purchasing the Hong Kong-based Regent International Hotels in 1992. But the worldwide recession continued into the mid-1990s and Four Seasons started struggling to turn a profit, a situation not helped by its new load of debt.

House of Sharp, house of Saud

Early in 1994, CEO Sharp hired Goldman Sachs to find a buyer for his company, but he still wanted to maintain control for at least the next three to five years. Later in the year, Sharp and Goldman Sachs found a miracle investor in Saudi Prince Al-Waleed Bin Talal, who in 2007 was ranked No. 13 on *Forbes*' list of The World's Billionaires. Prince Al-Waleed agreed to buy a 25 percent stake—enough to stabilize the firm's finances but also too small to reduce Sharp's status as primary shareholder.

Immediately after Prince Al-Waleed bought into Four Seasons, it rapidly transitioned from a business model of hotel ownership to one of hotel management. In 1997, for instance, the company sold Regent International, which it had purchased just five years earlier, to Carlson Hospitality Worldwide. Four Seasons continues to manage most of its former Regent properties, even though it no longer owns them. Not coincidentally, Four Seasons turned a profit again in 1997.

Also, Four Seasons' deep-pocketed new investor proved valuable in making some key acquisitions. In 1997, around the same time as the company sold Regent, Prince Al-Waleed largely financed the purchase of Paris' famed George V hotel. After renovations in characteristic Four Seasons' style—reducing the room-count from 300 to 245, so as to provide visitors with more luxurious accommodations—the hotel opened to acclaim in 1999.

Luxury means ... Bill Gates?

The company was not so fortunate to escape another mild recession after the attacks of September 11th, and occupancy rates in the company's American hotels hit a 15-year low point in 2003. However, the firm recovered in the next couple years, as the new era of globalization, large multinational firms and increased outsourcing led to a more active business travel market. Also, the first wave of baby boomer retirees began to travel in increasing numbers, and didn't mind laying their heads on Four Seasons' pillows. Although the firm lost $28 million during a down year in 2005, it raked in profits both in 2004 and 2006, reporting net income of $26 million and $50 million, respectively.

One of these baby boomer retirees was CEO Isadore Sharp himself, who turned 75 years old in October 2006. The next month, he led a $3.7 billion attempt to take the company private once more. This deal, which closed in early 2007, reduced Sharp to a minority shareholder for the first time since the company's founding in 1961.

The lion's share of funding for the deal came from Kingdom Hotels International, the holding company of longtime Seasons' investor Prince Al-Waleed, and Cascade Investment, a financial group backed by Microsoft co-founder Bill Gates. The prince and Gates have been rubbing shoulders since at least 2004, when the latter invited the former to dinner at his Bellevue, Wash., mansion to talk about expanding Microsoft into the Middle East.

They're going to Disney World!

In 2007, the company has gone about its regular business, with Isadore Sharp remaining chairman and CEO. In March, the Four Seasons announced plans for a new hotel near Disney World in Florida, which will open its doors in 2010. While the plans aren't finalized, Disney hopes the hotel will lure travelers to its theme park with posh accommodations, golf, shopping and probably a spa. The Four Seasons will have some competition, too—Intercontinental and the Waldorf-Astoria have both indicated interest in building near the park.

... And beyond!

The company is also looking to expand into India's booming market for hotels. While India has in recent years become a booming destination for business travelers, the number of hotels in the country hasn't kept up—the whole country has the same number of hotel rooms as New York City—leading to high prices for rooms and shortages during peak times. The new hotel will be built outside Delhi, and will include 230 rooms in addition to a golf course, a necessity for business travelers everywhere. Like the Disney World location, this hotel will be completed in 2010.

GETTING HIRED

Seek Seasonal employment

Four Season's employment site, at www.fourseasons.com/employment, provides aspiring hoteliers with information on job opportunities at the company. The Four Seasons believes in promoting from within—many of its managers have been with the company for 15 years or longer.

The hotel provides its employees with good benefits, well-fitting uniforms and an employee cafeteria. The company seeks employees to work in reservations, concierge, housekeeping, valet, uniform, in its spas and health facilities and in its restaurants and banquet halls.

The company recruits at Cornell, the CIA, the University of Denver and Northern Arizona University. It also recruits from the ranks of the National Society of Minorities in Hospitality (NSMH). If its recruiters aren't visiting a school near you, you can contact the nearest branch of the hotel to enquire about job opportunities by using the listings at www.fourseasons.com/employment/employment_contacts/index.html. Job openings can also be searched by location and function.

Visit Vault at **www.vault.com** for insider company profiles, expert advice, career message boards, expert resume reviews, the Vault Job Board and more.

VAULT CAREER LIBRARY   **193**

Global Hyatt Corporation

71 S. Wacker Drive
Chicago, IL 60606
Phone: (312) 750-1234
Fax: (312) 750-8550
www.hyatt.com

LOCATIONS

Chicago, IL (HQ)
Boston, MA
Dorado, PR
Los Angeles, CA
New York, NY
Phoenix, AZ
Washington, DC

Additional locations nationwide;
International locations in Argentina,
Azerbaijan, Australia, Brazil,
Canada, Caribbean, Chile, China,
Egypt, France, Germany, Greece,
India, Indonesia, Italy, Japan,
Jordan, Kazakhstan, Kyrgyz
Republic, Malaysia, Mexico,
Micronesia, Morocco, Nepal, New
Zealand, Oman, Phillippines, Poland,
Serbia, Singapore, South Africa,
South Korea, Switzerland, Taiwan,
Thailand, Turkey, Vietnam, Ukraine,
the UK, United Arab Emirates and
West Indies.

THE STATS

Employer Type: Private Company
Chairman: Thomas J. Pritzker
President & CEO: Mark S.
  Hoplamazian
2006 Employees: 85,000

DEPARTMENTS

Accounting/Finance/Tax
Administrative
Architecture/Design/Technical
  Services
Audio Visual
Casino/Gaming
Catering/Event Planning
Development
Facility Maintenance
Food & Beverage/Culinary
Front Office/Guest
  Services/Transportation
Golf/Health Club/Recreation/Spa
Hotel Room Operations
Housekeeping/Laundry
Human Resources
Information Systems
Legal
Loss Prevention/Safety
Property Management
Sending/Receiving
Quality Assurance/Hotel Operations
  Analysis
Revenue Management/Reservations
Sales/Marketing/Public Relations
Training Program

KEY COMPETITORS

Hilton Hotels
InterContinental Hotels
Marriott international

EMPLOYMENT CONTACT

www.explorehyatt.jobs

THE SCOOP

Hats off to Hyatt!

With over 700 hotels and resorts in 43 countries, Global Hyatt Corporation has built its fortune by accommodating the business travelers, convention-goers and upscale vacationers, who account for over half of the hotel chain's business. Hyatt runs hotels under the brands Andaz, Grand Hyatt, Hyatt, Hyatt Place, Hyatt Regency, Hyatt Resorts, Hyatt Summerfield Suites and Park Hyatt.

Redefining the hotel

The Global Hyatt Corporation started with the Hyatt House, a small motel near the Los Angeles International Airport. Local entrepreneur Hyatt R. von Dehn founded the hotel in 1954 and sold it to Jay Pritzker in 1957. The Pritzker family immigrated to America from Ukraine in the late 19th century and since the early 1900s had run a number of successful East Coast companies, mostly law and real estate firms. Jay Pritzker invited his family to help him run Hyatt on the West Coast, and by the mid-1960s the chain had airport hotels in West Coast cities like San Francisco, San Jose and Seattle.

Hyatt went public in 1967, and made industry history that year by opening the Hyatt Regency Atlanta, the world's first atrium hotel. It defied typical hotel architecture by featuring a 21-story tower lobby and grand, wide-open spaces. By the end of the 1960s, there were 13 Hyatt hotels in the U.S. In 1969 the company set up a separate company for overseas expansion, Hyatt International Corp., and opened its first international location, the Hyatt Regency Hong Kong.

A property Hyatt acquired in 1966 on Los Angeles' Sunset Strip, the Gene Autry Hotel, became famous in the 1970s for hosting major rock bands and their entourages, largely because of its proximity to clubs such as the Whisky a Go Go. Hyatt renamed it the Continental Hyatt House, but its nickname became the Continental "Riot House," for the kinds of parties that it witnessed.

The hotel was reputedly the spot of such famous moments as Led Zeppelin's Robert Plant proclaiming himself "a golden god" and the Rolling Stones' Keith Richards throwing a TV out of a window. The 2000 film *Almost Famous*, a fictionalized account of a 1970s rock band, shot a number of scenes inside the hotel. The name has since been changed to the more anodyne-sounding Hyatt West Hollywood and in April 2007 the property began a $30 million renovation.

Visit Vault at **www.vault.com** for insider company profiles, expert advice, career message boards, expert resume reviews, the Vault Job Board and more.

VAULT CAREER LIBRARY   195

Keeping it private

Jay Pritzker took the company private again in 1979, and the next year promoted his son Thomas J. Pritzker to company president. Also in 1980, the company premiered its Grand Hyatt and Park Hyatt brands, gearing Grand towards business travelers and Park on luxury vacationers. Hyatt opened its first resort location the same year, the Hyatt Regency Maui.

The company got terrible publicity in 1981, when a fourth-floor walkway collapsed in a Hyatt Regency atrium hotel in Kansas City, Mo. It killed 114 people and injured more than 200 others, at that time the deadliest structural collapse in American history. Hyatt was not the owner of the hotel in question—it was a franchise, owned by Hallmark Properties—so it wasn't found liable. Still, affected families filed over 2,000 lawsuits in the next years, and won settlements totaling $120 million.

A family affair

In the early 1990s Hyatt laid off approximately 1,000 employees and centralized many internal functions. Within four years, the company's profits increased by 50 percent. But Jay Pritzker died in 1999, setting off an epic struggle over the Pritzker family fortune. Pritzker had issued a memorandum in 1995, appointing three family members to run the business and ordering the even distribution of assets between 11 members of the family. In 2001, while the Pritzkers were parceling out the family fortune according to Jay's wishes, Jay's 16-year-old granddaughter, Liesel, sued the family for $6 billion. Her grounds for the lawsuit: she was not one of the 11 family members due to receive any money.

Shortly afterwards, the terrorist attacks of September 11th rocked the entire travel industry, and it took Hyatt more than a few hard quarters to regain profitability, never mind sort out the family drama. In March 2003 the company restructured, combining Hyatt Corp. and Hyatt International Corp. into Global Hyatt Corp. The move made financing easier and didn't involve any job eliminations.

In January 2005 Hyatt announced two news items: it settled the lawsuit, with Liesel Pritzker and her brother Robert receiving an undisclosed settlement (some news outlets reported it at $1 billion), and it completed the acquisition of the AmeriSuites hotel chain, and its 143 U.S. properties. With the lawsuit and restructuring out of the way, and armed with these valuable new assets, rumors swirled that the company might go public or that the Pritzkers might break up the company completely, but the Pritzkers stayed mum on their plans.

Hotel developments

In June 2006 Hyatt debuted its remake of the Amerisuites chain, renaming the brand Hyatt Place. Aimed at business travelers and families, Hyatt Place hotels feature lots of technological gadgets, such as a kiosk in the lobby where guests can check in, a mechanized takeout bar where guests can swipe a credit card and instantly get soups, sandwiches and other snacks, and 42-inch plasma TVs and Wi-Fi in each room.

In April 2007 Hyatt announced the creation of a new upscale brand, Andaz hotels. The first installment, in London, opened in fall 2007. And the next two, both in New York City, will open in late 2008 and late 2009. Andaz (which means "personal style" in Hindi) is designed to appeal to frequent travelers looking for a customized experience. Hyatt says that it oozes "casual luxury" yet is "uncomplicated." This translates to environmentally-friendly design (serving organic food, built out of recycled materials) and a combination of high-technology and no-frills presentation. For example, lobbies won't feature front desks; concierges will wander about with portable computers, taking care of their guests' needs.

To go with this "uncomplicated luxury," Hyatt recently developed its own brand of wine, with the help of wine-world hotshots Robert Mondavi and Andrea Immer. Known as Canvas, its beverages consist of three varietals chosen to be nonthreatening to even the most ham-fisted beer drinker—merlot, chardonnay and cabernet sauvignon. Starting July 2007, one can only buy Canvas drinks at Hyatt establishments.

What will become of Hyatt?

Since the Pritzker v. Pritzker lawsuit settled in 2005, industry analysts have been watching closely to see what will become of the Hyatt chain. After all, the lawsuit's 2001 filing interrupted the liquidation of the family's holdings, with the proceeds going to the 11 family members selected by Jay Pritzker. In late 2007, indications were that the liquidation is still under way. In August 2007, the family sold a $1 billion minority stake in Global Hyatt to a group of investors including Goldman Sachs. Thomas Pritzker, Hyatt's chairman, said the deal would allow the company "to further [its] restructuring efforts," which analysts say will eventually result in a public offering.

And then, in December 2007, the Pritzkers agreed to sell a 60 percent stake of its investing firm, Marmon Holdings, to Warren Buffett's Berkshire Hathaway for $4.5 billion. If the deal goes through, it would be Buffett's largest outside the insurance industry, and he would have the option of acquiring the remaining 40 percent of Marmon's shares over the next five or six years. Thomas Pritzker, who is also Marmon Holdings' chairman, said the deal with Buffett was "an elegant solution to a series of responsibilities that I had to the family, to the companies [and] to the management."

GETTING HIRED

Have a hospitable career

Hyatt maintains a careers page at www.explorehyatt.jobs. The site provides information on career paths, job opportunities and internships. Interns must be majoring in a field related to hospitality and must prepare for a 10-week commitment. The company also offers management-track positions. Hyatt visits students at Pomona, Florida State University, Temple University and the Culinary Institute of American. For experienced hires, jobs are searchable first by location and then by function. Job seekers must create a profile and upload their resumes in order to apply for a job at the company.

Straight to the interview

Hyatt's interview process seems to be very straightforward. "I applied online," reports one gent who worked as a waiter for Hyatt. "I went to two interviews. One with HR. One with a manager of the restaurant ... I was called and offered the job, but had to make it to the HR department to take a drug test. I started the job the next week." "I was asked if I had ever had customer service experience," added his front desk co-worker. "What did I think was good customer service, etc." "They ask if you are available on weekends and holidays, mornings and evenings," observes another.

OUR SURVEY SAYS

See yourself at a Hyatt

Several sources note that the more junior members of the hotel team generally work the less desirable shifts—nights, weekends and holidays. "It is not a cushy hotel job by any means," says one. "There are opportunities for advancement, but not usually within one's own hotel," notes a source in Michigan, "We must ask if there [are] any new jobs within available, as there are no bulletins on job openings." "The orientation went well," says another restaurant worker, "I made several friends from other departments in the first two days."

Visit Vault at **www.vault.com** for insider company profiles, expert advice, career message boards, expert resume reviews, the Vault Job Board and more.

V/\ULT CAREER LIBRARY   **199**

Harrah's Entertainment, Inc.

1 Caesars Palace Drive
Las Vegas, NV 89109
Phone: (702) 407-6000
Fax: (702) 407-6037
www.harrahs.com

LOCATIONS

Las Vegas, NV (HQ)
Atlantic City, NJ • Biloxi, MS •
Bossier City, LA • Boulder City, NV
• Cherokee, NC • Chester, PA •
Council Bluffs, IA • Elizabeth, IN •
Joliet, IL • Kansas City, MO •
Laughlin, NV • Memphis, TN •
Mound, LA • New Orleans, LA •
Phoenix, AZ • Reno, NV •
Robinsonville, MS • San Diego, CA
• St. Louis, MO • Stateline, NV

THE STATS

Employer Type: Private Company
Chairman, President & CEO:
  Gary Loveman
2006 Employees: 85,000
2006 Revenue ($mil.): $9,673.9

DEPARTMENTS

Accounting • Administration • Audit
• Casino Marketing • Casino
Operations • Communications •
Corporate • Corporate Development
• Customer Service • Entertainment
• Facilities • Finance • Food &
Beverage • Golf Operations • Hotel
Operations • Housekeeping • Human
Resources • Information Technology
• Leadout • Legal • Marine
Operations • Marketing • Operations
• Payroll/Accounts Payable •
Procurement • Race & Sports Book •
Retail • Room Service • Security •
Slot Marketing • Slot Performance •
Slots • Surveillance • Table Games •
Travel Services

KEY COMPETITORS

Las Vegas Sands
Trump Entertainment Resorts
Wynn Resorts

EMPLOYMENT CONTACT

www.harrahs.com/harrahs-
corporate/careers-home.html

THE SCOOP

Hurrah for Harrah's

Whether your vice is slot machines or Texas Hold 'Em, ponies or baccarat, Harrah's enables it. Harrah's is the largest casino company in the world, with a clutch of brands and properties like the Las Vegas mainstays Bally's, Caesar's Palace, the Flamingo, Paris Las Vegas, and Rio Hotel and Casino. In the nation's other gaming capital, Atlantic City, N.J., the company owns a Bally's, Caesar's Palace, Harrah's and Showboat. For the rest of the country, it's deuces wild: the company owns two in Reno, two near Chicago, two near New Orleans, two near St. Louis and two in Mississippi. The company is owned by the private equity firms Apollo Management and Texas Pacific Group.

Getting in on the "Reno Game"

During the Great Depression, financial reasons caused Bill Harrah to quit his undergraduate studies in mechanical engineering at UCLA. To make ends meet, he worked at the family business, which housed a hot dog stand, pool hall, shooting gallery and bingo-style game called the "Reno Game." Since bingo was illegal in California at the time, the business soon attracted the attention of California state attorneys. Bill's father grew agitated at the constant legal issues surrounding his business and sold it for $500 to his son, then 20 years old. Under Bill Harrah's leadership, annual sales improved to $50,000 in three years. However, Bill Harrah also tired of battling politicians and moved the "Reno Game" to its native city (Reno, Nev.) in 1937.

Harrah's first Reno venture was a modest bingo parlor, which failed after two months because of poor location. Harrah tried again in July 1938, and the new bingo parlor became popular due to Harrah's reputation for running an honest and fair operation. Harrah purchased Reno's Mint Club in 1946 and renovated the entire building. He added carpeting to the tiled floors, steam pipes under the front entrance sidewalks so customers wouldn't have to walk on snow or ice; he even imported Cuban cigars for high rollers.

Nearly a decade later, with the Mint Club roaringly successful, Harrah purchased the Gateway Club on Lake Tahoe's South Shore. After extensive remodeling, it opened in 1955 to profits of $1 million. Harrah arranged for plows to clear nearby roads and organized buses to bring customers from California. The Gateway helped transform

Visit Vault at **www.vault.com** for insider company profiles, expert advice, career message boards, expert resume reviews, the Vault Job Board and more.

VAULT CAREER LIBRARY   **201**

Lake Tahoe into a popular tourist destination, and served as the predecessor to today's Harrah's Lake Tahoe.

A casino mogul with ethics

Bill Harrah became a major advocate in Nevada for ethical gambling. He was instrumental in the 1955 creation of Nevada's Gaming Control Board, a regulatory agency. And in 1959, he helped establish an agency specifically targeted on eliminating crime from casino operations, called the Gaming Commission. Harrah expanded his Reno properties during the 1960s, building a 400-room hotel tower in 1962 and the Headliner Room in 1966. In the 1970s, Harrah invited big name performers, such as Bill Cosby and Sammy Davis Jr., to perform at his casinos. Harrah's made history in 1973 as the first casino company to be listed on the New York Stock Exchange. Bill Harrah passed away in 1978, just before his company acquired the rights to build and operate a hotel-casino in Atlantic City.

Harrah's new era

Soon after its founder's passing, Harrah's was acquired by the hotel chain Holiday Inns in 1980. After the deal, Holiday Inns renamed its Holiday casino as Harrah's Las Vegas. Holiday Inns changed its name to Holiday Corp. in 1985 and then sold its Holiday Inn brand and hotels in 1990 to Bass Plc (now InterContinental Hotels Group). Also in 1990, Holiday spun off the rest of its assets—including Harrah's and the hotel brands Embassy Suites, Hampton Inns, Homewood Suites and others—into a new entity called Promus Companies Inc. In 1995, Promus spun off its hotel brands and began trading publicly as Harrah's Entertainment, Inc. The company kept growing throughout the 1990s, adding an Illinois riverboat casino and launching new casinos in Kansas, Louisiana and Mississippi.

A new (or old) business plan

In the early 1990s, a Harvard Business School professor named Gary Loveman was working on an executive development program with Harrah's. He sent an unsolicited letter to then-CEO Philip Satre, suggesting the best way to build the company was through "same-store sales growth." This was basically Bill Harrah's philosophy of increasing sales at existing locations by increasing customer satisfaction, rather than opening new ones. Satre was impressed and hired Loveman as COO in December 1997. Harrah's also introduced its loyalty card program that year, which allowed customers to accumulate points and trade them in for slot machines or food. By 1999, Harrah's profits doubled.

Harrah's then embarked on a massive acquisitions streak. In 1998, the company purchased Showboat, a casino company with properties in Indiana, Atlantic City and Las Vegas. In 1999, Harrah's purchased Las Vegas' Rio Hotel and Casino, and the next year it bought Players International, with casinos in Illinois, Louisiana and Maryland. More locations followed: Arizona and Iowa in 2001, San Diego in 2002, Mississippi in 2003. These all seemed small in comparison to Harrah's nearly $10 billion buyout of Caesars Entertainment in 2005, acquiring the famous Las Vegas properties Bally's, Caesars Palace and the Flamingo, not to mention a Bally's and Caesars in Atlantic City.

Crossing the pond

In terms of acquisitions abroad, in August 2006 Harrah's acquired the U.K.'s London Clubs International and its seven British casinos for $532 million. These assets should grow in the future, as British gaming laws are currently deregulating, allowing for bigger casinos and larger payouts. Gambling analysts forecast that by 2010, the U.K. gaming industry's value will grow by 33 percent to about £11 billion, and Harrah's ownership of London Clubs will strengthen its chances for future operating licenses. London Clubs International also has sites in Egypt and South Africa.

Here, there, everywhere

Harrah's began work on two overseas casinos in 2007. The first, in Spain, will be located in Ciudad Real, a few hours from Madrid. It will include a casino under the Caesar's brand, 800-room hotel, theater, convention area and shopping, and is due to open in 2010. The second will be located in the Bahamas and boast a 1,000-room hotel, a casino and room for conventions. It should open in 2010.

But not in Macau

Unlike rivals Wynn Resorts and Las Vegas Sands Corp., Harrah's is not building a casino in Macau. It missed the last chance to win a contract in March 2006, when Wynn Resorts sold a building contract to Australian firm Publishing and Broadcasting for $900 million. This was the last contract available until at least 2009.

Visit Vault at www.vault.com for insider company profiles, expert advice, career message boards, expert resume reviews, the Vault Job Board and more.

VAULT CAREER LIBRARY   203

Harrah's is still getting in on the action in Macau, purchasing a golf course in the area in September 2007. At the time, Morgan Stanley analyst Celeste Brown told the Associated Press that Harrah's would either "turn it into a casino complex" or "sit on the land to sell later to concession holders." Michael Chen, Harrah's president of the Asia-Pacific region, said building a casino was out of the question, as "it's unlikely that any new licenses will be issued in 2009. But anything can happen in a long period of time. It wouldn't be my place to predict what would happen."

Now those are high rollers

In 2006, Harrah's revenue was $9.6 billion, with profits coming in at $500 million. Those numbers increased by 37 and 120 percent over the previous year, respectively. However, the company was weighed down by some $10 billion of debt, and analysts suggested the company being ripe for a takeover. Not surprisingly, the private equity firms Apollo Management and Texas Pacific Group offered to take Harrah's private for $17 billion in December 2006, and the company's shareholders agreed to the deal in April 2007. The deal closed in January 2008, more than a year after Harrah's first agreed to it. It was the largest ever privatization of a publicly held casino company and raised Harrah's debt to around $21 billion.

King of the Strip

If any company is well positioned to deal with such a high amount of debt, it is probably Harrah's, with its roster of profitable casinos. While preparing to go private in late 2006, the firm started talking of a massive redevelopment plan, involving the nearly 350 acres of downtown Las Vegas real estate that it owns—pretty much everything South from Harrah's Las Vegas to Paris Las Vegas, and then West to Rio Casino and Hotel.

In March 2007 the company swapped a 24-acre site to Boyd Gaming Corp. for the Barbary Coast Casino, gaining a key piece in between its Harrah's and Paris casinos. It renamed the Barbary as Bill's Gamblin' Hall, after the company's founder. Industry analysts say the company will eventually demolish Bill's and the neighboring Imperial Palace, but Harrah's hasn't yet released any specific plans.

GETTING HIRED

Take a chance on Harrah's

Harrah's careers web site, at www.harrahs.com/harrahs-corporate/careers-home.html, offers job seekers the chance to search open positions by location, keyword and job category. The site also offers some helpful interview tips and information about benefits, which include health and dental insurance, a 401(k) and internship programs for undergrads and MBA students.

Harrah's undergrad program includes internships in hotel, food and beverage, and IT, which are run by the HR department at a specific resort. There are also opportunities for seasonal employment over school vacations. Grad students are welcome to apply for internships after their first year. Job openings can be searched by function, location and a number of other criteria. In order to apply, job seekers must first create a profile.

Visit Vault at **www.vault.com** for insider company profiles, expert advice,
career message boards, expert resume reviews, the Vault Job Board and more.

VAULT CAREER LIBRARY   205

Hertz Global Holdings, Inc.

225 Brae Boulevard
Park Ridge, NJ 07656
Phone: (201) 307-2000
Fax: (201) 307-2644
www.hertz.com

LOCATIONS

Park Ridge, NJ (HQ)

International locations in Austria, Belgium, France, Germany, Ireland, Switzerland and the UK.

THE STATS

Employer Type: Public Company
Stock Symbol: HTZ
Stock Exchange: NYSE
Chairman & CEO: Mark P. Frissora
2007 Employees: 29,350
2007 Revenue ($mil.): $8,686

DEPARTMENTS

Accounting and Finance • Administration/Clerical • Customer Service • Driving • eBusiness Development • eBusiness Technology • Fleet Operations • Human Resources • Information Technology • Insurance • Maintenance • Operations Management • Mechanic • Pricing • Safety • Sales • Vehicle Cleaning & Service

KEY COMPETITORS

Avis Budget
Enterprise Rent-A-Car
United Rentals

EMPLOYMENT CONTACT

www.hertz.jobs

THE SCOOP

Rolling along

Hertz is a major player in the car-rental business, leading the U.S. airport rental industry and ranking only behind rival Enterprise in non-airport U.S. rentals. The company also has a worldwide presence, with outposts in 145 countries. Hertz rents out cars from a number of different collections, including a Green Collection of gas-sipping hybrids, a Fun Collection of convertibles and SUVs and, for those wanting the high life at a daily rate, a Prestige Collection of luxury cars. The company also rents out equipment for construction jobs, such as trailers, portable generators, pumps, cranes and concrete mixers. The majority of Hertz's 2007 revenue came from car rentals, while equipment rentals made up the remainder.

Any rental car you want, as long as it's black

In 1918, a 22-year old car salesman named Walter Jacobs opened a small car rental outfit with a fleet of 12 Ford Model Ts. By 1923, his operation pulled down about $1 million in sales annually, at which point Jacobs sold a majority stake to John Hertz, head of the Yellow Cab and Yellow Truck Company. General Motors (GMC) acquired the rental business in 1926, although Jacobs and Hertz continued to operate it.

At Midway, near Chicago, Hertz opened its first airport location in 1932, at the beginning of the passenger air travel era. The next year, Hertz debuted its first inter-city "rent it here/leave it there" plan. World War II hindered Hertz's expansion, but the company boomed with the growth of suburban car culture in the 1950s.

Who owned Hertz?

Hertz changed owners a number of other times, starting in 1953, when GMC sold it to another rental firm, Omnibus, which duly adopted the Hertz name and went public in 1954. In 1967, Hertz became a subsidiary of media conglomerate RCA (then the parent company of NBC), and in 1985 RCA sold it to UAL, the parent company of American Airlines. An investment group headed by Hertz executives and Ford Motor Co. purchased Hertz from UAL in 1987. Ford gained control of the firm in 1994 and issued some of its stock in 1997. Ford bought back all Hertz stock in 2001 and then sold the entire company to a private equity consortium in 2005, for a whopping $15 billion.

Visit Vault at **www.vault.com** for insider company profiles, expert advice, career message boards, expert resume reviews, the Vault Job Board and more.

VAULT CAREER LIBRARY   207

A cool reception

The company went public again in 2006, but its IPO failed to meet the expectations of its new private equity owners. While the company was expected to let go of shares at $16 to $18 apiece, it ended up selling 28 percent of its stock for a mere $15 per share. As such, the sale raised $1.32 billion for the firm, a less than satisfactory total when compared to the company's buyout debts of $12 billion. Despite the lackluster turnout for the company's IPO, Hertz had a perfectly respectable first year under its new boss. Revenue for 2006 came in at $6.3 billion, and profits at $115 million.

Employees are out ...

Stockholders and analysts, however, are a notoriously implacable breed. In order to fatten the company's profit margins (not to mention its stock price), Hertz announced in January 2007 that it would cut 200 management jobs at its Park Ridge, N.J., headquarters and its Oklahoma City service center. The next month, in February, 2007, Hertz announced 1,350 more job cuts, primarily in U.S. car rental outlets. This workforce reduction was expected to save the car rental company $125 million.

Hertz continued to roll back its employment numbers in June 2007, cutting 480 more jobs, as well as "financial and reservations-related" jobs in Oklahoma City, for a total of $24 million in savings. In September 2007, the company stated in a quarterly report that it expects to "implement other efficiency initiatives" in 2008, including reductions in European operations to save approximately $50 million. In February 2008, Hertz confirmed that it would cut some jobs over the course of the year, although it didn't specify the number of layoffs or when they would occur.

... Acquisitions are in

In July 2007, Hertz enlarged its U.K. footprint with the purchase of Autotravel, a former Hertz licensee. Autotravel is located in the northwestern part of England, near Manchester and relatively close to the Liverpool airport. The acquisition will increase Hertz's locations in England by around 25 percent.

GETTING HIRED

Put wheels on your career

Hertz's careers site can be reached by going to www.hertz.jobs. The site provides all manner of information for those seeking a career with the company. Its job offerings are divided into four divisions: rent-a-car local edition (which specializes in renting cars in the non-travel arena), corporate, financial, data and reservations. Jobs are searchable by keyword and location, among other metrics. While trainees' first jobs will be in their local area, subsequent career advancements typically require a willingness to move. Employee benefits include health, dental and life insurance, flexible spending accounts, vacation, savings bonds and tuition reimbursements for eligible hires.

Hertz also offers paid internships for college students. The company recruits at many colleges across the country, including most state schools. At press time, Hertz was recruiting at Suffolk University, Marist University, Loyola College, Georgia Southern University, Lamar University and Sonoma State University, among others.

OUR SURVEY SAYS

Putting their Hertz into their work

Sources report that Hertz's hiring process is fairly relaxed. "The interview was very sales and customer service oriented. 'Describe a time when you had to deal with an irate customer.' Other than that it is very corporate," says one management trainee. "Only one interview with the general manager," says another. "Hertz/Enterprise and many other rental companies are renowned for their management training programs," notes one hire enrolled in the program. Another management trainee adds, "My duties were varied, and I had to adjust to each situation, from answering the ringing phones, renting cars to customers, picking up and dropping off customers at hotels and auto repair shops, getting oil changes for cars, and … vacuuming and washing cars by hand."

A contact reports that most branches work "long hours. Trainees 50 hours per week. But managers, another story. If you're lucky 50, [if not] be ready to put in 11- to 12-hour days, working close to 60 hours per week. Let's not forget washing cars and dealing with stolen cars." Another respondent concurs: "The days were stressful and fast paced." Another hire, evidently from a less busy office, adds, "The hours were

Visit Vault at **www.vault.com** for insider company profiles, expert advice,
career message boards, expert resume reviews, the Vault Job Board and more.

VAULT CAREER LIBRARY   **209**

not bad. However, everyone had to work on some Saturdays." An insider notes that "Opportunities for advancement definitely depend on the region," and another observes that "Employee morale has suffered from [recent] layoffs." "Cost-cutting has been difficult for everyone," a co-worker agrees.

Hilton Hotels Corporation

9336 Civic Center Drive
Beverly Hills, CA 90210
Phone: (310) 278-4321
Fax: (310) 205-7678
www.hiltonworldwide.com

LOCATIONS

Beverly Hills, CA (HQ)

International locations in Africa,
Asia, Europe and the Middle East.

THE STATS

Employer Type: Private Company
Co-Chairman: Stephen Bollenbach
Co-Chairman: William Barron Hilton
President & CEO: Christopher
  Nassetta
2006 Employees: 105,000
2006 Revenue ($mil.): $8,162

DEPARTMENTS

Accounting/Finance/Tax •
Administrative & Clerical •
Architecture • Brand Management •
Call Center • Catering • Culinary •
Design & Construction • Food &
Beverage • Franchise Development •
Front Office/Guest Services • Guest
Assistance/Customer Service • Hotel
Operations/Management •
Housekeeping/Laundry • Human
Resources/Training • Information
Technology • Legal • Management
Trainee • Marketing • Project
Management • Property
Operations/Maintenance • Purchasing
• Real Estate • Recreation/Spa •
Retail • Revenue Management • Risk
Management • Sales/Event Services
• Security

KEY COMPETITORS

Choice Hotels
InterContinental Hotels
Starwood Hotels & Resorts

EMPLOYMENT CONTACT

hiltonworldwide1.hilton.com/en_US/
ww/people/employment.do

THE SCOOP

Conrad's clan

Hilton Hotels Corp. operates over 3,000 hotels worldwide, including the 1,302 hotels gained from the company's blockbuster 1999 acquisition of Promus Hotel Corporation for $3.7 billion. It operates in about 80 countries under the brands Conrad Hotels, Doubletree Hotels, Embassy Suites, Hampton Inn, Homewood Suites and, of course, Hilton. The firm primarily operates in the mid-market segment, although its Conrad and Hilton hotels offer upscale full-service lodging and its Embassy Suite chain was the first in the industry to offer upscale all-suite hotels. In July 2007, the private equity firm The Blackstone Group acquired Hilton for $26 billion, the largest deal in hotel industry history.

Taking the Hilton name worldwide

In 1919, Conrad Hilton bought his first hotel in Cisco, Texas, a region then being flooded by out-of-town oil prospectors who needed a place to sleep. Hilton's hotel was successful enough for him to purchase two other hotels in the area by 1920 and to open a high-rise hotel in El Paso, the Plaza Hotel, in 1925. The company suffered during the Great Depression, and Hilton sold off some properties to raise funds, while maintaining their management.

The company recovered in the 1940s, opening new hotels on the West Coast and purchasing New York City's Plaza and Roosevelt hotels in 1943 to become the country's first "coast-to-coast" hotel chain. In 1946, Hilton Hotels Corp. went public on the New York Stock Exchange and in 1949, Hilton purchased a majority stake in New York's Waldorf-Astoria Hotel. Also in 1949, Hilton opened The Caribe Hilton hotel in Puerto Rico, beginning the operations of the Hilton International Company. Between 1953 and 1966, Hilton International built 16 luxury hotels abroad.

In 1953 Hilton opened its first European hotel, Madrid's Castellana Hilton. The next year, Hilton became the largest hotel firm in the world with the $111 million purchase of Texas-based Statler Hotel Co. (it was also the largest real estate transaction in history, at the time). Hilton became an early proponent of airport hotels, opening the San Francisco Airport Hilton in 1959. In the mid-1960s, the company realized it could capitalize on its prestigious name and began offering franchises; it also spun off Hilton International as a separate company, in 1964.

Hilton: the next generation

Conrad Hilton passed away in 1979, after a decade in which his company entered Asia and Latin America (with The Hilton Singapore and The Hilton Caracas) and became sole owner of the Waldorf-Astoria. In honor of its founder, the company launched the Conrad luxury brand of hotels in 1985. In 1987, Hilton unveiled its customer-friendly frequent guest reward program, Hilton HHonors. By 1994, Hilton added the option of exchanging HHonors points for airline frequent flyer miles, called HHonors Reward Exchange. In 1995, Hilton launched its web site, www.hilton.com.

Bollenbach's symphony of acquisitions

In 1996, the company's 50th year as a publicly listed company, Hilton tapped Stephen Bollenbach to be its new chief—he was the first non-family member to occupy the corner office. Mere months after Bollenbach's appointment, Hilton acquired Bally Entertainment for more than $2 billion, making Hilton the world's largest gaming (i.e., casino) company. In 1998, Hilton spun off its gaming assets as Park Place Entertainment. (Park Place bought Caesars World Inc. in 2000, renaming itself Caesars Entertainment, and it was acquired by Harrah's, now the world's largest gaming concern, in 2005.)

Bollenbach oversaw another massive purchase in 1999, acquiring Promus Hotels for $3.7 billion. Promus was a 10-year-old company at the time, formed as a Holiday Inn spin-off in 1989. At the time of its acquisition by Hilton, Promus operated approximately 2,000 properties worldwide in the Doubletree Suites, Embassy Suites and Hampton Inn chains. In May 2004, Hilton's board of directors appointed Bollenbach as its co-chairman, alongside Conrad's son Barron Hilton.

Franchise power!

The hospitality industry faltered in the wake of the terrorist attacks of September 2001, and in third quarter 2001, Hilton's earnings and stock price each fell by about 60 percent. CEO Bollenbach claimed the chain would prevail in 2002, and it broke even as early as January 2002, when it reported a quarterly profit of $4 million. However, Hilton's earnings revival fell off the mark during early 2003, and the company lowered its forecast for the entire year in April. As reasons for the poor performance, Bollenbach cited the conflict in Iraq, a decline in business travel, the Asian SARS breakout and a weak U.S. economy.

Visit Vault at **www.vault.com** for insider company profiles, expert advice, career message boards, expert resume reviews, the Vault Job Board and more.

VAULT CAREER LIBRARY   213

The company has since boosted profits by opening more franchise locations and selling off wholly owned properties. In 2004, the company opened a grand total of 4,775 new rooms, in the form of two Doubletrees, two Embassy Suites, 14 new Hampton Inns, 13 Hilton Gardens, three Hiltons and two Homewood Suites. The next year, the company sold off 11 hotels for $416 million, and announced plans to move more assets at "attractive" market prices.

A Hilton reunion

In February 2006, Hilton completed a reunion more than 40 years in the making, purchasing Hilton International from Hilton Group plc for £3.3 billion. Hilton Hotels Corp. and Hilton International had operated as separate companies since a 1964 spin-off. The acquisition brought every Hilton brand back under the control of Hilton Hotels Corp.—some 2,800 hotels in 80 countries worldwide.

Peacock Alley

In January 2006, Hilton announced the creation of a new brand, using the name of its flagship New York City hotel: the Waldorf-Astoria Collection. The company bestowed the lofty title on three other hotels in 2006: the Arizona Biltmore Resort & Spa in Phoenix, the Grand Wailea Resort Hotel & Spa in Maui and La Quinta Resort & Club in Southern California.

The company is adding other Waldorfs through acquisitions and through renovations of existing properties. In December 2006, the collection acquired its first international hotel, Saudi Arabia's Qasr Al Sharq hotel. And Hilton is currently developing two other Waldorfs, in Beverly Hills and Bonnet Creek, Fla. (close to Disney World). For more information, one can visit the Waldorf-Astoria Collection's very own web site, at www.waldorfastoriacollection.com.

What next, Louis Vuitton sheets?

Not only is Hilton using the Waldorf-Astoria name to promote its hotels, in July 2007 the company announced a partnership with luxury conglomerate LVMH, which will stock Hilton's spas with its Acqua di Parma and Guerlain brands. Guerlain will brand the spa at Waldorf-Astoria Collection properties, while Acqua di Parma will lend its name to the spas at Hilton's Conrad brand. The company hopes to roll out 135 spas in its hotels by 2009.

Blackstone steps in

Hilton made another major announcement in July 2007, drawing back the curtain on an industry record $26 billion deal with The Blackstone Group to privatize Hilton's operations. The deal included assumption of Hilton's $7.5 billion debt and Bollenbach resigned in October 2007, when the deal was completed. Bollenbach will continue to co-chair Hilton's board of directors, alongside Barron Hilton, until 2010, and then provide consultation services until 2012. If the new boss is any indication, Hilton's future will be a continuation of its recent luxurious ways. In October 2007, shortly after wrapping up the deal, Blackstone appointed Bollenbach's replacement: Christopher Nassetta, former CEO of Host Hotels and Resorts, the largest luxury hotel chain in the world.

Current developments

In the future, the company plans to develop 50 more properties in its Conrad chain by 2010, which would make Conrad one of the largest luxury hotel brands in the world. Hilton is also developing properties in Macau, the burgeoning "Asian Las Vegas" where so many hotel and gaming companies are now building new attractions. (It has been a hot destination for development since the Chinese government awarded more contracts to Western firms for hotels and casinos.) The Las Vegas Sands Corp. owns the Sands Macau resort and casino, and is currently developing the Venetian Macau, and Hilton is one of the seven hotel companies providing these properties with lodging services.

GETTING HIRED

I want to be a Hilton (employee)

Hilton lists job openings on its main career site, hiltonworldwide1.hilton.com/en_US/ww/people/employment/us.do. Job openings are searchable by department and location. Job seekers are also encouraged to contact their local Hilton hotel for nonmanagement positions; since many are franchises, they usually conduct their own hiring. Benefits for workers in the U.S. include medical, dental and vision coverage, 401(k), credit union and paid vacation.

Visit Vault at **www.vault.com** for insider company profiles, expert advice, career message boards, expert resume reviews, the Vault Job Board and more.

VAULT CAREER LIBRARY

215

One for the students

Hilton sponsors an intensive full-time management training program, dubbed "Leader-In-Training," that typically lasts for six to eight months and offers competitive entry-level management salary. Potential candidates should be recent college graduates, preferably with a degree in the hospitality industry and a GPA of 2.8 or higher. The first half of the program offers rotations at various hotels; the second half specializes in a particular area of service. More information about Leader-In-Training can be found at www.hiltoncampus.com. For college undergrads between their junior and senior years, Hilton also offers summer internships; more information is posted on www.hiltoncampus.com.

OUR SURVEY SAYS

A large company with small benefits

"The people that I worked for and with [at Hilton] were excellent," says one contact, "[From] the general manager on down, [people] were excellent at their jobs and they loved to train and work with everyone." Another source notes that the interview process involved meeting with a "very nice" manager who had "a smile from cheek to cheek almost the whole time of the interview, but was very to the point and asked very efficient questions."

Upon closer inspection, not everything is so rosy at Hilton. "Because our hotel property is so large," says one, "it is very hard to be 'personal' to each and every guest. There are those who stay on the job for eons and seem to be just doing their job as to 'just get by.'" And it's hard to provide personal service when an operation is "run by minimum staffing," with "a lot of cuts in servicing the guests."

Also, all respondents had issues with Hilton's benefits. "Salary was very low," says one insider, continuing, "since I worked for a franchise, I had to wait six months before receiving any benefits, including vacation." Another says that, although "after six months of employment, as promised, I was given a 10 percent raise from when I started ... I did get a medical with a drug plan after three months of employment as stated in the contract. But [I] will have to wait until I hit the one year mark to be eligible for any sick paid [off-days] or paid vacation days."

InterContinental Hotels Group PLC

67 Alma Road
Windsor SL4 3HD
United Kingdom
Phone: +44-1753-410-100
Fax: +44-1753-410-101
www.ihgplc.com

LOCATIONS

Windsor, UK (HQ)
Atlanta, GA • Dallas, TX • Los
Angeles, CA • Miami, FL • Phoenix,
AZ • Richmond, VA • Sacramento,
CA • Washington, DC

International locations in American
Samoa, Australia, Austria, Azerbaijan,
Bahrain, Belgium, Cambodia, Canada,
China, Cyprus, the Czech Republic,
Egypt, Eritrea, Fiji, French Polynesia,
Gabon, Germany, Greece, Guam,
Hungary, India, Indonesia, Ireland,
Israel, Italy, Japan, Jordan, Kenya,
Korea, Kuwait, Lebanon, London
Malaysia,, Malta, Morocco, Nepal,
The Netherlands, New Zealand, the
Northern Mariana Islands, Oman,
Papua New Guinea, the Philippines,
Poland, Puerto Rico, Qatar, Romania,
Russia, Saudi Arabia, Scotland,
Singapore, Slovakia, Spain,
Switzerland, Taiwan, Thailand,
Turkey, the United Arab Emirates,
Uzbekistan, Vietnam, Wales, Yemen
and Zambia.

THE STATS

Employer Type: Public Company
Stock Symbol: IHG
Stock Exchange: London
Chairman: David Webster
CEO: Andrew Cosslett
2007 Employees: 11,456
2007 Revenue (£mil.): £923

DEPARTMENTS

Administration • Business Service
Center • Central Reservations •
Engineering • Executive/Corporate •
Finance & Business Support • Food
& Beverage • Front Office •
Internships • Housekeeping • Human
Resources • Information Technology
• Legal • Quality • Sales & Marketing
• Security • Spa/Recreation

KEY COMPETITORS

Accor
Marriott International
Starwood Hotels & Resorts

EMPLOYMENT CONTACT

www.ihgplc.com/index.asp?
pageid=7

THE SCOOP

Sit down and stay awhile

The InterContinental Hotels Group has the industry's largest number of rooms—some 590,000—in nearly 4,000 locations worldwide. Its brands include Holiday Inn, Intercontinental, Indigo, Candlewood Suites and Crowne Plaza. Although its headquarters are in the U.K., the majority of InterContinental's hotel rooms are located in the U.S.

From suds to lodgings

The InterContinental Hotels Group traces its origins back to a pub William Bass established in 1777. His beers—especially his pale ale—caught on, and in the 1800s, Napoleon requested the establishment of a Bass brewery in France. A few decades later, in 1876, Bass obtained the first trademark issued in Britain. In the following decades, Bass beer made its way to Antarctica with Ernest Shackleton's expedition and partway across the Atlantic on the Titanic.

Along the way, Bass became the biggest brewing company in England, and, as of the 1880s boasted a 145-acre brewery, one the largest in the world. The Bass family became noted Conservative politicians in the 19th century, with Michael Thomas Bass serving in Parliament for 33 years and his son, Michael A. Bass (later dubbed Lord Burton), serving for 21 years. Other Bass executives joined this so-called "beerage" of politically right-leaning, upper-class alcohol tycoons, including John Gretton Jr., a longtime company chairman who served as a Conservative MP from 1895 to 1943. All of these executives ran Bass with a characteristically tradition-minded approach, and the company steadily lost market share in the 20th century to more aggressively marketed and managed upstarts.

By the turn of the 1960s, Sir James Grigg became company chairman. A former cabinet minister for Winston Churchill, the 70-year-old Grigg appeared to be an all-too-typical Bass executive, but he brought the company into the modern brewing age, merging it with the upstart Mitchells & Butler in 1961. The firm undertook another major merger in 1967, with Charrington United Breweries (the makers of Canada Dry), but it retained much of its conservative management policies, such as its refusal to advertise to a younger demographic, promoting its family identity instead.

Visit Vault at www.vault.com for insider company profiles, expert advice, career message boards, expert resume reviews, the Vault Job Board and more.

VAULT CAREER LIBRARY   219

Sir Ian's Holiday

The firm named a new chairman and CEO in 1987—Sir Ian Prosser, who had worked at the company since 1969, when he answered a national newspaper advertisement for employment opportunities. Almost immediately afterwards, Prosser led a diversification effort, purchasing eight European Holiday Inn hotels for £152 million in May 1987. Apparently, he liked the investment, and the company spent £2.23 billion in 1989, purchasing much the rest of Holiday Inn.

The purchase was not as unlikely as it seems, due to the nature of the British beer industry. Brewers in the U.K. often owned their own "public houses," or "pubs," at which they would peddle their wares. This would be like Anheuser-Busch owning hundreds of bars in each of the 50 U.S. states (for obvious logistical reasons, the industry has not developed this way in America). For centuries, Bass had a large pub and hotel business; it also ran gambling establishments, which it divested in the late 1990s.

In the Holiday Inn deal, Bass gained rights to the Holiday Inn name, 55 wholly-owned establishments and the rights to over 1,400 franchises. The rest of Holiday Inn's former properties—Embassy Suites, Hampton Inns, Homewood Suites and more—were spun off to shareholders as Promus Companies Inc. (Hilton Hotels Corp. purchased Promus for $3.7 billion in 1999.)

Renovating an American classic, British-style

Holiday Inn was the brainchild of Kemmons Wilson, who brought clean, standardized motel rooms to America's brand-new highways under a single, recognizable, soon-to-be iconic brand. Holiday Inn's first location opened near Memphis in 1952, and within six years, 50 Inns were open for business. In 1972, the chain had achieved an unnerving ubiquity, as a new Holiday Inn opened every three days.

Bass poured a bunch of money into its new purchase, renovating the entire chain in the early 1990s for $1 billion, launching a budget brand called Holiday Inn Express in 1991 and expanding its upscale Crowne Plaza brand. Prosser also took Holiday Inns worldwide; by 1995, over 60 countries could boast billboards with the distinctive green and gold logo. The division's profits weren't up to snuff, however, and in 1992 Bass sued Promus, alleging it had intentionally withheld financial information during the acquisition discussions. Promus settled the lawsuit for $49 million in 1995.

To beer or not to beer

Bass agreed to merge with beverage rival Carlsberg-Tetley for £200 million in 1996; the deal would have made Bass the No. 1 brewer in the U.K. However, the British government intervened in mid-1997, blocking the merger for antitrust reasons. Bass reversed course and sold off a number of businesses in 1997 and 1998, which raised a total of $1.3 billion. Within a few years, Bass would sell off its brewery division entirely.

In March 1998, Bass spent $1.8 billion on the acquisition of InterContinental Hotels and Resorts. InterContinental dated back to 1946, when Pan American Airways founded the company to provide luxurious lodgings for its international travelers. Its owner in 1998 was the Saison Group of Japan, a major retailer, which put the group up for auction. Bass overcame fierce opposition to win the bid (its closest competition was Marriott).

In 1999, Bass launched a £900 million, five-year expansion plan, with the goal of quadrupling InterContinental's hotel facilities within two years. By 2000, Bass was the world's second-largest hotel group, and its brewing business seemed to be stuck in a downward spiral. In June 2000, the company cut the cord with over 100 years of history, selling Bass Brewers to European beverage giant Interbrew S.A. for £2.3 billion.

Suffering from "Incontinence"

Later that year, in September 2000, Sir Ian Prosser resigned as CEO while retaining his chairman status. Tim Clarke, his replacement as CEO, chose a new name for the company in 2001 (it could no longer be called Bass, for obvious reasons). After conducting an employee contest to come up with a new title, Clarke selected Six Continents. However, as noted at the time by London's *Telegraph*, "the company has already been dubbed 'Incontinence' by gleeful investors and anlysts."

The corporate breakup wasn't such a laughing matter to others, including executives at the U.K. grocery firm Sainsbury's, which named Ian Prosser its chairman-elect in February 2004. Shareholders revolted, one of whom was also a prominent former Bass investor, and accused Prosser of "ripping the heart out" of Bass/Six Continents. Amid further controversy, Prosser decided not to join Sainsbury's board.

Enter InterContinental

Six Continents was not fated to last very long, as by 2002 the firm's pubs and restaurants business was struggling in comparison to its hotels. Industry pundits wondered aloud why Britain seemed to be drinking less and less and advised investors to stay away from Six Continents, which had somehow managed (or mismanaged) to divest one of the most historic and successful brewing brands in beer brewing.

By February 2003, the company was looking seriously at the demerger that would result in InterContinental Hotels Group and Mitchells & Butlers PLC (as the pubs and restaurant business would be known). There was one problem: projected demerger costs would set shareholders back about £109 million. Factored into these costs were various executive bonuses and relocation fees, which Sainsbury's executives surely had in mind when they lobbied against Ian Prosser's appointment as that company's chairman.

The demerger was completed by April 2003, with former CFO Richard North taking over as InterContinental's initial CEO. He didn't last long in the job, stepping down in September 2004 by "mutual agreement," with InterContinental's board thanking him for his work "during its early life as a new and separate company." The management of the firm, befitting such a new company, was now almost entirely new itself. Chairman David Webster, who had joined the company's board in the midst of the demerger, took over for North as interim CEO. In February 2005 Webster appointed another outsider, former Cadbury Schweppes exec Andrew Cosslett, to the permanent post.

Hotels going Indigo

One of Webster's first moves as chairman was the premier of the Hotel Indigo line of hotels in late 2004. The Indigo hotels are based on the boutique hotel model, cheap but chic: the Target of the hotel world, sort of. They are located in central city locations, have cocktail lounges to draw guests and locals, rooms that are small but cozy, some extras such as a CD player and Internet, but no frills—no robes, no mini-bar, no pay-per-view and no DVD player.

The company's thinking for this line is evidenced by its name. It features a bold blue design, which SVP Kirk Kinsell said at the time was designed to mark "a departure from 'hotel-beige' properties," which he chalks up to "industry sameness and lack of a brand story." Again, like Target, the hotel's low cost goes with avant-garde design. Instead of wall-to-wall carpeting, for instance, its rooms feature hardwood floors.

Instead of bland, cookie-cutter paintings, the rooms feature colorful photo murals, blown up to fill entire walls. If this sounds a bit extreme, IHG institutes a regular change-over in each room's décor to keep a fresh feel in the hotel.

Bridging the InterContinental divide

Hotel Indigo is just one example of InterContinental overhauling its business. Since CEO Andrew Cosslett took over in 2005, he has traveled the globe looking for ways to invigorate the world's biggest provider of rooms. First on the agenda has been de-corporatizing the feel of its hotels, after shuttling through three different corporate parent entities in the last five years. This has meant training staff to be knowledgeable about their area, so that employees can offer local tips to business travelers all over the world. Also, Cosslett sympathizes with anyone who's ever been unhappy with rigid check-in procedures, removing InterContinental's traditional concierge lecterns in favor of a regular old desk.

Happy hoteliers

Financial returns have been pleasing since Cosslett became CEO, with annual revenue for 2005 clocking in at $1.4 billion, with $207 million in profits. The next year, IHG did even better business as revenue increased by 14 percent to $1.6 billion and profits more than doubled to $538 million.

The company's profits have been increasing so dramatically partly because global leisure travel is increasing, but also because InterContinental has been selling off its hotel properties, transitioning from a hotel owner to a hotel franchiser. From the 2003 formation of the company to 2007, the chain shed 174 properties for some $5 billion, with 25 left to sell off.

The franchise model has many advantages over directly owning the hotels— InterContinental is insulated from some of the vagaries of the market, while keeping fatter profit margins. It doesn't signal InterContinental's retreat from the hotel market, though—the company is planning on aggressively expanding its number of hotel rooms, opening hotels at the rate of one per day in June 2007. InterContinental hopes to add as many as 60,000 rooms by the end of 2008.

Road trips for a cooler planet

If cushy beds are a fading trend in the hotel industry (if only because everyone else already has them), then the move to environmental friendliness is hotter than a black

Visit Vault at www.vault.com for insider company profiles, expert advice, career message boards, expert resume reviews, the Vault Job Board and more.

VAULT CAREER LIBRARY   223

Prius in the sun in August. In 2007, management announced that it would be swapping out energy-hogging incandescent lights for more efficient florescent models. The company announced the change during an executive road trip, where four executives toured hotels in North America. Their car? A hybrid SUV, of course.

GETTING HIRED

Give your career some InterContinental flare

The careers site of the InterContinental Hotels Group (www.ihgplc.com/ index.asp?pageid = 7) provides information for hopeful hoteliers. Job applicants must select from three major regions, and then from corporate or hotel positions. Jobs are searchable by function, location and keyword.

If you're a management type hoping to break into InterContinental, be aware that the company takes its executive training very seriously. In 2005 it instituted a new "senior leadership program" that includes classroom teaching sessions and on-the-job training. Furthermore, the training differs for every one of the company's brands, as it insists on keeping brands separate to ensure the quality of each.

American CEO Tom Murray told *Commercial Property News* in 2005 that "We want our managers to be passionate brand champions. We want their careers, really, to be pegged to the success of the brand." Wherefore this brand emphasis? It's all part of IHG's attempt to reinvigorate its many properties. "We used to have the management of Crowne Plaza and InterContinental Hotels in one group," said Murray, "and I think InterContinental got more of the attention. Crowne Plaza suffered for it."

Intrawest ULC

200 Burrard Street, Ste. 800
Vancouver, British Columbia V6C 3L6
Canada
Phone: (604) 669-9777
Fax: (604) 669-0605
www.intrawest.com

LOCATIONS

Vancouver, Canada (HQ)
Anaheim, AZ • Ball Harbour, FL •
Bluffton, SC • Buckeye, AZ •
Camdenton, MO • Cooper, CO •
Corpus Christi, TX • Denver, CO •
Destin, FL • Dillon, CO • Florida Keys,
FL • Golden, CO • Keystone, CO • La
Jolla, CA • La Quinta, CA • Lake Las
Vegas, NV • Lake Placid, NY •
Mammoth Lakes, CA • Napa Valley,
CA • North Lake Tahoe, CA •
Orlando, FL • Palm Desert, CA •
Panama City, FL • Paradise Valley, AZ
• Pensacola, FL • Phoenix, AZ • Reno,
NV • San Diego, CA • Sandestin, FL •
Scottsdale, AZ • Silverthorne, CO •
Snowmass, CO • Snowshoe, WV •
Solitude, UT • Squaw Valley, CA •
Stowe, VT • Stratton, VT • Tampa,
FL • Temecula, CA • Tonopalo, CA •
Telluride, CO • Vernon, NJ • West
Palm Beach, FL • Winter Park, CO •
Hot Springs, VA

Canmore, Canada • Collingwood,
Canada • Kelowna, Canada •
Montreal • Panorama, Canada •
Toronto • Tremblant, Canada •
Vernon, Canada • Whistler, Canada

International locations in Africa,
China, the Caribbean, Europe and
Mexico.

THE STATS

Employer Type: Private Company
Interim CEO: Alex V. Wasilov
2007 Employees: 22,000

DEPARTMENTS

Attraction/Amusement • Business
Development • Call Center •
Community/Village Operations •
Corporate • Finance/Accounting •
Food & Beverage • General
Application • Golf • Guest Services •
Hotel/Resort • Human Resources •
Information Technology/Systems •
Legal/Administration • Maintenance •
Marketing/Sales • Owner Relations •
Product Development • Real
Estate/Development • Rental/Repair •
Retail • Ski/Mountain Operations •
Ski School • Timeshare •
Travel/Tourism

KEY COMPETITORS

Booth Creek Ski Holdings
Okemo Mountain Resort
Vail Resorts

EMPLOYMENT CONTACT

www.intrawest.com/employment

Visit Vault at **www.vault.com** for insider company profiles, expert advice,
career message boards, expert resume reviews, the Vault Job Board and more.

VAULT CAREER LIBRARY   225

THE SCOOP

Go play outside

Intrawest calls itself the company behind the world's greatest playgrounds, but it doesn't mean the kind with jungle gyms and swings. The company owns resorts that cater to every taste—assuming that all tastes run towards skiing, golf or the beach. Intrawest's ski properties include more than 20,000 acres of snowy and vertical terrain, mostly located in Canada, the Northeastern U.S. and in Colorado and California. Its golf and beach resorts are mainly located near Las Vegas and in Florida. The company also owns a share of Canadian Mountain Holidays, an outfit that drops skiers out of a helicopter onto a mountain (beat that, chairlift!).

Build it and they will come

Many resort firms started out with developers who went in search of property, but Intrawest took the opposite route. It started life in 1976 as a real estate firm with a portfolio of urban properties in Canadian cities. The company developed a handful of townhouses and broke into the retail real estate marketplace with a shopping center in 1981. Intrawest diversified its holdings again in 1986, purchasing a ski resort near Blackcomb mountain in British Columbia. Something in those mountains clicked—within four years, Blackcomb's skiing numbers increased by 75 percent. The company soon went public, in 1990.

The company parlayed its IPO funds into more white and hilly terrain, acquiring Quebec's Mont Tremblant in 1991 and British Columbia's Panorama Mountain Village in 1993, both ski resorts. Similar facilities in Stratton, Vt., and Snowshoe, W.V., joined the fold in 1993 and 1994, and Colorado's Mammoth, California and Copper came aboard in 1995. Intrawest cultivated warmer climes with the development of Floridian golf resorts in 1998, as well as purchasing a slew of ski and snowboard supply shops. The following year, Intrawest bought a share in Canadian Mountain Holidays, the aforementioned heli-skiing business.

The company continued blending snow and sun in 2000, when it developed another grown-up playground in Las Vegas and a resort in the French Alps. The following year, Intrawest developed two ski resorts in Colorado. Revenue fell off following the attacks of September 11th, but in 2003 the company was in fighting form again, opening a new ski resort in Blue Mountain, Ontario.

In 2005, Intrawest sold off its ski area in Mammoth, Calif., and began work on the Village of Imagine near Orlando, which resulted in a development of condos, high-end hotels, shopping and restaurants, sprinkled with native landscaping, lakes and canals. Also in 2005, Intrawest began construction on the facilities in Whistler, Canada, that will accommodate the Winter Olympics in 2010.

A good investment

The company took in a respectable $936 million in annual sales for 2006, a total 16 percent greater than the previous year. In August 2006, nearly simultaneous with these financial results, a private equity outfit, Fortress Investment Group, bought Intrawest for $2.8 billion.

While the deal with Fortress was under way, the folks at Intrawest didn't hesitate to make some deals of their own. In March 2007, Intrawest completed the $261 million acquisition of Steamboat, a ski resort near Steamboat Springs, Colo. (the purchase was first announced in December 2006). The town was named for the sound of the area's springs, which reminded settlers in 1865 of a steam engine. Skiers frequented the area as early as 1900 to float through its famous "champagne powder" snow, which is smooth, dry and especially good for skiing. Intrawest will run 13 restaurants in Steamboat as well as a hotel, and the company plans to develop the town enough to host 4,000 more people.

Tremblant express

In late 2007, Continental Airlines began daily direct flights from Newark Airport (near New York City) to Intrawest's Mont Tremblant in the coming ski season. The flights connect other Continental flights from elsewhere in the United States. Only chartered planes had ever flown this route before; commercial jets had to be routed into Montreal. Intrawest expected the Continental flights to boost attendance by several thousand people in the 2007-2008 season.

Lifting the Vail

In January 2008, Intrawest announced a new CEO, effective June 2008. The new chief will be Bill Jensen, former president and COO of main rival Vail Resorts, which owns four skiing resorts in Colorado and one in Northern California. Vail CEO Robert Katz spoke very highly of Jensen in the press release announcing his departure: "he has been a true leader within both the Vail community and the U.S. ski industry. Bill will be missed by everyone at our company."

Visit Vault at **www.vault.com** for insider company profiles, expert advice, career message boards, expert resume reviews, the Vault Job Board and more.

VAULT CAREER LIBRARY   227

GETTING HIRED

Add some champagne powder to your career

Intrawest hosts a large and informative site devoted to career opportunities with the company at www.wework2play.com. The site divides job openings into short- and long-term jobs. Short-term employees, who work during a resort's busy season, get benefits like free ski passes, inexpensive golf passes, and access to gyms. (Such perks vary between resorts.) The company also offers subsidized transport and discounts for friends who might want to drop in.

Seasonal positions include selling lift tickets, teaching ski or snowboard school, mountain maintenance, operating lifts; maintaining golf courses, teaching golf lessons, hotel positions like reservations, concierge, housekeeping, and retail and food service positions. Candidates should have a customer service or sales background and, ideally, a command of French or Spanish.

Long-term careers have many of the same perks that short-term ones do. Interested parties can search for jobs by type and function; in order to apply, they can fill out an online profile. People from overseas hoping to work in the U.S. or Canada must obtain the appropriate visa for the country in which they will work.

JetBlue Airways Corporation

118-29 Queens Boulevard
Forest Hills, NY 11375
Phone: (718) 286-7900
Fax: (718) 709-3621
www.jetblue.com

LOCATIONS

New York (HQ)
Atlanta, GA • Austin, TX • Boston,
MA • Buffalo, NY • Burbank, CA •
Burlington, VT • Charlotte, NC •
Chicago, IL • Columbus, OH • Darien,
CT • Denver, CO • Dulles, VA • Fort
Lauderdale, FL • Fort Myers, FL •
Garden City, NJ • Houston, TX •
Jacksonville, FL • Las Vegas, NV •
Long Beach, CA • Nantucket, MA •
Nashville, TN • New Orleans, LA •
Newark, NJ • Newburgh, NY •
Oakland, CA • Orlando, FL • Phoenix,
AZ • Pittsburgh, PA • Portland, OR •
Raleigh, NC • Richmond, VA •
Rochester, NY • Sacramento, CA •
Salt Lake City, UT • San Diego, CA •
San Francisco, CA • San Jose, CA •
San Juan, PR • Sarasota, FL •
Seattle, WA • Syracuse, NY • Tampa,
FL • Tucson, AZ • West Palm, FL

International locations in 11
countries.

THE STATS

Employer Type: Public Company
Stock Symbol: JBLU
Stock Exchange: NYSE
Chairman: David Neeleman
CEO: David Barger
President & COO: Russ Chew
2007 Employees: 9,909
2007 Revenue ($mil.): $2,842

DEPARTMENTS

Accounting & Finance • Audit •
Consulting • Customer Service •
Education & Training • Engineering •
Facility • Flight Operations • General
Management/Corporate Management
• Human Resources • Information
Technology • Legal • Marketing •
Pilots • Production & Manufacture •
Public Relations/Media •
Purchasing/Processing/Materials
Management & Logistics • Quality
Management • Research &
Development • Safety & Security •
Scheduling & Planning • System
Operations • Technical Operations •
Technical Publications

KEY COMPETITORS

American Airlines
Southwest Airlines
United Airlines

EMPLOYMENT CONTACT

www.jetblue.com/about/work

Visit Vault at **www.vault.com** for insider company profiles, expert advice,
career message boards, expert resume reviews, the Vault Job Board and more.

VAULT CAREER LIBRARY   229

THE SCOOP

The Jet Set

Consumers get a bang for their buck in the sky through JetBlue Airways, which keeps fares low by employing nonunion workers and only operating two types of planes—Airbus A320s and Embraer 190s—which require little upkeep and maintenance. The company flies to 50 cities in North America, mostly in the United States and the Caribbean. It also woos customers with goodies on board its planes, like leather seats, lots of legroom, free television, snack items and music.

A breath of new air

In February 1998 Chairman David Neeleman, a former Southwest Airlines employee, founded the company as New Air. His plan was to refine the budget airline travel experience by expanding amenities and in-flight entertainment. Or, as Neeleman himself put it, to "bring the humanity back to air travel."

The firm was (and is) based out of Forest Hills, in the Queens borough of New York City, very close to John F. Kennedy International Airport. This strategy is notably different from that of main low-budget rival Southwest, which uses more out-of-the-way airports. To play up its Gothamite connections, and emphasize its economic approach, the airline initially wanted to call itself "Taxi." Others disliked the idea, including investor JPMorgan, which threatened to yank its $20 million contribution from the airline's initial funding total of $128 million, and everyone settled on New Air. This name was dead within another year, as everyone settled on JetBlue instead.

In September 2000, the airline won takeoff and landing slots at JFK International and the government authorized its operation months later, in February 2000. The company's inaugural flight, between JFK and Fort Lauderdale, took place on February 11, 2000. By the next February, JetBlue had flown over a million customers, with sales of $100 million. Even after the September 11 attacks, when most U.S. airlines suffered, the airline's profits continued to rise.

The airline went public on the NASDAQ in 2002 and became one of the most popular airline stocks in history. JetBlue fliers everywhere quickly saw the results of the company's high stock price, as the company purchased LiveTV in 2002, outfitting every seat on its planes with DirecTV satellite television. Two years later, the airline announced the addition of XM Satellite Radio channels, Fox TV programs and 20th Century Fox movies to its in-flight entertainment.

© 2008 Vault.com Inc.

JetBlue—broadcasting itself!

The airline's avian comforts have, in some cases, transcended mere entertainment. A memorable example occurred in September 2005, when JetBlue flight 292 circled for three hours before performing an emergency landing at LAX. On their televisions, the flight's passengers were able to watch live coverage of the incident, and see the failure of the plane's front landing gear. Ouch—too much information.

Singin' the JetBlues?

JetBlue's winning streak ended in late 2004, as rising fuel costs combined with unforeseen events—like hurricanes in Florida, a state that accounted for almost 40 percent of the airline's routes—to chip away at profits. Also, JetBlue's struggling competition, such as then-bankrupt US Airways and then-bankrupt Delta, also affected the bottom line, as they lowered their fares dramatically to attract customers.

JetBlue announced its first ever quarterly loss at the end of 2005. The airline lost $42.4 million in fourth quarter of that year, wiping out any chance of making a profit that year; the loss was the airline's first since going public in 2002. But increased revenue and cost-cutting set the airline on the road to recovery, and by second quarter 2006, JetBlue was back in the black.

The company initiated a "return to profitability" plan in 2006, affecting cost-cutting measures hile continuing its habitual extension of its network (adding two to four new destinations per year). The airline removed a row of seats from all of its A320s in December 2006, which made possible a reduction in crew size from four to three (an FAA mandate requires one flight attendant per 50 seats). Over the course of the year, JetBlue cut 14 percent of the staff for every single one of its planes. This didn't sit well with employees, who launched various (unsuccessful) attempts to unionize— the baggage handlers filed a petition with the International Association of Machinists in May 2006 and flight attendants have contacted the Association of Flight Attendants.

Don't leave me hangin'

In February 2007, an enormous ice storm stranded a Cancún-bound JetBlue flight on the JFK tarmac for nearly nine hours. Naturally, supplies gave out, leading to horror stories about overflowing toilets and other dreadful conditions. The Cancún flight became known as JetBlue's "hostage crisis" and the situation turned into a public relations nightmare, as it was not then JetBlue policy to compensate any of the affected passengers. An absence of interline agreements (where one airline's ticket

Visit Vault at **www.vault.com** for insider company profiles, expert advice, career message boards, expert resume reviews, the Vault Job Board and more.

VAULT CAREER LIBRARY   231

can be used with another company) meant that all of the Cancún-goers were out of luck getting another ticket for free.

But JetBlue's problems didn't end there. As the days went by and the ice storm didn't abate, the airline canceled more and more flights. And then, the company's longtime thriftiness came back to haunt it, as reports trickled in of a staff totally unequipped for the disaster—JetBlue' s communications department, which locates flight crews and assigns them their next flights, was far too small for the company's size and thousands of JetBlue employees were unaccounted for, across the country. "We had so many people in the company who wanted to help who weren't trained to help," said then-CEO Neeleman, "We had an emergency control center full of people who didn't know what to do." The airline ultimately canceled nearly 1,200 flights, representing over $30 million of business. Union activists could be forgiven for snickering.

Neeleman immediately issued a public apology via video on the company's web site. He also unveiled a "Passenger's Bill of Rights," which obligates JetBlue to compensate passengers for such emergencies. Neeleman even issued a nationwide mea culpa on the *Late Show with David Letterman*, but it wasn't enough to save his job. In May 2007, Neeleman resigned as JetBlue's CEO, while remaining non-executive chairman. Dave Barger, company president since 1998, succeeded Neeleman as CEO. Later that May, according to SEC filings, Neeleman sold 2.5 million shares of JetBlue stock.

Share the air

In February 2007, ironically around the same time as the "hostage crisis," JetBlue was working to shore up its lack of interline agreements. That month, it announced an alliance with Irish carrier Aer Lingus and entered its first codesharing agreement, with Cape Air. Through the agreements, JetBlue fliers are now able to link up with Lingus' and Cape's flights around Ireland and to various destinations throughout Cape Cod and the surrounding islands.

The airlines expanded their alliance a year later, in February 2008, linking their flights together even more closely. When the partnership takes effect, probably in April 2008, flyers will be able to book connecting Jet Blue and Aer Lingus flights with one easy payment. JetBlue said it chose Aer Lingus as a partner because it has a similar low-priced business model, and offers the best value for customers.

Now flying the friendly skies: blue potato chips!

Despite the customer service controversies, JetBlue ranked as the No. 1 airline in consumer satisfaction in *Consumer Reports'* 2007 survey, scoring 87 out of a possible 100. Although the company has gone the route adopted by many similar airlines, charging for in-flight snacks, drinks, etc., its offerings are top-shelf, including blue potato chips, Dunkin' Donuts coffee and chocolate-chip cookies.

The company is also known for its clever marketing and communication measures (like its "letter ads," full page ads that address geographic regions directly and end with "Sincerely, JetBlue"). In August 2007 the company announced a partnership with the *The New York Times* for the launch of *Times On Air*, a monthly in-flight video magazine incorporating content from the *Times*.

The flight from Springfield is now boarding ...

As ever, JetBlue's marketing wizards were hard at work in 2007. In July, the airline once again showcased its unconventional marketing strategies by unveiling its first-ever specialty aircraft, the Woo-Hoo Jet Blue!, which features a picture of Homer Simpson and highlights the airline's new "Official Carrier of Springfield" status—a promotional tie-in with the release of the long-awaited, blockbuster *Simpsons* movie. The airline's web site was redecorated with Simpsons characters and their favorite JetBlue destinations.

Smaller = better?

Then, in October 2007, JetBlue reported its first third-quarter profit since 2005. Analysts attributed the figures to a change in strategy, as JetBlue and many rivals have recently scaled back their number of flights, leading to fuller planes and more efficient operations. The strategy continued to pay off through the year, as JetBlue posted its first year-end profits since 2004, despite a narrow fourth quarter loss. In 2007, the company earned $17 million on revenue of $2.84 billion, up from a loss of $1 million and revenue of $2.3 billion the previous year. The firm will continue its less-flights, more-full strategy in 2008, planning to sell some of its Airbus A320 aircraft. The company's third quarter report stated the firm's commitment to "cost discipline" and "a reduction in capacity."

The firm isn't spending less money, though, noting that "salary, wages and benefits" have increased by 19 percent in 2007, due to "changes" in the employee retirement plan and overtime considerations (surely during Valentine's Day). In March 2007, immediately after the February fiasco, JetBlue hired a new COO: Russ Chew, fresh

Visit Vault at **www.vault.com** for insider company profiles, expert advice, career message boards, expert resume reviews, the Vault Job Board and more.

VAULT CAREER LIBRARY 233

off a four-year stint as COO at the Federal Aviation Administration. In September, he was promoted to president of the company, and will bring all of his FAA expertise to the smaller, better-paying JetBlue.

GETTING HIRED

Join the Jet set

JetBlue's careers site, at www.jetblue.com/about/work, provides information for job seekers about opportunities and benefits. The company offers heath, dental and vision plans, as well as group discounts on home, pet and auto insurance. The company also offers a 401(k), profit sharing and discount stock purchase plan. Jobs are searchable by title, location and keyword. In order to apply, candidates must first create a profile.

Joie de Vivre Hospitality, Inc.

567 Sutter Street
San Francisco, CA 94102
Phone: (415) 835-0300
Fax: (415) 835-0311
www.jdvhotels.com

LOCATIONS

San Francisco, CA (HQ)

Berkeley, CA
Los Angeles, CA
Long Beach, CA
Napa, CA
Oakland, CA
Sacramento, CA
Santa Cruz, CA

THE STATS

Employer Type: Private Company
CEO: Chip Conley
President: Jack Kenny
2006 Employees: 3,000
2006 Revenue ($mil.): $200

KEY COMPETITORS

Global Hyatt
Starwood Hotels & Resorts
Las Vegas Sands

EMPLOYMENT CONTACT

www.jdvhotels.com/careers

THE SCOOP

Take a magazine and five adjectives ...

Joie de Vivre, the largest operator of boutique lodgings in California, brings its certain je ne sais quoi to small hotels in the Golden State. But what really sets JdV and its 34 hotels apart is that each of its properties is distinct from the others; indeed, there's nothing quite like any of them anywhere else.

CEO Chip Conley has devised a way to create environments that speak to people's interests, appealing to different "psychographics" instead of the usual demographics. For instance, Conley has described how his Phoenix Hotel was designed partially with readers of *Rolling Stone* magazine in mind ("funky, hip, young-at-heart, irreverent and adventurous"). And, to extend the publishing analogy, a loyal subscriber of the *New Yorker* would stay at the Hotel Rex ("worldly, sophisticated, literate, artistic and clever") and a reader of *Real Simple* could stay at the Hotel Vitale ("urbane, revitalizing, modern, fresh, nurturing").

Besides the Phoenix, Rex and Vitale, Joie de Vivre's other hotels include the Petit Auberge, aimed at Francophiles, the Miyako Hotel, for Japanophiles, and the newly opened Japanese pop culture-themed Hotel Tomo. The company also runs a number of spas, restaurants, clubs and lounges within its hotels, with names like Bambuddha, Dio Deka, Millennium and Café Andre.

A pink and green Phoenix rises from the ashes

It was in San Francisco in 1986 that a 26-year old Stanford MBA (with a massage license) left his job in real estate to purchase and refurbish a hotel. This renaissance man was Chip Conley, and the hotel he purchased was the Caravan, a run down establishment in the Tenderloin district of San Francisco. Conley fixed it up with the help of his friends, always with the intent of attracting a hip, musical crowd—for some reason, this included giving it a new green and pink paint job.

When the Caravan was reborn as the Phoenix in 1987, Conley contacted as many music promoters as possible (including über-promoter Bill Graham) and invited them to send their clients his way. The Phoenix had a few advantages for this demo-psychographic: it was hip, cheap and visiting rockers could be as loud as they wanted. The venture was a hit, as musicians, their tour managers and their entourages sometimes stayed for months while playing at various venues in the area. A decade after it opened, The Phoenix boasted a guest list including Kurt Cobain,

Sinéad O'Connor and Keanu Reeves (visiting with his non-band Dogstar), among others. It was also one of Timothy Leary's favorite hotels.

California dreaming

The Phoenix was Joie de Vivre's only property for a very profitable 10 years, and then Conley expanded in 1997, opening the Japanese-themed Kabuki Springs and Spa in San Francisco's Japantown. The next year the company moved into nearby Marin County with the Mill Valley Inn, nestled in a Redwood forest with a clear view of the San Francisco Bay.

The chain expanded again in 2000, opening three hotels in the rapidly growing Silicon Valley market. Unfortunately, the tech bubble that had made the Valley such a hotspot burst almost immediately afterwards. Joe de Vivre soldiered on in the diminished market and is still well established in the tech hub, which started humming again in 2003-2004.

The company's rapid expansion came to a halt between 2000 and 2005, as the entire travel industry suffered after the attacks of September 11th. In 2005, as the market started to pick up again, Joie de Vivre opened its first hotel in five years, the Hotel Vitale. It was also the firm's first luxury hotel, located in the Embarcadero Waterfront area. The same year, Joie de Vivre completed its renovation of Los Angeles' iconic downtown Holiday Inn, which reopened as the Hotel Angeleno.

Management that matters

Along the way, Chip Conley wrote three books, *The Rebel Rules: How to be Yourself in Business* (2001), *Marketing that Matters* (2006) and *Peak* (2007). The first book, *Rebel Rules*, featured a foreword from a kindred entrepreneurial spirit—Virgin founder Sir Richard Branson. In these books, Conley has detailed the roots of his management philosophy, particularly psychologist Abraham Maslow's hierarchy of needs. Maslow's hierarchy stipulates that humans have five sets of needs. The bottommost need is physical comfort—eating and sleeping—followed by the need for safety, love, self respect and respect of the community, and topped by self-actualization, creative expression and a sense of achievement.

Conley has applied this hierarchy to his management style. Employees are motivated by three things, which together account for Maslow's set of physical comfort, safety, love, self respect and respect of the community. Firstly, how well an employee is paid corresponds to his or her physical comfort and safety. Secondly, an employee's

Visit Vault at **www.vault.com** for insider company profiles, expert advice, career message boards, expert resume reviews, the Vault Job Board and more.

VAULT CAREER LIBRARY

237

career path satisfies self-respect and respect of the community. And lastly, an employee has a need for love—one must feel to be working towards a laudable goal, larger than one's self, which in the case of Joie de Vivre is the happiness of the hotel's guests. Conley takes his mission for happy employees seriously—he has even given up his own paycheck during rough patches so that he wouldn't have to lay anyone off.

Ohayou gozaimasu, Tomo!

Joie de Vivre's latest addition, the Japanese-themed Tomo, opened its doors in April 2007. But don't go there expecting Zen décor, rock gardens, ikebana and tinkly little fountains. The hotel, whose name translates as "friend" or "companion," has a decorating scheme inspired by the colors and images of anime and Japanese pop culture. Located in San Francisco's Nihonmachi Japantown neighborhood, the hotel fits right in to the area's Japanese shops, restaurants and spas. It also has meeting space, gaming rooms with Wii and PlayStation systems, and, naturally, a Japanese restaurant.

Citizen Conley

Tomo isn't the only new hotel Joie de Vivre has up its sleeve. In 2007, it announced a new hotel in Sacramento, to be located in a historic building on 10th and J streets and opening in fall 2008. The hotel will be called The Citizen Hotel, a name befitting its location in the state capital. A luxury hotel, the Citizen will have five penthouses and nearly 200 rooms, as well as rooms for meetings, a ballroom and a terrace.

Galleria de luxe

Joie de Vivre has also gussied up its Galleria Park Hotel, located in San Francisco's Financial District. The hotel underwent a $7 million refurbishment masterminded by Marni Leis and Oren Bronstein, a pair of designers. The hotel's guests are getting cushy new perks, like comfy office chairs, in-room selections of office supplies, mp3 alarm clocks and designer sheets. The renovations will be complete in the latter part of 2007.

GETTING HIRED

Add some joy to your career

Joie de Vivre's careers site, at www.jdvhotels.com/careers, provides information for job seekers about opportunities at the company. Openings are searchable by title and location. In order to apply for a position, job seekers must first create a profile.

The company offers many perks for its hires. Employees can stay at one of the company's hotels gratis for two nights every three months, and there are discount rates at hotels, spas and restaurants for employees and their friends. CEO Chip Conley makes efforts to make himself approachable, hosting regular dinners every three months. Job seekers can check out his web site at www.chipconley.com, where he explains his management philosophies, posts pictures of his family and has a blog.

Visit Vault at **www.vault.com** for insider company profiles, expert advice,
career message boards, expert resume reviews, the Vault Job Board and more.

VAULT CAREER LIBRARY   **239**

Kimpton Hotel & Restaurant Group, LLC

222 Kearney Street, Ste. 200
San Francisco, CA 94108
Phone: (415) 397-5572
Fax: (415) 296-8031
www.kimptonhotels.com

LOCATIONS

San Francisco, CA (HQ)
Alexandria, VA
Arlington, VA
Aspen, CO
Boston, MA
Burlingame, CA
Cambridge, MA
Chicago, IL
Cupertino, CA
Dallas, TX
Denver, CO
New York, NY
Portland, OR
Rosslyn, VA
Salt Lake City, UT
San Diego, CA
Scottsdale, AZ
Seattle, WA
Washington, DC
Vancouver
Whistler, Canada

THE STATS

Employer Type: Private Company
Chairman: Thomas W. LaTour
President & CEO: Michael Depatie
2007 Employees: 6,200

DEPARTMENTS

Administrative/Support
Building & Maintenance
Business & Financial Operations
Computer & Engineering
Construction
Customer Service
Food Preparation & Serving
Installation, Maintenance & Repair
Management
Protective Service
Sales/Marketing
Transportation

KEY COMPETITORS

Darden Restaurants
Fairmont Raffles Hotels
Starwood Hotels & Resorts

EMPLOYMENT CONTACT

www.kimptonhotels.com/emp_home.
aspx

THE SCOOP

A hotel to suit every taste

Kimpton Hotels and Restaurants operates 39 hotels in the U.S., which contain 45 restaurants and lounges and just over 7,000 rooms. Unlike other companies, where each hotel is a twin of the last, Kimpton specializes in boutique hotels, each with its own theme and often situated in historic buildings. The company's restaurants are equally diverse, featuring chef-driven menus and local ingredients, and designed to woo travelers from the surrounding areas as well as tickle the palates of hotel guests.

Themes of the company's hotels range from the Hotel Monaco's invitation to "Indulge your senses via guilty pleasures" in the otherwise anhedonic Salt Lake City to the Hotel Vintage Plaza's "Italian romance" in Portland, Oregon. One thing is common to every Kimpton hotel—a daily evening reception with wine and munchies.

From KFC to fine cuisine

Some hoteliers credit Bill Kimpton, the company's founder, with kickstarting a whole new era in the industry. His pioneering idea was the "boutique" hotel, essentially an effort to bring more personal service to middle class travelers, who increasingly had no alternative to bland, corporate chain hotels. It wasn't the lap of luxury but it wasn't the impersonal norm, either; it was something new.

The pioneering moment came in 1981, when Kimpton branched out after more than 10 years as an investment banker with Lehman Brothers and other firms, purchasing San Francisco's run-down Bedford hotel. Hotels weren't an entirely a new venture for Kimpton—as a financier, he had helped secure funds for famed developer Harry Helmsley, during the 1970s renovation of New York City's Palace Hotel.

Although hotels now commonly feature fancy restaurants with menus designed by celebrity chefs, they didn't when Kimpton launched the Bedford and Café Bedford in 1981. Also, the Bedford was the first hotel to feature a daily, complimentary wine hour for its guests. Kimpton had some experience with food service from his investment banking days, although of a very different stripe—he was instrumental in Kentucky Fried Chicken's 1964 IPO.

Travelers to the Bay area appreciated Kimpton's lodgings, and within two years the company opened a second hotel, the Vintage Court, in San Francisco's posh Nob Hill

Visit Vault at **www.vault.com** for insider company profiles, expert advice, career message boards, expert resume reviews, the Vault Job Board and more.

V/\ULT CAREER LIBRARY   241

neighborhood. This hotel had a wine theme, for people visiting the Napa Valley. (Kimpton sold the Vintage Court to another hotel company in 2003.) Also in 1983, Kimpton hired the company's current chairman, Tom LaTour, an executive with a wealth of hospitality experience. In 1989, the company opened the Prescott Hotel and its associated Postrio Restaurant, under the guidance of a young chef named Wolfgang Puck.

Kimpton's kibbles and bits

In 1991, Kimpton bought a former YMCA building in San Francisco; with a little fixing up, it became the Harbor Court Hotel. The following year, Kimpton extended the boutique hotel experience to family pets, when all of its hotels instituted a range of pet-friendly policies. The hotels become even more pet-friendly in 1993, when their front desks started offering fish to lonely travelers, upon request. Kimpton moved to accommodate their guests in every dimension in 1996, when they introduced rooms sized for taller travelers, with long beds, higher furniture and shower heads adjusted to avoid whacking them on the forehead.

In recent years, the company continued to cater to guests' sensitivities. In 2004, for instance, the chain developed environmentally-friendly hotel rooms and launched its Women InTouch program, to specifically address the needs of female travelers. Amenities include in-room spa services, Luna Bars and Altoids in rooms' honor bars, "fun, imaginative packages for women," and something called "Forgot It, We've Got It," which aims to replace all the little things that women might forget to pack, such as tweezers, sunscreen, nail care items, make-up mirrors and more. The company has another InTouch program, for customer loyalty that provides members with a complimentary night for every seven stays or 20 nights at a Kimpton hotel, whichever comes first.

Farewell, fearless leader

The group received some sad news in April 2001, when company founder and namesake Bill Kimpton passed away after a battle with leukemia. Longtime right-hand-man Tom LaTour became the company's chairman and CEO after his passing. LaTour was on hand in February 2002 to accept a posthumous honor for Kimpton: the International Society of Hospitality Consultants' Pioneer Award, for outstanding contribution to the industry.

Manifest destiny

In 2007, Kimpton announced an expansion plan, aimed at doubling its hotel holdings by 2012. The first new hotel, scheduled to open in 2009, will be located in Alexandria, Va., right near the city's shopping and dining district. It will have 107 rooms, some with terraces, as well as a wine bar and gourmet restaurant.

Kimpton is also developing a hotel in the Hell's Kitchen neighborhood of New York City, on 11th Avenue. The neighborhood, once a notorious slum, is gentrifying at a rapid rate, with chic bars and restaurants rapidly popping up. And it's close to New York's famous theater district, to boot. The hotel will be in a refurbished factory building, with large windows and high ceilings, and Kimpton is adding a rooftop bar, with a reflecting pool. Kimpton plans to have 10 hotels in the New York City area within a decade, some in areas off the well-beaten Times Square-Empire State Building-Statute of Liberty track, like Brooklyn and Jersey City.

Room + Board + Body + Soul

In 2007, Kimpton burnished its eco-friendly image yet again, when it teamed up with *Body + Soul*, an eco-friendly lifestyle magazine put out by Martha Stewart Omnimedia. Kimpton and the magazine rolled out two-day getaways for tired travelers that help revive them with ideas from the magazine. Travelers are treated to TV channels that broadcast yoga, meditation, Pilates workouts, healthy and organic foods (such as detoxifying cocktails), and spa treatments.

GETTING HIRED

Every career tells a story

Kimpton's careers page, at www.kimptonhotels.com/emp_home.aspx, provides information on the company's career advancement programs, benefits and job openings. The company encourages its workers to keep learning all through their careers, whether it's through internal courses at Kimpton University or with subsidies for courses at the local university. The company also offers its employees health and dental benefits, and work/life balance programs, which include sabbaticals and maternity and paternity leave. For those ready to apply, jobs are searchable by category and location.

Visit Vault at **www.vault.com** for insider company profiles, expert advice,
career message boards, expert resume reviews, the Vault Job Board and more.

VAULT CAREER LIBRARY   **243**

Las Vegas Sands Corp.

3355 Las Vegas Boulevard South
Las Vegas, NV 89109
Phone: (702) 414-1000
Fax: (702) 414-4884
www.lasvegassands.com

LOCATIONS

Las Vegas, NV (HQ)
Macau

THE STATS

Employer Type: Public Company
Stock Symbol: LVS
Stock Exchange: NYSE
Chairman & CEO: Sheldon G. Adelson
President & COO: William P. Weidner
2007 Employees: 28,000
2007 Revenue ($mil.): $2,951

DEPARTMENTS

Administrative/Clerical • Casino •
Construction • Corporate •
Engineering • Entertainment •
Executive Administration • Finance •
Food & Beverage • Front Office •
Guest Service • Hotel Operations •
Housekeeping • Human Resources •
Information Technology • Internship
• Maintenance • Marketing • Meeting
Services • Purchasing • Reservations
• Retail • Sales • Security •
Telecom/PBX

KEY COMPETITORS

Harrah's Entertainment
MGM MIRAGE
Wynn Resorts

EMPLOYMENT CONTACT

https://www.hrapply.com/venetian/
AppJobSearch.jsp

THE SCOOP

Hardly a desert of entertainment

The Sands Casino, for which the Las Vegas Sands Corporation is named, no longer exists. In the 1990s, the company built another casino in its place: The Venetian, a sprawling facility with a 4,000-room hotel, casino, restaurants and shopping galore. The Sands name lives on in other properties owned by the company, though. The Sands Expo Center is one of the largest convention facilities in the U.S., with over one million square feet of space for trade shows, expositions and other mass gatherings of salesmen. The Sands Macau is a new hotel and casino, opened in 2004. More recently, in 2007, the company added to its legacy with the launch of The Venetian Macau.

Home of the Rat Pack

Like many Las Vegas hotels and casinos of the 1950s, the Sands (established in 1952) became a chic hangout for entertainers in town, notably the "Rat Pack" of Frank Sinatra, Dean Martin, Sammy Davis Jr. and friends. In fact, Sinatra and Martin were actually shareholders in the original Sands and the original *Ocean's Eleven*, their most famous film as a group, was partially filmed inside the casino.

Billionaire Howard Hughes purchased the Sands in 1967 and promised to modernize the facility and add rooms and to it, neither of which he did. The Sands changed owners a few times in the 1980s, first when the Summa Corporation, Hughes' company, sold it in 1983 to the Pratt Corporation. Pratt attempted to expand into Mexico just as the Mexican economy took a nosedive and Summa reacquired the Sands later in 1983. Summa sold the property to Kirk Kerkorian in 1988, who renamed it the MGM Sands, and Kerkorian sold it to a group headed by Sheldon Adelson in 1989.

Sheldon Adelson made a fortune on computer industry trade shows in the late 1970s and early 1980s, and considered the Sands a perfect place to host visitors to his trade shows. But the iconic hotel, never sufficiently renovated, failed to woo many travelers. After repeatedly trying to revive the Sands, Adelson demolished it in November 1996. In April 1997, he began construction on a new hotel and casino in its place.

Home of singing gondoliers, wax and lots of suites

Where the Sands once stood, Adelson unveiled The Venetian in May 1999. The Vegas Strip's first all-suites hotel and casino, its construction cost about $1.5 billion. Patterned on Renaissance era Venice, the resort houses a replica Grand Canal, replete with singing gondoliers as well as an ersatz St. Mark's Square. In summer 1999, a branch of Madame Tussaud's waxworks museum opened inside, along with a Canyon Ranch spa. The Venetian's Guggenheim Hermitage Musuem, which borrows art from New York's Guggenheim and St. Petersburg's Hermitage Museums, opened in 2001.

Happy financial returns

The Venetian added a new tower in 2003 and Las Vegas Sands Corp. went public the following year. In the ensuing years, revenue soared and the Venetian became Vegas' leading attraction, in terms of operating cash flow. From 2003 to 2004, annual sales increased from $737 million to $1.2 billion, and revenue surpassed $2 billion for the first time in 2006, coming close to $3 billion the next year.

Las Vegas Sands' profits have also marched consistently upwards, going from $66 million in 2003 to a company record $495 million in 2004. They've tapered off in the years since, reaching $238 million in 2005 and $442 million in 2006. A good deal of the $200 million-plus drop in revenue between 2004 and 2005 was related to $2.4 billion in construction costs for the one-million-square-foot Sands Macau, which opened in May 2004. It was the first gaming facility to be operated by an American company in the region.

Asian invasion

Formerly a Portuguese colony, Macau is a major Asian gaming destination, which should only continue as Asian economies (and China's, in particular) experience tremendous economic growth. Certainly, the Sands has already become a major destination within Macau. By May 2005, it earned enough to pay off its construction costs, and in 2006 its casino expanded from 165,000 square feet to 229,000 square feet, a calculation Las Vegas Sands cites to claim it as the largest casino in the world.

The Sands Macau got a brother when Las Vegas Sands opened The Venetian Macau in August 2007. This Venice on the South China Sea has a shopping mall with three faux-Italian canals, complete with singing gondoliers, putting its Vegas namesake's one canal to shame. And The Venetian Macau's gaming floors are larger than anything in Las Vegas (though still not as large as the Sands Macau's).

Other hospitality companies, notably Wynn Resorts, are also chasing the Macau dream, building major casinos and hotels in the area, but the investment represents something of a risk for Western companies. While tourists usually spend about three days visiting Vegas—gambling, shopping, buying food and lodging all the while—visitors to Macau are tight-fisted by comparison, staying for only one day and generally packing a picnic lunch. The island also has yet to draw many visitors from far outside China. It generally receives day-trippers from the surrounding area, and its hotels aren't as full as those in Vegas.

Not a company to rest on its laurels, in May 2006 Las Vegas Sands landed a coveted bid to develop another international casino in Singapore. The Marina Bay Sands, slated to open in 2009, will be a resort with 3,000 rooms, pools, spas, restaurants and shopping, as well as an art and science museum. Sands is planning another resort in Hengqin, China, close to Macau, but although it signed an agreement with Hengqin in October 2005, Beijing has yet to hand down final approval. The plans call for it to be yet another version of The Venetian.

Sands and steel

Sands isn't only concentrating on Asia for growth opportunities. In early 2007, it announced the beginning of work on a casino at the abandoned Bethlehem Steel company building in Bethlehem, Pa. In 2005, the city issued gambling licenses to bring jobs to the area and relieve the city's debt, as well as renovate the Bethlehem Steel site. Several casino companies bid for the opportunity to build on the old industrial site and Sands' bid won.

The casino and hotel will feature chic postindustrial décor, incorporating the remains of the company's industrial machinery, exposed brick walls and metal bits. The site will include the tried and true trifecta of hotel, casino and shopping, in addition to a PBS station and a museum of industrial history. The casino is intended to lure shoppers and gamers (and their dollars) from the New York area.

Fit for a Doge

With all this activity far away from Nevada, the firm hasn't forgotten its big money-maker, The Venetian. In late 2006, Las Vegas newspapers learned that Sands was planning another all-luxury addition to the Venetian. Construction began in early 2007, and the expansion opened to the public in December 2007, having racked up $2.1 billion in construction fees. The 50-story, 3,066 suite Palazzo, as the expansion is called, includes 250 condominium apartments, the latest must-have addition for

Las Vegas hotels, and 14 restaurants (helmed by celebrity chefs, yet to be announced). The Palazzo will soon be importing the Tony award-winning Broadway show *Jersey Boys*. The construction negatively affected company earnings in 2007, which fell to $117 million from $442 million the year before.

GETTING HIRED

Add some Sands to your career

Las Vegas Sands' careers site, at https://www.hrapply.com/venetian/AppJobSearch.jsp, provides information on job openings and benefits. The company's benefits include options like heath, vision and dental insurance, disability and life insurance, and a 401(k) plan and a free lunch in the employee dining room. Nice perks include on-site child care and an on-site clinic. Job openings are searchable by location, keyword and department; in order to apply, job seekers must create a profile. The company also offers internships for undergraduate and graduate students in areas such as branding, marketing and HR.

Marriott International, Inc.

10400 Fernwood Road
Bethesda, MD 20817
Phone: (301) 380-3000
Fax: (301) 380-3969
www.marriott.com

LOCATIONS

Bethesda, MD (HQ)
Atlanta, GA
Austin, TX
Birmingham, AL
Boston, MA
Chicago, IL
Los Angeles, CA
Miami, FL
New York, NY
Washington, DC

Additional locations nationwide,
including the Virgin Islands.
International locations in Africa,
Asia, Europe and the Middle East.

THE STATS

Employer Type: Public Company
Stock Symbol: MAR
Stock Exchange: NYSE
Chairman & CEO: J. W. Marriott Jr.
President & COO: William J. Shaw
2007 Employees: 151,000
2007 Revenue ($mil.): $12,990

DEPARTMENTS

Accounting & Finance
Administrative & Support
Architecture & Construction
Facilities Management
Food & Beverage
Human Resources
Information Systems & Technology
Rooms Operations & Guest Services
Sales & Marketing

KEY COMPETITORS

Accor
Hilton Hotels
InterContinental Hotels

EMPLOYMENT CONTACT

www.marriott.com/careers

Visit Vault at **www.vault.com** for insider company profiles, expert advice,
career message boards, expert resume reviews, the Vault Job Board and more.

VAULT CAREER LIBRARY   249

THE SCOOP

There's room at this inn

Mariott is a leading company in the hotel industry, with nearly 3,000 hotels in over 60 countries. Marriott only owns 13 of these properties; all the rest are franchises. The company's brands cover nearly every segment of the market, from upscale to budget. These include Marriott (upscale), luxury (JW Marriott and Ritz-Carlton), all-suites (SpringHill Suites), extended-stay (Residence Inn and TownePlace Suites), mid-market (Renaissance and Courtyard) and budget-conscious (Fairfield Inns). Marriott also has a joint partnership with the Italian luxury company Bulgari to operate Bulgari-branded resorts in Bali and Milan.

From root beer to the Ritz

Marriott International, unlike most other hotel companies, started out in 1927 as a nine-stool root beer stand in Washington, D.C. The husband and wife duo behind the store was J. Willard Marriott and Alice Sheets Marriott, and they called the venture A&W, after their names. The stand was so successful that the Marriotts soon had an entire chain of restaurants, called Hot Shoppes Inc. In the 1930s Hot Shoppes went airborne, launching an airline catering unit.

The Marriotts stayed in the restaurant business for some 30 years before branching out into hotels in 1957, opening the Twin Bridges Motor Hotel in Arlington, Va. The couple had four hotels by 1964, and that year, they promoted their son, J.W. "Bill" Marriot Jr., to company president. Under the guidance of Marriott the younger, the company quadrupled its size by 1970. Along the way, it changed its name from Hot Shoppes to the Marriott Corporation, went public in 1968, purchased the Big Boy Restaurant chain and launched its own fast-food enterprise, Roy Rogers.

All kinds of hotels

Bill Marriott Jr. succeeded his father as CEO in 1972 and the firm invested some $3 billion in hotels over the course of the 1970s. Much of this investment came in the form of business-class hotels, located near cities and suburbs and armed with accommodations for large business meetings and conventions. Also, to complement its airline catering business, the firm started building hotels closer to airports. When Marriott purchased the airport-terminal catering firm Host International in 1982, it became the largest in the airport food services industry.

Marriott mainly focused on hotels throughout the 1980s as well, and began selling off its properties while maintaining their management to fuel further expansion. Marriott introduced a variety of new brands in all kinds of markets, such as the no-frills Courtyard in 1983 (without extras like banquet space or bellhops), timeshares in 1984 and the extended-stay chain Marriott Suites in 1987. By the time Marriott launched the budget-friendly Fairfield Inn in 1989, it managed nearly 500 hotels nationwide.

Marriott announced a major restructuring in 1989, selling off its restaurants division to Hardee's Food System for $365 million and its airline catering business to Caterair International for $570 million. As part of the process, the company also divided its real estate development and hotel management arms into two different companies. This reduced the company's tax load and allowed it to purchase the luxury hotel firm Ritz-Carlton in 1995. By 1997, Marriott operated nearly 1,500 hotels in every sector of the hotel industry.

Feeling disenfranchised

The terrorist attacks of September 11th greatly shook the travel industry in 2001, but Marriott recovered much sooner than many of its rivals. True, profits fell by more than half from 2000 to 2001, going from $479 million to $236 million, but they rebounded enough by 2003 to make a company record $500 million. Moreover, the firm didn't report any year-end losses in a notoriously bad period for travel companies. In May 2004, *Forbes* asked "What's the magic formula" that enabled Marriot to "recover nicely ... while its rivals floundered?" The magazine found that Marriott and its "hard-nosed executives ... exploited its size advantage as ruthlessly as a Microsoft or a Wal-Mart."

Some disgruntled franchisees actually sued the company for its operating methods in 2003 and 2004. Marriott settled nearly all of the lawsuits out of court, but the publicity negatively affected the company's stock price. In January 2003, in the midst of these legal issues, the company promoted CEO Marriott's son, J.W. "John" Marriott III, to chief of global sales and marketing. Industry analysts began floating John Marriott's name as a potential successor to his father, now 76 years old.

A new Marriott?

John Marriott is now vice chairman of the company's board, and *The New York Times* reported in mid-2003 that after his promotion to the executive ranks, "a new openness emerged in what many had considered a closed, even secretive culture at Marriott."

Visit Vault at **www.vault.com** for insider company profiles, expert advice, career message boards, expert resume reviews, the Vault Job Board and more.

VAULT CAREER LIBRARY   **251**

CEO Marriott seems to appreciate the need for change as well, telling *BusinessWeek* in September 2005 that the company is "not appealing to Generation X, even though [it has] a strong bond of loyalty with the baby boomers." In November 2005, Marriott moved to shore up its upscale brands, purchasing 38 hotels from rival Starwood Hotels and Resorts for $3.4 billion.

In 2006, Marriott continued to spruce itself up, and hopefully attract some Gen Xers. That year, it hired the "environmental design" firm IDEO to research improvements for its extended-stay TownePlace Suites chain. Among the innovations IDEO introduced to Marriott establishments: a sleeker lobby to keep guests moving in and out (eliminating the standard couch, coffee table and TV set) and a giant map of the surrounding locale, to keep customers plugged in to the community they are visiting.

The revamps keep on coming at Marriott. In August 2007, the company unveiled plans for a new brand of boutique hotels—a type of intimate, individualized hotel that started attracting mid-market travelers in the 1980s. Marriott is joining forces with Ian Schrager, the man behind New York City's achingly hip Gramercy Park Hotel, in order to develop its own flavor of boutique hotel. Marriott plans to feature this new brand (as yet unnamed) in 100 locations, including cities such as Las Vegas and New York, and in Asia and South America.

Chinese dreams

Marriott is rapidly expanding its Asian hotels in general, with plans to increase its number of Chinese hotels from 25 to 100 by 2012. In particular, Marriott will open 11 hotels in Beijing, just in time for all the business sure to come when that city hosts the 2008 Olympic Summer Games.

Mickey meets his match

In May 2007, the company inked a deal with kids' TV juggernaut Nickelodeon to create a theme park, complete with pools and water slides, musical productions and people wandering around in character suits. The resorts will also cater to grown-ups with things like spas and a kid-free lap pool. The first location is expected to open near San Diego in 2010, followed by 19 more within a decade. The parks will be located in areas as disparate as Europe, the Caribbean and the Middle East, to better blanket the world with cartoon characters. Marriott is aiming them at a generation of kids and their parents (who grew up watching Nickelodeon cartoons), as well as companies bored with the same old meeting spaces.

GETTING HIRED

A good place for everyone

The company's careers site, at www.marriott.com/careers/default.mi, provides plenty of information for the aspiring hotelier. There is ample information about the company's various hotel brands, as well as various career paths, such as accounting and finance, administrative and support, architecture and construction, facilities management, food and beverage, human resources, information systems and technology, rooms operations and guest services, and sales and marketing. The database of available jobs can be sorted according to location, category and keyword. Applicants can submit a resume and cover letter online. Benefits include the standard health, dental and 401(k), as well as tuition reimbursement and discounts on food and hotel rooms.

Marriott routinely gets kudos for its benefits and diversity programs. In 2007, *BusinessWeek* lauded it as one of the best companies to launch a career, while *LATINA Style* and *Black Enterprise* praised the company's diversity efforts.

A good place for students, too

Marriott also offers paid internship opportunities in the following divisions: accounting and finance, banquets and catering, culinary, front office, housekeeping, human resources, restaurants and sales. Internships are available throughout the year and typically last a minimum of 10 to 12 weeks; some last up to six months.

For students who might wish to speak to Marriott in person, the company's recruiting junket includes stops at Boston University, Brigham Young, the Culinary Institute of America, Hampton University, Johnson & Wales and San Diego University.

The merry life at Marriott

Insiders report that Marriott's interviews are "pretty intense." One business analyst recalls, "I went through three interviews—one with HR, one with [a] hiring manager and one with her manager. HR asked the personality type questions (strengths, weaknesses, tell me about a time ...). They also handled all the discussions regarding salary and benefits. The hiring manager asked technical questions and questions related to past experience and depth of knowledge as it related to the position I was interviewing for." A hotel manager says that she had a "full-day" interview, and was

Visit Vault at **www.vault.com** for insider company profiles, expert advice, career message boards, expert resume reviews, the Vault Job Board and more.

VAULT CAREER LIBRARY

253

"interviewed by six individuals. Most of the questions are 'fit' questions like, 'What are you looking for?' and, 'How could the company best utilize your skills?'"

OUR SURVEY SAYS

Diverse and engaged

While sources report that culture varies between locations, one satisfied insider notes that "The workforce is one of the most engaged workforces that I have been a part of." "Working at corporate headquarters is great," a colleague concurs. "Co-workers are easy to work with and there is a team atmosphere. [It's a] very diverse group of people." Interns at the company can be assured that they won't be spending time in front of the copier. "Interns here are regarded as associates who are capable of undertaking more work because they are, in theory, going to be entering the industry at a management level upon graduating from college," explains one program veteran.

A flexible firm

Sources say the hours are reasonable. "My typical work week is around 50 hours per week," says one manager, "and [it] is flexible enough if I need to take care of personal business in the middle of the day." "Some employees are given the opportunity to telecommute," adds another. "Marriott is a great place to work if you are a working mother. Most departments allow you to work flex hours, meaning you can set your own hours provided you are in the office during core business hours and those vary by department," notes an associate. The company makes balancing work and life obligations easy for its employees at headquarters with a number of nice perks. "The HQ campus has a child care center (although the wait list is long), nurses' station, large cafeteria, company store, dry cleaning, gas station and fitness facility," describes one happy worker.

MGM MIRAGE

3600 Las Vegas Boulevard South
Las Vegas, NV 89109
Phone: (702) 693-7120
Fax: (702) 693-8626
www.mgmmirage.com

LOCATIONS

Las Vegas, NV (HQ)
Atlantic City, NJ • Biloxi, MS •
Detroit, MI • Henderson, NV • Jean,
NV • Laughlin, NV • Primm, NV •
Reno, NV • Saucier, MS • Sloan,
NV • Tunica, MS • Macau

THE STATS

Employer Type: Public Company
Stock Symbol: MGM
Stock Exchange: NYSE
Chairman & CEO: J. Terrence Lanni
President: James J. Murren
2007 Employees: 54,700
2007 Revenue ($mil.): $7,692

KEY COMPETITORS

Harrah's Entertainment
Trump Entertainment Resorts
Wynn Resorts

EMPLOYMENT CONTACT

secure02.mgm-mirage.com/
employment/index.asp

DEPARTMENTS

Accounting
Accounts Payable
Administration, *M Lifestyle* Magazine
Administration, Risk Management
Aviation
Call Center
Corporate Services
Corporate Strategy
Diversity Education
Energy Management
Entertainment Reservations
Event Production—Technical
Financial Services
Graphic Arts
HR Labor Relations
Human Resources
Insurance Litigation
Internal Audit
Internet Marketing
IT
   Administrative • Business
   Development • Business Solutions •
   City Center • Computer Engineering
   • Customer Service • Data Security
   • IT—Governance • Internet
   Services • Network Engineering •
   Software Engineering • Systems
   Development • Systems Engineering
   • Systems Management
Loyalty Marketing
OCIP Administration
Production Services
Public Relations
Purchasing
Retail Accounting
Retail Administration
Retail Distribution Center
Securities Council

Visit Vault at **www.vault.com** for insider company profiles, expert advice,
career message boards, expert resume reviews, the Vault Job Board and more.

VAULT CAREER LIBRARY   255

THE SCOOP

The tiger of the Strip

MGM Mirage is the largest casino company in Las Vegas, owning 10 Casinos in Las Vegas and 12 elsewhere in the United States. Among its Las Vegas casinos are some of the Strip's most notable landmarks, including The Bellagio, Circus Circus, Luxor, Mandalay Bay, Mirage and MGM Grand. It also co-owns the Atlantic City luxury resort the Borgata, with Boyd Gaming Corp.

Transforming Vegas

Behind the titanic names of MGM Mirage's casinos are two notable figures in Las Vegas history: Kirk Kerkorian and Steve Wynn. Both started investing in Las Vegas real estate in the 1960s and both pioneered a new age of casinos as all-inclusive vacation destinies for families (as well as the usual high rollers). They didn't exactly work together, though: in 2000, Kerkorian's MGM Grand launched a hostile takeover of Wynn's Mirage Resorts, eventually winning control of the Bellagio, Mirage and other Wynn-developed properties for $6.4 billion. *Forbes* ranked Kerkorian (No. 7) and Wynn (No. 86) on its list of the Richest People in America in 2007.

Captain Kerkorian

A native of Fresno, Calif., Kerkorian had been visiting Las Vegas for his whole life when he invested in a strip of real estate in 1962. He rented it out to a group of developers building a casino called Caesar's Palace and then sold the land for an enormous profit in 1968. *Fortune* called it "one of the most successful land speculations in Las Vegas history." With these proceeds, Kerkorian bought the Flamingo Hotel in 1967 and built the International Hotel in 1969, then the largest hotel in the world.

Also in 1969, Kerkorian's company went public and bought a majority stake in the Metro-Goldwyn Mayer film studios. Kerkorian was more interested in MGM as a brand than an artistic venture, and in 1972 the company opened the MGM Grand, the world's largest resort hotel, in Las Vegas. The Grand Hotel opened at the MGM in 1973, and like the International before it, was the world's largest hotel at the time. Meanwhile, MGM film production slowed to about three or four films per year and Kerkorian's studio management attracted much criticism from Hollywood insiders.

However, MGM's casino-hotel resorts were immensely profitable, and came to dominate the Las Vegas landscape.

A Wynn-ing formula

Steven Wynn moved from the East Coast to Las Vegas in the 1960s and, like Kerkorian, invested in a few properties behind the scenes, amassing lots of capital for future deals. In 1972 he bought a stake in the classic Golden Nugget casino (which dated back to 1945). He instituted a redevelopment plan and opened a high-end hotel in 1977, kickstarting the Nugget's transformation from a one-trick pony (gambling) to the kind of all-inclusive, all-luxurious resort that populates Las Vegas today.

The Golden Nugget was far from Wynn's crowning achievement, however. The Mirage opened in 1989, replete with an indoor volcano and the famous magic show featuring Siegfried, Roy and their big cats (now on hiatus, due to an unprecedented big cat accident). The Mirage was such a success that Wynn's company changed its name to Mirage Resorts in 1991. Even more spectacular casinos followed, such as the marble confection known as the Bellagio, which opened in 1998. The company didn't lose sight of its middle-class demographic, though, opening the mid-market Monte Carlo in 1996 to attract visitors without enormous checkbooks.

Re-enter Kerkorian

While Wynn's resorts flourished, Kerkorian's MGM Grand was the site of Las Vegas' worst ever disaster in 1980. An electrical problem caused a fire in the hotel, ultimately killing 87 people and injuring hundreds more. The hotel reopened eight months later, but Kerkorian sold it to Bally Manufacturing Corp. in 1986, which renamed it Bally's (the current MGM Grand is a different property). Kerkorian turned his attention to his other assets—he sold and repurchased MGM studios three different times from 1986 to 1999, and has since become a major shareholder in all kinds of industries, most notably automobiles and oil.

Kerkorian returned to Las Vegas with a vengeance in 1993, opening a new MGM Grand that, again, boasted the world's largest hotel at the time. It was also the first Las Vegas property that cost $1 billion to build and included a theme park, called the Emerald City, as large as Disneyland when it opened in 1955. But it wasn't as successful as Kerkorian hoped, and he started rebuilding his Vegas portfolio through acquisitions. In 2004, Steve Wynn told the *Las Vegas Review-Journal* that Kerkorian "never had a bit of luck building hotels from scratch, but he has been the best acquirer of properties in the history of Las Vegas."

Visit Vault at **www.vault.com** for insider company profiles, expert advice, career message boards, expert resume reviews, the Vault Job Board and more.

VAULT CAREER LIBRARY   257

Let the wheeling and dealing commence!

In 2000, Kerkorian led MGM's $6.4 billion buyout of Wynn's Mirage Resorts, then the biggest merger in industry history (and one fiercely resisted by Steve Wynn). After the deal closed, Kerkorian's company owned outright five Las Vegas casinos, (the Bellagio, Boardwalk, Golden Nugget, Mirage and Treasure Island), 50 percent of the Monte Carlo, and a casino each in Biloxi, Miss., and Laughlin, Nev. (the Beau Rivage and another Golden Nugget). The company changed its name to MGM Mirage after the deal closed.

Shortly after the Mirage buyout closed, MGM partnered with rival Boyd Gaming Corp. to build Atlantic City, New Jersey's first new casino in 13 years—The Borgata. The property opened in July 2003 and features all the luxury resort amenities: hip restaurants, 300-thread count sheets, glass chandeliers and a 50,000-square-foot spa. The resort's marketing efforts courts young urban professionals instead of grizzled old timers, highlighting its nightclubs and restaurants, and keeping them open past midnight.

In 2004, Kerkorian spearheaded another huge acquisition, buying Mandalay Bay Resorts for $7.9 billion. In this deal, MGM acquired the Monte Carlo's outstanding shares, five more Las Vegas casinos (Circus Circus, Excalibur, Luxor, Mandalay Bay and Slots-a-Fun) and a smattering of casinos in Detroit, Illinois, Mississipi and elsewhere in Nevada. MGM Mirage was still a publicly traded company after each deal closed, and Kerkorian is still the firm's majority shareholder.

Farewell to one MGM ...

In April 2005, Kerkorian sold the MGM movie studios for $4.9 billion to a group of investors led by Sony Corporation. In the deal, Kerkorian made a personal profit of about $1.8 billion. It appears to signal an end to his on-again, off-again relationship with the studio since 1969, but Kerkorian has surprised industry-watchers before. He certainly isn't done investing in businesses outside of casinos and hotels. In 2007, Kerkorian-affiliated companies launched bids for stakes in two different oil companies, Delta Petroleuma and Tesoro, and for the Chrysler Group car company.

... and to the Boardwalk

In November 2005, MGM Mirage announced it would close its Boardwalk casino on the Las Vegas Strip, in preparation for a massive $7.4 billion development called Project CityCenter. As one might surmise from its name, it will be placed pretty much in the dead center of Las Vegas and constitutes a pretty large gamble on the city's long-term success. After hatching the plan, MGM hired consulting firm McKinsey & Co. to gauge whether the city could support such a large project. McKinsey confirmed the casino company's vision, which MGM Mirage likens to New York City's SoHo shopping area, rather than a mall.

The Boardwalk closed in January 2006 and construction on the city's new "Center" began in June 2006. The Boardwalk's demise affected 694 employees, more than 300 of which soon found employment at other casinos on the Strip. MGM Mirage hopes to create many more jobs through the project in the meantime: 7,000 for construction purposes and 12,000 permanent positions once the development opens, in late 2009.

Sandwiched between the Bellagio and the Monte Carlo, CityCenter will span 76 acres, feature two 60-story glass towers, a 4,000 room hotel-casino, three boutique hotels, 1,600 condos and over 500,000 square feet of retail space. MGM secured a major investor for CityCenter in August 2007, when the government of Dubai agreed to shell out $5.5 billion for a 50 percent stake in the project, as well as 9.5 percent of MGM's stock.

First stop: Macau ...

MGM Mirage has another major development pending on the island of Macau. Formerly a Portuguese colony, the island is a Special Administrative Region of China where gambling is legal, and gaming companies are feverishly developing casinos there in hope of a big payday. MGM Mirage is no exception, planning to build the MGM Grand Macau, a $975 million hotel-casino as a joint venture with Chinese businesswoman Pansy Ho. China's government approved the facility in April 2005 and construction is expected to be completed in early 2008.

Located adjacent to a site being developed by Wynn Resorts (Steve Wynn's new vehicle), the casino will be stocked with 300 tables and 1,000 slot machines, and the hotel will have 600 rooms. Construction will leave 50,000 square feet open for future development, depending on the MGM Grand Macau's initial success.

Build it, and they will come

MGM is spreading its love of construction to Atlantic City, too, currently developing a $5 billion hotel-casino by the boardwalk. The casino will aim for the higher-end Jersey gambler, with a spa, mall, theater and three hotel towers (each with a different demographic in mind). MGM hopes this project will reverse the downward slide of

Visit Vault at www.vault.com for insider company profiles, expert advice, career message boards, expert resume reviews, the Vault Job Board and more.

VAULT CAREER LIBRARY   259

gambling revenue in the Garden State by attracting a free-spending clientele from major cities nearby. The company is also building a $400 million hotel expansion to its co-owned Borgata property, which will add 800 rooms and suites in early 2008.

The opposite of Vegas

MGM's newest addition to the MGM Grand opened in May 2006. Called the Signature, it's a mixture of condominiums and hotel rooms, built on the remnants of MGM Grand's former theme park. It aims to gentrify the Sin City, featuring absolutely no gambling and no smoking, as well as the usual plush décor, brand-name bed sheets, spa, fitness center and pool. Condo owners can even make a profit, if they so choose—MGM provides an optional "rental program," through which condo owners can basically sublet their apartments into the hotel's room inventory, for use as luxury suites while they're out of town.

Raking it in

In 2007, the company racked up $7.6 billion in sales and more than doubled its profits to $1.6 billion, from $648 million the year before. MGM attributed the earnings disparity to the fact that Hurricane Katrina negatively affected its Gulf Coast properties during fiscal 2006. The firm also attributed its 2007 gains to a large investment from the government of Dubai and to a high number of international guests at its Las Vegas properties—in this respect, the weakened state of the U.S. economy and currency exchange rate has actually benefited MGM Mirage's business.

GETTING HIRED

Bet on a career at MGM

Candidates interested in working at the MGM Mirage should check out the job opportunities on the company web site, at secure02.mgm-mirage.com/employment. Job openings are searchable by title, department and hotel. For all jobs, the MGM Mirage requires candidates to provide picture identification, a detailed employment history and three personal references who are not family members or former employers. In order to apply, job seekers must first create a profile.

The site also provides information about benefits and job opportunities. Benefits include health and dental insurance, 401(k) accounts, flexible spending accounts and paid time off, tuition reimbursement and on-site child care.

Visit Vault at **www.vault.com** for insider company profiles, expert advice,
career message boards, expert resume reviews, the Vault Job Board and more.

V/\ULT CAREER LIBRARY   **261**

National Railroad Passenger Corporation

60 Massachusetts Avenue NE
Washington, DC 20002
Phone: (202) 906-3000
Fax: (202) 906-3306
www.amtrak.com

LOCATIONS

Washington, DC (HQ)
Boston, MA
Chicago, IL
Los Angeles, CA
Oakland, CA
Philadelphia, PA
Rensselaer, NY
Seattle, WA

Additional operations in 133
locations throughout the US.

THE STATS

Employer Type: Government agency
Chairman: Donna McLean
President & CEO: Alexander K.
  Kummant
2007 Employees: 19,000
2007 Revenue ($mil.): $2,153

KEY COMPETITORS

Greyhound
Southwest Airlines
US Airways

EMPLOYMENT CONTACT

jobs.amtrak.com
1-877-AMTRAK1 (1-877-268-7251)

THE SCOOP

Empire Builder

The National Railroad Passenger Corporation runs Amtrak, the United States' national intercity train service. Perennially unprofitable and dependent on government grants for a large portion of its budget, the company's funding is a hotly contested political football. Yet, somehow, the trains keep running.

In 2006, the company took in $1.35 billion in ticket sales, transporting a total of about 24 million people. If Amtrak were an airline, this total would place it in the top 10 in terms of ridership. The firm reported losses of about $1 billion for the year, as opposed to $1.1 billion the year before.

20th Century Limited

By the time Amtrak came onto the scene, rail travel's heyday was long over. The Pullman cars of the 1920s and 1930s, which whisked passengers across the American landscape in luxe comfort, were a distant memory by the 1950s. In that decade, the booming postwar economy gave rise to the most popular current means of transportation: airplanes and automobiles. By 1958, trains were carrying 4 percent of passengers traveling between cities, down from nearly 100 percent a decade earlier.

The railroad industry went through a period of consolidation, but even economies of scale could not render it profitable again—in 1970, American passenger railroads collectively lost about $500 million. The government intervened in 1970, passing the Rail Passenger Service Act and creating the National Railroad Passenger Corporation out of the remains of 15 train companies' passenger services. Only three train lines in the country, the Denver & Rio Grande Western, the Rock Island and the Southern, chose not to join the new corporation.

Riding rainbow

The corporation changed its name to Amtrak in 1971 for marketing purposes. At first, Amtrak didn't even own the trains or the tracks on which it ran—it leased the passenger cars from the struggling railroad companies and paid rent to the rail freight companies that owned the different stretches of track. One couldn't easily tell an Amtrak train, therefore, and the fleet's varied appearance earned it the "rainbow" nickname.

Rail passengers increased in number during the oil crisis of 1973, giving Amtrak some funds to invest in new locomotives and passenger cars, and the company began to resemble its current shape. The new trains had the recognizable red and blue Amtrak logo and color scheme, and employee ranks swelled with new hires, growing from 1,500 to 8,500 between 1972 and 1974.

Also in 1973, the federal government passed the Regional Rail Reorganization Act, reorganizing a mass of bankrupt Northeastern freight companies into the Consolidated Rail Corporation (Conrail). Another major piece of legislation, the Railroad Revitalization and Regulatory Reform Act of 1976 gave 621 miles of Conrail's tracks to Amtrak, including Pennsylvania Station in New York City and 30th Street Station in Philadelphia. With these additions, the firm's employee headcount doubled to 16,500.

A long, slow ride

However, tickets still failed to cover the company's costs and its transition from running the country's rail lines to owning and operating them progressed slowly, especially as government vacillated between different budget considerations. When Ronald Reagan became president in the 1980s, he clearly wanted to cut Amtrak down to size. "On the New York to Chicago train," he declared, "it would cost the taxpayer less for the government to pass out free plane tickets." Amtrak continued to operate as a sort of national safety net, as evidenced by Reagan's run-in with an air traffic controller's strike in 1981, during which Amtrak ticket sales increased dramatically.

The company began to look for other sources of income in the 1980s, including transporting mail and packages as well as allowing phone companies to bury high-speed data lines near train tracks. Things began to look up in 1984, as nearly half of people traveling between New York and Washington, D.C., opted to take the train rather than fly or fight the traffic on I-95. Any improvements in these regional services were more than offset by money-losing routes—like the one that runs from Florida to California—and Amtrak's lack of profits attracted governmental criticism until well into President Clinton's tenure in the 1990s.

Despite the passing of several governmental ultimatums that the firm start turning a profit, the most recent of which expired in 2002, the government continues to float Amtrak's boat. In 2002, then-President David Gunn argued to Congress that all forms of transport require government support. Expenses for air traffic control and road maintenance are both handled by government-run trust funds, the details for which hardly ever get hashed out during annual budget debates. In the 34 years between 1971 and 2005, Amtrak received $29 billion in government funding, which seems like a great deal—but not when compared to the $15 billion that airlines received from the government in 2001 after the terrorist attacks of September 11th.

I want my TGV!

One perennial Congressional complaint is that the richest country in the world doesn't have train service to rival the high-speed trains of Europe, China and Japan. The larger cities in those areas are all laced together with glistening ribbons of well-maintained track, frequented by blisteringly fast trains. What Congress often fails to mention is the oodles of money spent by foreign governments in the 1970s and 1980s to fund those trains' and rail lines' development, the same period that the American government idly watched 15 historic rail roads lapse into bankruptcy.

In the 1980s, while Congress griped about Amtrak actually gaining complete ownership of its own trains and tracks, France was building special extra-long and extra-flat tracks for TGV, the world's fastest train. (One current TGV route averages a speed of 160 mph.) These tracks, needless to say, are not shared with any other train or freight service, a luxury few Amtrak trains can claim. Almost all of the tracks Amtrak uses are still owned by freight companies, and many were laid out in the earlier half of the 19th century. The oldest tracks used by Amtrak date back to 1826 and were designed to accommodate trains going a stately 30 mph.

Amtrak's answer to the TGV is Acela, a high-speed train running on the Boston-New York-Washington, D.C., route. The model uses tilted train cars to keep passengers relatively unaware of the high G forces incurred in going around tight corners at high speeds. The Acela, which debuted in 2000, has a top speed of 150 mph in places, but only averages around 70 mph due to engineering difficulties (Amtrak accepted the lowest bid for the train's design) and because it doesn't run on an exclusive track.

You only have to take your shoes off if you want to

Amtrak carried about 2.6 million more passengers in 2006 than in 2005, a trend that continued in the first half of 2007, increasing by a rate of 6 percent. Analysts suggest that train passengers don't need to worry about gas prices or loud engine noises, but a more probable cause of so many people hitting the tracks is the recent increase in airline security. Passengers can board trains without having to remove their shoes and can freely transport such contraband as nail clippers, knitting needles and containers holding more than three ounces of liquid. Luggage is also less likely to

Visit Vault at **www.vault.com** for insider company profiles, expert advice, career message boards, expert resume reviews, the Vault Job Board and more.

VAULT CAREER LIBRARY   265

go missing when traveling by train, since passengers generally keep their bags with them when traveling.

Trains are also increasingly en vogue with the green set, which opts for choo-choos because they are one of the most fuel-efficient modes of transport per capita. A train uses one-fifth less fuel to travel any given distance than a car or a plane. Many scientists believe that planes may be more harmful for the environment than ground-based modes of travel, since they emit carbon higher in the atmosphere.

Some Amtrak routes experienced a tremendous boom in terms of passengers. The route between Chicago and St. Louis increased its passenger figures more than 50 percent in the first half of 2007, and the Acela's amount increased by a fifth. In fact, the Acela train now transports more people between New York and Boston than airplanes do.

Going long

But Amtrak's long-distance routes are a different story. They consistently lose money, perhaps because of a disturbing trend reported in the company's 2006 annual report: for the full year, only 30 percent of them arrived on time. "Approximately 80 percent of delay minutes outside of the Northeast Corridor," wrote Amtrak in its annual report, "[are] due to insufficient rail capacity and the need for additional infrastructure improvement."

And, of course, Amtrak doesn't even own most of these rails, so it will need a lot of help in repairing them. Unfortunately, after almost 40 years of existence, the company still owes $3.5 billion in debt to its leases on locomotives and other forms of rolling stock. So, while its increased number of passengers is very good news, Amtrak will operate the way it always has: negotiating with the government for annual grants, attempting to pay down more of its debt and continuing its eternal quest to gain control of the tracks on which it runs. (For now, turning a profit is still out of the question.)

Affairs of state

Yet even the same old, same old represents a victory of sorts for Amtrak, as it has resisted repeated attempts by the second Bush administration to do away with its existence altogether. In early 2005, the White House released its annual budget, with nothing allocated for Amtrak. The idea was to cut funding completely and see what would become of its constituent parts. Both the House and the Senate rejected these plans, with the latter voting later in the year to pay $11.6 billion to the company over the next six years.

Also in late 2005, November to be exact, Amtrak's board "released" CEO David Gunn from his duties. Democrats in office were furious, with New York Senator Charles Schumer even questioning the board's legal authority to fire Gunn. The departing executive, who is credited with reviving New York City's subway system in the 1980s and came out of retirement in 2002 to attempt a similar feat with Amtrak, released his own statement: "I did not resign [from Amtrak]. I was removed. It's been fun. Good luck." In a subsequent interview with *The New York Times*, Gunn described the motives of the Bush administration and the Amtrak board, saying that "it's been their goal from the beginning … to liquidate the company."

The company replaced Gunn in August 2006 with Alexander Kummant, a former executive at freight carrier Union Pacific Railroad, and Amtrak-boosters suspiciously eyed him as a President Bush appointee. However, Kummant has stated a commitment to preserve the controversial long-distance routes and fighting for governmental aid in improving track conditions.

Seeking all Amtrak-friendly politicians

Surprisingly, Kummant and governmental Amtrak-boosters (i.e., Democrats) have succeeded in winning more and more support for increasing subsidies. The driving factor surely hasn't been any philosophical agreement, but rather the sound of tickets being sold as the number of passengers continues to rise.

In October 2007, the Senate passed (by 70 to 22) the Passenger Rail Improvement and Investment Act, which would give the company about $3 billion annually over the next six years, thus sparing the railway its annual lobbying efforts to win federal grants. However, the bill has yet to pass the traditionally less Amtrak-friendly House, not to mention the veto pen of President Bush.

Luxury cars and

In the meantime, CEO Kummant is working with other interests to shape up Amtrak. He is leaning on his old employer, Union Pacific, to repair stretches of poorly-maintained track that cause delays. And he has tried sprucing up the company's offerings, launching a joint venture in November 2007 with GrandLuxe Rail Journeys, a private rail tour operator. GrandLuxe is attaching seven of its spiffy sleeping, dining and lounge cars to regularly scheduled Amtrak routes—including Chicago to San Francisco, Los Angeles to Chicago and Washington, D.C., to Miami.

Kummant has his hands full with another old Amtrak issue, which came to a head in November 2007, just as GrandLuxe cars went out around the country. The vast majority of Amtrak's employees, about 15,000 out of the grand total of 19,000, have been working without a contract since 1999, and threatened to go on strike, effective December 1st. For the last eight years, they had been negotiating a new contract with the company (talk about protracted), often in the form of courtroom mediation.

The employees would have gone on strike years ago, but the Railway Labor Act prohibits any strike until federal officials deem mediation attempts unsuccessful. On November 28th, just three days before workers across the country were set to walk off the job, President Bush created a "presidential emergency board," sort of as another form of mediation. Following the government intervention to preserve rail service over the holiday season, the unions reached an agreement with Amtrak in mid-January 2008, preserving Amtrak's strike-free record.

GETTING HIRED

Train yourself for Amtrak

Amtrak's careers site, at www.jobs.amtrak.com provides information about employment and open positions at the company. During summer 2007, the company announced it was recruiting security officers, but there are many other positions available. Jobs can be searched by keyword, location, schedule and amount of travel. To apply for a job, candidates must first create a profile. Some jobs may require membership in a union.

Hopeful employees might also want to check out back issues of the Amtrak employees' newsletter, *Amtrak Ink*, which are archived at www.amtrak.com/servlet/ContentServer?pagename=Amtrak/am2Copy/Title_Image_Copy_Page&c=am2Copy&cid=109355406 7060&ssid=603.

OUR SURVEY SAYS

Amtrak.com or Amtrak.gov?

While Amtrak is not a "government entity" survey respondents admit that "there is a strong political undercurrent" and that "politics at the management level [are] pretty bad." One source even characterized the firm as sharing "many of the hierarchical and bureaucratic characteristics of a government entity—so employees must be comfortable having one foot in the private sector and one foot in the public sector."

The firm's highly regulated nature has resulted in several workplace realities, both good and bad. "The majority of the workforce is unionized," notes one person, and is "highly paid compared to other industries." And "at the worker bee level," claims another, "everybody got along [and] the color of your skin made very little difference." Another agrees, noting that "diversity among employee ranks seemed to be good." Yet again, the political nature of Amtrak is never far from sight: "there appeared to be fewer female and/or ethnic minorities at the executive level than overall employee demographics would suggest."

Amtrak's penchant for pensions

And, like government employees, Amtrakers enjoy major retirement benefits (the longer the tenure, the better) and "Historically, many of the staff had 30—or more—year careers." The bureaucracy can weigh down on employees, however, as "Information was controlled and not readily shared beyond the immediate staff having a 'need to know,'" which resulted in a lack of communication: "new people were seldom taken around and introduced … and most of the company probably didn't even know about many of the major projects and initiatives that were already underway."

Laying tracks for slow-moving careers

A similar lack of communication, or opportunity, arises in respect to career advancement. With the company attempting to change its culture into less of a subsidized, government-dependent entity, "there appears to be a lot of opportunity for midlevel managers" but "current staff have not found rapid advancement opportunities. Advancement was too slow for many, thus [resulting in pretty high] turnover."

Visit Vault at www.vault.com for insider company profiles, expert advice, career message boards, expert resume reviews, the Vault Job Board and more.

VAULT CAREER LIBRARY 269

In the near future, respondents stress patience as the company changes its business model. One reports that "the required skill sets will change faster than the corporate culture, which could lead to a good deal of frustration for the most qualified individuals." Another notes that a standard workweek clocks in at 40 hours, but as "many of the staff [appear] to be over-allocated, [they often work] much longer hours."

Northwest Airlines Corporation

2700 Lone Oak Parkway
Eagan, MN 55121
Phone: (612) 726-2111
Fax: (612) 726-7123
www.nwa.com

LOCATIONS

Eagan, MN (HQ)
Anchorage, AK • Baltimore, MD •
Boston, MA • Chisholm, MN •
Detroit, MI • Dulles, VA • Hong
Kong • Honolulu, HI • Indianapolis,
IN • Memphis, TN • Minneapolis,
MN • New York, NY • San Antonio,
TX • San Francisco, CA • Seattle,
WA • Sioux City, IA • Tacoma, WA
• Tampa, FL • Amsterdam •
Bangkok • Beijing • Manila • Osaka
• Singapore • Taipei • Tokyo

THE STATS

Employer Type: Public Company
Stock Symbol: NWA
Stock Exchange: NYSE
Chairman: Gary L. Wilson
President & CEO: Douglas M.
  Steenland
2007 Employees: 34,000
2007 Revenue ($mil.): $12,528

DEPARTMENTS

Administrative
Customer Service
Engineering
Financial & Accounting
Flight Attendant
Human Resources
Information Technology
Luggage Handling
Maintenance
Pilots
Security

KEY COMPETITORS

American Airlines
Delta Air Lines
US Airways

EMPLOYMENT CONTACT

www.nwa.com/corpinfo/career

Visit Vault at **www.vault.com** for insider company profiles, expert advice,
career message boards, expert resume reviews, the Vault Job Board and more.

VAULT CAREER LIBRARY   271

THE SCOOP

Some people just know how to fly

Northwest Airlines is the fourth-largest airline in the U.S., with a fleet of 500 planes traveling to airports in 160 countries. The airline has hubs in Minneapolis-St. Paul, Detroit, Memphis, Amsterdam and Tokyo. Northwest is also a major player in Asian air travel, flying 200 flights weekly between the U.S. and Asia. Northwest is part of the SkyTeam alliance of airlines.

They have liftoff

In 1926, Colonel Lewis Brittin (member of the Minnesota Aviation Hall of Fame) organized a group of Midwestern businessmen to purchase the faltering airmail service between Minneapolis-St. Paul and Chicago. Within a year, the airline provided passenger service along the same route, and by 1928 it offered its first international service, going along a Northwestern route from Fargo, N.D., to Winnipeg, Canada.

In the 1930s, the company expanded its service across the Midwest, conducting its first "northern transcontinental" route to Seattle and Tacoma, Wash., in 1933. NWA common stock went public in 1941, the same year that annual passenger revenue exceeded mail revenue for the first time.

Also in 1941, the United States entered World War II, and the American government assigned Northwest the task of facilitating its flights to cold Northwestern areas, like the Aleutian Islands. The government also employed Northwest in outfitting Army bombers for cold weather and long-distance routes. The airline's employee headcount grew dramatically during the war, from a prewar total of 881 to 10,439 by war's end in 1945.

Travel Northwest to Asia!

After the war, Northwest won governmental approval to start flying to Asian cities via Alaska on its "great circle" route. At that time, the only competing service to Asia was Pan Am's slower route through the Philippines and China. By the mid- to late 1960s, the "Northwest Orient" service arranged flights from Philadelphia, Detroit, San Francisco and the Twin Cities to Hong Kong, Osaka, Hawaii and other Pacific destinations. In 1968, the firm was the most profitable in the industry for the first time, and won the profit race again in 1969.

Northwest looks East

The airline added service from Los Angeles to Tokyo in the early 1970s and went public on the New York Stock Exchange in 1973. The time to start looking eastwards arrived in 1978, when the American airline industry underwent deregulation, and in 1979, Northwest began offering trans-Atlantic routes to Copenhagen and Stockholm. By the mid-1980s, Northwest added over 20 U.S. markets and international routes to Pacific cities, like Shanghai and Kuala Lumpur, and Atlantic ones, like Frankfurt and Dublin.

In 1986, Northwest nearly doubled its size with the $884 million purchase of Republic Airlines, the largest acquisition in company history. The merger narrowly won federal approval, as Republic was a major regional competitor to Northwest, having purchased the West Coast-based Hughes Airwest in 1980. The acquisition brought Northwest a fair amount of debt, and in 1989, financiers Alfred Checchi and Gary Wilson led a $3.8 billion leveraged buyout, taking Northwest private.

Indebted Northwest

The airline's debt only grew in the early 1990s, reaching $4.2 billion by 1992. Not coincidentally, the firm gained a reputation among business travelers for poor customer service, earning the nickname "Northworst" and suffered massive losses in 1991 and 1992, totaling $618 million. In late 1992, the state of Minnesota struck a deal with Northwest, agreeing to invest $670 million in return for Northwest's commitment to remain in the state. Northwest used $310 million from the package to pay down some debt and the remainder on construction of new facilities in the Great Lakes State. In 1993, the firm struck a last-minute agreement with its unions to cut costs, and went public in 1994, just as the industry pulled out of a slump.

In 1995, Northwest reported $902 million profits on sales of $9 billion. However, labor issues re-emerged in September 1998, when all of Northwest's pilots went on strike, forcing the airline to cancel 1,700 daily flights for over two weeks. Northwest laid off a staggering 31,000 employees during the strike, inviting them back to work after its conclusion.

The firm hired a new CEO and a new president in February 2001, Richard Anderson and Douglas Steenland, respectively. The two worked together to restore (or create) a high level of morale among company employees. They looked to be making headway by April 2001, when they resolved a contract dispute with mechanics that dated back to 1996. But then, the following September 11th, terrorist attacks sent the airline industry into one of its worst slumps in history.

A dark day

In the weeks following the September attacks, Northwest reduced its flight schedule by 20 percent and announced about 10,000 job cuts. Congress quickly enacted grants for the industry, totaling $5 billion in immediate funds and $10 billion more in loan guarantees. Northwest's share of the grants was $461 million. The airline reported annual losses of $423 million in 2001, actually a better result than much of its competition. To attract customers in 2002, Northwest increased flight frequency on popular routes, established an "interline" electronic ticketing capabilities with American Airlines and expanded its Biz Perks corporate rewards program.

Crisis mode

Things didn't look up for the company in the following years. In 2002, Northwest cut 1,000 jobs and, after failed negotiations with Expedia prompted the firm to stop selling tickets online, announced a second round of job cuts, asking 1,600 flight attendants to take voluntary leave. The next year, Northwest negotiated with its workers' unions to cut costs, asking its pilots to take a pay cut of 20 percent and its unions to approve $950 million in job cuts. In March 2004, ALPA, the pilots' union, recommended that pilots agree to $200 million in annual cuts through 2006, less than half of Northwest's plans to save $442 million on pilot costs. In November 2004, the two sides settled on $300 million in savings, to be realized through a 15 percent pay reduction over two years.

CEO Anderson departed Northwest in October 2004, in favor of a job at UnitedHealth Group. Douglas Steenland, the company president, added chief executive to his job titles. In August 2007, Anderson resurfaced in the airline industry as Delta's new CEO.

Making concessions

In February 2005, Northwest cut complimentary food from its domestic coach service and revealed plans to eliminate 930 mechanics' jobs. Also that month, Northwest hiked fares by as much as $40. In April 2005, the airline revealed losses of $450 million for its first quarter, and CFO Bernard Han resigned shortly afterwards.

In August 2005, the cost of jet fuel surged past $100 per barrel and Hurricane Katrina, the nation's largest ever natural disaster, devastated much of the Gulf Coast. Northwest filed for bankruptcy protection the next month, in September 2005, shocking Wall Street analysts who thought the airline was better equipped to avoid it than many rivals. Company stock plummeted over 50 percent on the news. Without

Chapter 11 protection, Steenland said, the firm faced "heavy losses," on top of the $3.6 billion it had lost since 2001.

A week later, Northwest began restructuring efforts, announcing the layoffs of 1,400 flight attendants, mostly from hubs in Detroit and Minneapolis-St. Paul. In early 2006, the company laid off 5,400 striking mechanics and replaced them with non-unionized workers. The company outsourced some maintenance in the meantime, to make up the difference. In January 2005, in the midst of bankruptcy proceedings, Northwest agreed to acquire the similarly bankrupt Mesaba Airlines, which, as Northwest Airlink, had operated feeder service to Northwest hubs for 22 years.

Due North

Northwest emerged from bankruptcy at the end of May 2007 with a plan to retain top management, compensating its top 400 executives with a 5 percent stake (worth nearly $300 million) in the reorganized company. The company's employees didn't appreciate this news: as a result of the bankruptcy proceedings, their pay and benefits were cut by $195 million.

Besides salary decreases, Northwest employees will also have to get used to the firm's policy switch from a traditional pension plan to a 401(k) program. They probably won't strike again for awhile, though, as another union contract won't expire at Northwest until 2011. Industry-watchers have expressed concern that employees' disgruntlement could lead to poor customer service and more worker-related trouble for the airline.

It didn't take long for such worker-related trouble to occur, as an apparent pilot shortage in June 2007 resulted in the cancellation of nearly 1,000 flights. Flights continued to be dropped throughout July—over 500 were tallied over the course of one particular weekend—due to what the Associated Press called "a higher-than-normal rate of absentee calls" from "sick" pilots. Union representatives at the time claimed that its pilots were legitimately sick, as Northwest had recently increased pilots' workload to 90 hours per month, just 10 hours short of the FAA's utmost limit. The two sides reached an agreement in August, when Northwest agreed to pay pilots time-and-a-half after flying 80 hours per month and to cap flying schedules at 90 hours.

Visit Vault at **www.vault.com** for insider company profiles, expert advice, career message boards, expert resume reviews, the Vault Job Board and more.

VAULT CAREER LIBRARY   275

Back to basics

Northwest is trying to return to what it does best: flying people to Asia. Immediately after emerging from bankruptcy in spring 2007, the firm began lobbying lawmakers for the newest air route to China, which is allowed by regulators relatively infrequently. Northwest proposed flying nonstop from its hub in Detroit to Beijing, via the North Pole. Despite its best efforts, however, United won rights to the route. The next route to China will open up in 2009. In November 2007, Northwest announced plans for direct flights between its Memphis hub and Tokyo, probably starting up in 2009 when new aircraft arrive in the airline's fleet. The firm currently flies to Japan from Detroit, Minneapolis, Los Angeles and San Francisco.

Also, "Northworst" appears to have gotten the message about its recent past, in November announcing a dramatic attempt to improve customer service during the 2007-2008 holiday season, the Comprehensive Holiday Travel Reliability Program. It includes an online customer database that maintains contact info in case of delays or problems, updates of airport gates every 15 minutes in case of a delay, booking agents waiving flight-changing fees in case of delay or cancellation, and other helpful policies.

In January 2008, media reports stated that Delta Air Lines was in "serious" talks with both Northwest and United Airlines about a potential merger, with Continental Airlines also named as a potential merger-mate. Except for Continental, all of these firms recently emerged from bankruptcy and, without much cash on hand, a merger would do the most to boost their services and business outlook. Also in January, Northwest released its year-end financial results, with revenue slightly decreasing (by 0.3 percent) and profits more than doubling year-over-year, from $301 million to $764 million. The talks with Delta reportedly grew more serious in February, even settling on the executive leadership of Delta CEO Richard Anderson, with Northwest CEO Steenland remaining underneath him. Anderson and Steenland partnered as CEO and president of Northwest in 2001, and this would be a return to form, of sorts.

GETTING HIRED

Get your flight on

Northwest has an informative careers site at nwa.com/corpinfo/career/summary, which provides information on opportunities at the company for everyone from the greenest intern to the most seasoned pilots. The company divides its recruiting into corporate jobs, luggage handlers, reservations agents, flight attendants, pilots, interns and college graduates. Some positions may require joining a union, and flight attendants must adhere to guidelines about height and appearance. Northwest recruits MBA and BA candidates from the University of Michigan, Michigan State and the University of Minnesota. MBA candidates are also sought from the University of Chicago and Wharton.

Omni Hotels Corporation

420 Decker Drive
Suite 200
Irving, TX 75062
Phone: (972) 730-6664
Fax: (972) 871-5665
www.omnihotels.com

LOCATIONS

Irving, TX (HQ)
Atlanta, GA • Austin, TX • Boston,
MA • Broomfield, CO • Champions
Gate, FL • Charlotte, NC •
Charlottesville, VA • Chicago, IL •
Corpus Christi, TX • Dallas, TX •
Detroit, MA • Fort Worth, TX •
Houston, TX • Indianapolis, IN •
Jacksonville, FL • Los Angeles, CA
• New Orleans, LA • New Haven,
CT • New York, NY • Pittsburgh,
PA • Richmond, VA • San Antonio,
TX • San Diego, CA • San
Francisco, CA • St. Louis, MO •
Tucson, AZ • Washington, DC

THE STATS

Employer Type: Subsidiary of TRT
  Holdings
CEO: James D. Caldwell
President: Michael J. Deitemeyer
2006 Employees: 9,500

DEPARTMENTS

Administrative • Art •
Clerical/Secretarial • Communications
• Culinary • Customer Service •
Finance • Food & Beverage • Front
Desk • Housekeeping • Human
Resources • Information Systems •
Legal & Governmental Affairs •
Marketing • Network Administration
• Operations • Planning • Production
• Public Relations • Quality
Assurance • Restaurant Operations •
Revenue Management • Rooms •
Sales • Technical Support

KEY COMPETITORS

Four Seasons Hotels
Marriott International
Starwood Hotels & Resorts

EMPLOYMENT CONTACT

www.omnihotels.com/AboutOmni
Hotels/Employment

E-mail: recruiting@omnihotels.com

THE SCOOP

All hotels to all people

Omni Hotels operates a small chain of 40 resorts in Canada, Mexico and the U.S., varying from historic hotels in New York, Chicago and Washington, D.C., to modern spa and golf complexes. Omni mainly focuses on upscale leisure and high-end corporate travel.

An epic story of clams and cracker barrels

Omni Hotels began in 1945 as a single clam stand, operated by the five Dunfey brothers in Hampton Beach, New Hampshire. After a few summers of brisk sales, the natural next step was a restaurant, and the brothers pooled their clams and purchased Lamie's Tavern, a combo restaurant and, thrown into the deal, a motor inn. The brothers committed to providing their guests with "good old New England hospitality" and advertised their restaurant as a "cracker barrel lounge." The brothers preferred the hotel side of the business and in 1958 purchased a 332-room hotel. They adopted the name Dunfey Hotels Corp. for the venture, although they still offered "cracker barrels" for years to come (no relation to the restaurant chain).

By 1964, Dunfey Hotels operated 16 establishments throughout New England, most of them as Sheraton franchises. While franchising is now the industry standard, this was somewhat revolutionary at the time—Dunfey's 16 hotels made it the world's largest franchisee. The Dunfeys were ambitious to expand further, but lacked capital. They sold their hotels and "cracker barrel" lounges to Irish airline Aer Lingus in 1976. The Dunfeys continued to run the company, and under Aer Lingus started acquiring and restoring historic American hotels for its "Classic Hotel Division," which is still part of the company's operations.

Dunfey Hotels Corp. gradually acquired a select group of East Coast hotels, with a few historic assets in Chicago (the Ambassador East Hotel), New York City (the Berkshire Place) and Washington, D.C. (the Shoreham Hotel). The company continued purchasing antique lodgings nationwide and, in 1983, acquired Omni International Hotels, an operator of three hotels in the Southern states. Aer Lingus seized on Omni as a new brand name for its hotels and began divesting Dunfey motor inns and franchises to finance the purchases of other historic hotels. Omni sold off the last Dunfey property in 1992, and the Dunfey brothers retired from the hotel

Visit Vault at **www.vault.com** for insider company profiles, expert advice, career message boards, expert resume reviews, the Vault Job Board and more.

VAULT CAREER LIBRARY   279

business and founded Dunfrey Brothers Capital Group, a venture capital firm devoted to socially responsible causes.

An Omni-vorous company

By 1987, Omni Hotels was an attractive candidate for acquisition, with a low debt-load from a decade of cautious purchases and an enviable roster of 36 hotels, most of them with a high pedigree. That year, Aer Lingus sold Omni to World International Holdings and Wharf Holdings, two Hong Kong-based conglomerates. Wharf Holdings rebranded its upscale hotels in Hong Kong and Singapore as Omni establishments.

The company began to grow at a faster rate, often through management and franchise agreements, bringing its now-prestigious Omni brand to hotels across the country. Omni picked up nine more locations by 1991, and then co-owner World International cashed out during an industry slump, selling its 50 percent ownership to Wharf Holdings. The downturn actually benefited Omni Hotels, as it picked up new franchises and locations at rock-bottom prices in the early 1990s. In 1992 it added hotels in Florida, New York, Ohio and Texas. The next year, it started managing the Chicago Hyatt Regency Suites, renaming it the Omni Chicago Hotel.

In 1996, Wharf Holdings sold Omni to TRT Holdings, a Texas-based holding company with interests in gyms and oil prospecting. With the spending power of its new parent company, Omni snapped up eight more hotels in 1998, including its first foray into Canada. TRT's gym holdings also resulted in some synergy, supplementing Omni's hotels with fitness equipment in 2002. Two years later, TRT Holdings purchased Gold's Gym from private equity firm Brockway Moran & Partners.

Getting bigger all the time

In recent years, Omni has increasingly opened hotels near convention centers and sport arenas, including the 2004 opening of the Omni Hotel San Diego, directly connected to the Padres' baseball team's stadium. In August 2006, Omni began work on a site in Fort Worth, Texas, which will include a luxury hotel and condominiums.

Getting bigger all the time

In July 2007, Omni announced construction on two new hotels, one in Mexico and the other in Houston. The Mexican site, located on 90 oceanside acres near Puerto

Vallarta, will have a small hotel, condominiums and private houses, in addition to golf and spa facilities. The first part of the development is due to open in 2010. The Houston hotel will be located downtown, within walking distance of the city's convention center. It will also be close to the Houston Pavilions area of offices, restaurants and shopping. The hotel will have a gym with nutritionists and trainers, as well as a spa.

Scents and sensibility

In an attempt to differentiate its brand from every other high-end hotel out there, Omni offers the Sensation Bar to stimulate each guest's interests (and some of its enses). The bar is a tray of little keepsakes, placed beside the regular old mini bar. The things inside are geared to the location of the hotel, such as items related to the local sports team or local point of interest (e.g., voodoo dolls at Omni's New Orleans branch). Other items include the edible (jellybeans, chocolates), mildly amusing (deck of cards, mini Zen garden) and girly (lip balm, bath salts, pillow spray).

In addition to these little gifts, however, guests should be on the lookout lest unexpected sources inside Omni hotels blindside their sensory stimuli. In a summer 2007 promotion, the company started scenting its newspapers. Each paper came with a sticker, ostensibly shilling the hotel's coffee and muffins, and emitted a berry aroma when touched.

Kids rule Omni

Naturally, traveling with small children in such a stimulating environment must be trying to the nerves of the most patient of parents. To aid them in their quest for contented, quiet youngsters, Omni rolled out special accommodations for kids in 2007. Not only do children get a whole sack of toys, including a kaleidoscope and (horrors!) kazoo, but Omni also prepares rooms in child-friendly splendor, down to a kid-sized bathrobe and fish-shaped bathmat. If that doesn't remind Mom and Dad enough of home, the concierge desk provides an assortment of toys, surely to be strewn about under unsuspecting adult feet.

Visit Vault at **www.vault.com** for insider company profiles, expert advice, career message boards, expert resume reviews, the Vault Job Board and more.

VAULT CAREER LIBRARY

281

GETTING HIRED

Omnify your career

Omni's careers site, at www.omnihotels.com/AboutOmniHotels/Employment, provides information about openings at the company. The company employs people in the areas of culinary arts, food and beverage, finance, HR, rooms operations, and sales and marketing. Job openings are searchable by keyword, location and department. In order to apply, job seekers must fill out an online profile. Benefits include a 401(k), health and dental, paid time off, relocation assistance and tuition assistance, and nice perks include discounts on rooms.

Omni encourages college students to apply for jobs, though it does not post a list of colleges at which it recruits. Along with submitting a resume to a specific position, college students are invited to send a resume and cover letter to the recruiting department, at:

College Recruiting Department
Omni Hotels
420 Decker Drive, Ste. 200
Irving, Texas 75062
Phone: (972) 730-6664
Fax: (972) 871-5669
E-mail: recruiting@omnihotels.com

Penn National Gaming

825 Berkshire Boulevard, Ste. 200
Wyomissing, PA 19610
Phone: (610) 373-2400
Fax: (610) 373-4966
www.pngaming.com

LOCATIONS

Wyomissing, PA (HQ)
Alton, IL
Aurora, IL
Bangor, ME
Baton Rouge, LA
Bay St. Louis, MS
Biloxi, MS
Black Hawk, CO
Chambersburg, PA
Charles Town, WV
Freehold, NJ
Grantville, PA
Hobbs, NM
Joliet, IL
Lancaster, PA
Lawrenceburg, IN
Monmouth, NJ
Reading, PA
Riverside, MO
Sioux City, IA
Toledo, OH
Tunica, MS
York, PA
Orillia, Canada

THE STATS

Employer Type: Public Company
Stock Symbol: PENN
Stock Exchange: Nasdaq
Chairman & CEO: Peter M. Carlino
2007 Employees: 15,289
2007 Revenue ($mil.): $2,437

DEPARTMENTS

Corporate
Gaming Facilities
Race Tracks
Off-Track Wagering Facilities

KEY COMPETITORS

Harrah's Entertainment
MGM MIRAGE
Trump Entertainment Resorts

EMPLOYMENT CONTACT

www.pngaming.com/main/
employment.shtml

THE SCOOP

Making a wager on the gaming business

So much for Quaker sobriety. Out of the unassuming-sounding town of Wyomissing, Penn., comes Penn National Gaming. The company owns properties in Indiana, Mississippi, Missouri, Maine, Ohio, New Jersey and, of course, Pennsylvania. Despite not having locations in Las Vegas or Atlantic City, Penn National is the third-largest gambling company in the country, behind Harrah's and MGM Mirage.

Penn National specializes in everything from slots to ponies, with 12 casinos, three racetracks with slot machines and six non-slot racetracks, evenly divided between harness and thoroughbred racing.

And they're off!

The Carlino family has been with Penn National Gaming since its first incarnation in 1972 as a thoroughbred racetrack in Grantville, Penn., about 15 miles north of Harrisburg. After a decade of enjoyable equine entertainment, in 1982 the track debuted Pennsylvania's first telephone-based betting system, "Telebet." The next year, Penn National started recording its races on film and simulcasting them to other tracks in the region, enabling gamblers miles away to register their bets with Penn National. It was all part of a strategy, described in 1997 by then-CFO Robert Ippolito as "bring[ing] the track to the people."

Penn National opened a number of off-track betting parlors throughout Pennsylvania in the 1990s, starting with one in Reading in 1992 and five more by 1996. Penn National got involved in another form of wagering in 1994, going public on the Nasdaq. In 1996, flush with IPO and OTB cash, the company purchased the Pocono Downs racetrack. The new investment soon turned a profit and Penn National purchased another racetrack in 1997, in West Virginia. The company's first purchase outside of Pennsylvania, it was closely followed by the 1999 acquisition of a harness-racing facility in New Jersey.

The company diversified into a major gaming firm by 2003, snapping up four other gaming companies in Mississippi, Colorado, Illinois and Louisiana. Revenue increased along with the company's size, surpassing $1 billion annually by 2003. In 2005, Penn National sold Pocono Downs and acquired a racetrack in Bangor, Maine, which pushed revenue past $1.3 billion for the year.

A winning perfecta

Penn National had a winning year in 2006. Its perfecta of horses and gambling took in $2.2 billion that year, and the company walked away with winnings of $327 million. Revenue increased nearly 70 percent from 2005, while profits were up 170 percent over the year previous. Now that will usher you into the winner's circle!

A private affair

Penn National continued its acquisition spree in November 2006, acquiring a thoroughbred racetrack and the Black Gold Casino in New Mexico. Little did Penn National realize that its expansion might make it the object of someone else's acquisition spree. In summer 2007, two private equity firms—the Fortress Investment Group and Centerbridge Partners—offered more than $6 billion to take Penn National private. Penn National agreed, and the deal is expected to close in summer 2008. Current CEO Peter M. Carlino, son of company co-founder and former CEO Peter D. Carlino, will remain in his post afterwards.

Looking ahead

Regardless of going private, Penn National is continuing to do what it does best: acquire and retool casinos and racetracks, often together, in rural and suburban areas. In November 2007, the firm petitioned the state of Kansas for the authority to operate a state-owned casino and hotel, a few miles south of Wichita. If approved, it would complement another pending Kansan casino, for which the company requested approval in August 2007.

GETTING HIRED

Take a chance on Penn National

Penn National's careers site, at www.pngaming.com/main/employment.shtml, divvies up its job openings by location. Job seekers can opt to work at a racetrack, at a gaming facility, in an off-track betting parlor or in corporate HQ. In order to apply, job seekers must create an online profile.

Benefits offered by the company include health, vision and dental insurance, disability insurance, 401(k) and flexible spending accounts for child care and health care.

priceline.com, Inc.

800 Connecticut Avenue
Norwalk, CT 06854
Phone: (203) 299-8000
Fax: (203) 299-8948
www.priceline.com

LOCATIONS

Norwalk, CT (HQ)
New York, NY
San Francisco, CA

THE STATS

Employer Type: Public Company
Stock Symbol: PCLN
Stock Exchange: Nasdaq
Chairman: Ralph M. Bahna
President & CEO: Jeffery H. Boyd
2007 Employees: 1,324
2007 Revenue ($mil.): $1,409

DEPARTMENTS

Finance
Human Resources
Information Technology
Legal
Marketing
Operations
Travel

KEY COMPETITORS

Expedia
Orbitz
Travelocity

EMPLOYMENT CONTACT

hostedjobs.openhire.com/epostings/
jobs/submit.cfm?company_id=15787

THE SCOOP

Name your price

It's a simple problem of economics. Every day, on average, planes take off with 10 percent of their seats empty. Since airplanes only make money when there are people paying to fill those seats, these seats become worthless as soon as the plane takes off. That's where Priceline steps in. The company allows people to bid on travel products—like rental cars, hotel rooms and airplane tickets—and score deals during low-demand times, when they otherwise might sit empty. So, far from Priceline being a "negotiator," as its commercials with William Shatner attest to, it is merely an online demonstration of the invisible hand of the marketplace.

Priceline also sells package vacation deals and cruises through its web site. It operates Booking.com as an outlet for European travelers and, for those more inclined to be homebodies than world travelers, the company owns part of Priceline mortgage, a mortgage lending company.

Towards a more efficient marketplace

Priceline began with a stunningly simple idea: let consumers bid on the 500,000-odd airplane seats that go unsold each day. When founder Jay Walker first put his idea online in April 1998, he believed his concept could usher in a new era in airline pricing. And indeed, it caught on rapidly with flyers, particularly those seeking cut-rate deals on last-minute travel. But demand far outstripped supply in the early days, with only 7 percent of bidders in 1998 actually "winning" a flight.

Such problems were partially alleviated in summer 1998, after Walker signed up his first major American carrier, Delta. It was the breakthrough that Priceline was waiting for—Northwest and Continental signed on almost immediately thereafter, and the company soon received an infusion of $55 million in private funding, from the likes of financier George Soros and Microsoft co-founder Paul Allen. Priceline spent the money wisely, signing up a spokesman in the former Captain Kirk (a/k/a William Shatner), who promptly enjoyed an Emmy-winning career renaissance on ABC's *Boston Legal*.

Priceline's wavering revenue line

Walker's company started expanding its product offerings in mid-1999, first with a name-your-price deal on hotel rooms in over 1,000 U.S. cities, and then into name-

Visit Vault at **www.vault.com** for insider company profiles, expert advice, career message boards, expert resume reviews, the Vault Job Board and more.

VAULT CAREER LIBRARY

287

your-price gambles on everything from mortgages to groceries to gas. The little Priceline engine that could wasn't quite up all of these tasks, and phased out groceries and gas in 2000.

The next year, the attacks of September 11th caused a large dip in the market for travel bookings, and Priceline's revenue for the year fell by $64 million, resulting in year-end losses of $7 million. Things were more or less back on track by the end of 2003, as Priceline turned an $11 million profit, despite revenue decreasing from $1 billion to $863 million.

Revenue increased each year from 2004 to 2006, surpassing $1 billion again in 2006, although profits were down 61 percent that year. The company blamed falling market share and a slowdown in airline capacity for this drop. It may face more trouble ahead, as Delta, Southwest and United all announced in 2007 that they will cut capacity (i.e., number of flights they will offer) in 2008, which means less potential seats for Priceline customers.

Enter the Negotiator

What's the solution to Priceline's falling profits? Gaining market share, of course. In early 2007, Priceline gave its celebrity spokesman William Shatner a new role as The Negotiator, the go-to guy for all your discount travel needs. The company's spots, which air on television and are available on the Internet, feature an over-the-top Shatner boldly fighting for discounts on behalf of anguished bargain-seekers everywhere, often talking down travel agents with typical Shatnerian gusto. Shatner shortly got a MySpace page, complete with downloadable ring tones, backgrounds and disparaging comments about a certain well-traveled gnome.

Their survey says

William Shatner alone won't woo customers in the Web 2.0 era. In March 2007, shortly after premiering The Negotiator, Priceline announced that it would team up with Zagat Surveys to give its customers access to reviews of airlines and hotels on its web site. Priceline will also get Zagat-powered travel guides, giving the inside dish on what to see and do (and what not to), as well as printable summaries that travelers can take with them.

GETTING HIRED

Prepare to meet the Falcon of Truth

Priceline.com advertises available job opportunities under the "jobs" section of its web site, at hostedjobs.openhire.com/epostings/jobs/submit.cfm?company_id= 15787. Priceline offers its employees health and dental coverage, 401(k) with company match and the potential of a bonus. Job seekers can browse positions, or set up a job search that will e-mail them appropriate openings as they come up.

Visit Vault at **www.vault.com** for insider company profiles, expert advice, career message boards, expert resume reviews, the Vault Job Board and more.

VAULT CAREER LIBRARY   289

Qantas Airways Limited

Qantas Centre
Level 9, Building A
203 Coward Street
Mascot, New South Wales 2020
Australia
Phone: +61-2-9691-3636
Fax: +61-2-9691-3339
www.qantas.com.au

LOCATIONS

New South Wales, Australia (HQ)
Apia, Samoa • Bali • Bangkok •
Beijing • Dubai • Hanoi • Ho Chi
Minh City • Hong Kong • Jakarta •
Johannesburg • Kuala Lumpur •
London • Manila • Mumbai • Seoul
• Shanghai • Singapore • Surabaya,
Indonesia • Tahiti • Taipei • Tokyo
Vanuatu

Additional locations in Argentina,
Australia, Austria, Bahrain, Brazil,
Canada, Chile, Fiji, Finland, France,
Germany, Greece, Ireland, Italy,
Mexico, The Netherlands, New
Zealand, Papua New Guinea, Serbia,
Slovenia, Switzerland and the US.

THE STATS

Employer Type: Public Company
Stock Symbol: QAN
Stock Exchange: Australian Stock
Exchange
Chairman: Margaret Jackson
CEO: Geoff Dixon
2007 Employees: 33,342
2007 Revenue (A$mil.): A$15,166

DEPARTMENTS

Aboriginal & Torres Strait Islander
Initiatives
Airport Service Operators
Engineering & Maintenance
Flight Attendants
Graduate Program
Telephone Sales

KEY COMPETITORS

American Airlines
Singapore Airlines
Virgin Blue

EMPLOYMENT CONTACT

www.qantas.com.au/info/about/
employment/index

THE SCOOP

The thunder from Down Under

The Australian-based airline Qantas carried some 25 million passengers on its 215 airplanes in 2006. Along with its low-fare subsidiary, JetStar, and its shuttle airline, QantasLink, the company operates regional routes to 58 cities within Australia and to nearly 90 cities in Asia, Europe and the U.S. Qantas' other subsidiaries provide in-flight catering, air freight services (notable pieces of cargo have included Formula One cars and equipment for a Rolling Stones tour), plane maintenance and overhaul, and wholesale travel packages. The airline also maintains the QANTAS Founders Outback Museum, which features an exhibit where visitors can tour a retired 747.

Take the Kangaroo Route

As airlines go, Qantas is one of the oldest still in operation. In 1920, two flying buddies from the Great War, W. Hudson Fysh and Paul McGinness, founded the Queensland and Northern Territory Aerial Services (QANTAS) to carry cargo, mail and passengers across the wild stretches of Australia's outback. In 1921, Fysh and McGinness bought their first planes (surplus military craft) and began making flights. Qantas flew its first passengers in 1922, carrying them two at a time in open seats in a biplane. (Conditions on Qantas planes have since improved.) In 1928, the airline instituted a program to fly doctors to patients in the outback.

Business grew rapidly in Qantas' first years, as flights reached one million miles by 1930. It started adding international routes as early as 1935, when it flew from Darwin to Singapore. Longer routes, like the 14-day undertaking between Australia and England, were inaugurated in 1946. The path taken by all of these planes, going eastwards over the Indian Ocean, became known as the Kangaroo Route.

During World War II, despite lacking in artillery, Qantas' planes moved people and supplies around the Pacific Theater. In 1953, once peace returned to the region, the airline began flights to North America. The next step, in 1958, was a flight around the world; the six-day trip went from Australia, over India, to England, to the U.S., and then back to Australia. In 1959 the airline acquired its first jets, Boeing 707s, and began its first nonstop flights. About three decades later, in 1989, one of the airline's 747 jets became the first to make the flight between London and Sydney without stopping; it took 20 hours. Qantas' flights from Australia to the U.K. served the airline well throughout the 1970s, often in conjunction with a low-fare policy that offered customers charter-level ticket prices with first-rate service.

Shifting alliances

After electing a new Labor government in 1983, the Australian government purchased a majority stake in Qantas the same year. And in 1988, after five years of modernizing Qantas' fleet and enjoying record-setting profits, the government struck a deal with New Zealand to merge their state-owned airlines: Australian Airlines, Qantas and Air New Zealand. This plan met opposition in New Zealand and that government decided to privatize Air New Zealand instead. A number of bidders fought over the rights to Air New Zealand, including British Airways and a consortium led by (ironically) Qantas. The latter group won, and Qantas took a 19.9 percent stake in Air New Zealand.

In 1990, the news emerged that Qantas and its investment partners—American Airlines, Brierley Investments and Japan Air—had a secret financial arrangement to prevent British Airways from winning the auction. Also that year, Qantas ran headlong into a financial crisis, due to a labor dispute with its pilots and the crisis in the Persian Gulf. The airline suffered greater losses in 1991, and laid off 5,000 employees to cut costs. By 1992, the Australian government was looking to sell the flagging airline. Understandably, there were few takers and the government merged together Australian Airlines and Qantas, with plans to go public in 1993. These plans changed in late 1992, when (also ironically) British Airways purchased a 25 percent stake in Qantas for $470 million. The road ahead was still difficult—a number of anti-BA executives swiftly departed Qantas and the company lost $250 million in 1993.

Qantas went public in 1995, after two years of delays. Within another two years, in 1997, the company recorded a profit again. However, this was immediately followed by the Asian financial crisis of 1998, but Qantas managed to stay viable through a number of international codesharing agreements, facilitated by its association with British Airways. These included alliances with firms such as American Airlines, Japan Airlines and Emirates.

Feeling Blue

Qantas relinquished its 19.9 percent stake in Air New Zealand in 1997, upon learning that ANZ planned on purchasing rival Australian carrier Ansett Airlines. This actually worked to Qantas' advantage, as Ansett went bankrupt following the terrorist attacks of September 11th, and Qantas snapped up the majority of its roots. However, a powerful new competitor came on the scene in 2000: low-fare Virgin Blue, an offshoot of Sir Richard Branson's Virgin Atlantic. The airline's cheap, local routes rapidly ate away at Qantas' market share, becoming Australia's second-biggest airline and leading budget carrier.

Qantas introduced a series of its own budget airlines, either through acquisition or wholesale launches. In 2001, Qantas purchased the low-fare Impulse Airlines and took over its routes. In 2002, it relaunched the Australian Airlines brand (which it purchased in 1992) as an international carrier, offering discounted rates to vacation hotspots like Bali and Hong Kong. After attempts to integrate Impulse into the QantasLink fleet, Qantas rebranded Impulse Airlines as JetStar in 2004. Australian Airlines' operations were added to the JetStar routes in 2006, in light of increased competition from the upstart Virgin Blue. JetStar currently handles all of Qantas' discount routes, both domestic and international.

Taking off, but for the fuel

In 2006, Qantas took in just over $11 billion in sales, a 15 percent increase over 2005. Profit declined nearly 30 percent on the year, to $394 million, largely because of rising fuel prices. Qantas hedges some of its fuel supply (i.e., buys it in advance for a set rate), but the airline is at the mercy of the marketplace for the majority of its jet fuel.

Plane dealing

In 2007, Qantas began beefing up its fleet with new planes. While some airlines have opted for Boeing's sleek and fuel-efficient 787 Dreamliner over Airbus' beleaguered superjumbo A380 (held up in endless manufacturing delays), Qantas is taking a few of each: 65 of the 787s and 20 of the A380s. The A380s, due to be delivered in winter 2008, will feature lounge areas for business-class passengers, flat beds, larger entertainment screens and Internet access. The seats in all classes are manufactured by Recaro, the company that also makes seats for zoomy cars like Porsche and Aston-Martin. The superjumbo was originally due to be in Qantas' fleet in 2006, but production ran two years late, prompting Qantas to place its orders with Boeing.

The 787s will be used for direct flights, both within Australia and overseas. The plane is designed for more comfortable flights, as its higher carbon-fiber fuselage can support a higher internal air pressure. In January 2008, however, Boeing notified Qantas of a further three-month delay in the delivery of the 787s—they are now

Visit Vault at www.vault.com for insider company profiles, expert advice, career message boards, expert resume reviews, the Vault Job Board and more.

VAULT CAREER LIBRARY 293

scheduled to arrive in May 2009. This news angered Qantas CEO Geoff Dixon, who was an outspoken critic of the Airbus' repeated delays. He mentioned that Qantas might seek compensation, according to the company's original contract with Boeing.

Training wings

Whenever these new planes arrive, Qantas will need pilots to fly them. In early 2007, the company announced the founding of a pilot school, with the aim of producing 3,000 trained pilots by 2017. The airline expects a great deal of air travel as Australia's economy grows alongside that of Asia in general. While the details have not yet been hashed out, the school may involve a partnership with the Royal Australian Air Force.

GETTING HIRED

Add a little bounce to your career

Qantas' careers site, www.qantas.com.au/info/about/employment/index, provides job seekers with information on open positions at the company. At press time, the company had openings for pilots, flight simulator instructors and cabin crew in the U.K. and in New Zealand. Cabin crew must meet a minimum height requirement, pass a swim test and show their ability to lift a 60-pound plane door in the event of an emergency.

Perks include generous vacation time and free or discount travel privileges. Pilots must have a bachelor's degree, and must pass a psychometric assessment. Pilots and cabin crew must also hold permanent residency in the country out of which they operate. A job line, at +61 (2) 9691 3200, also provides information on open positions.

Royal Caribbean Cruises Ltd.

1050 Caribbean Way
Miami, FL 33132
Phone: (305) 539-6000
Fax: (305) 539-0562
www.royalcaribbean.com

LOCATIONS

Miami, FL (HQ)
Fort Lauderdale, FL
Seattle, WA
Springfield, OR
Washington, DC
Wichita, KS

Additional locations nationwide and in Canada, Spain and Portugal.

THE STATS

Employer Type: Public Company
Stock Symbol: RCL
Stock Exchange: NYSE
Chairman & CEO: Richard D. Fain
President: Adam Goldstein
2007 Employees: 45,936
2007 Revenue ($mil.): $6,149

DEPARTMENTS

Accounting/Finance • Administrative/Clerical • Air/Sea • Architecture/Design • Auditing • Call Center • Consulting • Corporate Communications • Culinary • Customer Service • Education/Training • Entertainment • Executive • Hospitality/Travel • Human Resources • Information Technology • Internet/e-Commerce • Internships • Legal • Logistics • Management • Marine • Purchasing • Revenue Management • Safety & Environment • Sales/Marketing • Supply Chain • Total Guest Satisfaction

KEY COMPETITORS

Carnival
Holland America Line
Star Cruises

EMPLOYMENT CONTACT

www.royalcaribbean.com/our Company/career

Visit Vault at **www.vault.com** for insider company profiles, expert advice, career message boards, expert resume reviews, the Vault Job Board and more.

VAULT CAREER LIBRARY   295

THE SCOOP

Give your vacation the Royal treatment

Royal Caribbean is the world's second-largest cruise line. Its 34 ships visit nearly 200 destinations in the Americas, Asia, Europe and naturally, the Caribbean. The company's brands include the family-oriented Royal Caribbean, Spain-based Pullmantur Cruises and its premium line, Celebrity Cruises. Royal Caribbean has a partnership with U.K.-based First Choice Holidays to attract British visitors to its Caribbean line Island Cruises. In 2007, the company racked up $6.1 billion in sales.

From Norway to the Caribbean, by way of the West Coast

Two Norwegian shipping companies founded Royal Caribbean in 1968, after realizing their Caribbean cruises were constantly their most popular and most in demand. Song of Norway, Royal Caribbean's first ship, set sail for the Caribbean in 1970, and it was joined by two other ships in the next two years.

In 1986 the company opened a destination unique to Royal Caribbean cruises— Lacadee, located on a Haitian peninsula. Royal Caribbean started offering cruises from the U.S.'s West Coast in 1990, and it went public in 1993. The company has periodically added new ships to its fleet since 1988, when it ordered three new ships. It ordered other shipments in 1995 and 2001, and currently has plans to take delivery of five ships by 2010.

Losing its Princess

The attacks of September 11th greatly hurt the tourism industry, and in its aftermath many cruise companies either merged together to cut costs or stopped operating completely. In December 2001, Royal Caribbean announced plans to merge with Europe-based P&O Princess Cruises, the world's third-largest cruise firm, made famous for its appearances on the 1970s TV show *The Love Boat*. The companies actually insisted that it was a "merger of equals" and unrelated to the financial uncertainty of the era, as they had been discussing the merger for at least a decade.

Both Princess and Royal Caribbean were then surprised when No. 1 cruise firm Carnival launched a hostile $4.6 billion takeover attempt of Princess, dwarfing Royal Caribbean's offer of $2.9 billion. Both Princess' and Royal Caribbean's executives were committed to the deal and they resisted Carnival's attempt. In January 2002,

Carnival responded by increasing its offer to $5.3 billion. Princess rejected this bid the following month, and continued to recommend the Royal Caribbean deal to its shareholders. The shareholders had a clear choice: loyalty or an extra $2 billion.

All parties involved then waited for word from regulatory authorities on whether any merger of the world's biggest cruise lines would clear antitrust concerns. The European Commission approved both mergers by July 2002, and the Federal Trade Commission followed suit in October 2002. Finally, in January 2003, Royal Caribbean's worst fears came true: Princess' board recommended Carnival's offer. The merger wrapped up in April 2003, although Princess paid Royal Caribbean $62.5 million, according to the terms of their original merger agreement.

Although it missed out on Princess, Royal Caribbean acquired Spanish-based cruise operator Pullmantur in November 2006 for €430 million. Based in Spain and Portugal, the deal represents a step forward for Royal Caribbean in the European market, although certainly not as large as the Princess acquisition would have been. The company offers cruises around Europe, the Caribbean and Latin America. Royal Caribbean will be transferring some ships into Pullmantur's fleet in late 2008.

Freedom sets sail

Also in 2006, Royal Caribbean received shipment of Freedom of the Seas, the largest passenger craft ever constructed in terms of tonnage. The ship weighs in at 160,000 tons and measures about 1,100 feet from stern to stern, with room for about 4,000 passengers. It has a rock climbing wall, mini golf course, a suite that can sleep 14 people (for those cruises *en famille*), three pools, a boxing ring, Jacuzzis cantilevered over the sides of the ship and even an ice skating rink. The size of the Freedom makes it too large to fit in the locks of the Panama Canal, and therefore it must go around Cape Horn en route to the Eastern hemisphere. For the time being, Freedom operates out of Miami and cruises in the Caribbean. Her sister ship, the European-route serving Liberty of the Seas, began service in May 2007.

If you think Freedom's frickin' huge, Royal Caribbean has two even bigger ships on order. The $1.3 billion Genesis Class of ships (their names are undecided, but won't be Genesis of the Seas), will be 40 percent larger than the Freedom class and will have room for more than 5,000 people. The boats are under construction in a Finnish shipyard, and the first ship will take its maiden voyage about 2010.

Not just shuffleboard and mai tais

Royal Caribbean's a large company with lots of large ships, but it hasn't lost sight of life's (or cruising's) small pleasures. In May 2007 the company debuted Azamara, a new cruise brand allied with its Celebrity line, featuring much smaller ships than the Royal Carribean line. They sleep around 700 passengers and travel to exotic locales in Asia and South America, occasionally making 'round-the-world jaunts. The brand is aimed at passengers traveling without children—better known as retirees—eager for luxurious and sophisticated experiences. To pamper the guests, Azamara offers butler and concierge service, better food than the usual cruise ship fare, a spa, martini bar and lectures on the local sights, wine pairing and other high falutin' topics.

... and not the same old markets, either.

Asia isn't just an exotic destination for Azamara cruise passengers, however. Increasingly, it's a destination for Royal Caribbean and its cruise line competitors (especially the Hong Kong-based Star Cruises, which essentially introduced cruising to the region). In fact, industry analysts forecast that 1.5 million Asians will take annual cruises by 2010. Royal Caribbean opened a regional headquarters in Singapore in July 2007, and stationed its Rhapsody of the Seas ship there in December 2007.

GETTING HIRED

All hands on deck

Royal Caribbean's careers site, at www.royalcaribbean.com/ourCompany/career.do, provides information for people seeking jobs at the company. Not surprisingly, it takes a huge number of people to make these ships run smoothly. The site divvies up jobs by function—landlubbers can opt for jobs at corporate HQ, while those granted permanent immunity from seasickness can opt to work on a ship. Shipboard jobs include hotel and restaurant-type jobs like waiters, chefs and sommeliers, though there are also options for technical marine jobs in navigation and the like, as well as positions in the cast and crew of the onboard shows. To apply for a position, job seekers must first create a profile.

Employees usually work six months onboard, and then receive two months of vacation with an allowance. The company offers stock options and health insurance, although some sources report insurance is only offered when an employee is working onboard.

OUR SURVEY SAYS

Fair treatment, fancy ships

"With regards to the cruise line industry," says a ship-bound casino dealer, "Royal Caribbean is one of the best companies to work for, I know based on experience because I also worked for other cruise lines." Why is it the best? It could be the "newest, largest and most beautiful ships in the world," but most of all, it is how "they care about their employees ... it doesn't matter where you're from and what you do on the ship—everyone is [treated] the same."

Visit Vault at **www.vault.com** for insider company profiles, expert advice, career message boards, expert resume reviews, the Vault Job Board and more.

VAULT CAREER LIBRARY 299

Sabre Holdings Corporation

3150 Sabre Drive
Southlake, TX 76092
Phone: (682) 605-1000
Fax: (682) 605-8267
www.sabre-holdings.com

LOCATIONS

Southlake, TX (HQ)
Denver, CO • Las Vegas, NV • Los
Angeles, CA • Newton, MA • North
Palm Beach, FL • San Antonio, TX •
San Francisco, CA • San Juan, PR •
Scottsdale, AZ • Wilkes-Barre, PA •
Winston-Salem, NC • Bangalore •
London • Krakow • Montevideo,
Uruguay • Singapore

Other International locations in
Argentina, Australia, Bahamas,
Barbados, Belgium, Bolivia, Brazil,
Canada, Chile, China, Colombia,
Costa Rica, Denmark, Dominican
Republic, Ecuador, El Salvador,
France, Germany, Greece, Guatemala,
Honduras, India, Ireland, Italy, Japan,
Malaysia, The Netherlands, Nicaragua,
Norway, Peru, Russia, South Korea,
Spain, Sweden, Switzerland, Taiwan,
Thailand, the UK, Venezuela and the
West Indies.

THE STATS

Employer Type: Private Company
Chairman, President & CEO:
  Michael S. Gilliland
2007 Employees: 9,000
2007 Revenue ($mil.): $2,823.8

DEPARTMENTS

Administrative
Accounting
Airline Scheduling/Planning
Business Systems
Call Center
Corporate Solutions
Design
Editorial
Flight Operations
Human Resources
Market Research
Marketing/Communications
Product Management
Quality Control & Testing
Revenue Management
Sales
Software Development
Web Development

KEY COMPETITORS

Amadeus
Pegasus Solutions
Travelport

EMPLOYMENT CONTACT

www.sabre-holdings.com/careers

THE SCOOP

You'll never roam without a gnome

A one-stop destination for travel products, Sabre Holdings Corporation derives its name from a system that tracks airline, rental car, railroad and hotel reservations. The firm still books reservations of all sorts under a variety of names; the Sabre Travel Network handles the company's traditional air travel reservations, its Synxis subsidiary handles hotel reservations and Vistrio lends the company's database expertise to corporate clients.

But Sabre covers many other travel needs, especially ones that can be answered online. Sabre's online outlet, often distinguished by a gnome mascot, is known as in North America as Travelocity.com and in Asia as Zuji.com. Sabre's other web sites are the travel-review site IgoUgo, and the (aptly named) last-minute travel arrangement site lastminute.com. Other subsidiaries include the travel marketing firm Jurni, an organization that provides bookings to travel agents, Nexion, and a consulting firm for airlines all over the world, Sabre Airline Solutions. In 2006, the company handled over $10 billion worth of reservations and racked up over $2 billion in revenue.

A Magnetronic Reservationator for the modern age

The groundwork for Sabre was laid after a chance meeting in 1953 between American Airlines President C. R. Smith and IBM sales representative R. Blair Smith (no relation). In a discussion regarding the travel industry, the two men developed plans for a data processing system that could create and manage airline seat reservations, then send such information to ticket agents across the country.

American and IBM set to work, and in 1960 the two companies jointly debuted the Semi-Automatic Business Research Environment—Sabre for short. With its Briarcliff Manor, N.Y.-based mainframe processing 84,000 telephone calls daily, it was the nation's second-largest data processing system by the mid-1960s, trailing only the U.S. government. The Sabre system hit travel agencies in 1976, and recorded over one million fares by 1978. Sabre proved instrumental in American Airlines' launch of the airline's first frequent flyer program in 1981, and the program reached personal computers in 1985.

AMR, American Airlines' parent company, purchased Sabre in 1986, the same year the system debuted in the European travel market. In 1988, Sabre Airline Solutions began providing software, consulting and systems management services to other airlines, and eclipsed storage capabilities of 36 million fares. Among its innovation highlights in the 1990s were a flight rescheduling system, the RESARAIL system for European rail reservations and the establishment of the SabreSonic passenger solution in Asia, a joint venture with ABACUS International.

Comings and goings

To kick off the new millennium, AMR spun off Sabre completely in 2000, and the new company immediately purchased GetThere, an online corporate travel booking tool. The following year, it acquired the Sabre Pacific travel distribution business from TIAS, a travel alliance between Qantas, Air New Zealand and Ansett Airlines, thus expanding the firm's presence in the South Pacific region.

Expansion was on the company's mind again in 2002, as Sabre picked up Travelocity, an online travel-booking portal, in a hostile takeover worth $345 million. The purchase added Site59, an online purveyor of last-minute model air, hotel and rental car inventory (now known as lastminute.com).

Also in 2002, Sabre announced plans to reduce costs as the travel and tourism industry attempted to regain footing following the September 11 terrorist attacks, cutting about seven percent of its workforce. In 2003, Sabre remained "cautious" with regards to hiring, and announced plans to let go of about 500 more workers that October, its fourth round of layoffs in as many years.

Same plane, different pilot

The world's largest travel agent became the largest privately held one in December 2006, when Sabre announced its acquisition by Texas Pacific Group and Silver Lake Partners. Sabre was the last of the three-largest reservation firms to go private, after Worldspan and Travelport were privatized in March 2003 and August 2006, respectively. In fact, Travelport and Worldspan announced plans to merge in December 2006, just weeks before Sabre went private, creating a massive new reservation company.

Sabre's $4.5 billion buyout closed in March 2007, taking on about $550 million in debt, although it gave Sabre's shareholders 115 percent of their original share price. At a time when reservations were up, analysts said that the purchase could enable Sabre to launch takeover bids for competitors such as Expedia.com.

The Internet can take you anywhere

Also, the company's drive to make Travelocity the most popular online booking site continued in 2007. That March, the Roaming Gnome, Travelocity's mascot, got his own MySpace page. He currently has more than 13,000 friends, who keep up with all of his latest travels through his blog, which also contains pictures of his gnomic travels (gnome snorkeling with a dolphin, gnome on Bourbon Street, etc.). And, for the completely gnome-obsessed, the site hosts ringtones and computer wallpapers as well.

Show me the money

A few months later, in mid-2007, Sabre teamed up with rival European travel distributor Amadeus to set up MoneyDirect, a system for funneling payment to the correct travel vendors. The aim is to make MoneyDirect's system the industry standard for payments. The system already funnels $2 billion per annum to the right people at the right time. It's not as easy as it sounds—the system has to deal with different payment methods (e.g., credit or debit) in various countries and currencies.

E-site in sync with Synxis

Sabre has only made one acquisition since going private, buying up the major Internet marketing firm E-site Marketing in June 2007. The unit specializes in "business solutions exclusively for the hospitality industry," and Sabre is integrating it into its hotel reservation arm, Synxis. The addition of E-site will expand Synxis' online presence, beefing up its web site design, online advertising efforts, E-business plans and more.

Convergence and sacrifice

More of the company's operations under its new owners in 2007 were marked by the philosophy of "convergence," which sometimes meant investing more money to make the company more efficient, but often meant cost-cutting. In December 2007, CEO Michael Gilliland told Fort Worth's *Star-Telegram* that the company's "technological convergence," to bring its online businesses onto a "single platform," involved spending "around $10, maybe $15 million more this year [2007] than we originally had in our budget."

The convergence has also meant downsizing and outsourcing, as the firm opened up a new office in Montevideo, Uruguay, and moved about 800 people there from all over the world. Employment is down 3 percent at Sabre's Southland, Tex.,

Visit Vault at **www.vault.com** for insider company profiles, expert advice, career message boards, expert resume reviews, the Vault Job Board and more.

VAULT CAREER LIBRARY   **303**

headquarters, which will increase as the firm goes forward with plans to vacate one of its three buildings in the region. The company's convergence has also democratized the workplace somewhat. CEO Gilliland "polled the employees in a town hall [meeting]" and decided to move into a cubicle. He said it went along with the company's philosophy: "as we ask our entire team to make sacrifices about how they do business, we all need to be making the same sacrifices."

GETTING HIRED

Make the cut

The career section of Sabre's web site, www.sabre-holdings.com/careers, divides jobs by location (U.S. and abroad), and allows job seekers to create a profile and upload a resume (recruiters routinely scan the profile database for candidates). In addition, the company runs a summer internship program for students with placements in the fields of finance, marketing and technology. It currently recruits at Cornell University, Florida Institute of Technology, Indiana University, Massachusetts Institute of Technology, Southern Methodist University, Texas A&M University, Texas Christian University, the University of North Texas and the University of Texas at Arlington, Austin and Dallas. Benefits for employees include health and vision insurance, 401(k), and flexible work programs like telecommuting, compressed work weeks and job sharing.

OUR SURVEY SAYS

Friendly and casual

Sabre provides its "hardworking and friendly" employees with the "latest in technology." The company has a relaxed dress code—most employees wear business casual or even jeans—and workers feel that the policy is indicative of a "congenial" and "laid-back" atmosphere. Others, however, are still feeling the effects of recent layoffs. "Not many opportunities to advance; very top heavy; lot of job insecurity as layoffs are an annual theme," explains one hire. "Management is not concerned with employee growth," adds his colleague.

SAS AB

Frösundaviks Allé 1, Solna
SE-195 87 Stockholm
Sweden
Phone: +46-8-797-00-00
Fax: +46-8-797-16-03
www.sasgroup.net

LOCATION
Stockholm (HQ)

THE STATS
Employer Type: Public Company
Stock Symbol: SAS
Stock Exchange: Stockholm Stock
  Exchange
Chairman: Egil Myklebust
President & CEO: Mats Jansson
2007 Employees: 26,538
2007 Revenue (SEKmil.):
  SEK 52,251

KEY COMPETITORS
American Airlines
British Airways
Finnair

EMPLOYMENT CONTACT
www.sasgroup.net

THE SCOOP

Take wing

The SAS (Scandinavian Airlines System) Group is the parent company of four airlines: Blue1, Scandinavian Airlines, Spanair and Widerøe. It also owns part of airBaltic, Latvia's national airline. In 2006, their combined fleets transported nearly 40 million passengers to 179 airports in 37 countries. SAS was formerly the parent company of the Rezidor hotel company, whose properties include the Country Inn, the Hotel Missoni, the Park Inn, the Radisson SAS and the Regent.

A secret consortium of Scandinavian aviators

In the 1930s, three independent airlines from Denmark, Norway and Sweden struck a deal to offer a trans-Atlantic service from the Danish city of Bergen to New York City. The flight didn't take off before World War II broke out, however, and the Nazis invaded Denmark and Norway. Sweden remained neutral during the war, and the airlines secretly continued negotiating with each other. They placed covert orders on American B17 "Flying Fortress" jets, planning to convert them into passenger planes, and the Danish and Norwegian partners smuggled their shares of the down payment through occupied territory at great risk.

Two months after fighting ended with the 1945 invasion of Germany, the airlines started flying from Stockholm to New York. The next year, the company adopted the SAS name and logo for international flights, featuring the three flags of Denmark, Norway and Sweden. Each airline was 50 percent owned by its respective government. In 1951, SAS began flying European and domestic services as well, although SAS contracted with some pre-existing carriers, such as current subsidiary Widerøe, a regional Norwegian airline since 1934.

A small but SAS-sy airline

Despite representing the three-largest Scandinavian countries, SAS remained a relatively small European airline for much of its history. British Airways and the continental giants Air France and Lufthansa had much greater resources and routes at their disposal. SAS constantly innovated in the face of these obstacles, and was an early advocate of airline alliances and the use of new technology.

SAS struck an unusual deal in 1959, solving its problem of having a relatively large fleet (three different airlines' pooled fleets) and a relatively small route network (primarily European cities). That year, governmental officials from Thailand approached SAS with a proposition: SAS would loan its excess planes to an Asian air service, and Thailand would provide a hub (Bangkok) and an extensive route network in the area. In 1960, Thai Airways Ltd. took flight with a fleet of SAS-manufactured and -maintained aircraft. This arrangement continued for the next 15 years, and although SAS does not currently own any part of Thai Airways, it continues to provide the airline with technical and operational support.

The company continued innovating in the 1960s, diversifying into hotels with the 1960 purchase of Copenhagen's Royal Hotel and debuting the first Europe-wide computerized reservation system in 1965. In 1970, SAS formed its next major alliance: the KSSU group, with KLM (Royal Dutch Airlines), Swissair and UTA (France's Union de Transports Aeriens). The alliance pooled maintenance and technical services, allowing each member to concentrate on updating its fleet and charting new routes.

Calling all business travelers

Competition for SAS' trans-Atlantic routes heated up in the late 1970s, after the U.S. government deregulated its airline industry. And in 1980, SAS posted its first year-end losses in 17 years. The company responded in 1981 by appointing a new CEO, Jan Carlzon, who stressed the importance of business travelers. "The first purpose of a Scandinavian airline," he said in an early press conference, "must be to serve business." He dubbed SAS "the Businessman's Airline," and introduced first business class in 1982. SAS also became the first airline to offer separate check-in counters and special (Scanorama) airport lounges for business travelers. The company employed its other assets in this strategy, too, introducing SAS Business Hotels around Scandinavia with easy phone-call-reservations and adding Business Travel Systems to its computerized reservations system.

The company reported profits again in 1982 and unveiled a new employee seminar, nicknamed "charm school," in 1983. The company culture started stressing that its employees make decisions themselves, asking them to "work smarter, not harder." The company launched the regional carrier Spanair in 1986 as a joint venture with Spanish travel agency Viajes Marsans, and now owns 100 percent of the airline. By the late 1980s, SAS flew to 90 cities and earned comparisons with the U.S. carrier Delta Air Lines for its emphasis on customer service.

Recessionary measures

A recession in the late 1980s spurred job cuts and reorganization at the company, which continued into the early 1990s, with the beginning of the Gulf War. SAS returned to airline alliances to boost the bottom line, forming the European Quality Alliance (EQA) with Austrian Airlines and Swissair in 1987, to share operating expenses and ramp up marketing efforts.

The EQA soon developed into something else altogether: the Alcazar project, an attempt to merge AUA, SAS and Swissair together with KLM. (The airlines chose the code-name Alcazar in honor of a famous Spanish fortress.) The merger looked all set to go through in 1992 but the news leaked to the press in 1993, which responded with numerous editorials against the idea. The plan was dead by November 1993. CEO Carlzon left SAS in the midst of this drama, after a company record 12-year tenure.

Carlzon's replacement, Jan Stenberg, continued making deals. SAS inked an agreement with Radisson Hotels in 1994, joining together to create the major European chain Radisson SAS Hotels. The next year, SAS launched airbaltic as a joint venture with the Latvian government and shook hands with Lufthansa and United Airlines to synchronize travel in Germany and the U.S. SAS brought these two partners together into a new codesharing network, the Star Alliance, in 1997. Other inaugural Star members were Air Canada and Thai Airways. Star now has more than 18 member airlines, flying to 850 destinations worldwide. In 1998 SAS snapped up the regional Finnish airline Air Botnia and renamed it Blue1; it is now Finland's second-largest carrier.

A new millennium

SAS looked set to grow in 2001, acquiring the Norwegian carrier Braathens, with routes to Asia and South America. However, the terrorist attacks of September 11th severely depressed air travel, and in October, the combination of heavy fog and human error resulted in an SAS jet colliding with a private jet. It was the worst ever crash in Scandinavian commercial air traffic, killing all 110 people onboard. These incidents hurt SAS more than its rivals, and the company posted its worst ever year-end losses in 2003.

SAS entered the fray of low-cost European carriers in 2003, announcing a new brand with the charming and unique name of Snowflake. Unfortunately, Snowflake melted in the harsh light of the airline industry, and SAS reabsorbed it in 2004. Also that year, the airline's mechanics went on strike for 10 days, causing hundreds of flight cancellations.

A new structure

In the name of cost efficiency, SAS organized a new legal structure in 2004. It split itself up into three regional airlines: Norways' SAS Braathens, Denmark's SAS Scandinavian Airlines Danmark and Sweden's SAS Scandinavian Airlines Sverige. The company also founded an international carrier, SAS Scandinavian International. (SAS Braathens adopted a more national-sounding name in June 2007, changing to SAS Scandinavian Airlines Norge.) These developments only applied to operations carrying the SAS name; subsidiaries such as Spanair and Widerøe were unaffected. As a result of the high costs of all this rearrangement, SAS lost $50 million in fiscal 2005.

Keeping the planes, losing the hotels

The company restructured again in November 2006, spinning off its hotel division into a publicly traded company, and raising $600 million in the process. The company's revenue and profits increased in 2006 to $8.8 billion and $25 million, respectively. SAS' number of passengers increased by more than 6 percent year-over-year.

Hug it out

Despite the enthusiastic reception to the hotel division's IPO, labor problems plagued SAS in spring 2007. The airline's union wanted to take control of hiring and firing, to have a workers' holiday on December 26th (a popular travel day) and to constrain working hours in the early morning and late evening. SAS didn't agree, and a three-day strike in May 2007 grounded most of SAS' fleet.

The labor problems continued throughout 2007, and the company's announcement in December that it was considering the elimination of its technical services (SAS Ground Services and SAS Technical Services) and parts of SAS Cargo. Unions representing the units feared as many as 10,000 job cuts and, later that month, an unusual number of employees called in sick. When contacted, union representatives claimed they weren't organizing any strikes. Whether a strike or not, these absences had their desired effect, as SAS' board postponed voting on the restructuring until February 2008.

Visit Vault at **www.vault.com** for insider company profiles, expert advice, career message boards, expert resume reviews, the Vault Job Board and more.

VAULT CAREER LIBRARY   **309**

GETTING HIRED

Say hej to SAS

SAS maintains its worldwide careers page at www.sasgroup.net/SASGroup. Applicants can browse all open positions or search them; they must have a valid work permit for the country in which they will be based, and have a command of Finnish, Norwegian or Swedish—or all three. Flight attendants must meet minimum height requirements, have previous customer service experience and be able to swim. SAS is in the process of revising its management trainee program, but will post information about it when it becomes available. Applicants must fill out a form online.

Six Flags, Inc.

1540 Broadway, 15th Floor
New York, NY 10036
Phone: (212) 652-9403
Fax: (212) 354-3089
www.sixflags.com

LOCATIONS

New York, NY (HQ)
Arlington, TX
Atlanta, GA
Baltimore, MD
Chicago, IL
Jackson, NJ
Lake George, NY
Los Angeles, CA
Louisville, KY
San Antonio, TX
San Francisco, CA
Springfield, MA
St. Louis, MO
Washington, DC

THE STATS

Employer Type: Public Company
Stock Symbol: SIX
Stock Exchange: NYSE
Chairman: Daniel M. Snyder
President & CEO: Mark Shapiro
2007 Employees: 2,094
2007 Revenue ($mil.): $972.8

KEY COMPETITORS

Cedar Fair
Universal Parks
Disney Parks & Resorts

EMPLOYMENT CONTACT

www.sixflags.com/national/Jobs

Visit Vault at **www.vault.com** for insider company profiles, expert advice,
career message boards, expert resume reviews, the Vault Job Board and more.

VAULT CAREER LIBRARY   311

THE SCOOP

They just wanna have fun

With nearly 30 parks across the U.S., Six Flags is the largest amusement park operator in the country. Its parks feature everything from animal safaris to water parks to roller coasters fit to please kids of all ages, and Six Flags has a deal with Time Warner to ensure that its parks are populated by characters like Bugs Bunny and Superman. Company revenue comes from three virtually equal sources: food, park admissions and souvenirs sold inside the park.

A Wynne and Wood creation

Angus Wynne II, owner of the Texas-based real estate investment firm Great Southwestern Corporation (GSC), was the man behind Six Flags. He hired Charles Wood Jr., engineer of the original Disneyland in 1955, to help assemble the park, and it opened to the public as Six Flags Over Texas in 1961. The park was divided into six themed sections, each represented by a country (or political interest) that had once claimed Texas for its own. These were France, Mexico, Spain, the Republic of Texas, the Confederate States of America and the United States of America. In 1963 the park introduced the world's first log flume ride (now an industry standard) and in 1966 a steel rollercoaster.

A turnaround project

In 1967 Six Flags' parent company, GSC, was acquired by the Pennsylvania Railroad, which merged with New York Central in 1968 to become Penn Central Corporation. Penn Central declared bankruptcy in 1970, the largest in American history. The investment bankers presiding over the bankruptcy hired Victor Palmieri to run GSC. Palmieri was a former lawyer, real estate entrepreneur and government employee. His work on GSC so impressed Penn Central that it hired him to divest all the company's non-rail holdings. Palmieri launched an entire career off this reputation, founding the Palmieri Company, a consulting firm specializing in large-scale turnarounds of bankrupt companies. Six Flags benefited from Palmieri's work as well, expanding across America in the 1970s into California, Missouri and New Jersey, and adding another Texas location. Penn Central sold Six Flags to Bally Manufacturing Corp. in 1982 for $142 million.

In 1984, Bally opened a new Six Flags location in Illinois, but the company was soon distracted by its 1986 acquisition of MGM Grand's casinos and hotels. After the MGM deal, Bally's debt swelled to $1.6 billion and Six Flags was a prime candidate for divestiture. In 1987, Six Flags' management teamed with private equity firm Wesray Capital to buy the company for $350 million. As part of the deal, Six Flags assumed $250 million of debt.

Don't forget the debt!

A recession in the late 1980s left Six Flags floundering, and by 1991 the company admitted it was having trouble making repayments and might declare for bankruptcy. That year, Time Warner partnered with two private equity firms (The Blackstone Group and Wertheim Schroder & Co.) to buy the entire company for about $700 million. Time Warner bought the remaining 50 percent of Six Flags in 1993 for about $70 million. Ever since, Time Warner's superheroes, such as Batman and Superman, and Looney Tunes characters, like Bugs Bunny and Daffy Duck, have been fixtures in Six Flags locations. In the mid-1990s, Six Flags soon opened Batman: The Ride in parks nationwide.

However, Time Warner's debt load was enormous and it sold a controlling share (51 percent) of Six Flags in 1995 to private equity firm Boston Ventures for $1 billion. Six Flags went public in 1996 and Premier Parks Inc. purchased a majority stake in 1998, for $965 million (Time Warner sold off its remaining shares in the deal). This purchase involved taking on a lot of debt, again, but Premier Parks hasn't sold Six Flags yet. It expanded the firm internationally, purchasing parks in Düsseldorf and Mexico City in 1999 and in Montreal in 2001. Also in 2001, Premier changed its name to Six Flags Inc.

After the terrorist attacks of September 11th, Six Flags' sales plummeted. The company acquired another park in 2002, the Jazzland theme park near New Orleans, but sold off more properties than it acquired over the next few years. In 2004, Six Flags divested all of its European properties and a theme park in Ohio, and in 2005 it sold Houston's AstroWorld.

Fire sale

The company's divestiture strategy continued in January 2007, when it sold seven of its parks for $312 million to PARC 7F Operations Corp. The deal included locations in California, Colorado, New York, Oklahoma, Texas and Washington.

The company also announced aggressive marketing measures to increase attendance. Families with older kids are getting roller coasters endorsed by celebrity skateboarder Tony Hawk, and a ride based on a new Batman film, *The Dark Knight*, due to hit theaters in 2008. The company is courting families and their little ones with shows featuring The Wiggles and Thomas the Tank Engine rides. Other promotions feature celebrities, such as "America's legendary daredevil," Evel Knievel, who lent his name and image to a new wooden rollercoaster set to open in Six Flags St. Louis in spring 2008. Knievel passed away in November 2007, but Six Flags will continue with construction of the coaster.

1. Eat funnel cake. 2. Get on rollercoaster

Youngsters visiting Six Flags will receive another, more traditional youth-targeted promotion: junk food. Six Flags is adding outlets with all the foodstuffs parents (and nutritionists) don't recommend, including Cold Stone Creamery, Papa John's and Sara Lee. The company is spreading its brand outside of its parks, too, recently launching a cross-promotional campaign in summer 2007 that featured discounted admission coupons on boxes of Kraft's macaroni and cheese.

And for the retro- and hamburger-loving patron, Six Flags launched a joint venture with the Johnny Rockets restaurant chain in March 2007. Six Flags will set up 26 Johnny Rockets restaurants at its theme parks by 2010; the restaurant will promote Six Flags on its regular menus, kid's menus, receipts and even those little plastic trays that waiters use to bill people. This strategy is notably different from Six Flags' main rival Walt Disney, which started emphasizing healthier food items at its parks in 2006.

Escalating losses

In 2007, Six Flags took in $973 million in revenue. This was a slight improvment over the past several years; revenue was on a slight, but steady decline since the turn of the century. Losses increased dramatically in 2006, from $110 million to over $300 million in 2006. The company staunched some of the money hemorrhage in 2007; losses decreased to about $250 million. The company is still operating under a high amount of debt, and the company also points to increasing operating costs as a cause of its unfavorable results. Six Flags is cautiously optimistic about 2008, and hopes to become a value proposition for families sticking closer to home and cutting back on summer vacation costs.

GETTING HIRED

Park yourself at Six Flags

Six Flags' careers site, at www.sixflags.com/national/Jobs/index.aspx, provides information on seasonal and permanent employment at its parks. Jobs are sorted by park location, and then by function. Aspiring actors are welcome to audition for the parks' live shows and costumed characters that wander about. Students from overseas seeking seasonal employment can also apply to Six Flags to work for the summer through a seasonal work exchange program. Benefits for seasonal workers include free park admission and discounts on merchandise.

OUR SURVEY SAYS

A lean organization

Sources recommend the Six Flags experience, noting that it "offers a good corporate culture with a very diverse work environment" and that it held "huge opportunities to grow professionally and personally." Another theme is the company's slowing rate of expansion. "The [company's] growth spurt came to an end," says one Los Angeles insider, "and now Six Flags is actually considering selling off some properties in order to retire some debt." "The company runs pretty lean," remarks another, which results in a wealth of opportunities: "I have a degree in marketing but Six Flags has [moved me] into several different departments for growth. So far in my career at Six Flags I have worked or managed, seasonally and full time, in the retail, food service, finance, guest relations, human resources and marketing departments." Unsurprisingly, another source says that "there are opportunities for overtime" and "there are always new jobs opening up."

Visit Vault at **www.vault.com** for insider company profiles, expert advice, career message boards, expert resume reviews, the Vault Job Board and more.

VAULT CAREER LIBRARY   315

Southwest Airlines Co.

2702 Love Field Drive
Dallas, TX 75235
Phone: (214) 792-4000
Fax: (214) 792-5015
www.southwest.com

LOCATIONS

Dallas, TX (HQ)
Albany, NY
Baltimore, MD
Chicago, IL
Detroit, MI
Hartford, CT
Houston, TX
Las Vegas, NV
Manchester, NH
Oakland, CA
Orlando, FL
San Antonio, TX
San Francisco, CA
San Jose, CA
Springfield, MA

THE STATS

Employer Type: Public Company
Stock Symbol: LUV
Stock Exchange: NYSE
Chairman: Herbert D. Kelleher
CEO: Gary C. Kelly
2007 Employees: 34,378
2007 Revenue ($mil.): $9,860

DEPARTMENTS

Technology Professionals
Facilities Maintenance
Finance
Flight Operations
Flight Operations Training
General Counsel
Ground Operations
In-flight
Internal Audit
Maintenance
Marketing
People & Leadership Development
Provisioning
Reservations
Safety, Environmental & Federal
 Airport Security
Schedule Planning
Strategic Planning & Implementation

KEY COMPETITORS

AMR Corporation
Continental Airlines
JetBlue

EMPLOYMENT CONTACT

www.southwest.com/careers

THE SCOOP

Love is in the air

Southwest Airlines is the largest domestic carrier in the U.S., flying over 2,800 flights a day to 60 destinations, which adds up to 65 million passengers a year. The airline has long prided itself on its low costs and number of passenger complaints, both among the smallest in the industry. Southwest keeps costs down in part because its fleet has only one type of plane—Boeing 737s—which eliminates the need to train pilots and mechanics for multiple aircraft. The airline also operates on a direct-flight model, so most Southwest flights are of the coveted nonstop variety, sparing customers the necessity of bolting through strange airports to catch connecting flights. In turn, this eases the customary anxiety about lost luggage. The airline aims to keep things light inside its planes as well—flight crews are trained to sing upon takeoff and crack jokes while giving preflight safety instructions.

A cocktail napkin and a dream

As Southwest Airlines likes to tell it, the company started out with a cocktail napkin and a dream. Rollin King, owner of a floundering commuter airline, was sitting in a San Antonio bar with his lawyer, Herb Kelleher, and the two decided to start a new, short-haul air carrier. When King and Kelleher's airline first took flight in 1971, it served three Texas cities: Dallas, Houston and San Antonio. Southwest Airlines, as they called it, turned its first profit in 1973, and it hasn't had an unprofitable year since. The company went public in 1977.

By 1983, the airline was transporting 9.5 million people annually. In a decade's time, Southwest acquired other airlines, gaining routes to Western cities like Portland, Salt Lake City and Boise. To follow were routes to Florida, in 1996, and to the New York City area, in 1999. For its success, many industry-watchers credited Southwest's corporate culture, which they (perhaps enviously) identified as "partying" and hard-working. Chairman Kelleher was famous in industry circles for his unabashed love for cigarettes and alcohol, and Southwest's offices were widely reputed for practical jokes and a similar love for alcohol (after 5 p.m., naturally).

Southwest even managed to remain profitable after the terrorist attacks of September 11th, posting profits of $550 million in 2001 and $180 million in 2002. The attacks didn't stop the company from rolling out its first coast-to-coast flights, either, which debuted in 2002. Two years later, the company debuted a Spanish-language version of its web site, an unusual amenity in the airline industry.

Hedge hog

Southwest has insulated itself somewhat from fluctuations in fuel prices through its longtime program of "fuel hedging," paying cash upfront for future years' worth of fuel, at forecast prices. This has worked to Southwest's advantage, since few could have foreseen in November 2001, when the price of oil per barrel was $17, that by January 2008, the price would rise to $100. As of 2008, Southwest calculated its fuel hedging had saved $3 billion since 1999, and was set to save another $2.5 billion until 2010, with fuel prices at current levels. Analysts still find fault with the strategy, pointing out that it amounts to speculative energy trading, which is inherently risky.

Behind the hedges

Discount fuel notwithstanding, Southwest is still feeling the pinch of a more competitive market for discount air travel—and it still has to pay the going rate for a large proportion of its jet fuel. The airline faces other problems as well. Its staff is one of the highest paid in the industry, and labor costs have cut into profitability. In 2006, Southwest raised its ticket prices six different times, and in 2007, it raised prices five times.

In 2006, the airline reported $9 billion in revenue and profits of nearly $500 million—a profit margin of 5.4 percent. By comparison, Southwest's profit margin between 2005 and 2003 hovered around 6.4 percent. Due to these declining results and the airline industry's slow recovery after September 11th, Southwest warned in June 2007 that it would slow its growth, acquiring only about seven new aircraft by 2008, instead of the budgeted 34. At the time, CEO Gary Kelly also admitted that projected returns on invested capital would be lower than expected.

Southwest wants to get away from its old business model

At the end of 2007, Southwest began moving away from its no-frills, low-cost tradition. One of Southwest's signature policies, of non-assigned seating, where first arrivers could sit wherever they chose, was discontinued in November 2007. Now, the highest-paying "business" class of traveler receives first choice in seating, along with the gift of a free alcoholic beverage and credits on an improved frequent-flier plan. Some aspects of Southwest's new seating plans resemble the old free-for-all, as the passengers board in three groups—once the first group seats itself, the next one gets on, and so forth.

Southwest raised fares for its new "Business Select" tickets accordingly, and expects the change to bring in an additional $100 million annually. The company also changed the available ticket columns on its web site, which used to include labels such as "refundable anytime" and "discount fare," but now only consist of "Business Select," "Business" and "Wanna Get Away," the first two of which are not discount tickets. In November 2007, Southwest rebutted concerns that it was turning away from its core demographic by noting that low-fare fliers can qualify for the "Business Select" treatment—once they record 16 round-trips in a year.

In an unrelated decision that also affects passengers, the firm announced in December 2007 that, to save costs, it would reduce capacity for the next year, meaning less flights and more crowded planes. In yet another cost-cutting move, the company offered in December 2007 to buy out 9,000 of its employees. Due to its continual cost-cutting and price-increasing efforts, Southwest's year-end revenue improved to $9.8 billion in 2007, and profits improved to $645 million, a new company record.

The "company mom" and "lawyer" move on

It is a new era at Southwest in more ways than one, as the company announced in July 2007 that Herb Kelleher and Colleen Barrett, the company's co-founder and chairman and the company's president, respectively, would retire in May 2008. The company offered no clues on who would replace them, but stated that CEO Gary Kelly was under contract through February 2011.

News sources were quick to note that the changes were not indicative of any inner turmoil. *The New York Times* wrote that they "promise management continuity as the airline faces a number of difficult challenges." Kelleher broke the news to investors in a conference call, and stated that the change was not the result of any pressure from Southwest's board and that "there won't be multitudinous changes." He also revealed that he and Barrett would remain Southwest employees for five years after leaving the board, in as-yet unspecified positions. It all sounds like a fond farewell for both figures, with Kelleher adding that Barrett is the "company mom" and that he "can't imagine that will ever change."

Actually, insiders say the pressure is on for CEO Kelly to prove that he can keep Southwest's signature wacky culture intact. Perhaps that's why he surprised employees at the October 2007 company Halloween party, appearing in drag as Edna Turnblad, the mother character from the musical *Hairspray* (played by John Travolta

Visit Vault at **www.vault.com** for insider company profiles, expert advice, career message boards, expert resume reviews, the Vault Job Board and more.

VAULT CAREER LIBRARY

319

in the most recent film of the same name). Stories of unusual gags at Southwest offices abound, such as a fund-raising contest that resulted in company executives being dunked, in front of employees, into a giant tank of water. The company also proudly notes that its wages are the highest in the industry and its workers are some of the most dedicated. At Southwest, "You have to work hard," a union officer told *The New York Times* in February 2008. He said airline veterans who come to Southwest often quit, simply because "They're not used to working that hard."

GETTING HIRED

Love to work for Southwest?

In 2006, Southwest hired 2,360 people out of nearly 284,827 hopeful applicants. How can you improve your chances? Firstly, check out Southwest's careers page, at www.southwest.com/careers. The page provides descriptions of various jobs within the company, as well as information about benefits, perks and internships. Benefits include 401(k) with profit sharing, discount stock purchase plan, health and dental insurance, free flights on Southwest (space permitting) and discount trips on other carriers. Southwest's internship program is designed for undergraduate college students and takes place at the company's headquarters in Dallas.

For even more information, pick up a copy of the popular book *Nuts*, written by Kevin and Jackie Freiberg, which chronicles the astonishing rise of Southwest and offers some inside information on the running of the company. Quite a few contacts at the company recommend reading the book before you go in for an interview, as it gives an insiders' account of how the company is run. Interested applicants might also want to check out the Southwest blog, at www.southwest.com/jp/blog.html?ref=blog_fgn.

Star Cruises Limited

Suite 1501, Ocean Centre
5 Canton Road
Tsimshatsui, Kowloon
Hong Kong SAR
Phone: +852-2378-2000
Fax: +852-2314-3809
www.starcruises.com

LOCATIONS

Hong Kong (HQ)
Ahmedabad • Auckland • Bangkok •
Beijing • Dubai • Guangzhou, China
• Jakarta • London • Manila,
Philippines • Mumbai • New Delhi •
Pelabuhan Klang, Malaysia • Phnom
Penh • Seoul • Shanghai •
Singapore • Sydney • Taipei •
Tokyo

THE STATS

Employer Type: Public Company
Stock Symbol: 0678
Stock Exchange: Hong Kong Stock
  Exchange
Chairman & CEO: Tan Sri Lim Kok
  Thay
2006 Employees: 20,600
2006 Revenue ($mil.): $2,343.1

KEY COMPETITORS

Crystal Cruises
Holland America Cruises
Royal Carribean Cruises

EMPLOYMENT CONTACT

www.starcruises.com/newweb/
about_starcruises/job_opportunities.
aspx

Visit Vault at **www.vault.com** for insider company profiles, expert advice,
career message boards, expert resume reviews, the Vault Job Board and more.

VAULT CAREER LIBRARY   321

THE SCOOP

Hong Kong bound

Star Cruises offers its customers a chance to escape to the balmy waters of the South China Sea, not to mention destinations in the Caribbean, Europe, North America and beyond. Its cruise brands include Norwegian Cruise Lines (sailing to Alaska and the Caribbean), Orient Lines (Africa, Antarctica, Scandinavia and South America) and Star Cruises (Southeast Asia). With 20 ships, Star Cruises is one of the top five cruise lines by capacity. The company has 25 offices worldwide.

Ship shape

Star Cruises was established in 1993 by the Genting Group, a Malyasian conglomerate. Both of its other brands, Norwegian and Orient, are older entities, dating back to 1966 and 1991, respectively. Norwegian Cruise Lines (NCL) began as the Norwegian Caribbean Line, co-founded by the Norwegian entrepreneur Knut Kloster and the Israeli Ted Arison. Arison left in 1972to found rival Carnival Cruise Lines, now the world's largest cruise line; Carnival's current CEO, Micky Arison, is Ted's son. Kloster continued running NCL and made headlines with the 1979 purchase of the SS France. His $100 million remodeling resulted in the Norway, then the world's largest cruise ship.

In 1993 the British entrepreneur Gerry Herrod launched Orient Lines' first cruise, traveling from Mombasa to Cape Town. Orient helped create the niche of "destination cruising," which stressed stops at many destinations instead of one basic stop. The line still bills itself as "the destination cruise specialists" and NCL purchased a majority stake in 1998, keeping its management intact.

Meanwhile, Star Cruises slowly assembled a fleet of used ships in the 1990s and began building a route network in Southeast Asia, where cruising was virtually unknown as a vacation choice. By the late 1990s, it took delivery of its first new ships, the Superstar Leo and Superstar Virgo. And then, much to the industry's surprise, it started filling them with middle class Asian customers. Then Star Cruises shocked the industry by acquiring all of NCL and Orient Cruise Lines for an undisclosed sum in February 2000. With the addition of the U.S.-based NCL and the U.K.-based Orient, Star immediately started billing itself as the "first global cruise line"

Stormy weather

In 2006, Star Cruises' revenue increased by 30 percent to $2.3 billion, largely because it added two new ships to Norwegian Cruise Lines' fleet. This has become the company's main operational strategy: feeding new ships into Norwegian's larger and more profitable fleet, and eventually transferring them over to Star Cruises. Orient Lines maintains a fleet of one ship: the Marco Polo, its inaugural vessel. The company recorded year-end losses of $30 million in 2006, which it attributed to rising fuel costs.

A sure bet

Star Cruises, backed by some other investors, is taking a gamble on a casino in Macau. Sort of a Las Vegas of the East, Macau is an island off the coast of Southern China where gambling is legal—and where gaming companies are duking it out to start building casinos. In January 2007, Star Cruises established a subsidiary for the purposes of building a hotel and casino on the island, which will be called Resorts World at Macau.

Hong Kong bound

In June 2007, Star began operating its cruise ship Superstar Aquarius out of Hong Kong, just in time to celebrate the 10th anniversary of Hong Kong returning to Chinese rule. As the population of China becomes increasingly wealthy, Star is hoping that more individuals will opt to go on cruises. As of 2007, the Chinese middle class constituted roughly 150 million people, and is expected to grow to 280 million by 2017.

Full of surprises

Star Cruises also seems to love surprising the cruise industry. In August 2007, the company sold 50 percent of NCL for $1 billion to U.S.-based Apollo Management. Star said the cash injection will be used to reduce debt and pay for NCL's new ships arriving in 2009 and 2010, which it says are roughly the same size as Royal Caribbean's Freedom of the Seas and Liberty of the Seas, the largest ships in the business. NCL will continue to operate as part of Star until the end of 2008, and then Apollo and Star will make a decision on the future of the brand. The deal also gives Apollo the right to name a majority of NCL's board members.

Visit Vault at www.vault.com for insider company profiles, expert advice, career message boards, expert resume reviews, the Vault Job Board and more.

VAULT CAREER LIBRARY   323

GETTING HIRED

Add some Star power to your career

Star's careers site, at www.starcruises.com/newweb/about_starcruises/ job_opportunities.aspx, provides information about job openings. Ship-based postions are staffed by crewing manager, and contact points in several countries are listed on the site. At press time, there were only a few postings in the company's shore-based jobs in Hong Kong; applicants can send materials via e-mail or by post. The company prefers people with good English skills, as well as a command of Cantonese or Mandarin to work onboard its ships.

Starwood Hotels & Resorts Worldwide, Inc.

1111 Westchester Avenue
White Plains, NY 10604
Phone: (914) 640-8100
Fax: (914) 640-8591
www.starwoodhotels.com

LOCATIONS

White Plains, NY (HQ)

Additional locations across the US;
International locations in Albania,
Algeria, Anguilla, Argentina, Aruba,
Austria, Australia, Bahamas, Bahrain,
Bangladesh, Belgium, Brazil, Brunei,
Bulgaria, Cambodia, Cameroon,
Canada, Cayman Islands, Chad,
Chile, China, Colombia, Congo,
Croatia, Cyprus, Denmark, Djibouti,
Dominican Republic, Ecuador, Egypt,
El Salvador, Ethiopia, Finland, Fiji,
France, French Polynesia, Gabon,
Gambia, Georgia, Germany, Greece,
Guatemala, Guyana, Hungary, India,
Indonesia, Ireland, Israel, Italy, Japan,
Jordan, Kuwait, Lebanon, Lithuania,
Malaysia, Maldives, Malta, Mauritius,
Mexico, Monaco, Morocco, Nepal,
Netherlands, New Caledonia, New
Zealand, Nigeria, Oman, Pakistan,
Panama, Paraguay, Peru, Poland,
Portugal, Qatar, Russia, Saudi Arabia,
Senegal, Seychelles, Singapore,
South Africa, South Korea, Spain, St.
Lucia, St. Maarten, Sweden,
Switzerland, Syria, Taiwan, Thailand,
Tunisia, Turkey, Uganda, the UK,
United Arab Emirates, Uruguay,
Vanuatu, Vietnam and Yemen

THE STATS

Employer Type: Public Company
Stock Symbol: HOT
Stock Exchange: NYSE
Chairman & CEO: Bruce W. Duncan
2006 Employees: 155,000
2006 Revenue ($mil.): $6,153

DEPARTMENTS

Accounting, Finance & Tax •
Administrative & General •
Architecture, Design & Construction •
Banquets, Catering & Convention
Services • Call Center & Telemarketing
• Creative Services • Development &
Real Estate • Engineering, Maintenance
& Facilities • Food, Beverage &
Culinary • General Manager/Hotel
Manager • Guest Services & Front
Office • Housekeeping & Laundry •
Human Resources • Information
Technology/Systems • Legal •
Marketing & Public Relations •
Procurement, Purchasing & Receiving •
Retail & Gift Shop • Revenue
Management • Sales • Security & Loss
Prevention • Six Sigma • Spa, Golf,
Health Club & Recreation

KEY COMPETITORS

Hilton Hotels
Marriott International
Wynn Resorts

EMPLOYMENT CONTACT

www.starwoodhotels.com/corporate/
careers

THE SCOOP

Get your rest in at Westin (or St. Regis, or W)

Wherever you go, there they are. Starwood owns nearly 900 hotels in 100 countries, offering cushy perks to weary travelers, wherever they may be. The company's luxury brands include such venerable names as the St. Regis (of New York and Beijing) and Le Meridien, and such chains as Sheraton, Sheraton Four Points and Westin. It also operates the W hotels so beloved of bright young things. Finally, Starwood owns 25 timeshare resorts in vacation hot spots like Aruba, the Bahamas and Mexico.

A Stern-licht hand

Starwood shot to the front ranks of the hotel industry in the 1990s, under the guidance of CEO Barry Sternlicht and his keen eye for real estate investments. Five years after graduating with an MBA from Harvard Business School, Sternlicht found himself heading up Starwood Capital Group in 1991, a real estate investing firm named after an exclusive neighborhood in Aspen, Colo. Starwood made a killing off investments in apartments until 1993 and then switched its focus to hotels, which were selling at bargain prices after a period of overdevelopment in the 1980s. Starwood bought the Westin hotels chain in 1994, adding such luxury hotels as San Francisco's St. Francis.

The REIT stuff

In 1995, Sternlicht recognized an opportunity to reorganize Starwood's hotel properties into a real estate investment trust (REIT), a type of public company with a lighter tax burden, required to generate 75 percent of its revenue from real estate assets. Most hotel companies didn't meet these requirements, as any income generated from hotel management was not classified as related to real estate. However, Sternlicht noticed that some existing REITs both owned and managed hotels, as they were grandfathered in when REIT regulations changed in 1984. Starwood purchased a majority stake in one of these, Hotel Investors Trust Corp., transferred Starwood's hotel properties into it, and renamed the company Starwood Lodging Trust and Starwood Lodging Corp.

Soon after Starwood became an REIT, ITT Corp. started entertaining bids for its hospitality assets, including the Sheraton hotel chain, Caesars Palace and a number of other casinos, and a string of hotels around the world. *Fortune* called the ensuing bidding war between Starwood and Hilton "one of the nastiest takeover battles of the [19]90s," and Starwood eventually won the day with a bid of $10 billion in 1997. During the bidding, Sternlicht also launched the W hotel chain in 1997, a small, urban offshoot of Westin that still enjoys tremendous popularity.

In the late 1990s, Starwood adjusted to its new ownership of Sheraton, a company seven times larger than itself. But Hilton's CEO, Stephen Bollenbach, was frustrated at losing the bid and visited Washington, D.C., to lobby for the closure of Starwood's REIT tax loophole. Sure enough, the federal government passed an IRS Restructuring Bill in 1998 and Starwood adopted a traditional corporate structure. To defray some debt, the company sold Caesars Palace and ITT's other former casinos to Park Place Entertainment for $3 billion in 1999. (Ironically, Park Place was a former Hilton property; it is now part of Harrah's, the largest casino company in the world.)

Starwood retools

In 2000, Starwood began a $400 million renovation of its Westin hotel chains into an upscale brand. It also announced plans to convert the Ciga Group of European palaces (another ITT acquisition) into Westin. Also in 2000, the company adopted the "Six Sigma" quality improvement management style, made famous by General Electric. It was the first company in the hotel industry to adopt the system.

In 2001, the events of September 11th and a faltering economy depressed revenue and the demand for business travel, and Starwood's revenue fell each year from 2001 to 2003. The company shifted its focus to the better performing sectors of Asia and Europe. Starwood remained profitable, but profits were stagnating in the $300 million range, and in 2004 CEO Sternlicht replaced himself with Steven Heyer, former president and COO of Coca-Cola. (Sternlicht remains with the Starwood Capital Group, investing in real estate projects and sometimes hotels.)

Heyer made some notable purchases, such as the November 2005 acquisition of European chain Le Meridien for $225 million. (Le Meridien operated 130 hotels worldwide, most of them concentrated in Africa, Asia-Pacific, Europe and the Middle East.) However, his strategy was less reliant than Sternlicht's on big buys. He recognized that Starwood's upscale clientele was highly appealing to advertisers, and struck rich advertising deals with Apple, BMW, Yahoo! and others. Also, he reduced costs by selling off the company's real estate and transitioning to a franchise and management model. In 2006, Starwood sold 43 hotels for a total of $4.5 billion. No doubt this sale helped the company to its impressive financial results in 2006: profits of $1 billion, more than double the previous year's total of $422 million.

The wrong side of the bed

The following year began eventfully, when CEO Heyer resigned his post in April 2007, after less than three years in the job. Starwood said the decision was due to a clash of styles, not a lack of results. Many company sources felt Heyer was inaccessible—he never moved to the company's White Plains, N.Y., headquarters, preferring to commute from Atlanta by private plane, and he was rarely available, save for quarterly conference calls. On an interim basis, the company replaced Heyer with its chairman, Bruce Duncan. Analysts reflected that this could mean a return by former CEO Barry Sternlicht, still with the Starwood Capital Group. Others speculated about Starwood putting itself up for sale.

In their Element

Executive shake-ups notwithstanding, Starwood began launching two new hotel brands in 2007. The first new brand is "aloft" hotels, aimed at the mid-price hotel market in general and urban 30-something types in particular. Allied to the trendy W hotel brand, aloft hotels will be stocked with non-capitalized features that sound straight out of an Ikea catalogue: the hotel's pool area is known as "splash," the patio as the "backyard." The car wash is accurately labeled "rinse." And the snack bar and gym are called refuel and recharge, respectively.

Starwood's aloft hotels open their slick stainless-steel doors to reveal minimalist décor with bright colors—Design Within Reach meets Lily Pulitzer, if you will. The hotels will have trendy lounges, fireplaces and outdoor "backyard" patios. The plan is for aloft hotels to pop up in a number of cities, inlcuding Beijing, Houston, Las Vegas, Montreal and Sydney. The company had 50 spots lined up for 2008, and plans to expand to 500 by 2012.

Starwood's other new hotel brand, aimed at the extended-stay market, is known as Element—yes, like the Honda. Hyped on its site as a "smart, renewing haven experience," the hotel rooms have open floor plans, full kitchens and large desks. The brand is yoked to Westin, but departs from it on a number of levels. The hotels will feature a sleek, Zen-inspired aesthetic, areas for socializing, large windows and minimalist, nature-inspired décor. The hotels are also aiming for the environmentally-friendly dollar: rooms will have low-flow faucets, compact fluorescent lights, recycling bins and shampoo dispensers instead of those cute little shampoo bottles, which will be depressingly hard to stick into one's luggage. Like aloft, the first Element hotel will open in 2008.

Also, Starwood's Le Meridien chain is undergoing a style change. Over the course of 2007, Le Meridien's SVP Eve Ziegler worked with French marketing agency iKône to hire notable names to spruce up the brand, including contemporary art expert Jérôme Sans, chef Jean-Georges Vongerichten and even furniture maker Nick Dine, who's premiering a new bed in 2008. Le Meridien even hired the perfume design firm Le Labo to give the brand its own fragrance. Ziegler told *The New York Times* in November 2007 that "Starwood's mission is to transform the hotel industry from a functional business to a lifestyle business," and that the new Le Meridien will be "chic, cultured and discovery-oriented."

Asian invasion

Starwood also continues aggressively expanding its hotel properties in Asia. As of 2007, hotels there contributed less than 10 percent to the company's revenue, but that might soon change. In 2007, the company announced a new resort in Lhasa, Tibet, to open in 2010, and hotels in Beijing, Guangzhou, Jakarta and Macau.

GETTING HIRED

Join a rising Star

Candidates interested in working for Starwood should look at the company's web site at www.starwoodhotels.com/corporate/careers. The site provides information about job openings and benefits. Benefits include health insurance, 401(k), life insurance and a stock purchase plan, as well as an extensive menu of training programs in everything from computer skills to languages. Perks include the option to stay in a Starwood hotel for $29 a night, free or discount meals, and discounts on the company's products. Jobs are searchable by country and then by function, brand and location. In order to apply, job seekers must fill out an online form.

In addition to seeking experienced hires, Starwood recruits from a number of schools, including Brigham Young, New York University, San Diego State and Cornell's School of Hotel Administration. Internships are aimed at business and hotel school students; in addition, there are brief externships offered during spring and fall. The company also offers a management training program with rotations through the various departments.

Travelport Limited

Morris Corporate Center III
400 Interpace Parkway
Building A
Parsippany, NJ 07054
Phone: (973) 939-1000
Fax: (973) 939-1096
www.travelport.com

LOCATIONS

Parsippany, NJ (HQ)
Bradenton, FL • Broomfield, CO •
Centennial, CO • Chicago, IL •
Englewood, CO • Greenwood
Village, CO • Rosemont, IL •
Washington, DC • Brussels •
Blagrove, UK • Copenhagen •
Frankfurt • Glasgow • Kings
Langley, UK • London • Madrid •
Nagoya, Japan • Osaka • Paris •
Stockholm

Other locations in 130 countries
worldwide.

THE STATS

Employer Type: Private Company
Chairman: Paul C. Schorr IV
President & CEO: Jeff Clarke
2007 Employees: 6,000
2007 Revenue ($mil.): $2,780

DEPARTMENTS

Accounting/Finance/Tax
Administration
Communications
Computing/Information Technology
Customer
Care/Reservations/Operations
E-commerce/Design
Engineering
Human Resources/Facilities
Legal
Marketing
Procurement
Product
Sales
Sourcing
Tourism

KEY COMPETITORS

Expedia
Priceline.com
Sabre Holdings

EMPLOYMENT CONTACT

www.travelport.com/en/careers

THE SCOOP

You can't go far without Travelport

Travelport's brands allow its customers to get where they're going and have someplace to stay when they arrive. Its subsidiaries include inexpensive retail travel bookings firms Cheaptickets.com, Octopus Travel and ebookers.com, travel product wholesaler Gullivers Travel Associates and the automated airline seat reservation system Galileo.

Travelport began in 2001 as a subsidiary of the Cendant Corporation, which dissolved its operations in 2006 into four separate companies: Avis (rental cars), Realogy (real estate), Wyndham Worldwide (hotels) and Travelport. As part of this dissolution, Cendant sold Travelport to private equity firm The Blackstone Group in July 2006.

Between this privatization and the end of its fiscal year, Travelport took in revenue of $839 million and posted $150 million in losses. The company currently operates under $3.6 billion of long-term debt, related to its corporate inheritance from Cendant and from buyout funds. Other figures offer the company more comfort, however: bookings for flights in the U.S. and Canada increased 7 percent during 2006, and U.S. vacation bookings increased by 10 percent. Travelport's bookings, in particular, grew by 25 percent throughout the year.

Galileo charts an electronic path

Although the Travelport name is relatively new, its core business, the Galileo computer reservation system (CRS), dates back to 1971. That year, United Airlines developed the Apollo CRS, which became one of the leading CRS systems in the late 1970s, behind rival Sabre. In 1986, United renamed Apollo as Covia and spun it off as an independent company. Also in 1986, Sabre debuted on the European market, prompting European airlines to find their own computerized reservation systems, and fast.

In 1987, one consortium of six airlines founded the CRS Amadeus, and another consortium of three airlines teamed with Covia to start work on what would become Galileo. Galileo's founding airlines were British Airways, KLM and Swissair. By the time the system became operational in 1989, Aer Lingus, Alitalia, Austrian Airlines, Olympic Airways, TAP Air Portugal and other European carriers had joined the group. The Galileo Co. and Covia merged together entirely in 1993 and went

Visit Vault at **www.vault.com** for insider company profiles, expert advice, career message boards, expert resume reviews, the Vault Job Board and more.

VAULT CAREER LIBRARY   331

public on the New York and Chicago Stock Exchanges in 1997, the same year that Cendant Corp. formed out of the merger of hotel firm Hospitality Franchise Systems and e-commerce firm CUC International.

Cendant's spending sense

In June 2001 Cendant acquired Galileo for approximately $2.9 billion and renamed it Travelport, combining its operations with CUC's e-commerce assets and a host of new acquisitions. These included the $425 million purchase of discounted airline ticket web site Cheaptickets.com in August 2001. In November 2004, Cendant added the online travel site Orbitz for $1.1 billion. Cendant struck again in December 2004, paying $1.1 billion for Gullivers Travel Associates, a wholesaler of hotel rooms, travel packages and group tours, and $404 million for ebookers.com, a U.K.-based online travel site.

Aiming for orbit

In July 2007, Travelport spun off its Orbitz brand as a separate company, maintaining a majority stake in the company. Orbitz's IPO raised $500 million, which Travelport will use to pay back some of its debt. Travelport hoped to raise even more money in the spin-off, forecasting Orbitz's stock at $17 per share. However, trading opened at $14 and fell to the $10 range in the stock's second month. The future is bright for Orbitz, though, as the worldwide travel market is projected to grow dramatically along with an increasingly large and wealthy global population—by 2020, tourism is projected to be a $2 billion industry.

Spanport? Travelworld?

Travelport also used a portion of Orbitz's IPO cash to fund its merger with Worldspan, a provider of travel technology, first announced in December 2006. The deal closed for $1.4 billion in August 2007, bringing together two of the largest CRS firms in the world, and the No. 2 and No. 3 firms in the U.S. Worldspan was founded in 1990, when Delta, Northwest and TWA merged together their own respective CRS systems. These systems had an impressive pedigree—one of them, PARS, was developed by IBM and had been in use since 1964.

The Galileo-Worldspan merger is expected to save $100 million in annual operating costs. It came amid major changes in the CRS industry, as Sabre itself went private in March 2007; Amadeus has been privately owned since 2005. In January 2008, the company announced the consolidation of Galileo's and Worldspan's operations from three offices in Denver, Colo., Parsippany, N.J., and Rosemont, Ill., into a new North American headquarters in Atlanta. The company hasn't stated whether it will be reducing headcount along with the move, or when the move will be finalized.

GETTING HIRED

Let your career take off with Travelport

Travelport's careers site, at www.travelport.com/en/careers, provides job seekers with information about openings and benefits at Travelport. Jobs can be searched by numerous criteria, including brand, keyword, location and possibility of working at home. In order to apply for a job, candidates must first create a profile.

Travelport offers benefits including a choice of health insurance plans, a retirement savings scheme, a flexible work schedule and education benefits. Perks include discounts on travel and other merchandise.

Visit Vault at **www.vault.com** for insider company profiles, expert advice,
career message boards, expert resume reviews, the Vault Job Board and more.

V/\ULT CAREER LIBRARY   333

Trump Entertainment Resorts, Inc.

1000 Boardwalk
Atlantic City, NJ 08401
Phone: (609) 449-6515
Fax: (609) 449-6586
www.trumpcasinos.com

LOCATION
Atlantic City, NJ (HQ)

THE STATS

Employer Type: Public Company
Stock Symbol: TRMP
Stock Exchange: Nasdaq
Chairman: Donald J. Trump
CEO: Mark Juliano
2007 Employees: 6,800
2007 Revenue ($mil.): $988.24

DEPARTMENTS

Administrative/Professional
Cashiering
Entertainment
Food & Beverage
Gaming
Hotel Operations
Marketing
Transportation

KEY COMPETITORS

Columbia Sussex
Harrah's Entertainment
Wynn Resorts

EMPLOYMENT CONTACT

www.trumpemployment.com

THE SCOOP

Good times with The Donald

Trump Entertainment Resorts is famed real estate mogul Donald Trump's gaming business. It operates three casinos in Atlantic City, New Jersey: the Trump Marina, Trump Plaza and Trump Taj Mahal. The crown jewel of this assemblage of gaming palaces is the Taj Mahal, featuring 1,250 hotel rooms, nine restaurants, shopping, a nightclub, a theater, a health spa and a swimming pool, in addition to plenty of gambling options. In 2006, the Taj Mahal took in about half of the company's revenue, racking up $500 million in sales. The Trump Marina, located on the water, has 728 hotel rooms, seven restaurants and a cabaret theater, among other attractions. Finally, the Trump Plaza has 900 hotel rooms, a health spa, restaurants, shops and gaming. Both the Trump Marina and the Trump Plaza took in about $250 million in 2006. Trump Entertainment Resorts is separate from Donald Trump's real estate interests.

Higher stakes, bigger hair

In 1980, Donald Trump wasn't satisfied with the progress of his plot to cover Manhattan with bronze-colored glass, so he acquired some properties near Atlantic City's Boardwalk. After four years of development, Trump Plaza opened to the public in 1984. Trump purchased another casino the next year, eventually reopening it as the Trump Marina in 1986. And in 1988, Trump purchased Atlantic City's largest casino, the Taj Mahal—it reopened in 1990.

These properties came at a steep price. They were all financed with high-yield debt (a/k/a "junk bonds"), and an economic downturn in the early 1990s left them unable to pay off their debt loads. The Taj Mahal filed for bankruptcy protection in 1991, followed by the Marina and the Plaza in 1992. The resorts emerged from bankruptcy as a publicly traded company, Trump Hotels & Casino Resorts Inc. (THCR), in 1995, raising $140 million in a public issuance of stock. The company still operated under great amounts of debt, however, and despite the healthy operations of its casinos, continued reporting annual losses.

In 2001, the attacks of September 11th greatly affected the entire American economy, and the already faltering THCR racked up even greater losses. Donald Trump seemed resigned to a second bankruptcy declaration and started working on restructuring THCR in early 2004. A deal was in place by August 2004, involving

Visit Vault at **www.vault.com** for insider company profiles, expert advice, career message boards, expert resume reviews, the Vault Job Board and more.

V/\ULT CAREER LIBRARY   **335**

the reduction of interest rates on the company's bonds, writing off some of the company's debt and reducing Trump's personal stake from 56 percent to about 25 percent.

Other perks of the deal angered shareholders, such as Trump retaining $2 million in annual "service payments," as well as the chairman's seat, despite going bankrupt twice in 12 years. Trump himself angered shareholders further in August 2004, when he told New York's *Daily News* that bankruptcy "doesn't matter," classifying it as a "modern-day thing, a legal mechanism." THCR declared bankruptcy in November 2004 and emerged just six months later, in May 2005, due to the restructuring deal already in place. The company renamed itself Trump Entertainment Resorts Inc. (TER), and one of its first acts was appointing a new CEO in July 2005: gaming executive James Perry, formerly of Argosy Gaming Co. Later that month, TER hired current CEO Mark Juliano as its COO.

It will take more than an apprentice to turn this around

In November 2005, TER agreed to sell its Gary, Ind., riverboat gambling subsidiary to The Majestic Star Casino LLC, netting $200 million of much-needed cash. The company then launched a two-year, $140 million investment plan to improve its services and amenities. The plan includes sprucing up hotel rooms, overhauling the Taj Mahal's shopping area, enlarging its gaming areas and adding more stores. It also called for a bunch of new eating options at the Taj, among them a candy store, burger restaurant and noodle bar. The plan's largest feature is the construction of a new hotel wing, with 786 rooms, to open in late 2008. The company is also working on leveraging its brand equity (hey, all those seasons of *The Apprentice* aren't for naught!) in order to draw customers.

In 2006, the company took in just over $1 billion, most of which came from gaming. Revenue increased about two-thirds over the previous year (which was five months shorter than fiscal 2006 due to bankruptcy proceedings). The company posted losses of $22 million for the year, 30 percent less than in the previous fiscal year. The company still owes $1.4 billion in debt and cut costs through layoffs, eliminating about 200 jobs in 2006.

TER faces increased regional competition from neighboring states that have loosened their gambling restrictions to attract business, like New York and Pennsylvania. The company has attempted to compete, applying for gaming licenses in Mississippi, Pennsylvania and Rhode Island in 2006. It only succeeded in gaining regulatory approval in Mississippi, and signed a letter of intent to develop with locally based Diamondhead Casino Corp. in June 2007. However, TER ultimately decided not to go through with the project.

You're fired!

With such a subpar balance sheet, it's no surprise that TER hired Merrill Lynch in early 2007 to look into a possible buyer for the company. After a considerable lack of interest, TER announced in July 2007 that "previous discussions with prospective acquirers of the company have concluded, and there are currently no ongoing discussions with the parties that submitted [any] indications of interest."

Perhaps in a related move, CEO James Perry retired in June 2007, replaced on an interim basis by COO Mark Juliano. In August 2007, Juliano became TER's new chief, exchanging his "O" for an "E." Simultaneous with that announcement, TER's board named a new director: Ivanka Trump, daughter of the company's chairman. After months of deliberation, New Jersey's Casino Control Commission approved Ivanka Trump's appointment in January 2008. While awaiting word on Ivanka's seat on the board, the company refinanced its debt in December 2007, taking a $492 million loan from Beal Bank Nevada.

GETTING HIRED

You're hired!

You don't need to be the next apprentice to work for Mr. Trump. Candidates can visit the company's employment web site, www.trumpemployment.com, and can apply online or by mail. Trump Entertainment Resorts offers job opportunities in a number of areas, including: administrative and professional, entertainment, food and beverage, gaming, hotel operations, marketing, secretarial/clerical and transportation. Benefits include direct deposit, health insurance, free cafeteria, 401(k) and vacation time, as well as perks like an employee party. College students can get their foot in the door with a summer internship in any one of the group's three Atlantic City hotel-casinos. Interns must be enrolled in a graduate or undergraduate program, and be pursuing a course of study related to their internship.

Visit Vault at **www.vault.com** for insider company profiles, expert advice, career message boards, expert resume reviews, the Vault Job Board and more.

V/\ULT CAREER LIBRARY   **337**

TUI AG

Karl-Wiechert-Allee 4
D-30625 Hanover
Germany
Phone: +49-511-566-00
Fax: +49-511-566-1901
www.tui-group.com

LOCATIONS

Hanover, Germany (HQ)
Mulhouse, France
Rengsdorf, Germany

THE STATS

Employer Type: Public Company
Stock Symbol: TUI; TUIFF
Stock Exchange: Frankfurt; London
Chairman: Michael Frenzel
2007 Employees: 68,521
2007 Revenue (€mil.): €21,866

DEPARTMENTS

Administrative
Category Management
Development Services
Finance
FIRST Business Travel
Flight Planning/Flight Service
Human Resources
Information Technology/Operations
Legal
Marketing
Web Strategy, Business Development
& Tourism

KEY COMPETITORS

Accor
American Express Travel Related
Services
Thomas Cook

EMPLOYMENT CONTACT

www.tui-group.com/en/jobkarriere

THE SCOOP

The road most traveled

If it floats or flies, TUI's into it. The conglomerate is a leader in Europe's tourism industry, handling more vacations in 2006 than any other travel firm. Vacationers can reach their destinations on a TUI airline, drive a TUI rental car, cruise on a TUI ship or stay at a TUI hotel. The company owns 100 brands, 279 hotels and offers tours to nearly 60 countries. TUI's tourism unit merged with U.K.-based First Choice holidays in September 2007, creating the world-leading travel firm TUI Travel plc.

TUI's cargo shipping subsidiary, Hapag-Lloyd, is the fifth-largest line in its industry, in terms of capacity. Its fleet of 140 ships plies the sea routes between the Americas, Asia and Europe.

One if by sea, two if by air

TUI's antecedents date back as far as the 19th century, to major players in the shipping industry's golden age, during the industrial revolution. Hamburg-Amerikanische Packetfahrt-Actien-Gesellschaft (Hapag) began sending steamships across the Atlantic in 1847, 10 years before competitor Norddeutscher Lloyd appeared on the scene. Besides providing the principle means of transport across the Atlantic, Hapag and Norddeutscher offered pleasure cruises by the turn of the century, starting with Hapag's tour of the Mediterranean that first set sail in winter 1891.

World War I slowed each company's activities and the German government eventually commandeered each firm's ships for the war, which recurred in World War II. Both companies managed to survive, only to see airplanes revolutionize the travel industry in the late 1940s and 1950s. The future quite obviously lay in pleasure cruises, and Hapag and Norddeutscher both began providing more tropical routes. In 1970, the two companies were unable to survive independently and merged to form Hapag-Lloyd. Two years later, Hapag-Lloyd started a passenger airline, to complement its cruise division. Hapag-Lloyd joined TUI in 1998.

It takes mettle to succeed in travel

TUI took the scenic route to becoming a major tourism company. It was initially founded in Germany in 1923 as the mining and smelting conglomerate Preussag, short for Preussische Bergwerks-und Hütten-Aktiengesellschaft. Over the next few

Visit Vault at **www.vault.com** for insider company profiles, expert advice, career message boards, expert resume reviews, the Vault Job Board and more.

VAULT CAREER LIBRARY 339

decades, Preussag's economic fortunes were dramatically affected by German political developments—booming in the 1930s as the government prepared for war, then heavily damaged by allied bombing in the 1940s.

After the war, the company's remains were effectively split up between occupying forces in East and West Germany. Administration of Preussag was ceded to West German authorities in 1946 and the company had its first stock offering in 1959. It used the proceeds to diversify into other industries during the 1960s, acquiring businesses in the chemical, firefighting, oil prospecting and shipbuilding industries. These purchases insulated the company somewhat from the vagaries of the metal markets, but the 1973 oil crisis still took a big chunk out of company revenue.

Exiting industry

In 1989, Preussag merged with a major steel firm, Salzgitter, only for the steel market to take a downturn in 1993. This was the last straw for Preussag as an industrial concern; the company retained its cargo shipping interests but increasingly switched its focus to travel and tourism, acquiring such firms as TUI in 1997 and Hapag-Lloyd in 1998. TUI stands for Touristik Union International, which formed in 1968 out of the merger of German tour operators Dr. Tigges-Fahrten, Hummel Reise, Scharnow-Reisen and Touropa.

In 2000, Preussag sold off its mining interests and officially rebranded itself as a travel firm in 2002, shedding the industrial-sounding Preussag in favor of TUI. With Preussag's shipbuilding interests, Hapag-Lloyd's considerable cruise assets and TUI's large tour business, TUI was instantly transformed into a major travel conglomerate. It purchased stakes in other major European tour operators, such as the U.K.'s Thompson Travel Group and France's Nouvelles Frontiers. In 2003, TUI set up companies specializing in tours of Germany and Russia for Chinese tourists. In 2005, TUI acquired the Canadian shipping firm CP Ships, supplementing Hapag-Lloyd's logistics division.

TUI gooey

In 2006, TUI took in $27 billion in revenue, up nearly 7 percent from 2005. However, the company reported $1.1 billion losses that year, compared to profits of nearly $674 million the previous year. While travel sales remained flat for the year, the CP Ships acquisition boosted the shipping division's figures by 63 percent. The company is working to cut costs in its tour division in order to save $400 million by 2008.

The company is involved in strongly growing industries; 147 million Europeans used travel services in 2005, and that number is expected to grow to 159 million in 2008. The container shipping industry is growing as well, with 98 million TEU (Twenty-foot Equivalent Units, or standard-size containers) shipped in 2005, projected to grow to 114 million TEU in 2008.

Getting its First Choice

In early 2007, TUI placed a bid for a majority share of British tourism firm First Choice Holidays, one of the top four firms in the European travel industry. The EU tentatively approved the merger, on the condition that First Choice and TUI each divest Irish assets, for antitrust reasons. After the firms sold off their emerald isle holdings in May 2007, the EU approved the deal in June. The new company, TUI Travel plc, began trading on the London Stock Exchange in September 2007. The new firm considers itself "the world's leading travel group," with operations in 180 countries and 30 million customers combined. TUI AG has a 51 percent stake in the venture, and First Choice shareholders own the other 49 percent.

Your own Tuscan town

TUI's getting its first choice in more ways than one. In May 2007, TUI announced that it had purchased an entire town in Tuscany—Montaione and its environs. The area, approximately six square miles in size, already contains a golf course, a town with a church and a picturesque castle, and is surrounded by vineyards and olive groves. In a resort titled Toscana Resort Castelfalfi, TUI plans to add a spa, boutiques, restaurants and hotels (without which any quaint Italian village is incomplete). The town will be built to environmentally friendly standards, with solar power, food from local farms and a wastewater treatment plant.

Let's go for a cruise ...

And coming soon to an ocean near you will be TUI Cruises Ltd., a joint venture between TUI and Royal Caribbean Cruises. The firms announced the partnership in December 2007, and TUI Cruises will release its first cruise ship in 2009, to be followed by two each in 2011 and 2012. TUI and Royal Caribbean will each hold a 50 percent interest in the company, which has yet to gain regulatory and board approvals. TUI Cruises will be based out of Hamburg, Germany. The deal allows TUI and Royal Caribbean powerful partners as they attempt to break into the cruise industry and the European travel market, respectively.

GETTING HIRED

Have a ship shape career at TUI

TUI's careers page, at www.tui-group.com/en/jobkarriere, provides information on job openings and the company's training and student programs. The company hires in the areas of corporate centre (headquarters) IT, distribution, tour operator, airlines, destination management, hotels and animation (a child care program for people on vacation). Jobs are searchable by keyword, location and function. Job postings are in German, so applicants should have a command of German and authorization to work in the country in which they will be employed. Hapag-Lloyd has its own careers site, at www.hapag-lloyd.com/en/hr/21116.html, which features a boat-themed Flash game.

Although student programs are set up according to the German education system, the company offers internships during the school year as well as opportunities for business school students to write dissertations on its business. The company recruits at the University of Tilburg, the University of Hannover and at the European Business School International University Schloß Reichartshausen.

UAL Corporation

77 W. Wacker Drive
Chicago, IL 60601
Phone: (312) 997-8000
www.united.com

LOCATIONS

Chicago, IL (HQ)
Austin, TX • Cleveland, OH •
Columbus, OH • Denver, CO •
Detroit, MI • Fort Meyers, FL • Las
Vegas, NV • Newark, NJ • Oakland,
CA • Orange County, CA •
Portland, OR • San Francisco, CA •
Tucson, AZ • Washington, DC

International locations in Argentina,
Australia, Brazil, Belgium, Canada,
Chile, China, Costa Rica, El
Salvador, France, Germany,
Guatemala, Hong Kong, India,
Ireland, Italy, Japan, Kuwait,
Mexico, Netherlands, New Zealand,
Singapore, South Korea, Thailand,
the UK, Uruguay, US Virgin Islands,
Venezuela and Vietnam.

THE STATS

Employer Type: Public Company
Stock Symbol: UAUA
Stock Exchange: Nasdaq
Chairman, President & CEO: Glenn
F. Tilton
2007 Employees: 55,000
2007 Revenue ($mil.): $20,143

DEPARTMENTS

Administrative
Airport Operations—Flight Crew
Airport Operations—Leadership
Airport Operations—Ramp
 Service/Plane Side
Contact Centers—Reservations
Engineering
Finance/Accounting/Auditing
Financial Planning & Analysis
Human Resources
Information Services
Internships
Maintenance
Marketing
Operations
Resource Planning
Route Planning/Revenue Management
Sales
Worldwide Sales Strategy

KEY COMPETITORS

American Airlines
Delta Air Lines
Northwest Airlines

EMPLOYMENT CONTACT

www.united.com/page/middlepage/
0,6823,1383,00.html?navSource =
aboutunited&linkTitle = 1careers

Visit Vault at **www.vault.com** for insider company profiles, expert advice,
career message boards, expert resume reviews, the Vault Job Board and more.

VAULT CAREER LIBRARY   343

THE SCOOP

It's time to fly

For decades, UAL Corp.'s subsidiary United Airlines was the largest airline in the U.S. and worldwide, but it has recently fallen to No. 2 in both categories, behind American Airlines. United operates around 4,000 flights per day under the Ted, United Express and United names. The airline's hubs are located in Chicago, Denver, Los Angeles, San Francisco and Washington, D.C., from which it flies to over 200 destinations worldwide.

Pioneer in flight

United Airlines claims to be the oldest commercial airline in the United States, due to its 1930 purchase of Varney Airlines, flyer of the first contract airmail service in 1926. Another United predecessor, Boeing Airplane Co., traces its roots back to 1917, when William Boeing founded it as Pacific Aero Products Co. to build aircraft for World War I. Pacific Aero changed its name to Boeing Airplane in 1929, and also changed its focus to airmail, buying up a large number of airmail carriers such as Varney. Due to the act of, well, uniting all of these carriers, Boeing changed its name to United Air Lines in 1931.

United's prominence in the airmail trade worked against it in 1934, when President Roosevelt found that American Airlines, TWA and United had consolidated the country's airmail routes between them. To punish these powerful airlines, Roosevelt cancelled all existing airmail contracts and banned the common ownership of airlines and manufacturers. United then split into three companies: a parts supplier (United Technologies, owner of Pratt & Whitney engine maker), an aircraft manufacturer (Boeing Airplane Co.) and an airline (United Air Lines).

The newly constituted United became America's leading airline, establishing routes to major cities such as Chicago, Los Angeles and New York. It also set industry standards, such as hiring the industry's first stewardesses (of a sort), when it brought nurses onboard to help passengers cope with unpressurized cabins and turbulent flights. The U.S. government called upon United to participate in the war effort during World War II, and the company trained pilots for long distances and airlifting supplies.

After the war

In the postwar economic boom, the American public clamored to fly the friendly skies and United obliged. Booming revenue enabled United to adopt much of its modern appearance in the 1950s, incorporating advances in aviation technology developed during the war for use in bombers—like pressurized cabins and jet engines—resulting in larger, faster and more comfortable planes. Stewardesses, then wearing uniforms that required girdles, high heels and gloves, agitated against sexist impositions in the workplace, like not being allowed to work after becoming pregnant, getting married or reaching the age of 32, among other pre-feminist prejudices.

During the 1960s, new jet propulsion technology and a merger with Capital Airlines fueled United's further growth, though the company received a huge blow in 1969, when the Civil Aeronautics Board denied its application for routes to Asia. The company posted a $50 million loss the following year, due to a flagging economy and high fuel costs. Around this time, in 1968, United created UAL Corp. as a holding company for its non-airline businesses, and UAL officially became United's parent company in 1969.

A budding conglomerate?

In the deregulated era of the airline industry after 1978, United dropped its services to smaller, less profitable destinations and acquired a number of non-airline enterprises in a bid to become a travel conglomerate. In 1970 it purchased Westin Hotels, in 1978 and 1979 Hawaii's Mauna Kea Properties and Olohana Corp., in 1985 Hertz Rent-A-Car, and in 1987 Hilton International. The firm also added to its aviary assets, purchasing Pan American Airways' Pacific Division in 1985.

The company added a new name to this new identity in 1987, the computer-generated moniker Allegis. However, investor groups noticed that Allegis' constituent parts would be worth more separate than apart. One private equity firm, Coniston Partners, even launched a takeover bid in May 1987. These investors ultimately won, as the firm divested a number of non-aviation assets (and fired its executives) in late 1987. The firm renamed itself UAL Corp. in June 1988.

The industry's largest

At the start of 1990, United received U.S. government approval to serve Paris via Chicago and Washington, D.C., and later launched a Newark-Tokyo route. In October 1990, United placed a $22 billion aircraft order, the largest in commercial

Visit Vault at www.vault.com for insider company profiles, expert advice, career message boards, expert resume reviews, the Vault Job Board and more.

VAULT CAREER LIBRARY   345

aviation history, and acquired the defunct Pan Am's routes from America to London, as well as all of its South American operations.

Fuel prices rose due to military activity in the Persian Gulf, and competition in the airline industry increased due to a spate of new carriers. United forged ahead, inaugurating a low cost West Coast-based airline in 1995 and joining forces with Air Canada, Lufthansa, SAS, Thai Airways and Variq to form the Star Alliance codesharing organization in 1997. UAL launched an ambitious $4.3 billion plan to acquire competitor US Airways in May 2000. However, the Justice Department blocked the deal in July, sending the stock prices of both companies tumbling. United was particularly affected by the fallout, reporting quarterly losses of $292 million in July 2001. At the time, UAL's CFO told analysts that "none of us have seen this type of downturn before."

And then, just months later, the terrorist attacks of September 11th rocked the industry. They involved two United aircraft, and the picture grew even bleaker for UAL after the attacks. It reported two straight years of losses in 2001 and 2002 equaling $4 billion, and filed the largest bankruptcy in aviation history in December 2002.

Airborne once again

The company finally emerged from bankruptcy in February 2006 and announced its first quarterly profit, of $119 million, six months later. A 2005 settlement between United and the Pension Benefit Guaranty Corp. called for the government to take over UAL's under-funded pension plans in exchange for securities worth $1.5 billion. The deal saved UAL $1.3 billion for 2005, and another $3.1 billion over the next six years, releasing it from over $990 million in funding claims and another $800 million in administrative claims. All previous employees' pensions survived, but were cut by between 20 and 50 percent. United continues to provide a pension plan, although much diminished from its former state. In the remainder of 2006, United took in revenue of $17.8 billion and managed to turn a $32 million profit.

Silk road

United scored a coup in February 2007, winning government approval for a route between Beijing and Washington, D.C. Air travel between the U.S. and China is regulated by a treaty, which allows the addition of a new route every few years. Naturally, with China's economy booming, there's a lot of demand for seats on the route—nearly 100,000 people traveled back and forth between the countries in 2006.

Daily flights began in March 2007, and United expects the route to reap about $30 million in annual profits.

In September 2007, the company won approval to become the first U.S. carrier to fly daily nonstop service to Guangzhou, China. Flights out of San Francisco will begin in June 2008. United isn't winning all bids for Chinese travel, though. In January 2008 the U.S. government passed over United's bid to fly a major new route from Los Angeles to Shanghai in favor of archrival US Airways, which will fly out of Philadelphia starting in 2009.

To buy or not to buy, or merge

Freshly out of bankruptcy court, United execs have some tough choices to make. Many airlines in better financial shape are buying up the latest, greatest planes from Boeing and Airbus, and United will be left with a rapidly aging fleet unless it figures out how to finance new orders. United has the option to snap up some short-range Airbus jets, but may opt to merge with another airline instead.

The entire airline industry is watching to see what United will do, especially considering the rapidly developing situation between itself, Delta, Continental and Northwest Airlines, which the *Chicago Tribune* called a "high-stakes and unprecedented contest." In January 2008, Delta approached both Northwest and United with merger proposals, and analysts predicted that Continental would soon join in the discussions. The talks between Delta and Northwest grew more serious in February, and consequently, so did those between United and Continental. News reports claimed United CEO Glenn Tilton has been vocal about wanting to merge with another carrier. Of the named airlines, only Continental has not declared bankruptcy since September 11th, and analysts point to any potential merger as hugely significant for the industry's future.

GETTING HIRED

Come staff the friendly skies

United's careers site, at www.united.com/page/middlepage/0,6823,1383,00.html, provides information for job seekers about career openings at the company. Opportunities are sorted by division: administrative, airport operations and contact centers-reservations, flight attendant, pilot, internships, MBA, professional and technical. They can also be sorted by location, function and keyword. In order to apply for a job, candidates must first create a profile. Benefits include a 401(k), heath and dental insurance, and perks like free flight privileges.

In 2007, shortly after exiting bankruptcy and dodging the bullet of pension funding, United announced it had slots to hire 100 experienced pilots. Turnout was quite impressive—in the first 10 days, over 1,000 people applied for the positions. The company continues to seek qualified applicants to fly on its international routes. Pilots must have at least a high school diploma, a valid passport, recent flight experience and must have spent 1,500 hours flying fixed wing planes.

OUR SURVEY SAYS

1970s flashback

Contacts say UAL has a "great work environment" and is "a great company, professional and well known." On the other hand, some report the "management style hasn't changed since the 1970s" and "through bankruptcy, this company lost a lot of its flair and joy." Still "there is a tremendous sense of loyalty within the company ranks," even if "most people have [forgotten] why the love is there."

A sense pervades that management is aloof. "It felt like no matter how hard we tried to do our job," says a source in Las Vegas, "[managers] never recognized any success or great achievement of [their] employees." A San Franciscan reports a similar atmosphere: "Most people are overworked and spend far more hours in the office than they are paid for ... [management] tend[s] to hold their cards very close to their chests and transparency is lacking as part of culture." The source continues, saying that United employees are "always waiting for the other shoe to drop," and that, although "the company looks poised to do fine over the next cycle ... with merger talk abound[ing], I don't expect the current employee situation to get any better, given how opaque management are about the future."

Cool perks

Still, other insiders are less concerned about these matters: "working with airplanes is really cool, and the flight benefits [are] a pretty nice perk." One contact notes that United flight benefits extend to every employee, as well as his or her parents and dependents.

US Airways Group, Inc.

111 West Rio Salado Parkway
Tempe, AZ 85281
Phone: (480) 693-0800
Fax: (480) 693-5546
www.usairways.com

LOCATIONS

Tempe, AZ (HQ)
Mazatlán, Mexico
Montreal
Ontario
Ottawa
Saint Thomas
Toronto

THE STATS

Employer Type: Public Company
Stock Symbol: LCC
Stock Exchange: NYSE
Chairman & CEO: William Douglas
  Parker
President: J. Scott Kirby
2006 Employees: 37,000
2007 Revenue ($mil.): $11,700

DEPARTMENTS

Accounting
Customer Service
Finance
Fleet Services
Human Resources
InFlight
Legal
Maintenance
Pilot
Professional
Reservations
Reservations—Tourism
US Technologies

KEY COMPETITORS

American Airlines
Delta Air Lines
JetBlue

EMPLOYMENT CONTACT

www.usairways.com/awa/content/ab
outus/employment/default.aspx

Visit Vault at **www.vault.com** for insider company profiles, expert advice,
career message boards, expert resume reviews, the Vault Job Board and more.

VAULT CAREER LIBRARY 349

THE SCOOP

From sea to shining sea

US Airways is the fifth-largest airline in the U.S. In 2006 it flew 36 million people to roughly 90 airports across the country, mostly from its hubs in Charlotte, Phoenix and Philadelphia. The company's three subsidiaries, MidAtlantic Airways, Piedmont Airlines and PSA (the former Pacific Southwest Airlines), operate a regional feeder network under the name US Airways Express, along with a number of independent partners. Overall, US Airways operates 280 mainline jets systemwide.

In the purple mountains of the Allegheny ...

Like many American airlines, US Airways formed during the 1930s, when the U.S. government parceled out airmail routes to a number of small independent companies. Initially known as All American Aviation, the company was founded in Delaware in 1937 by Richard du Pont, an aviating enthusiast and member of Delaware's famed du Pont family. In 1939, All American began an airmail service in rural areas of Western Pennsylvania and the Ohio Valley, which were hard to reach by more traditional mail delivery methods, and it established headquarters in Pittsburgh soon afterwards. All American's mail service expanded rapidly—it was carrying over half a million letters per year by 1941. In 1949, All American Aviation changed its name to All American Airways and switched from airmail to passenger service. The government assigned it passenger routes within and around its Pittsburgh headquarters, and in 1953 it changed its name to Allegheny Airlines, a name locals had already been calling it.

Improvements in aircraft technology helped the firm grow in the 1950s, but government regulation limited significant expansion. Allegheny Airlines found a way forward in 1967, when it began subcontracting its rural assignments to smaller, independent airlines, which the government allowed, as it meant the discontinuance of subsidies to the airline. For passengers, this practice led to a decline in service and they soon started calling it "Agony Air." It was a boon for the company, though, as the extra cash lying around enabled it to expand beyond its purple mountain purview. The firm purchased Indianapolis-based Lake Central Airlines in 1968 and upstate New York- and New England-focused Mohawk Airlines in 1972.

Deregulation nation

In 1978, the U.S. government deregulated the airline industry, removing itself from an active role in assigning particular routes. Allegheny Airlines expanded its service dramatically, adding stops in Arizona, Texas, Colorado and Florida. To reflect its expanding network, and perhaps to shed its "Agony Air" reputation, the company changed its name to USAir in 1979.

At the dawn of the 1980s, USAir was mainly an East Coast operation, and much smaller than rivals United and TWA, to name a few. In a bid to become a truly national airline, USAir merged with two other firms in 1987, first the West coast-based Pacific Southwest Airlines and then the international carrier Piedmont Airlines.

However, immediately after USAir announced the Piedmont merger—at $1.6 billion, then the largest in industry history—corporate raider Carl Icahn launched a hostile takeover bid for USAir. The airline responded by changing its merger plans—instead of financing the deal half with stock and half with cash, it borrowed an extra $800 million to eliminate stock from the deal and negate Icahn's plans. After the Piedmont deal cleared, USAir had about $2 billion in debt, and chose not to cut down on labor costs, raising fares instead. Unfortunately, the economy slowed significantly in the early 1990s and USAir didn't report a profit from 1988 to 1995.

A name change and numerous suitors

In 1993, as an attempt to get back in the black, USAir sold 24.6 percent of its stock to British Airways for $400 million. As part of the deal, USAir agreed to give up its rights to London-based routes. The agreement seemed to work, as USAir reported a profit for fiscal 1995, earning $119 million on $7.5 billion revenue.

USAir gained a new CEO in 1996, naming former United Airlines executive Stephen Wolf to the position. USAir and United, Wolf's old employer, had been in serious merger since 1995, and industry analysts suggested that Wolf was brought aboard to consummate the deal.

Later in 1996, British Airways announced a potential partnership with American Airlines. USAir cried foul and took the airline to court, seeking BA's divestiture of USAir stock and the restoration of rights to London's Heathrow Airport. In May 1997, British Airways sold off its holdings in USAir, ending the legal relationship between the two airlines. Also, USAir started flying to London again. Coincidentally or not, three directors resigned from BA's board soon afterwards.

Visit Vault at **www.vault.com** for insider company profiles, expert advice, career message boards, expert resume reviews, the Vault Job Board and more.

VAULT CAREER LIBRARY   351

Also in 1997, USAir changed its name to US Airways and adopted a spiffy new blue, red and silver color scheme.

Although the airline was still profitable, costs began to spiral out of control in the late 1990s, exemplified by the firm's policy of paying its pilots at least 1 percent higher than major rivals. Also, low-fare regional firms such as JetBlue and Southwest started to attract ever greater business. US Airways' attempt to offer low-budget flights, called MetroJet, only lasted from 1998 to 2001. Finally, in 2000, US Airways and United agreed to a merger, but federal regulators soon put the kibosh on the deal.

Two bouts with bankruptcy

After the terrorist attacks of September 11th, US Airways reduced its flight schedule by 23 percent, retired aircraft and eliminated 11,000 jobs. The company plunged into bankruptcy in 2002, and new CEO David Siegel, who came aboard that year, instituted a drastic restructuring program. The airline cut 200 more flights, grounded 31 planes and eliminated over 2,500 more jobs. Along the way, the company closed a Tampa maintenance hangar just days before Thanksgiving 2002, infuriating employees. The airline came out of bankruptcy in March 2003.

CEO Siegel's demand for further cuts soon lost him the support of US Airways employees. In December 2003, a number of unions, including the Air Line Pilots Association, called for Siegel and CFO Neal S. Cohen to resign. Siegel stepped down in April 2004, followed closely by the company reporting $89 million in losses for fiscal 2004, and US Airways entered bankruptcy again in late 2004. The firm lost $537 million in fiscal 2005, and this time, the airline looked to be headed for liquidation—in January 2005, a bankruptcy judge terminated the pension plans of over 53,000 US Airways retirees. However, in May 2005, West Coast budget airline America West swooped to the rescue, acquiring the soon-to-be ex-company for $1.5 billion.

Takeover turbulence

The America West merger closed in September 2005, with each airline maintaining its own name and routes. The new company, known as US Airways Group, proudly heralded itself as the nation's leading low-budget, coast-to-coast carrier and fifth-largest overall airline.

In November 2006, the company unexpectedly bid $8 billion (half-cash and half-stock) for bankrupt rival Delta, but the other airline wasn't receptive to the deal, even though the deal would create the world's largest airline. By December, US Airways CEO Doug Parker said the deal wasn't worth the trouble—US Airways would have to submit a merger plan to a bankruptcy judge and battle with Delta's management at the same time. If Delta executives didn't change their minds, he said, the deal was dead, which is exactly how it played out.

In the meantime, US Airways still faced troubles integrating its operations with the former America West Airlines. In March 2007, after struggling for nearly two years to combine the airlines' reservation systems, the company's check-in kiosks briefly crashed nationwide. And US Airways still hasn't combined employee contracts for its pilots, flight attendants, mechanics and fleet service workers. The airline will continue to negotiate with all parties concerned in 2008, which probably won't be easy. In August 2007, for example, US Airways pilots (internally known as "East" pilots) walked out of negotiations, insisting on higher pay; despite these setbacks, the two sides continue to work on a solution.

The company has actually performed well financially, exceeding analysts' expectations by posting $11.7 billion in 2007 revenue, with profits of $427 million. However, the firm's stock price took a beating in 2007, dropping 74 percent from January 2007 to January 2008 ($56.30 per share to $14.71). J. Scott Kirby, the airline's president, spoke at an investor conference in December 2007, and reassured troubled US Airways stockholders that the firm would turn things around in 2008. In particular, he stated that integration efforts would take a backseat to providing good service. "Integration was distracting," he said, "we're happy to be focused on getting back to the basics and running an airline instead of trying to integrate two airlines."

Do the Hustle!

US Airways redoubled its customer service focus the previous month, in November 2007. That month, it instituted a "Holiday Hustle" program, with the goals of fewer than seven mishandled bags per 1,000 passengers and an on-time departure rate of 60 percent. Successful completion of the program, at the end of December, would result in a $100 bonus for every employee, along with other incentives. The company was on pace to meet its goal, but its rate of mishandled bags spiked on December 23rd, just a few days before Christmas.

Orient Express

US Airways had some good news in January 2008, when the U.S. government awarded it flying rights to China. US Airways had lodged its bid for the flight in July

Visit Vault at **www.vault.com** for insider company profiles, expert advice, career message boards, expert resume reviews, the Vault Job Board and more.

V/\ULT CAREER LIBRARY

353

2007, when the U.S. and Chinese governments agreed to expand their flying relationship. The company emphasized the size of its airplanes and the fact that Philadelphia had no direct service to China. American, Continental and Northwest Airlines also won flight approval, and they will operate routes out of Chicago, Newark/New York and Detroit, respectively. The flights will begin in 2009, and promise to have a great deal of traffic for decades to come, considering China's burgeoning economy.

GETTING HIRED

Take your career on a spin with U.S.

The company's careers site, at www.usairways.com/awa/content/aboutus/employment, provides a job search function. Jobs can be searched by keyword, function and location, though pilots and flight attendants are expected to be able to spend nights on the road. Flight attendants must be at least 20 years of age, and may have to meet minimum height requirements. In order to apply, job seekers must first create a profile.

Vail Resorts, Inc.

390 Interlocken Crescent
Suite 1000
Broomfield, CO 80021
Phone: (303) 404-1800
www.vailresorts.com

LOCATIONS

Broomfield, CO (HQ)
Arrowhead Mountain, CO
Aspen, CO
Avon, CO
Bachelor Gulch Village, CO
Beaver Creek, CO
Breckenridge, CO
Broomfield, CO
Colter Bay Village, WY
Edwards, CO
Grand Teton National Park, WY
Heavenly Mountain, CA
Keystone, CO
Lakewood, CO
Santa Fe, NM
Teton Village, WY
Vail, CO

THE STATS

Employer Type: Public Company
Stock Symbol: MTN
Stock Exchange: NYSE
Chairman: Joe R. Micheletto
CEO: Robert A. Katz
2007 Employees: 14,900
2007 Revenue ($mil.): $940.5

DEPARTMENTS

Accounting
Administration
Children Services
Conference Services
Craft/Trade/Maintenance
Executive
Finance
Food & Beverage
Golf
Human Resources
Information Systems/Technology
Legal
Lodging Operations
Mountain Operations
Purchasing
Resort Services
Retail Operations
Risk Management
Sales & Marketing
Ski & Ride School
Sports & Recreation

KEY COMPETITORS

American Skiing Company
Booth Creek Ski Holdings
Intrawest

EMPLOYMENT CONTACT

skijob1.snow.com

THE SCOOP

Avant-ski, apres-ski

Beloved of the jet set and people who use "winter" as a verb, Vail Resorts controls five of the chicest ski resorts in the U.S. These are the Coloradan mountains and hotels of Beaver Creek, Breckenridge, Keystone and Vail, and the Lake Tahoe, Calif.-based Heavenly Mountain. The company's operations include building and maintaining ski lifts, half-pipes and pistes and renting out space for shops and restaurants. Vail Resorts also maintains trails and facilities for non-snow-related activities, like golf courses, hiking and mountain biking trails. The company also has a concession to operate hotels near Wyoming's Grand Teton National Park.

Vail-proof strategy

After entering World War II, in 1942 the U.S. government set up a center in Colorado to train soldiers for ski-bound fighting in the Alps. It was called Camp Hale and located about 23 miles away from where the Vail resort is based today. A former Camp Hale trainee, Pete Seibert, studied hotel management after the war and returned to Colorado in 1955 with the dream of starting his own ski resort. At the time, U.S. skiing was relatively unsophisticated, with few of the all-purpose ski villages common in Switzerland and other Alpine countries.

In Colorado, Seibert met a local named Earl Eaton who showed him an unnamed mountain (Vail). Seibert was so awestruck that he purchased the mountain and started secret construction of a resort that opened in 1963, much to the surprise of local residents. Less than two weeks after opening, the resort scored a public relations coup when the U.S. ski team used it as a training camp. By 1964, *Sports Illustrated* claimed that "never in the history of U.S. skiing has a bare mountain leaped in such a short time into the four-star category of ski resorts." Analysts attributed Vail's success to its resemblance to traditional European ski villages. "With bed, board and bars close at hand," wrote *The New York Times* in 2002, Vail "established a style that has since become familiar at American ski resorts."

A downward slope

Vail was incorporated as a town in 1966, placing it somewhat out of the control of Vail Associates, Seibert's company. Partly to counteract this development, Vail

Associates purchased 2,200 acres of land 10 miles away, which opened to the public after extensive development in 1980 as the more luxurious Beaver Creek ski resort.

However, despite the healthful and outdoorsy reputation of the sport, Vail fared badly in the age of aerobics and conspicuous consumption—the 1980s. Revenue fell and Vail Associates nearly declared bankruptcy before finding a benefactor in Gillett holdings, a company with interests in TV stations and meat packing. The company's namesake, George Gillett, later became famous to sports fans across the world as owner of the Montreál Canadiens hockey team and co-owner of the Liverpool, U.K., soccer team.

Gillett was also an avid skier, and reinvented Vail Resorts with the principle that "the customer is king." He criticized the company for focusing on real estate at the expense of customer service and personally led every employee-training program. The company also invested in faster lifts and an expansion plan called the China Bowl that, when finished in 1989, doubled the mountain's skiing space. By the early 1990s, Vail was the largest ski resort in the U.S., surpassing California's Mammoth Mountain.

Goodbye to Gillett?

Just as Vail recovered its world-class form, its parent company Gillett Holdings ran into financial trouble, due to the high-interest ("junk") bonds Gillett had used to finance acquisitions in the early 1980s. Gillett Holdings filed for bankruptcy in 1991 and transferred Vail Associates to the New York-based investment firm Apollo Advisors LP, although George Gillett remained Vail's chairman.

By the mid-1990s, Vail faced increasing competition from resorts like Colorado's Aspen and British Columbia's Whistler and Blackcomb, which featured a number of mountains close to each other. In 1996, Vail Associates purchased two nearby mountains from real estate firm Ralcorp Holdings for $310 million, adding them to Vail and Beaver Creek as the Breckenridge and Keystone resorts. The company went public in 1997, the first North American ski resort to do so, adopting the name Vail Resorts, Inc. In the process, George Gillett retired after 10 years as the company's chairman.

In 1999 the company completed its acquisition of the Grand Teton Lodge Co., which operates hotels in Wyoming's Grand Teton National Park. After the terrorist attacks of September 11, 2001, the nation's fear of flying and the accompanying economic downturn in 2002 led Vail Resorts to post losses in 2003 and 2004. But things got back on track in 2005, when the company posted a profit of $23 million.

They're on TV!

In February 2007, Vail Resorts teamed up with LX.tv in order to promote its resorts to a new generation of skiers. LX.tv is an online video network of lifestyle advice— sort of a YouTube for the rich and famous, just the sort of customer Vail Resorts wants to attract. A series of short video clips, updated regularly, shows off the merits of Vail's various towns, from the nightlife in Breckenridge to dining in Vail the spa in Tahoe.

Aspen aren't the only thing that's green

In March 2007, Vail Resorts announced it would begin building Ever Vail, the first ever sustainable, Leadership in Energy and Environmental Design (LEED)-certified ski village. The $1 billion project is to be located on a 10-acre parcel West of Vail Village, and will include around 200 condominiums, a hotel, restaurants, offices and shops. The company has not yet set a date for the development's opening.

On the up and up

Vail Resorts posted strong financial results in 2007, increasing its revenue by more than $100 million to $940.5 million, and profits by about $15 million to $61 million. CEO Robert Katz expects to increase on these totals in 2008, championing the conclusion of real estate construction at Vail—The Arrabelle and The Lodge, part of a Vail Chalets project that will wrap up itself in early 2009. The company will also add to its children's ski and snowboard school in Beaver Creek, opening the Buckaroo Express Gondola.

Introducing ... the new CEO of Intrawest!

In January 2008, Vail announced that Bill Jensen, the president of its mountain division, was leaving the company to become the new CEO of rival Intrawest, effective June 2008. Intrawest owns and operates a number of ski resorts, including Mont Tremblant and Whistler in Canada. Vail bid him a fond farewell in the press release announcing his departure, with CEO Katz saying that Jensen "has been a true leader within both the Vail community and the U.S. ski industry. Bill will be missed by everyone at our company."

GETTING HIRED

Put on your powder suit

Vail Resort's careers site, at skijob1.snow.com, provides job seekers with information on the various opportunities—everything from winter work to careers—in addition to tips on housing and information about benefits. Jobs range from sales associates, who sell everything from lift tickets to ski equipment, to stable hands, security personnel and waiters for the resorts' many restaurants. There's demand for people well-versed in PR, HR and administration, in addition to chefs and ski school instructors. Most jobs require a commitment to work for the entire season.

Interviews take place at the resorts, but the company also has a recruiting crew that makes stops in Boston, Dallas, Orlando, Seattle and Washington, D.C., among other cities. Benefits include free ski passes (of course!) as well as discounts on merchandise, subsidized housing for some positions and health insurance for full-time employees.

Visit Vault at **www.vault.com** for insider company profiles, expert advice, career message boards, expert resume reviews, the Vault Job Board and more.

VAULT CAREER LIBRARY   359

Virgin Atlantic Airways Ltd.

The Office, Crawley Business
Quarter
Manor Royal
Crawley, West Sussex RH10 9NU
United Kingdom
Phone: +44-1293-562-345
Fax: +44-1293-538-337
www.virgin-atlantic.com

LOCATIONS

Crawley, UK (HQ)
Norwalk, CT

Additional locations in Australia, the
Caribbean, China, Hong Kong, India,
Japan, Nigeria, South Africa, the
United Arab Emirates and the UK.

THE STATS

Employer Type: Private Company
Chairman: Sir Richard Branson
CEO: Steve Ridgway
2006 Employees: 9,000
2006 Revenue ($mil.): $3,330.2

DEPARTMENTS

Administration
Airport Services
Call Centre
Cargo
Engineering
Finance
Human Resources
Marketing
Sales

KEY COMPETITORS

American Airlines
British Airways
Continental Airlines

EMPLOYMENT CONTACT

www.virgin-atlantic.com/en/us/
allaboutus/workingforus

THE SCOOP

Pure player

Virgin Atlantic Airways, jointly owned by Sir Richard Branson and Singapore Airlines, is one of the three largest airlines to ply the North Atlantic's airspace. In addition to its New York-London route, it reaches nearly 30 destinations around the globe, including Delhi, Hong Kong, Mauritius, Nairobi, Sydney and Tokyo.

The airline has a fleet of 37 planes of recent manufacture, bearing such names as Tubular Belle, Varga Girl and Bubbles. These planes feature three classes of seats: Upper Class, with flat beds, a stand-up bar and other cushy amenities like massages, Premium Economy, which gives customers the option of a larger seat and more legroom, and economy, which is as you'd expect. All of the seats feature in-flight entertainment like music and movies, as well as multi-player video games, children's entertainment, SMS messaging and seat-to-seat messaging.

A breath of fresh air for a stuffy business

Sir Richard Branson began what would become the Virgin empire as a mail-order record service in 1970. A year later, he opened his first record store on London's Oxford Street. In 1972, Branson opened a recording studio on a converted squash court, and he launched the Virgin record label and music publishing company in 1973. Mike Oldfield was the first artist to sign with Virgin, and recorded the highly successful album Tubular Bells in 1973, one of the biggest selling records of the 1970s (also well known as the theme music to the film *The Exorcist*). More established acts followed in the 1970s and 1980s, such as the Rolling Stones, (ironically) the Sex Pistols, Phil Collins, and Boy George and the Culture Club.

Branson's next move—the creation of Virgin Atlantic Airways in 1984—was deemed "completely mad" by fellow employees and industry analysts, who were befuddled by an entertainment company that started an airline. But Branson brought the same fun, youthful and irreverent ethos to the trans-Atlantic puddle jump that he did to the music business. The fledgling airline forged ahead, with its first 747 flying between London and Newark that June. The following year, the airline established its cargo division and began flights from London to Miami.

By 1989, Virgin had shuttled over one million passengers between London, Miami, New York and Tokyo. After selling his Virgin record label for $800 million in 1992, Branson invested the proceeds in his airline, buying a clutch of new planes and adding amenities like TV screens and larger seats. The airline received a major publicity boost in 1993, when it settled a libel suit against archrival British Airways for £610,000, exposing BA's "dirty tricks" campaign to smear Virgin and Branson in the process. Also in 1993, *Executive Travel* voted Virgin its Airline of the Year for the third year in a row.

Engaging in many Virgin pursuits

While taking his airline company global, Sir Richard Branson did a little bit of everything, both in and out of the business world. Virgin became a ubiquitous brand name in and beyond entertainment, launching its retail Virgin "Megastores," and operations in engineering, finance, publishing, radio and even cola. Branson himself dabbled in daredevil pursuits, for instance setting a Guinness World Record in 1986 by crossing the Atlantic Ocean in a speedboat, and starring in *The Rebel Billionaire* reality TV show, on Fox in 2004.

"It's better inside the plane"

Like its founder, and most of its sister Virgin companies, Virgin Atlantic cultivates an image of youthful, carefree fun. In 2006, for example, the firm advertised new amenities on its planes by rolling out an ad campaign warning passengers of a condition known as "disembarkaphobia," or "the desire to stay onboard a Virgin Atlantic flight." In 2007, the airline poked fun at its competitors with billboards that mocked their taglines, with messages saying, "The skies would be much friendlier if you had an onboard bar like us." Other ads plugged the company's in-flight massages and other first-class perks.

Dreaming bigger and cleaner

In addition to plying first-class customers with bars, massages, manicures and the like, the cherry-red company is also emphasizing greener pursuits. In April 2007, Virgin agreed to spend $2.8 billion on 15 of Boeing's fuel-efficient 787 Dreamliner aircraft, with an option for eight more and purchasing rights for 20 more. Additionally, Virgin is working to take maize to the air with an experimental jet powered by corn-derived biofuel, which may be cleaner and less costly than ordinary jet fuel. In January 2008, the company announced a test flight (with no passengers) from London to Amsterdam, using biofuel—the first commercial carrier to attempt an eco-friendly flight.

Let there be Virgin America!

More aerial news came in the form of the creation of Virgin America, a new low-fare airline. Its initial proposal hit objections from entrenched, high-fare airlines, in addition to falling afoul of regulations that stipulate that three-quarters of any American airline be controlled by U.S. citizens. After some executive and ownership restructuring, which reduced the company control of Branson in particular and British interests in general, Virgin America gained approval in March 2007. It was an opportune moment for Virgin to expand its trans-Atlantic offerings, as the U.S. and the European Union signed an "open skies" agreement in April 2007, significantly liberalizing the market.

Virgin America's first flight, from San Francisco to New York, took off in August 2007. Months later, in November 2007, the annual Zagat survey ranked all U.S. airplane firms in terms of customer satisfaction: Virgin America came in first for its pricier premium seats, and second for its economy section. Customers might be satisfied with its extremely low prices, which already rank at the forefront of the U.S. marketplace with such low-cost carriers as JetBlue and Southwest.

GETTING HIRED

Give your career a lift

Virgin Atlantic's careers site, at www.virgin-atlantic.com/en/us/allaboutus/working forus/index.jsp, provides information for job seekers on job openings and benefits. Nice perks include seven free flights per year, one-third off at Virgin Megastores and a profit-sharing plan, on top of more standard benefits like a 401(k), health insurance and tuition assistance. The company also provides profiles of various positions at the company, including cabin crew and in-flight beautician.

Virgin requires that its cabin crew and beauticians speak fluent English, hold an EU passport and have a minimum height of 5'2". Beauticians also require licenses appropriate to their duties. Jobs are searchable by department. In order to apply to a position, job seekers must first create a profile.

Walt Disney Parks & Resorts, LCC

1375 E. Buena Vista Drive
Lake Buena Vista, FL 32830
Phone: (407) 828-1750
Fax: (407) 934-8889
disney.go.com/destinations

LOCATIONS

Lake Buena Vista, FL (HQ)
Anaheim, CA
Burbank, CA
Celebration, FL
Glendale, CA
Kissimmee, FL
Orlando, FL
Tampa, FL

THE STATS

Employer Type: Business Segment
of The Walt Disney Company
Chairman: James A. Rasulo
President: Allen R. Weiss
2007 Revenue ($mil.): $10,626

KEY COMPETITORS

Royal Caribbean Cruises
Six Flags
Universal Parks

EMPLOYMENT CONTACT

corporate.disney.go.com/careers

DEPARTMENTS

Accounting/Finance •
Administrative/Support/Call Center
Services • Architecture & Design •
Associates/Internships •
Banking/Credit Union • Broadcast
Sales • Broadcasting • Business
Development & Planning •
Construction Management •
Creative/Artistic/Animation •
Engineering • Entertainment •
Facilities/Security • Food &
Beverage/Culinary • Hotel Operations
• Human Resources • International
Business • International Production •
Laundry • Legal/Legal Affairs •
Lodging • Maintenance •
Marketing/Promotions/Publicity/Adver
tising • Merchandise • Movie
Production • Music and
Entertainment • New Media/Internet
• Nurse/Medical/Healthcare • Parking
& Transportation •
Procurement/Logistics/Inventory •
Product/DVD Development &
Merchandising • Production &
Programming • Production &
Technical Operations •
Public/Community Relations •
Publishing • Radio Production • Real
Estate/Development • Research •
Resort/Theme Park Operations •
Sales • Sciences/Horticulture/Zoology
• Security Operations • Sports &
Recreation • Technology &
Information Services • Theatrical &
Stage Production • Travel & Sales •
Travel/Maritime • TV Marketing • TV
Production • TV Research •
Wireless/Mobile

THE SCOOP

Where dreams come true (especially if they involve large rodents)

Ever wanted to dance with Cinderella, sail with the *Pirates of the Caribbean* or shake Mickey's hand? Well, you can, at one of Disney's resorts. Disney's parks and resorts segment runs several theme parks, including the famed Disneyland and Walt Disney World, with outposts in Hong Kong, Paris and Tokyo, as well as a cruise line, complete with private island, a lot of sand and a hot Caribbean band. The company's Imagineering unit is responsible for the design and construction of the rides and animated dioramas that populate the park. The division brings in about a third of the Walt Disney Company's revenue.

Another world

After achieving his fame in the movie business, Walt Disney built Disneyland at a cost of $17 million on 160 acres of Californian orange groves. Originally conceived as a small amusement park near Disney's animation studios, plans for the park grew until it required its own piece of real estate. The park first opened its doors in 1955. Similar theme parks had actually existed since the 1890s, but they usually attracted unsavory characters and Disney certainly didn't want that. When Disneyland opened in 1955, it included Main Street USA, Adventureland, Fantasyland, Frontierland and Tomorrowland. The park was centered around Main Street USA, reputedly based on the main street of Marceline, Missouri, Walt Disney's hometown.

Within two years, Disneyland drew 10 million visitors, but they were mainly from California. To reach audiences on the densely populated East Coast, Disney started researching possible East Coast locations for another park in 1958. The company began buying land in Florida in 1964 and, after some media speculation, announced plans for a theme park the next year. Walt Disney died soon afterwards, in 1966, and his brother, CEO Roy Disney, took over the construction. Walt Disney World opened its gates in 1971. And unlike California's Disneyland, a relatively stand-alone operation, the World was located near two golf courses, as well as hotels and resorts where vacationing families could stay.

In 1982, Disney World realized one of its founder's ambitions for the park, opening the Epcot exhibit. It features several different pavilions showcasing the culture of various countries as well as exhibitions about technological progress in the realms of physics, chemistry and biology. The attraction received its name from Walt Disney's

Visit Vault at **www.vault.com** for insider company profiles, expert advice, career message boards, expert resume reviews, the Vault Job Board and more.

V/\ULT CAREER LIBRARY **365**

notes, where he called it the Experimental Prototype Community of Tomorrow (EPCOT). It was the park's most expensive addition yet, costing over $1 billion. Disney World got another addition in 1998: the Animal Kingdom park, sort of a Disney-fied zoo.

Disney Worlds around the world

In 1983, Mickey said konnichiwa to Tokyo and opened a Walt Disney World in Japan, which attracted five million visitors in its first year. But Disney wasn't done spreading the house of mouse all over the globe. To make a corner of France that would forever be America, the company opened Euro Disney on the outskirts of Paris in 1992. The site featured six hotels (5,000 rooms), each representing a region of the U.S. It also included many of its California cousin's most popular rides.

French activists protested Euro Disney's opening as cultural imperialism, an unwanted imposition of American values and an infringement on French culture—the restaurants, for example, committed the dreadful faux pas of not serving wine. Attendance was low in the European location, although that probably had more to do with Europe's flagging economy at the time. Euro Disney started turning a profit in 1995 and it was Europe's most popular tourist spot in 2007.

Scrapped Westcot

In the 1990s, Disney tried to bring California's Disneyland up to the level of Florida's Disney World. In 1991 it announced plans for a $3 billion development, sort of a West Coast version of Epcot, called Westcot. But financial problems associated with the launch of Euro Disney led Disney to scrap the project in 1995. Disney eventually built an attraction on Westcot's property for about $1.4 billion, a Golden State-themed park named Disney's California Adventure. It hasn't been a roaring success, and in 2007 Disney announced a massive renovation of the park (more on this below).

Sailing the high seas of Disney

In 1998, Disney took delivery of the Disney Wonder, one of the largest cruise ships in the world. The Wonder, along with its sister ship Magic, holds 2,400 vacationers and has three swimming pools, a spa and a theater with a different show every night. In 1999, Disney purchased Gorda Cay, a Bahamian island previously used by drug smugglers, and renamed it Castaway Cay. The company dredged the island's naturally deep harbor to accommodate a cruise ship and enlarged its beach.

Hong Kong dreams

In 2005, with the rest of the world effectively conquered, Disney set its sights on capturing an audience in the world's most populous country. That year, it opened a Disneyland in Hong Kong, but the venture was fraught with problems. Locals objected to the project, saying that the city was footing too much of the construction costs.

And, similar to Euro Disney's first years, the project met opposition along cultural lines, as most Chinese people didn't grow up with Mickey, Belle, et al., and certainly didn't grow up on Main Street, USA. Also, it might simply not be thrilling enough, as Disney and its partner in the venture, the Hong Kong government, only built the park with 16 attractions, far less than Disneyland Paris' 52 rides. Disney has dropped hints about opening a theme park near Shanghai, but recently stated that no construction will begin in the area before 2010, or until it works out operational issues at its Hong Kong location.

Mickey's slimming down

In 2006, Disney moved to serve better food in its parks—or at least food that's better for its visitors. Sensitive to America's obesity epidemic, Disney announced in October 2006 that it would change the menu at its theme parks' snack stands to encourage healthier eating. During market testing, an overwhelming majority of parents opted to feed their kids a healthier lunch in lieu of soda and fries, and Disney changed its kids' meals to come with low-fat milk and a side of fruit by default. Disney is also putting limits on the amount of fat and calories in the food it serves, expected to take effect in 2008.

Pirates of the Caribbean (and Mediterranean)

Food isn't the only thing getting an upgrade at Disney. In February 2007, Disney announced that its two cruise ships, Magic and Wonder, would be getting two sister ships by 2012. The new, $800 million-plus ships (which don't yet have names) will have 12 decks, two more than Disney's current ships, and over 1,200 rooms onboard. Disney will then expand its fleet's destinations, which currently includes itineraries in the Caribbean, Mediterranean and Gulf of Mexico.

Be our guest

Disney isn't neglecting its land-bound properties, however. In 2006 and 2007, it announced plans to build upscale hotels near Florida's Walt Disney World. In May

2006, it announced plans with Hilton Hotels Corp. to build two hotels adjacent to Walt Disney World, one of them a 1,000 room Hilton and the other a 500-room addition to Hilton's Waldorf-Astoria Collection. The project broke ground in April 2007, and is expected to open in late 2009. On the other side of the resort, Disney is developing 450 acres into moderately-price hotels, restaurants and stores, expected to open in 2010.

Son of Disneyland

In October 2007, Disney announced that it would be giving its California Adventure theme park—the park that opened after the failure of Westcot—a $1.1 billion, five-year makeover. The project is aimed at increasing the park's magic quotient, which visitors say is lacking. The entrance of the park will get a focus area like Disneyland's Main Street, 250 more hotel rooms and rides based on animated movies like *The Little Mermaid* and *Cars*.

By far, the most exciting (and important) new addition to California Adventure will be a ride called Toy Story Mania, set to debut in June 2008. Estimated at $80 million and three years of construction, the ride will be based on the successful Disney animated film of the same name and put 3-D glasses-wearing riders through a ride that combines physical and digital thrills. It promises to be nothing less than *Toy Story* come to life, with revolutionary digital animation technology thrusting riders directly into the world of the movie. Every Disney division is chipping in on Toy Story Mania: the Pixar animation studio provided animation and creative advice, the video game unit Disney VR Studios offered customized software, the media networks division ABC will promote the ride after it opens and, of course, the parks and resorts division handled the bulk of construction and design.

California Adventure isn't the only park slated for some upgrades. In October 2007, Disney announced plans for a new luxury resort in Hawaii. The company has already snapped up 21 acres of oceanfront property in Ko Olina, near Honolulu (for $144 million). The finished result will have 800 hotel rooms, cottages, shopping and dining, and is expected to open in 2011. It will have competition, though—seven new hotel, timeshare or condominium towers are either currently open or under construction, and Disney's property is located directly next to Marriott Corp.'s Ihilani resort.

GETTING HIRED

Whistle while you work

Disney maintains separate sites for those who wish to work for its theme parks and cruise ships. Walt Disney Imagineering is the brains behind the parks' operations, creating the effects and animatronics that delight theme park visitors. The Imagineers are located in Orlando and Anaheim, and their careers page is located at: corporate.disney.go.com/careers/who_imagineering.html.

If you like Mickey so much that you'd like to be him, at least in half-hour increments, visit disney.go.com/disneycareers/disneyland/home/index.html for jobs at Disneyland, or www.disney.go.com/DisneyCareers/wdwcareers, for jobs at Walt Disney World. In addition to hosts, ticket takers and waiters, the company wants to hire lots of actors—especially ones that can credibly act and sing as Disney characters, and hopefully with some acrobatic ability, too.

If *Pirates of the Caribbean* was your favorite Disney movie, then perhaps the seafaring life is for you. Disney Cruises maintains a site of job openings on its ships, as well as permanent positions on Castaway Cay, at www.dcljobs.com. But the life aquatic is no song and dance—cast members are expected to work 10-hour days, seven days a week, for at least three months at a time.

Disney has very stringent standards for how its employees must look and act. While employees of diverse backgrounds are, of course, welcome at the company, the company places restrictions on employees' piercings and visible tattoos, hairstyles and footwear.

OUR SURVEY SAYS

Whistle while you work

Apparently, there are two constants to working at Disney: nonexecutive salaries 20 percent below industry average ("just because it's Disney"); and an extracurricular commitment to the company's many entertainment products. So, if you greatly prize the company's history—or, as one source puts it, "drink the Kool-Aid"—Disney could be a great place to work. If not, it's probably just another underpaid entertainment job.

Visit Vault at **www.vault.com** for insider company profiles, expert advice, career message boards, expert resume reviews, the Vault Job Board and more.

V/\ULT CAREER LIBRARY   **369**

One corporate communications associate feels "very, very underpaid at $55,000." Two others, a software engineer and analyst, respectively, remarked that "Disney pays about 20 percent below market as a general rule" and "they try to cheap out a bit on salaries because they're Disney and they have a good brand name. If you're a director or above, you are being very well compensated, with good benefits." And although "people always say that Disney has good benefits," the analyst disagrees: "if you're an office desk jockey it's a pretty typical benefits package. You have to pay for some medical and dental each week through [your] paycheck."

A perk-y place

What about all those great perks of working at Disney? "Pretty lame from what I've seen," remarks a rather sour source at Disney corporate, "unless you're into super touchy-feely stuff … if you don't have kids, how often do you really want to go to [Disney World]? What's that worth, a couple hundred bucks?"

Other survey responses underline how committed to the Disney ideal one has to be at the company. For theme park employees, "There is a Disney 'look' and you spend a lot of time during training discussing [it]." But a corporate source also mentions that, with "room[s] full of MBAs" at Disney, "perception is more important than reality" and "there are many pressures to fit in to the culture. You need to help out in the park during busy times. This can involve sweeping, parking, etc."

Another agrees, saying that "opportunities for advancement are very political" and that "the company is filled with sales types who are very competitive and catty." However, the same source added that the culture is "casual," "fun" and "creative." A theme park insider had only good things to say about Disney, calling it "a wonderful place to be" and that employees "felt honored to be there."

Wyndham Worldwide Corporation

7 Sylvan Way
Parsippany, NJ 07054
Phone: (973) 753-6000
Fax: (973) 753-7537
www.wyndhamworldwide.com

LOCATIONS

Parsippany, NJ (HQ)
Atlanta, GA
Las Vegas, NV
Orlando, FL
Phoenix, AZ
San Diego, CA

Additional locations nationwide;
International locations in Argentina,
Australia, Belgium, Brazil, Canada,
Chile, China, Colombia, Czech
Republic, Denmark, Egypt, England,
Finland, France, Germany, Greece,
Hungary, India, Indonesia, Ireland,
Italy, Japan, Jordan, Korea, Kuwait,
Malaysia, Malta, Mexico, Morocco,
Netherlands, New Zealand, Oman,
Philippines, Poland, Portugal, Qatar,
Romania, Russia, Scotland,
Singapore, South Africa, Spain,
Taiwan, United Arab Emirates,
Uruguay and Venezuela.

THE STATS

Employer Type: Public Company
Stock Symbol: WYN
Stock Exchange: NYSE
Chairman & CEO: Stephen P. Holmes
2007 Employees: 33,200
2007 Revenue ($mil.): $4,360

DEPARTMENTS

Administrative
Architecture/Design & Construction
Communications
Compliance
Customer Service
Call Center
Event Planning
Executive
Facilities
Finance
Hotel/Resort Operations
Human Resources
Information Technology
Legal
Maintenance
Marketing
Operations
Product Management
Project Management
Procurement/Purchasing
Quality Assurance
Real Estate & Development
Revenue Management
Sales
Telecommunications
Training

KEY COMPETITORS

Hilton Hotels
Marriott International
Starwood Hotels & Resorts

EMPLOYMENT CONTACT

www.wyndhamworldwide.com/careers

Visit Vault at **www.vault.com** for insider company profiles, expert advice,
career message boards, expert resume reviews, the Vault Job Board and more.

VAULT CAREER LIBRARY   371

THE SCOOP

Lodgings for work and play

You can wander, but you'll never be far from Wyndham, the world's largest hotel chain. Wyndham's 500,000-plus rooms are so ubiquitous, they account for one of every 10 hotel rooms in the U.S. If the name Wyndham doesn't ring any bells, the firm's locations operate under other names: AmeriHost Inn, Baymont, Days Inn, Howard Johnson, Knights Inn, Ramada, Super 8, Travelodge, Wingate Inn and Wyndham Hotels and Resorts. Most of these locations are franchises.

A long and Wyndham road

Wyndham Hotels & Resorts was founded by Texas-based real estate developer Trammel Crow in 1981, as an operator of vacation properties. The company moved into mid-market hotel management in 1990 with its acquisition of the Howard Johnson hotel chain. In 1992, the company moved into budget lodgings with the acquisition of Days Inn, a position strengthened by the 1993 purchase of Super 8. The company debuted its business travel brand, Wingate, in 1995, featuring such amenities as conference rooms and Internet access. The same year, it acquired the Knights Inn line of hotels.

There was a price to the company's rapid expansion in the 1990s—it was about $3 billion in debt by the end of the decade. In 1999 the firm agreed to a $1 billion restructuring plan, with private equity firms including Apollo Real Estate Advisors and Thomas H. Lee Partners taking control of the company. When the entire tourism industry suffered a major downturn after the terrorist attacks of September 11, 2001, Wyndham was hit especially hard. By the beginning of 2002, the company laid off 1,600 employees and put 20 percent of its workforce on reduced hours. Wyndham squeaked through 2001, posting $451 million in revenue and $300 million in profits, partly due to divesting a number of its properties. In 2004 Wyndham moved to save more costs, shedding nine underperforming hotels and starting to offer timeshares.

Many owners, only one Wyndham

The Blackstone Group, a private investment firm, took over the chain for around $3.2 billion in August 2005. The ink on the deal was barely dry in October 2005, when Blackstone sold Wyndham to Cendant Corp., a travel conglomerate with interests in car rentals (Avis), travel booking web sites (Orbitz) and real estate (Century 21).

But Cendant was going through a transitional period of its own, restructuring its assets and weathering shareholder and investor lawsuits concerning some financial funny business in the mid-1990s. (Cendant settled with shareholders for a record $2.83 billion in 1999.) Weeks after acquiring Wyndham, Cendant split itself into four operating segments, and in 2006 divested three of them. Wyndham was one of these, spun off to Cendant shareholders in July 2006. (The other spin-offs were Realogy and Travelport Ltd., and Cendant renamed itself Avis, after its rental operations.) Wyndham is still dealing with Cendant's legal baggage, most recently settling a lawsuit with Cendant's former accounting firm Ernst & Young in December 2007.

They're off!

In 2006, much to the benefit of the newly independent Wyndham, the hotel industry recovered much of its pre-downturn form. In July of that year, Wyndham acquired the Baymont hotel brand, aimed at value-conscious travelers. The company ended the year with $3.8 billion in revenue and $300 million in profits. Revenue increased 10 percent over the year previous, while profits fell by a third, mostly because of costs associated with breaking apart from Cendant.

Sharing time with Wyndham

Wyndham's timesharing unit, Wyndham Vacation Ownership, touts itself as "the world's largest vacation ownership business," and has driven much of the company's recent growth. Over the course of 2007, it began renovation on a San Francisco hotel and opened in Florida's Panama City Beach. And in January 2008 alone, the company either opened or acquired timeshare properties in Colorado, San Diego and South Carolina. The South Carolina property in particular will see extensive development, as Wyndham is signed on to acquire over 78 units by early 2009, when they will open with lakefront access.

Lucky No. 8

From South Carolina to China, Wyndham has opened 50 motels in China since 2005, seeking to capitalize on the region's increasing importance as a destination for business travel and as the site for the 2008 Olympic Summer Games, to be held in Shanghai. All recent Wyndham hotels in China have opened under the Super 8 brand—the company is keeping the Western name because eight is considered a very lucky number in China. Wyndham isn't the only firm breaking ground in China—the country's number of hotels is expected to double between 2006 and 2008. In

Visit Vault at **www.vault.com** for insider company profiles, expert advice, career message boards, expert resume reviews, the Vault Job Board and more.

VAULT CAREER LIBRARY

373

December 2007, Super 8 reported that it had exceeded its development goals in China for the third straight year.

L'heure bleu

And, if Super 8 and timeshares don't seem diverse enough, Wyndham launched its own line of spas in June 2007. Known as The Blue Harmony, its facilities marry spa treatments with dance. Treatments include facials designed for people whose phones are permanently welded to their faces, massages for people who cannot let go of their PDAs, as well as a customized aroma experience and a specialized menu. There will be a virtual private trainer in a gym setting, which will also be available in hotel rooms, for guests who want to get their groove on there. Piggybacking on another hot trend, the spas will have organic cotton robes. The first of the spas-cum-dance-studios will be located in one of the company's hotels near Orlando, but will soon spread to more locations.

GETTING HIRED

Check in to a career at Wyndham

For more information on starting a career with Wyndham International, visit its careers site at www.wyndhamworldwide.com/careers. The site provides information about the company's benefits, which include a choice of consumer-directed health plans, 401(k), flexible hours, and benefits for domestic partners. The site also features employee testimonials and information on diversity and awards. The site lists job openings and descriptions of the positions available, and is searchable by location. In order to apply for a position, job seekers must first create a profile.

Wynn Resorts, Limited

3131 Las Vegas Boulevard South
Las Vegas, NV 89109
Phone: (702) 770-7555
Fax: (702) 697-5009
www.wynnresorts.com

LOCATIONS

Las Vegas, NV (HQ)
Atlantic City, NJ
Macau

THE STATS

Employer Type: Public Company
Stock Symbol: WYNN
Stock Exchange: Nasdaq
Chairman & CEO: Stephen A. Wynn
President: Ronald J. Kramer
2007 Employees: 16,500
2007 Revenue ($mil.): $2,687

KEY COMPETITORS

Harrah's Entertainment
Las Vegas Sands Corp
MGM MIRAGE

EMPLOYMENT CONTACT

www.wynnjobs.com

Visit Vault at **www.vault.com** for insider company profiles, expert advice,
career message boards, expert resume reviews, the Vault Job Board and more.

VAULT CAREER LIBRARY   375

THE SCOOP

Everybody's a winner at Wynn

With locations in Las Vegas and Macau, Wynn Resorts brings a touch of luxury to gaming. Wynn Las Vegas—a $2.7 billion playground in the desert—features amenities such as an 18-hole golf course, a 2,700-room hotel with spa, nightclubs and five pools, a 111,000-square-foot casino and 22 restaurants that satisfy desires for everything from a multicourse Daniel Boulud feast to a quick snack.

Wynn Las Vegas also has a shopping mall with high-end retail, two resident shows—Spamalot and Le Reve, an Esther Williams-meets-Cirque du Soleil extravaganza—and, to top it all off, a Ferrari and Maserati dealership. Wynn Macau is similarly outfitted, with a slightly smaller casino than the Las Vegas location, 600 hotel rooms, five restaurants and a pool and spa.

The Wynn era

Perhaps more than any other casino mogul, Steve Wynn turned Las Vegas from a down-and-out gaming and drinking town into a destination for shopping and family entertainment (not to mention gaming and drinking). The *Las Vegas Review-Journal* named Wynn among The First 100 Persons who Shaped Southern Nevada, crediting him with nothing less than creating "a new era." The "new" Vegas can be seen in popular culture, in TV shows like *Las Vegas* and films like the 2001 remake of *Ocean's Eleven*. Fittingly, one of the characters in *Ocean's*, the casino owner Terry Benedict played by Andy Garcia, was reportedly based on Steve Wynn.

Wynn's father, Michael Weinberg, ran bingo parlors in the Eastern U.S. in the 1940s and 1950s, funneling his profits into the fun and games of Vegas, where he first took his 10-year-old son Steve in 1952. An older Steve Wynn moved to Las Vegas in 1967 and began his career of wheeling and dealing the same year, investing in the Frontier Hotel. But that was the "old era" of Las Vegas, and apparently some of Wynn's partners were connected to the mob. Although Wynn was never cited for wrongdoing, state authorities soon intervened and the group sold the Frontier to billionaire (and aviator) Howard Hughes. In the process, Wynn befriended E. Parry Thomas, a prominent Vegas banker who was known for his casino investments.

Wynn became the youngest casino owner in the country in 1972, purchasing a stake in the centrally located Golden Nugget casino that year and adding a high-end hotel to it five years later. As soon as gambling became legal in Atlantic City, N.J., Wynn purchased an aging hotel and completely remodeled it as another Golden Nugget in 1980. But the biggest moment of Wynn's career arrived in 1989, when he opened the Mirage.

Success or Mirage?

In 1986, Wynn purchased a valuable property on the Vegas strip from Howard Hughes' estate, then sold his Atlantic City Golden Nugget for $440 million to raise development funds for the Vegas property. After $750 million worth of construction, the property began life as the Mirage in 1989, the first major new hotel on the Strip since the MGM Grand in 1973. Because of its high cost, the venture would have to earn $1 million per day to pay down its debt.

Simply put, the Mirage was spectacular, with an indoor forest and volcano (!) and a magic act featuring Siegfried, Roy and their big cats. It set a new standard for size and extravagance among casinos, helped redefine what Las Vegas offered. The Mirage didn't just pay off its debts, it annihilated the competition: Caesars Palace, located immediately next door, reported an 80 percent drop in revenue in 1990.

Wynn struck again with an even bigger, bolder hotel in 1998: the marble confection known as the Bellagio, reportedly a $1.5 billion project. Modeled on Lake Como, it featured its own art museum (then worth about $100 million) and a shopping mall with astronomical prices. At the time of its opening, Wynn was quoted as saying "If we could build a hotel that, regardless of the century, was clearly, unequivocally, overwhelmingly the most lovely, elegant, beautiful hotel ever built in the history of the planet, a place where even the people in Johannesburg or Singapore would say, 'It's a wonderment,' well, wouldn't that be something?" But such a hotel was not exactly profitable, and in 2000, when rival casino mogul Kirk Kerkorian (majority shareholder in MGM Grand) launched a hostile takeover bid, Wynn's investing partners sold the Mirage and Bellagio for $6.4 billion. MGM Grand duly renamed itself MGM Mirage, after its new star property.

Back in the saddle

In 2002, Wynn obtained a license to operate a casino in Macau, a "special administrative region" off the coast of China where gambling is legal. Also in 2002, he started building the Wynn Las Vegas, which opened in April 2005. The Macau site opened a few months later. For fiscal 2005, the new Wynn Resorts Ltd. racked up $712 million in revenue, with losses of $90 million.

Visit Vault at **www.vault.com** for insider company profiles, expert advice, career message boards, expert resume reviews, the Vault Job Board and more.

V/\ULT CAREER LIBRARY   377

Due to ongoing construction, financial results have been inconsistent ever since. In 2006, the company took in sales of $1.4 billion and profits of $628 million, and the next year reported $2.7 billion and $258 million in the same categories. The firm was boosted by the September 2007 opening of Wynn Macau, which offset approximately $998 million of construction-related costs, spent throughout the year.

Bis, bis!

In April 2007, the firm announced an addition to the Wynn casino in Las Vegas, aptly called Encore. The new addition will be located right next door to Wynn, on the famed Strip. The building will be the tallest in Vegas, at 60 stories, and will feature over 2,000 suites, with bathrooms larger than most New York apartments.

The complex, to be constructed at a cost of $2 billion and opening in 2009, will hopefully attract big spenders—at $400 a night—from the luxuries at the Bellagio, that other Steve Wynn brainchild. Encore will also have a full complement of restaurants, meeting rooms, pools and other amenities.

Wynn's Macau location is getting some renovation attention, too, with the Wynn Diamond Suites, a new tower of high-end hotel suites. The suites will cost $1.2 billion and provide an additional 100,000 square feet of gambling, restaurants and a movie theater. The new addition will open in December 2007.

The artful Mr. Wynn

The colorful Mr. Wynn is making news almost as fast as his new properties are making lots of money. An avid art collector, he attracted a great deal of attention in October 2006 for agreeing to sell Picasso's "La Rêve" for $139 million—at that point, the highest ever selling price for a single piece of art. But Wynn, who suffers from an eye disease that obscures his peripheral vision, succeeded in putting one of his fingers through the painting, about a week later. The value of the painting dropped to around $85 million, and when his insurer, Lloyd's of London, refused to compensate him for the difference, Wynn took the firm to court for $54 million in January 2007.

GETTING HIRED

Gain the house advantage in your job search

Wynn's careers site, www.wynnjobs.com, provides information for job seekers on benefits (which include health and dental insurance, 401(k) with company match, and paid vacation) as well as open positions. Job seekers may apply online at the company's web site, or in person at the company's recruiting center at 3720 Howard Hughes Parkway, Suite 170 in Las Vegas. After three months on the job, employees can request a transfer to Macau.

Visit Vault at **www.vault.com** for insider company profiles, expert advice,
career message boards, expert resume reviews, the Vault Job Board and more.

V/\ULT CAREER LIBRARY   379

About the Editors

Michaela R. Drapes graduated from the University of Texas at Austin and has degrees in radio/TV/film and english. Before joining Vault, she was an editor at award-winning business publisher Hoover's Inc. and covered an array of industry sectors, including pharmaceuticals, amusement parks, real estate, and international banking and finance. Michaela is one of the founders of fashion startup Kindling & Tinder and is an irreverent music critic; she also occasionally DJ's at independent rock shows around New York City.

Nicholas R. Lichtenberg holds degrees from the University of Syracuse in drama and history. Before working at Vault, he covered and canvassed trial court bureaucracies in select states as an assignment editor at the legal publishing company ALM Media Inc. He lives in New York.